THE
LANCASTER STORY

Built as a Mk I, DV379 was delivered to
BOAC in November 1943 and re-registered
G-AGJI. The gun turrets were omitted, with
the nose and tail sections faired over. The
aircraft retained its wartime camouflage and
was used for long-range development.

THE LANCASTER STORY

PETER JACOBS

To Christopher and Matthew

A Cassell Book

Published in 2002 by Silverdale Books
An imprint of Bookmart Limited
Registered Number 2372865
Trading as Bookmart Limited
Blaby Road
Wigston
Leicestershire LE18 4SE

Text copyright © Peter Jacobs 1996
Design and compilation copyright © Cassell & Co 1996

Reprinted 2003

ISBN: 1-85605-703-8

This book was designed for
Cassell & Co
Wellington House, 125 Strand
London WC2R 0BB
by Roger Chesneau/ DAG Publications Ltd

Printed and bound in Dubai

Contents

Foreword

Marshal of the Royal Air Force Sir Michael Beetham GCB CBE DFC AFC DL FRAeS

Few would question that the Lancaster was the most effective bomber on either side in World War II. Born out of the ill-fated Manchester, the Lancaster formed the backbone of Bomber Command at that time and made a major contribution to victory. Such was the success of the design that from it grew the Lincoln, York and Shackleton, all three being important elements of the Royal Air Force front line for many years after the war.

Anyone who flew the Lancaster had a deep affection for it. It was certainly my favourite aircraft, and the one Lancaster still flying today, PA474 in the Battle of Britain Memorial Flight, always evokes a warm response from the crowd at any of the numerous displays in which it participates.

Peter Jacobs tells the story of the Lancaster in all its many facets. Tracing the origins of the design through production to operational service, we are treated to a full complement of technical and operational data which is all set in the context of the time, together with personal experiences of the aircrew and, importantly, the oft-forgotten but vitally important groundcrew.

The book makes fascinating reading both for the Lancaster enthusiast, for whom it will bring back warm feelings of nostalgia, and for the wider readership, who I am sure will enjoy learning about this great aircraft.

Introduction

I was delighted when given the chance to write *The Lancaster Story*. There can be no doubts among air historical enthusiasts that the Avro Lancaster is one of the greatest aircraft of all time and certainly one of the most famous: books and films about such exploits as the Dambuster Raids have all made the Lancaster a household name from 1943 until the present day. In fact, if any non-enthusiast were asked to name a famous bomber it is certain that the Lancaster would be the most frequently quoted.

Much has already been written about the aircraft. Two of the best (and most complete) works to date are *The Avro Lancaster* by Francis K. Mason and *Lancaster: The Story of a Famous Bomber* by Bruce Robertson. These have both described the aircraft and its history in similar ways and both are thoroughly recommended for the Lancaster enthusiast. There has also been the *Lancaster at War* series published by Ian Allan, and several other works over the years have also covered the wartime experiences of people associated with the aircraft. However, few have told the history of the Lancaster in full.

The origins of the heavy bomber stretch back to the First World War and so the Lancaster story begins as early as 1916. As to the end of the story, there is none: examples of the Lancaster still fly today, and others are to be found in museums, maintained and preserved by enthusiasts across the world. In the present book the story is covered chronologically, although specific areas such as the development of the aircraft's armament and specialist equipment are discussed in individual chapters, while extensive appendices give details of, for example, production and service use.

Several people have helped me throughout my research and without their help the book would not have been possible. My personal thanks are due to the many wartime personnel of my acquaintance who either flew or maintained the Lancaster during its finest days and some of whose memories are included in a later chapter: John and Mike Chatterton, Les Bartlett, Bill Spence, Alan Rowe, Frank Cornett, Ron Irons, Bert Dowty, 'Buck' Rogers and Eric Howell to name but a few. There has also been much help from the staffs of the RAF Museum, the Imperial War Museum, the Public Record Office and the Air Historical Branch (in particular Graham Day, who has provided me with so much assistance over the years). Thanks go also to those who have helped with photographs for the book, in particular to Steve Barker for his superb cover illustration and for his assistance; to Peter Green and the Air Historical Branch; and to *FlyPast* magazine for access to their ar-

chives (from which the photographs in this book are taken, except where credited otherwise). During my research I was given access to two surviving Lancasters, this being made possible through the kind offices of Fred and Harold Panton at East Kirkby and of the Battle of Britain Memorial Flight at RAF Coningsby.

I also thank Marshal of the Royal Air Force Sir Michael Beetham GCB CBE DFC AFC DL FRAeS for kindly agreeing to write the Foreword to the book; few have risen from wartime operations as Lancaster pilots to command at every possible level within the RAF. Finally, my personal thanks go to my former RAF colleague Ken Delve, now Editor of *FlyPast*, for his help over the years: without his support and advice I would never have been given the chance to tell *The Lancaster Story*.

Peter Jacobs

The author in the cockpit of Lancaster NX611 at East Kirkby.

Bibliography

Ashworth, Chris, *Action Stations*, vol. 5, PSL 1982

Bowyer, Chaz, *For Valour: The Air VCs*, William Kimber 1978

Bowyer, Michael J. F., *Action Stations*, vol. 1, PSL 1979

———, *Action Stations*, vol. 6, PSL 1983

Clarke, R. Wallace, *British Armament*, 2 vols, PSL 1993 and 1994

Currie, Jack, *Augsburg Raid*, Goodall 1987

Delve, Ken, *Source Book of the RAF*, Airlife 1994

Delve, Ken, and Jacobs, Peter, *The Six Year Offensive*, Arms & Armour Press, 1992

Garbett, Mike, and Goulding, Brian, *Lancaster at War*, Ian Allan 1971

Gibson, Guy, *Enemy Coast Ahead*, Michael Joseph 1946

Halley, James J., *Lancaster File*

———, *Squadrons of the RAF and Commonwealth*, Air Britain 1988

Halpenny, Bruce Barrymore, *Action Stations*, vol. 2, PSL 1981

———, *Action Stations*, vol. 4, PSL 1982

Harris, A., *Bomber Offensive*

Holmes, Harry, *Avro: The History of an Aircraft Company*, Airlife 1994

Mason, Francis K., *Avro Lancaster*, Aston 1989

Middlebrook, Martin, and Everitt, Chris, *Bomber Command War Diaries*, Penguin 1985

Musgrave, Gordon, *Pathfinder Force*, Macdonald & Jane's 1976

Onderwater, Hans, *Operation Manna/Chowhound*, Roman Luchvaart 1985

Robertson, B., *Lancaster: The Story of a Famous Bomber*

Smith, David J., *Action Stations*, vol. 3, PSL 1981

———, *Action Stations*, vol. 7, PSL 1983

Sweetman, John, *Dambusters Raid*, Arms & Armour Press 1982

Tanner, J., (ed.) *The Lancaster Manual*, Arms & Armour Press 1977

Williamson, Arthur, 'Bomber Command Losses', 1995

Air Historical Branch (various records, papers and documents)

Public Record Office (various articles and records)

Roe, A. V. & Co., Flight Engineer's Notes

1. Origins

Following the end of the First World War, much was written and debated about the lessons that had been learnt. What had become increasingly obvious as the war progressed was that the employment of air power had become one of the major factors in helping to decide the outcome of a specific battle or a prolonged campaign. With the development of the long-range bomber, a nation could no longer regard itself immune from attack. Indeed, as early as 1916, the General Officer Commanding the Royal Flying Corps (RFC) in France, Major-General Sir Hugh Trenchard, had outlined a possible doctrine for the RFC: 'Even with an unlimited number of machines for defensive purposes, it would still be impossible to prevent hostile machines from crossing the line if they were determined to do so, simply because the sky is too large to defend.'

Trenchard had been a firm believer in the potential of the aeroplane as a weapon of war since the early days of the RFC. He was a veteran of the Boer War in South Africa, during which he had been awarded the Distinguished Service Order, and served with the Corps only as a result of his ill-health: two years before hostilities began in Europe he had nearly died as a result of a fever in Nigeria and had been given a staff appointment to see him through until retirement. However, with the formation of the RFC, Trenchard had seen the opportunity to become deeply involved with a new military era—from its beginning.

At the outbreak of war Trenchard had been given command of the RFC at home to set up the vast training programme required to ensure that the right number of men and aeroplanes were sent to the front line. His tremendous leadership resulted in his being sent to France in person, to command the 1st Wing RFC, and within a year of war breaking out he was appointed to command the entire RFC on the Western Front. Although he was strong in personality, his ideas and methods in command sometimes upset other Army commanders. After all, military flying was still in its infancy and had no definite future—at least, that was the view of some of the more senior 'traditional' Army officers who believed that wars were fought by cavalry, infantry and artillery. Nevertheless, Trenchard believed in the future of air warfare and his methods, although not always favoured by the rest of the Army, certainly became popular with the men he commanded, and he quickly developed the respect of the Corps. However, the RFC on the Western Front had been unable to take the war beyond the immediate battlefield due to the lack of suitability of its aircraft at that time. But, by early 1917, one of the main developments in the Corps had been the increasing use of bombing aircraft.

The D.H.4, designed specifically for bombing duties, first appeared in August 1916. The first unit to receive the aircraft was No 55 Squadron, which in March 1917 moved to Fienvillers in France to commence bombing and reconnaissance operations along the Western Front. Powered by the Rolls-Royce Eagle engine, the D.H.4 was capable of a good operational speed at a good height and proved a difficult target for German fighters. It was rugged and reliable and it became generally popular with its crews. It was soon realised that bombing could not only be carried out by day but also by night, and the first night-capable bombers, F.E.2bs, arrived in France in March 1917.

Under the guidance of Trenchard a new unit of the RFC, the 41st Wing, was formed in October 1917 at Ochey in France to commence a bombing offensive against German towns and industrial targets within reach of Allied airfields along the Western Front. In addition to the D.H.4s and F.E.2bs, the Wing was equipped with the Handley Page O/400. This big aircraft was a development of the HP O/100 which had earlier entered service for shipping attacks with the 3rd Wing, Royal Naval Air Service (RNAS), in April 1917. Capable of carrying sixteen 112lb bombs, the O/400 had a greater bomb load than any other RFC bomber at the time and became the first of the 'heavies'. When it first formed, the 41st Wing comprised No 55 Squadron RFC (D.H.4s), No100 Squadron RFC (F.E.2bs) and No16 Squadron RNAS (O/400s). The three squadrons began the bombing offensive during the winter of 1917/18 but the build-up was slow because of the obvious problems with weather, target intelligence and reconnaissance and just 'finding their feet' in this new and demanding role.

Within weeks of the D.H.4's commencing bombing operations, plans for a modified variant were discussed. Designated the D.H.9, the prototype (a revised D.H.4) was air-tested in July 1917. Although powered by a new BHP engine, the aircraft did not seem as capable as the existing D.H.4 but, despite protests by many (including Trenchard) at the time, the D.H.9 went into full production and the first deliveries were made during late 1917 and early 1918. The D.H.9 was very similar in appearance to the D.H.4, but the BHP engine proved unreliable and was lacking in performance. Apart from the obvious problem of suffering an engine malfunction deep over enemy territory, a fully loaded D.H.9 could not reach an operating height of much more than 10,000ft and therefore became an easy target for defending German fighters. It did, however, have some design improvements over the D.H.4, notably the cockpit layout which allowed the two crewmen to communicate better than was possible in its predecessor. This point demonstrates the requirement, in the very early days of the bomber, for good communication between the crew members. Nevertheless, despite being a pleasant aeroplane to fly, the D.H.9 was not in general well received and many of its crews would be killed or wounded in it before the war was over.

In February 1918 the 41st Wing was upgraded and became VIII Brigade. Following the formation of the Royal Air Force (RAF) on 1 April 1918, the Brigade was expanded and renamed the Independent Force of the RAF, under the direct command of Trenchard, with the role of carrying out a strategic bombing offensive against Germany. By September 1918 the Force had expanded to nine squadrons, of which five were equipped with O/400s. Three of these 'heavy' squadrons were located at Xaffevillers (Nos 97, 100 and 215 Squadrons), with one squadron at Roville-sur-Chenes (No 115) and one at Autreville (No 216), all with the capability of carrying out night bombing. From Azelot, two squadrons of D.H.9s (Nos 99 and 104) and one squadron of D.H.4s (No 55) carried out day attacks. In addition to the bomber squadrons, No 45 Squadron (Sopwith Camels) moved to the Western Front from Italy in September to carry out bomber escort duties from Bettoncourt, a role in which it continued until the end of the war.

It had originally been intended that the Independent Force would be a large formation of over 40 squadrons, although this number was far from being achieved before the end of hostilities. It had not altogether proved successful in its early days and a large number of bombers had been lost as a result of enemy action as well as in flying accidents. There were several reasons for the relatively scant success of the

Force during its brief wartime experience. First, the bomber of the First World War had proved little or no match for a defending fighter. Secondly, the lack of accuracy in bombing methods meant that more often than not a long and hard journey to a target proved fruitless in terms of the final delivery of the weapon; greater accuracy often meant flying lower, therefore making the aircraft and crew more susceptible to ground fire. Finally, there was often little or no pre-target intelligence or post-target reconnaissance. However, despite the losses and setbacks, and the fact that the British heavy bombing offensive was still in its early stages when the war came to an end, the point had been made: there was a future in long-range bombing.

The Aftermath of War

At the end of the First World War the Independent Force consisted of some 150 bombers including many of poor performance and inadequate bomb load. Despite the lack of conclusive answers to many vital questions, it was nevertheless a widely held belief that the future of air operations lay with the bomber. In the inter-service wrangling over the post-war composition of the armed forces, when the Navy and the Army tried to see off the young RAF and absorb those parts of air power which they considered important, the need for independent control of the bomber was one of the factors used by Trenchard to secure the future of his Service. He was convinced in his idea that 'to win a war it would be necessary to pursue a relentless offensive by bombing the enemy's country, destroying his sources of supply of aircraft and engines, and breaking the morale of his people'. The British Air Staff needed no convincing. Their theory was that 'The strategic air offensive is a means of direct attack on the enemy state with the object of depriving it of the means or the will to continue the war. It may in itself be the instrument of victory or it may be the means by which victory can be won by other forces. It differs from all previous kinds of armed attack in that it alone can be brought to bear immediately, directly and destructively against the heartland of the enemy.'

The period following the First World War proved to be very difficult for the planners as it appears that the politicians had little interest in military matters, working on the assumption that 'no major war was likely for at least ten years'. Although the stability of Europe suggested the lack of urgency in developing a home bomber force, the RAF was still very much committed overseas. It was not long after hostilities had ceased in Europe before the bomber was to play an important role in resolving a potentially awkward situation. In British Somaliland a bandit known as the 'Mad Mullah' had for a considerable time been causing unrest, and so it was decided to oust him and his supporters. British Somaliland had been a source of military difficulty for the British ever since its acquisition as a Protectorate in 1898. It was a large country with an inhospitable climate and terrain, conditions in which the British soldier had been battling for years in an attempt to keep the native tribes at peace. A Colonial Office appraisal in early 1919 came up with two options, give up the area or mount a major expedition—although the latter, according to the War Office, would be expensive and was likely to tie up three Army divisions for at least a year. At that time, when there were other more pressing colonial problems, this was simply not viable. More in hope than expectation, the War Office approached the RAF for ideas. At a time when the RAF was still under pressure from the Navy and the Army to try and justify its peacetime existence, it was decided that the new Service would mount an expedition in conjunction with existing local forces.

Trenchard dispatched a special unit known as 'Z Force', under the command of Group Captain R.Gordon, and by November 1919 an advance party was in British Somaliland to select suitable landing grounds and to liaise with local land force commanders. In the meantime a force of twelve D.H.9s had sailed to Somaliland aboard the seaplane carrier HMS *Ark Royal* and arrived at Berbera on 30 December. Bombing and reconnaissance operations commenced on 21 January 1920 and within just a few days the Mullah had fled from his defences; he was eventually killed in neighbouring Abyssinia. As a result of the bombing operations against the Mullah, the RAF units returned to Berbera by 18 February, the situation having been resolved in less than four weeks. Although this one incident was short-lived and far away from the RAF's home bases, word soon spread of its success. The Colonial Office expressed their delight at the outcome and low financial cost in concluding what had become a most awkward situation. It had also given the RAF the evidence that it needed to support its case for the air policing of colonial disturbances.

The post-war division of the Ottoman Empire had given Britain control of various parts of the Middle East, all of which were potentially volatile. One of the most vociferous anti-British leaders was Sheik Mahmud with his dream of an independent Kurdistan. The revolt had begun in May 1919 and by October 1922 eight RAF squadrons were involved in the Mesopotamia theatre. The British were learning the lesson that inter-tribal conflict was a natural state of affairs in Mesopotamia and that to prevent such happenings would require almost continuous operations. As with Mesopotamia, India was continually to involve the RAF in active operations, although most of the actions were small-scale, anti-tribal affairs. The

degree of involvement varied from the support of local forces to suppress riots, to a major role such as the Third Afghan War. In the period up to 1922 the main trouble spots were Waziristan and Mahsud, although the Afghans continued to make border raids from time to time. Waziristan remained the major operational area until 1924, although much of the frontier district was peaceful. By the outbreak of the next crisis, in 1928, the RAF in India was still awaiting re-equipment with new types. It was not until 1929 that Nos 11 and 39 Squadrons arrived with the new Westland Wapiti, a single-engine biplane with a top speed of 135mph. Throughout the early 1930s, the RAF's main bomber on the North-West Frontier remained the Wapiti, which, although a rugged aircraft that proved ideal for frontier operations, was capable of carrying a bomb load of just 500lb under its wings and fuselage. In 1932 the newer Hawker Hart arrived in-theatre, and it would be a further six years before these would be replaced by twin-engine monoplanes.

There was, however, some concern within the RAF in the way the bomber force was organised and employed. In May 1928 Trenchard had highlighted his belief that 'it would be better to attack military targets at source, i.e. the factories, rather than in the field as it would have

greater effect for less effort'. However, his comments were not supported by the other Service chiefs as there were severe doubts about bombing accuracy, with the probable destruction of civilian, rather than military, establishments. The period was, generally, one of peace, with little support for any military expansion. Europe had, after all, just come out of 'the war to end all wars' and there was a reluctance to start planning for the next one, should it occur.

The RAF's commitments abroad had, however, ensured that bomber development had not been completely abandoned. New specifications continued to be issued in an attempt to keep up with technical improvements, but these did not lead to any production contracts. However, although there had been no great plans for changes in policy by the end of the 1920s, it soon became increasingly obvious that the RAF's bombing force was limited to single- or twin-engine biplanes of various sizes and capabilities. These ranged from relatively agile but less capable aircraft, such as the Wapiti, to the larger bombers with little or no agility, such as the Handley Page Heyford and the Vickers Virginia.

Early heavy bombers such as the Handley Page Heyford were only capable of carrying bomb loads of up to 3,500lb and of achieving about 140mph. (*Lincolnshire Echo*)

There was clearly a need to move on in all aspects of aircraft and weapon design. The biplane was starting to appear somewhat dated as more manoeuvrable and faster monoplane designs were taking shape. Earlier ideas that monoplanes were either unsafe or just 'not suitable' for military purposes were proving unsound. With the expected development of the fighter, it was clear that for a bomber to survive it would have to fly high and fast, be manoeuvrable when required and be able to defend itself if necessary. Technology was also advancing, such that it was conceivable that a bomber force would be able to fly deep into enemy territory, in all weather and at night, and be able to deliver a large bomb load accurately on target. The next generation of bombers would have to represent a significant improvement on its present force if the RAF were to prepare itself for any future conflict—and by the mid-1930s it was apparent even to the politicians that Europe was not as stable or as peaceful as might have been expected ten years earlier. With Adolf Hitler becoming Chancellor of Germany in 1933, and his Nazi Party's rise to power, the stage was set for a future conflict. It was probably only a question of when.

Expansion

At the beginning of 1933 the RAF's operational home bomber force consisted of just five night- and six day-bomber squadrons. This force appears even less capable when considering the fact that the day bombers, the Wapiti and Hart, although very capable in their time, were by then somewhat outdated. Even the heavier night bombers, such as the Virginia, were only capable of carrying a bomb load of just over 3,000lb at an operating speed of little more than 100mph and at a altitude of a mere 5,000ft. Not only were the aircraft outdated, the bombing methods had changed little since the end of the First World War. In addition the Air Staff had stated that there was no requirement for a single bomb to be heavier than 500lb and that the 250lb bomb would remain the standard weapon.

Recognising the need for a new bomber, the Air Ministry had issued Specification B.9/32 in October 1932 for a twin-engine, long-range, daytime medium bomber. Because of international agreement, the aircraft's all-up weight was to be limited to just 6,300lb and its range to just over 700 miles. One point of emphasis in the specification concerned the operating

Handley Page Hampdens of No 49 Squadron being prepared for operations at Scampton. Having entered service with the RAF in 1938, the Hampden played an important part in Bomber Command operations during the early years of the war. (*Lincolnshire Echo*)

speed of the bomber, and here an attempt was made to improve considerably upon the bombers in service at that time. Although the specification would hardly bring about the performance and bomb load capabilities of the later heavy bombers, it was, nevertheless, a significant advance. Despite answering the same specification, the design and performance of the two prototypes, produced by Vickers and Handley Page, were quite different when the aircraft appeared in 1936. The Handley Page HP 52 was very much designed to the performance in the specification as a medium bomber, enhanced by its speed and manoeuvrability. In contrast, the Vickers Type 271 appeared more along the lines of a heavy bomber, with a far greater range and bomb load than the original requirement. These two designs, later named the Hampden and Wellington, would see Bomber Command through the early and difficult years of the

Second World War. The Hampden entered service with the RAF in August 1938 and went on to play an integral part in the full range of Bomber Command's operations during the first years of the war. It was obvious from the early days of the war that the aircraft had severe limitations, but for two years the Hampden squadrons of No 5 Group carried out their operations, often under extreme conditions and against determined opposition. The Hampden was withdrawn from operations on the night of 14/15 September 1942; nevertheless, the tremendous contribution made by the aircrews and groundcrews cannot be overstated. The Wellington entered service with the RAF in October 1938 and was without doubt the single most important bomber of the early years of the war, shouldering the responsibility for the Bomber Command offensive until the introduction of the four-engine 'heavies'. In all, 11,461 Wellingtons were built, the largest total ever of any British multi-engine aircraft.

The requirement for a medium bomber was soon followed by Specification B.3/34 issued in July 1934 emphasising the need for a night-capable heavy bomber intended to replace the RAF's heavy bi-planes. The result was the ordering of two prototypes in 1935. The Handley Page concept, the HP 51 (later named the Harrow), was a high-wing monoplane capable of carrying troops as well as a bomb load. However, the fixed undercarriage and, perhaps, too much emphasis on its troop-carrying capability meant that its role would later be more suited to that of transport rather than heavy bombing. The second prototype was the Armstrong Whitworth AW 38, later named the Whitley, which was a different design altogether. The wing was not mounted as high as the HP 51's, which gave it a larger fuselage bomb bay and an eventual bomb load of 7,000lb. Unlike other bomber designs throughout the mid-1930s, the Whitley was designed for night operations. With a crew of five, it was a great improvement over the aircraft it replaced and went on to become a pioneer in night bombing operations. Having played its part, the Whitley eventually bowed out from Bomber Command's front line on the night of 27/28 April 1942, although it continued to serve with operational training units and Coastal Command. The Whitley demonstrated the rapid progress of military aviation during the mid-1930s

The Handley Page Harrow was designed to meet Specification B.3/34, which outlined the need for a night-capable heavy bomber. However, the aircraft's fixed undercarriage and, perhaps, too much emphasis on its troop-carrying capability meant that its role was more suited to that of transport. (*Lincolnshire Echo*)

and the inherent problems of getting aircraft from the original specification to operational service before they became obsolete. Following the Air Ministry's specifications, bomber production was often ordered before the prototypes had made their first flights, such was the urgency to build the RAF's bomber force with the continuing threat to Europe of Germany's Nazi Party.

Because of the lack of stability in Europe, the Government suggested that the military should draw up and present for consideration a series of expansion plans for rearming all the armed forces to assure the security of Britain's world-wide commitments. In 1934 Expansion Scheme A, approved on 18 July, proposed a maximum front-line strength and stated that the RAF would be ready for war in eight years' time. With Germany identified as the most likely opponent, there was a need to develop aircraft with the range and performance to attack targets in the Ruhr and Rhineland. Budget constraints ensured that a policy of quantity rather than quality would be agreed; better quality would come later as more funding became available and improved types of aircraft entered production. The Scheme also stated that there should be 84 home-based squadrons, with a total of 960 aircraft. Of these 84, sixteen would be either medium or heavy bomber squadrons and 25 light bomber squadrons. A further 27 squadrons, with a total of 292 aircraft, would be based overseas.

More Expansion Schemes followed, in particular Scheme F, approved on 25 February 1936, which indicated an overall increase in aircraft strength and the first increase in overseas establishment. The number of home-based squadrons should increase to 124, with a total of 1,736 aircraft, plus a further 37 squadrons based overseas, with a total of 468 aircraft. The Scheme also stated that the bomber element of the RAF was to be an offensive, rather than a counter-offensive, weapon and provided for 68 bomber squadrons with a total of 990 aircraft scheduled for completion by March 1939.

In July 1936 a major change in RAF structure and commands saw the birth of Bomber Command under of Sir John Steel. With the Germans marching back into the Rhineland, more Expansion Schemes followed, in particular Scheme H approved on 14 January 1937 which recommended an increase to 145 home-based squadrons with a total of 2,422 aircraft. In these figures, the Scheme required an increase in the fighter element to meet the probable scale of attack and an attacking force not inferior to that of Germany. The number of bomber squadrons was increased to 90, with a total of 1,659 aircraft scheduled for completion by 1943. The 90-squadron plan was questioned by some on the grounds of cost and also from a conviction that the strategic concept was wrong. Some felt that the RAF should adopt a more defensive doctrine and have a greater percentage of fighters, balanced only by light and medium bombers. The

Air Staff were dismayed and, although they held to the offensive doctrine, had to accept a cut in the proposed size of the bomber force. This resulted in Scheme K, which was approved on 14 March 1938 as a more realistic scheme, with a provision for 77 bomber squadrons, of which 58 were to be heavy bomber squadrons with an establishment of sixteen aircraft per squadron.

However, doctrine had to be turned into plans, and although the year 1937 brought great advances in this area, much remained to be done. The starting point for the planners was the doctrine of independent bombing of Germany to achieve victory. The original assumptions made by the Joint Planning Committee suggested a three-phase campaign which involved countering the German air offensive, countering the land offensive and carrying out an air offensive against German industry and transport. The need to attack the *Luftwaffe* was stressed in view of the degree of destruction it could inflict. The Committee stated in a paper in October 1936 that 'the offensive employment of our own bombers is the only measure which could affect the issue during the first weeks of the war' and went on to indicate three categories of objectives—'demoralise the German people, attack vital targets

and inflict casualties upon German aircraft or their maintenance organisation'. However, the paper later stated that none of these categories was particularly suitable for attack by the British bomber force mainly because of Germany's superior air power and the vulnerability of Britain herself to air attack. Britain would, therefore, have to adopt a defensive air strategy. This general philosophy had been translated into planning for war with Germany. The Air Targets Intelligence Sub-Committee issued appreciations on certain industrial and military targets, although the data on which they based their assessments were very limited. By the end of 1937 these initial summaries were being issued as definite plans, known as the Western Air Plans, and Bomber Command was instructed to commence detailed planning, to be completed by 1 April 1938. As a result Bomber Command was reorganised during early 1938 to reflect the requirements of the Western Air Plans, and, although modified several times, these became the basis of Bomber Command strategy.

The Vickers Wellington first appeared in 1936. More than 11,000 would eventually be built—the largest total ever for a British multi-engine aircraft.

Towards the 'Heavies'

Nevertheless, the problem still existed that large numbers of bombers were still not available, and the earlier policy of quantity rather than quality was reconsidered. To many, the concept of fewer but more capable bombers seemed the way ahead. One squadron of light bombers could deliver, for example, 6,000lb of bombs on target whereas a squadron of heavy bombers could, perhaps, deliver three or four times that amount. This theory was backed up by the Air Ministry when Specification B.1/35 was issued for a large twin-engine heavy bomber. Two designs were selected, one from Vickers and the other from Armstrong Whitworth, although the latter concept was later abandoned. The Vickers design, later named the Warwick, was not a successful bomber design although it did later enter service as a maritime reconnaissance aircraft.

Private ventures such as the Bristol 142, which later developed into the Blenheim, showed what the manufacturers were capable of if given the right amount of support. The 142 was designed as a high-speed, twin-engine monoplane and immediately impressed the Air Staff as a potential light/medium bomber. In mid-1936 the Blenheim was capable of out-performing the RAF's current front-line fighters, although, had its performance been compared to that of a more capable fighter, such as the Spitfire or Hurricane being developed at that time, then the aircraft would not have seemed quite so impressive. This fact was to prove costly during the early days of the Second World War when the Blenheim came up against high-class fighter opposition. The same was true of the Fairey Battle, which also first appeared in 1936: as a light bomber it appeared an excellent prospect, but it proved unsuccessful against good fighter opposition.

Although Specification B.1/35 did not produce a heavy bomber, it did make designers consider what was necessary in a future heavy bomber. Ideas varied from that of a high-performance aircraft with only a modest bomb load to the other extreme, an aircraft with a large bomb load but lesser performance. Consequently two further specifications were issued in 1936 to consider both aspects of heavy bomber design. Specification B.12/36, issued in July, specifically addressed the bomb-load capability and P.13/36, issued in September, concentrated on aircraft performance. For the competition for Specification B.12/36, the requirement was for a four-engine aircraft with a crew of six, capable of carrying a bomb load of 12,000lb at more than 200mph, at a height of 12,000ft and over an operating range of 1,500 miles. Its wingspan was limited to 100ft, due to the size of RAF hangars at that time, and this remained a design constraint throughout the period. The aircraft was also to be equipped with the latest navigation equipment and three power-operated gun turrets, including a four-gun tail turret. For various reasons the RAF decided to put its faith in the 0.303in machine gun for both offensive and defensive purposes. The one innovation that went with this was the development of power-operated turrets to take multiple gun settings, the idea being that the bomber with its heavy turret armament would be able to look after itself.

B.12/36 was a considerable advance on any previous specification and it would be some years before the design would reach operational service. Two prototypes were ordered from Short Brothers, which resulted in the Stirling, and two prototypes from Supermarine, which resulted in the Types 317 and 318, both of which were severely damaged during a German air raid on Southampton in 1940 and later written off. Powered by four Bristol Hercules engines, the Stirling became the first of the RAF's heavy bombers to enter service and it made its operational début on the night of 10/11 February 1941. Initially the aircraft achieved a reasonable reputation for survivability, both in its ability to take punishment and for its self-defence capability against German fighters. However, it was to exhibit severe limitations which restricted its operational life to less than four years. Improving German defences, particularly flak, meant that the aircraft's poor operational ceiling gave increasing cause for concern, with the Stirling squadrons taking the brunt of the punishment. This, and the fact that the largest bomb it could carry was 4,000lb, eventually led to most Stirling squadrons re-equipping with newer and more capable heavy bombers, although it was not until September 1944 that the last Stirling bomber operation was flown. For Specification P.13/36 the requirement was for a heavy bomber, also with a crew of six, to be powered by two Rolls-Royce Vulture engines and capable of carrying a bomb load of 8,000lb. It would also have to be capable of operating from existing RAF airfields without any operational limitations or changes to existing runways and hangars.

One of the most immediate problems during the 1930s Expansion Schemes was the lack of suitable airfields. A programme to provide more airfields, to combat the threat from Germany, began in 1935, resulting in a remarkable increase in their number over the next few years. Even as the programme was getting under way, the requirements were changing. The later specifications for the heavier bombers meant that the layout of the older airfields was unsuitable. The Wellington, for example, was about 32,000lb in weight and required a take-off run of over 500yd; however, the later heavy bombers would weigh twice as much and require over 800yd of runway for take-off. It was clear that the extra weight of the new aircraft, and the amount of runway activity in a prolonged campaign, would soon make the standard grass runways and airfields unsuitable. Although Specification P.13/36 stated that the aircraft would have to be capable of operating from existing airfields, it was essential that the long-term solution to the problem—the development of all-weather airfields—be addressed. The standard pattern for a bomber airfield was for three runways, each of 1,000 yards, at 60 degrees to each other. Dimensions changed frequently to meet the requirements of new aircraft, resulting in the Class A airfield becoming standard for the heavy bombers. This layout included a main runway of 2,000yd and two secondary runways of 1,400yd of tarmac and concrete construction, plus extensive trackways and hardstandings.

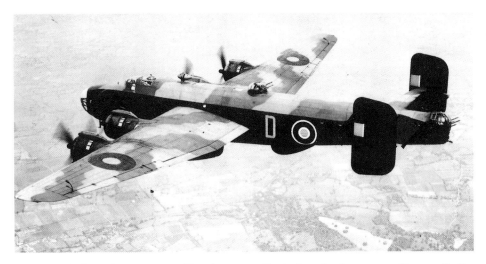

Although built to the same specification as the Avro Manchester, the Handley Page Halifax differed radically in being equipped with four Rolls-Royce Merlin engines.

A further requirement of P.13/36, which later proved most significant, was that the aircraft should be capable of carrying two 21in torpedoes for anti-shipping attacks as an alternative to its standard bomb load. This meant that the aircraft would be designed with a large bomb compartment—which would facilitate the carriage of larger weapons later in the war; one of the problems the Stirling would later meet was that the aircraft was designed with a neat arrangement of cells in the fuselage which later prevented it from carrying larger bombs. The two preferred designs to meet P.13/36 were proposed by Handley Page and A. V. Roe. The Handley Page proposal, the HP 56, was origi-

nally designed to be powered by two Rolls-Royce Vultures (as stated in the specification), but the aircraft was later redesigned as the HP 57, to be powered by four Rolls-Royce Merlins instead. This significant change in design was initially due to the likely shortage of Vulture engines in view of the increasingly high demand at the time. Later designated the Halifax, the prototype HP 57 (L7244) made its first flight on 25 October 1939. The Halifax was the second of the four-engine 'heavies' to undertake bombing operations when its first sortie took place in March 1941. The squadrons of No 4 Group, Bomber Command, gradually re-equipped over the next twelve months as the Halifax played an increasingly important part in the Command's offensive, although its loss rate was often quite high. Nevertheless, the aircraft proved to be sturdy and reliable, and generally well liked by its crews. The Halifax also had a successful career in other roles,

including Special Duties, although it was mainly employed as part of the Main Force of Bomber Command. A total of 6,176 Halifaxes were built and the aircraft served with 34 squadrons of Bomber Command throughout the war.

The Avro Manchester

On 1 January 1910 two brothers, Edwin Alliott Verdon Roe and Humphrey Verdon Roe, had established A. V. Roe and Company in Manchester. More commonly known as Avro, it was the first company ever registered as a manufacturer of aeroplanes, and since its very first day it had been at the forefront of aeronautical progress. The firm's original proposal in response to Specification P.13/36 was for an aircraft 69ft in length, of 72ft wingspan and with a gross weight of 37,777lb, a top speed of 330mph at 15,000ft and a service ceiling of 24,000ft. This original proposal led to the development of the Avro Type 679, which, unlike the Handley Page proposal, continued to utilise two Vulture engines. It was designated the Manchester, and two prototypes were ordered on 8 September 1936. The aircraft was designed with an 80ft wing span, with the main spars passing through the fuselage at the mid-position, and two fins. The two Rolls-Royce Vulture 24-cylinder, liquid-cooled engines were mounted in nacelles either side of, and close to, the fuselage section, with the undercarriage designed

The first Manchester prototype, L7246, shown with twin tail and no turrets.

to retract into them. The Vulture had originated from the idea of joining two 12-cylinder Peregrine engines, one on top of the other, in an 'X' type arrangement; in this way a lower power-to-weight ratio and an increased power output was achieved—the engine was expected to develop 1,700–1,800hp—and such a powerplant would result in a less costly aircraft than the alternative four-engine bomber.

The specification had stated that the aircraft should accommodate a crew of six in order to carry out a number of duties, some of which were new and more specialised than had been previously em-

Roy Dobson, who joined A. V. Roe in 1914 and went on to become the company's managing director in 1941. (BAe)

ployed in RAF bombers. The requirement was for two pilots, with other duties such as those of navigator, bomb aimer, wireless operator and air gunners being shared among the other four crew members. The Manchester design accommodated the front crew of four positioned forward of the wing spar in a sizeable compartment. These crew positions comprised the two pilots, a navigator/bomb aimer and a wireless operator/front gunner; the remaining two crew members, both air gunners, were positioned aft of the main spar, one in the tail gun position and the other in the ventral gun position.

The design of the Manchester continued under Avro's Chief Designer, Roy Chadwick, throughout 1937, although in the early stages the exact crew composition and bomb load were unclear (it was decided that the first prototype should be built without gun turrets). Roy Chadwick was what can only be described as a brilliant aircraft designer. Born at Urmston, Manchester, in 1893, he had, quite simply, devoted his life to the world of aviation. After school he worked in the drawing office at the British Westinghouse Company at Trafford Park in Manchester. Such was his determination to succeed, Chadwick had introduced himself to the great pioneer aviator, Alliott Verdon Roe, in 1911 and persuaded the latter to take him on as a draughtsman. So began Chadwick's long association with the A. V. Roe aircraft company. By the outbreak of the First World War Chadwick was just 21 years old but already commanded a workforce of 100. One young man work-

The second Manchester prototype, L7247, with the interim central fin fitted—a result of lateral instability following the aircraft's maiden flight on 26 May 1940.

ing for him during the early months of the war was Roy Hardy Dobson. Born in 1891 at Horsforth, Yorkshire, Dobson had served an engineering apprenticeship in Manchester before joining A. V. Roe in 1914. Within two years he was in charge of the Experimental Department and at the end of the First World War he became works manager. In 1934 Dobson was appointed general manager, and he went on to become the company's managing director in 1941.

Roy Chadwick had been instrumental in the design of the Avro 500 series, in particular the Avro 504 which had carried out the first bombing raid on Germany. After the First World War he remained with A. V. Roe, where he not only designed aircraft but actually flew them as well. This personal conquest had nearly led to his death in 1920 when he survived a crash in an Avro Baby (which was said to be the first truly light aeroplane). When the company was sold to J. D. Siddeley 1928, Chadwick was appointed Chief Designer. He continued to develop his quite brilliant career, working particularly closely with Dobson. The 'two Roys' worked in harmony, both becoming directors in 1936, and were undoubtedly the reason for the company's continuing success, with Chadwick looking after aircraft design and Dobson looking after the production.

The first Manchester prototype, L7246, was built at Newton Heath and the main sections were transported to Ringway for final assembly during May. L7246 made its maiden flight on 25 July 1939 at Ringway in the hands of A. V. Roe's chief test pilot, Captain H. A. 'Sam' Brown. The flight showed that the aircraft suffered many handling faults, including a problem with lateral stability. Similar comments were made when the aircraft was later delivered for RAF evaluation at the Aeroplane and Armament Experimental Establishment (A&AEE) at Boscombe Down. It was further revealed that the early Vulture I engines fitted in the first prototype were boost-limited and lacking in overall power. However, the design was generally praised, in particular its overall performance in speed and altitude, although it was hoped that the unrestricted engines proposed for the next prototype would improve the aircraft's overall performance.

The second prototype, L7247, differed aerodynamically from its predecessor in that it included a redesigned and extended outer wing along with new fins and rudders. It was intended that the second prototype would be as close in its final design to the proposed production airframe. The maiden flight of L7247 took place on 26 May 1940 and was generally successful, in particular the improvements to the aerodynamics. However, there was still some concern about the lateral stability of the aircraft. This concern resulted in a central fin being fitted to L7247 almost immediately, a modification which proved partially, but not completely, successful in solving the problem. With these significant changes to the second prototype, it was decided that there was little or no further use in the development trials for the original prototype and so L7246 was delivered to the Royal Aircraft Establishment (RAE) at Farnborough for other trials.

During the summer of 1940 continuous improvements and modifications to L7247 were made—the installation of Vulture Mk II engines, the fitting of an improved central fin and the fitting of three hydraulically powered Nash & Thompson gun turrets which would, it was

hoped, provide good all-round defence against attacking enemy fighters. The front turret was the FN5, as fitted to the Wellington, which was armed with two 0.303in Browning machine guns. The rear turret was the FN4, armed with four Brownings, which would later prove to be one of the best developments in defensive armament for the heavy bomber. The third turret was the FN21 ventral turret, known as the 'dustbin', but its value on the aircraft was a cause for concern. Fitted with two Brownings, it was a heavy and crude design which was lowered for use. When extended into the airflow, the turret caused drag which was sufficient to slow down the aircraft by some 15kt. Nevertheless, the Manchester had taken shape and, with its relatively large bomb bay capable of carrying bombs of 1,000lb or 2,000lb, or a single bomb of 4,000lb, it was ready for production.

The relative size and complexity of the Manchester at that time meant that initial production was slow. This was further hampered by the continuation of flight trials, which highlighted the need for additional modifications to the design. The proposed number of Manchesters eventually amounted to some 1,200 airframes, the building of which was originally to be shared between A. V. Roe at Newton Heath and Metropolitan-Vickers at Trafford Park. The initial contract awarded to A. V. Roe was for 200 Manchesters built to Air Ministry Specification B.19/37 under Contract No B.648770/37, and the initial contract awarded to Metropolitan-Vickers was for 100 Manchesters, also built to Specification B.19/37, under Contract No B.108750/40. This order was later distributed further to include another 300 airframes to be built by the Fairey Aviation Co. and Sir W. G. Armstrong Whitworth.

The first production Manchester, L7276, was delivered to Boscombe Down on 5 August 1940. Initial trials were generally successful, with only minor modifications being made. These modifications were incorporated into the second production airframe, L7277, which was delivered to Boscombe Down in October. This air-

craft then went through a complicated trials programme which included the carriage of various bomb loads. Initially it was decided that the aircraft could operate successfully, and safely, at a ceiling of about 13,500ft (although this was later revised to 12,000ft).

Into Service

Production of the Manchester had slowly improved to an acceptable rate. With the long and hard summer of 1940 past, during which time the heroics of 'The Few' had ensured that Britain was safe from invasion (at least for the time being), the concentration of effort began to swing from defence to attack. It was clear that the Manchester offered Bomber Command the chance to take the war back to Germany, deep into its industrial heart, which the shorter-range and less capable bombers could not reach. There did not seem enough time to develop the Manchester further as a weapon of war, and the feeling was generally one of getting the aircraft into service and that 'everything would work out all right.' There was a definite urgency to hit back at the enemy as soon and as hard as possible.

The Manchester trials carried out by late 1940 suggested no hints that the aircraft would be anything but very successful in its role. Nevertheless, by any standards the bomber was rushed into operational service. This was particularly true in the case of the Vulture Mk II engines which, although considerably improved from the early Mk Is, still lacked power and were prone to overheating. The aircraft, and therefore the engines, had simply not flown enough hours to make a complete assessment of the capabilities and limitations of the Vulture engines in a likely combat environment.

It had been decided that No 207 Squadron would be the first to equip with the RAF's latest bomber. Not only would this unit be the first to receive the new aircraft, but it would also be responsible for bringing it up to an operational standard. This would involve assessing the airframe and engine performance, and include crew training and the development of new tactics. The decision to make No 207 Squad-

An early-production Manchester (L7277), with central fin but no dorsal turret.

ron the first to be equipped with the new Manchester was an interesting one. Just prior to the Second World War the Squadron became a Group training unit, equipped with Ansons, and it had remained in this role until April 1940, when it became part of No 12 Operational Training Unit. The Squadron re-formed on 1 November 1940 at Waddington as part of No 5 Group, Bomber Command, under the direction of Squadron Leader Noel Hyde and initially included some of the most experienced crews in the Command. The first aircraft, L7279, was delivered on 6 November, followed by the second, L7278, four days later. Over the next six weeks the Squadron accumulated a total of eleven aircraft and sixteen crews. However, the introduction of the Manchester into service suffered early setbacks. Problems with the Vulture's cooling system and also with the airframe delayed the Squadron's operational work-up period well into early 1941.

The first Manchester operations took place on the night of 24/25 February when six aircraft from the Squadron took part in an attack against the French port of Brest where the German cruiser *Admiral Hipper* had been detected. For the Manchesters the raid was reported as successful inasmuch as the aircraft had performed more or less as expected. However, it soon became clear that the *Admiral Hipper* was not hit or even damaged in any way. Nevertheless, the Manchester had finally taken part in its first operation, some eighteen months after the first prototype had made its maiden flight back in July 1939.

All of the early Manchesters delivered into squadron service were of basic Mk I design with the original three tail fins and no dorsal turret fitted. They were also unable to carry any of the larger 2,000lb bombs which had been one of the early design advantages of the aircraft. This problem was solved within a month of commencing bombing operations when No 207 Squadron received more updated airframes. The slightly later design of airframe also included the Nash & Thompson FN7 dorsal turret, armed with two Brownings. Despite the relatively long delay into operational service, the prob-

lem of the Vulture engines still remained and it was not long before the Squadron suffered its first loss due to a technical defect. On the night of 20/21 March, Manchester L7278 crashed following a fire after take-off. Although the four rear crewmen baled out, two had vacated the aircraft too early and were killed before their parachutes could fully deploy. In an attempt to land the aircraft the two pilots had remained with the stricken bomber, but they were killed when the aircraft struck an obstacle on landing and blew up.

On the day following the first operational sorties by the Manchesters of No 207 Squadron, the second Manchester unit formed. Under the command of Squadron Leader Denys Balsdon, No 97 Squadron formed at RAF Waddington on 25 February. Initially, pilots with brief Manchester experience with No 207 Squadron formed the 'backbone' of the new unit. Throughout the next six weeks the Squadron took delivery of its aircraft and crews and completed its operational work-up. Its first operations took place on the night of 8/9 April when four Manchesters participated in a raid against Kiel. All four of No 97 Squadron's aircraft returned safely, but one of No 207 Squadron's Manchesters, captained by its commanding officer, Wing Commander Hyde, failed to return. This was a most tragic incident and felt by the crews to be a setback in the Manchester's early operational life:Hyde had, after all, been instrumental in seeing the RAF's new bomber into service. Unfortunately, his loss would not be the last amongst the early Manchester pilots and crews.

Problems with the Vulture persisted. By April 1941 the engine had flown sufficient hours to enable detailed diagnoses of its performance, capabilities and weaknesses to be made. Close examinations of stripped-down engines revealed that the problem of overheating appeared to be caused by the 'X' type arrangement of the 24 cylinders, restricting cooling and affecting the lubrication of the big-end bearings. All Manchesters were grounded until the problem could be resolved. This temporary hiatus in the aircraft's operational career gave engineers the chance to make additional design changes to the existing airframes to bring the Manchester further towards its design specification. These modifications included the fitting of dorsal turrets to the early airframes and improving the capability of the aircraft to carry the larger 4,000lb bomb.

The first raid following the grounding was flown on the night of 2/3 May 1941 and was significant for the fact that one aircraft from No 207 Squadron dropped the new 4,000lb bomb. Although this raid marked the first operational release of the 4,000lb 'Cookie' by a Manchester, earlier drops had been made by Wellingtons. The successful release of the 'cookie' meant that, from that night, the 4,000lb bomb would be available for use by the Manchester crews.

By the end of the month Manchesters had flown over 100 operational sorties. It is difficult to assess the Manchester's overall performance and effectiveness during the first three months of its operational life. It had undoubtedly suffered setbacks and losses, but then that would be expected following the introduction of any aircraft into operational service. Any assessment is made trickier because of the problem of determining the exact reasons for the losses, particularly those over hostile territory. However, what does seem clear is that the Vulture engines were often the reason for aborted sorties. In the first three months of Manchester operations the abort rate was as high as one in five during operational sorties. Not all of these were attributable to problems with the engines, but many were. In the same period it appears that more Manchesters were lost as a result of mechanical failure than to enemy activity. With three aircraft coming to grief on training flights, the total number of losses rose to eleven. Thus, as a result of continuing engine failures, the Manchesters were once more withdrawn from operations in the summer of 1941.

With this further break from operations, doubts were expressed over the future of the Manchester and whether or not it should remain in service. After much discussion it was decided to persevere, although it was decided to improve the Vulture engines and to remove the central vertical fin and increase the size of the tailplane and the two remaining fins in order to improve lateral stability. Aircraft incorporating these modifications were designated Manchester IA.

This period also saw the establishment of the third Manchester squadron. Under the command of Wing Commander George Valentine, No 61 Squadron formed at North Luffenham on 17 July. With Manchester operations having resumed on the night of 7/8 August, this Squadron flew its first operational sortie on the night of 14/15 August when Valentine and his crew joined six other Manchesters in a raid on Magdeburg. Valentine failed to return from an operation less than three weeks later. His aircraft is believed to have crashed near Berlin on the night of 2/3 September with the loss of the entire crew. Flying with Valentine that night, as an observer on the raid, was North Luffenham's Station Commander, Group Captain J. Barrett, and the loss was a double tragedy for both the Squadron and the station.

The Manchester squadrons continued their operational work-up of new crews throughout the remainder of 1941, resulting in a gradual increase in the number of Manchester operational sorties. The fourth squadron to operate the aircraft was No 83, under the command of Wing Commander Stewart Tudor DFC, which re-equipped at Scampton in December 1941 and commenced operations the following month. Already an experienced Bomber Command unit, No 83 had been flying Hampdens since the outbreak of the war, during which time Sergeant John Hannah had been awarded the Victoria Cross for courage following an attack on the port of Antwerp on the night of 15/16 September 1940. At just eighteen years of age, the youthful wireless operator/air gunner was the youngest ever airman to receive the award.

Despite the increase in the Manchester's operational sorties, the aircraft's contribution to the overall effort mounted by Bomber Command during the last months of 1941 remained small. This is in no way

The cockpit of the Manchester, showing the dual controls for the two pilots.

disrespectful to the individual efforts by the Manchester crews, as these proved as determined as ever, but merely a reflection of the number of sorties flown. This period of introducing the Manchester into operational service had proved very slow and frustrating, and the brunt of the bomber effort had to come from the other aircraft of the Command. Despite having been in service for ten months, there were still only a relatively small number of Manchesters flying and few crews carrying out operations. By the end of 1941 there were just four Manchester squadrons, representing a mere 7 per cent of Bomber Command's operational strength, compared to 21 Wellington squadrons, which still formed the backbone of the Command's effort. However, a point in the Manchester's favour during the last four months of 1941 was that just five aircraft were lost on operations—a reasonable statistic.

Owing to the unsatisfactory performance of the Vulture engines of the Manchester Mk I and Mk IA, the design team at A. V. Roe had given consideration to replacing the Vultures with either two Bristol Centaurus radial engines or two Napier Sabre I inlines. As a result, one Manchester airframe was sent to Napiers at Luton for Sabres to be installed. When it was found that the Sabre would require lengthy development it was discarded for the Bristol Centaurus, a more powerful derivative of the Hercules radial engine as fitted to the Stirling. Two of these engines were installed and the variant was designated Manchester Mk II. But the aircraft was never flown, because of the satisfactory performance of a four-engine variant, the Manchester Mk III, already being unofficially referred to as the Lancaster.

One of the most significant raids by Manchesters was the daylight attack against the German warships *Scharnhorst*, *Gneisenau* and *Prinz Eugen* at Brest on 18 December. The warships had been in dock for some time and Bomber Command had made several attempts to prevent them from returning to sea. During the previous week a number of raids had been carried out, including minelaying operations in the Channel immediately off Brest. These raids took place by day and by night

but proved largely unsuccessful. Only the previous night, a force of 120 bombers had carried out attacks, again without any apparent success. The daylight raid on 18 December was carried out by 47 bombers, including nine Manchesters of No 97 Squadron, with cover provided by Fighter Command. The Manchesters were led by Wing Commander Balsdon, who flew as second pilot to Flight Sergeant G. Pendrill for the raid. Each Manchester carried three 2,000lb armour-piercing bombs and, despite heavy flak and cloudy conditions, pressed home a most determined attack for the loss of one aircraft over the target area. During his attack Balsdon's aircraft was hit by flak over the target but managed to return to its base at Coningsby. However, the aircraft crashed on landing with the loss of the entire crew.

The raid initially appeared unsuccessful, although it was later determined that the *Prinz Eugen* had suffered some damage. It also appeared that damage had been inflicted on the lock gates, which prevented the *Scharnhorst* from putting to sea for some considerable time. The warships finally made their dash from Brest through the English Channel on 12 February 1942. Using bad weather to conceal their escape, the ships were not spotted until late morning. Throughout the remainder of the daylight hours Bomber Command flew 242 sorties against the warships in a final attempt to stop them. Most of the bombers were unable to locate the ships but Manchesters of Nos 61 and 207 Squadrons were amongst some which did attack. This final sortie against the warships brought to an end a prolonged period of sustained operations against Brest, during which Bomber Command had dropped nearly 3,500 tons of bombs and lost 127 aircraft. All three ships had at some time suffered some damage and had, at least, been kept away from sea for several weeks —something for which the Royal Navy and merchant shipping were grateful.

The Period of Change

For Bomber Command, the year 1942 marked the turning point of the war. In February, after frequent changes of commander, the Command acquired at its

Air Marshal Sir Arthur ('Bomber') Harris assumed the leadership of Bomber Command in February 1942 and remained at its head until the end of the war.

head the man who was to inspire and lead it for the rest of the war—Air Marshal Arthur Travis Harris.

Born in 1892, Harris went through a relatively unremarkable schooling, leaving when sixteen to go to Rhodesia. When the First World War broke out he became a bugler with the 1st Rhodesia Regiment and took part in campaigns in South-West Africa, after which he returned to England and joined the RFC. Tours in Home Defence and artillery-spotting over the Western Front saw him end the war as a Major. One of the few to be given a post-war position, Harris went to the North-West Frontier Province of India. It was there as a Squadron Commander that he developed his theories of air power. By 1922 he was the Officer Commanding No 45 Squadron in Iraq, where he converted his Venom and Victoria transport aircraft into 'long-range heavy bombers' by cutting sighting holes in the nose and bolting on 'home-made' bomb racks. Harris's connection with bombers continued in 1925 when he was the Officer Commanding No 58 Squadron in the United Kingdom, equipped with the Vickers Virginia, the RAF's first post-war heavy bomber. A period at the Army Staff College at Camberley and a tour in Egypt were followed by another Squadron Commander tour, this time with No 210 at Pembroke Dock with flying boats. A series of staff appointments gave Harris his chance to influence air policy. As a member of the Joint Planning Committee in 1936 he helped formulate the strategic bombing policy for the event of war with Germany. With the reorganisation of RAF Commands and Groups, he took over the newly formed No 4 Group in 1937, based at Linton-on-Ouse. However, it was a short-lived appointment as he was sent to the United States with the Purchasing Mission to acquire American aircraft, followed by another tour in the Middle East as Air Officer Commanding Palestine and Trans-Jordan. Harris was promoted to Air Vice-Marshal in July 1939 and appointed Air Officer Commanding No 5 Group. He became Deputy Chief of Staff and was promoted to Air Marshal in June 1941.

As the war progressed, Harris became more concerned about the way that the bombing offensive was being conducted. He appreciated the great strain under which crews were operating and tried to adopt a policy of 'two nights' rest between each mission'. His opinions were to stand him in good stead when he took over control of Bomber Command, which, he was determined, should be run his way: the decisive nature of its offensive power should not be misused or bled away to other areas. It was a policy that brought him many heated arguments but it was undoubtedly one that, in general terms, was correct. He was convinced of the value, and the necessity, of the bombing offensive and he gave a tremendous boost to the morale of the Command at a time when its fortunes and spirits were at a low ebb.

February 1942 also saw a slight change in the Manchester's order of battle, with No 97 Squadron losing its aircraft preparatory to receiving the new Lancaster which was about to enter service. However, the number of Manchester squadrons remained at four as No 106, under

Table 1. Manchester Production by A. V. Roe at Newton Heath

Serial nos	Marks	No of aircraft
L7246	Prototype	
L7247	Prototype	
L7276–L7325	Production MkI	50
L7373–L7402	Production MkI	30
L7415–L7434	Production MkI/IA	20
L7453–L7497	Production MkI/IA	45
L7515–L7526	Production MkI/IA	12
Total		**157**

Table 2. Manchester Production by Metropolitan-Vickers at Trafford Park

Serial nos	Marks	No of aircraft
R5768–R5797	Production MkI/IA	30
R5829–R5841	Production MkI/IA	13
Total		**43**

the command of Wing Commander Robert Allen DSO DFC*, re-equipped with the aircraft at Coningsby. Like No 83 Squadron, No106 had previously operated the Hampden, initially from Finningley and then from Coningsby since February 1941. The Squadron's association with the Manchester was only a brief one, operationally lasting from March to June. However, its success with respect to the number of operations flown during this period was comparatively good. Incidentally, the Squadron's new commanding officer was a young 23-year-old pilot, Wing Commander Guy Gibson DFC*.

By the following month it had been decided to re-equip all the heavy bomber squadrons of No 5 Group with the Lancaster. By the end of March the number of Manchester squadrons had been reduced to three, with No 207 having ceased operations in preparation for receiving its Lancasters. However, two more units briefly re-equipped during March and April, bringing the total number of squadrons to have received the Manchester to seven, although they never all operated the aircraft at the same time. No 50 Squadron based at Skellingthorpe commenced operations on the night of 8/9 April and No 49 Squadron at Scampton on the night of 2/3 May. With No 49 operational, this brought the number of Manchester squadrons at any one time back up to five.

The period April–May 1942 saw a great change in Bomber Command's order of battle. It had seen the passing of the Whitley from the front line, the last operation having taken place on the night of 27/28 April. For the Manchester this was the peak period in terms of the number of operational squadrons, and the aircraft was about to make an appearance in the new bombing strategy of the 'Thousand Bomber' raids. For some time Harris had planned a very large raid as a demonstration of the full power of a coordinated bombing plan. The target chosen for the first of these raids was the city of Cologne on the night of 30/31 May. By scraping together every possible asset a force of 1,047 bombers, including 46 Manchesters from No 5 Group, was dispatched to the target. One of the Manchesters taking part in the raid was flown by Flying Officer Leslie Manser, a 23-year-old pilot serving with No 50 Squadron. Cologne was his fourteenth 'op'.

In Manchester L7301, Manser and his crew took off from Skellingthorpe just after 2300 hours. Owing to the full bomb load and overheating engines, he found that he could not climb above 7,000ft. At that point he would have been perfectly justified in aborting the sortie and returning to base. Instead he decided to continue. Overhead Cologne Manser released his bombs and turned for home, and al-

most immediately his aircraft was hit by flak. To avoid the searchlights and further damage, he dived the aircraft to 1,000ft. Having escaped immediate danger, he climbed to 2,000ft, where it would have been possible for the crew to bail out, but Manser was determined to return the aircraft and crew to base. Then the port engine caught fire. The fire was eventually controlled but the Manchester, on just one engine, began to lose height. Manser hung on as best he could, every minute taking him and his crew nearer to safety. When a crash became inevitable, Manser ordered the crew to bail out. One of the crew

handed him his parachute but Manser waved it away, saying that he could only hold the aircraft steady for a few more seconds. As the crew descended to safety they saw the aircraft, still with Manser on board, plunge to earth and burst into flames. The Manchester had crashed three miles east of Bree, a tiny Belgian village close to the Dutch border. Apart from one crew member, who was injured and subsequently taken prisoner of war, the remainder of the crew escaped capture and returned to Britain, via Gibraltar, on 1 July. It was only then that the story was told by the crew, and it was subsequently announced that Leslie Manser had been awarded a posthumous Victoria Cross, the only occasion that a VC was awarded to a member of a Manchester crew. In a personal letter to Manser's family, Harris wrote that 'no Victoria Cross has been more gallantly earned'.

Although just under 900 of the bombers claimed to have attacked Cologne, the damage inflicted was lighter than had been hoped. Nevertheless, a number of impor-

Later production Manchesters included the FN7 dorsal turret, followed by the removal of the central fin, which resulted in the designation Manchester Mk IA. Shown here is L7466, which served with No 97 Squadron at Coningsby before being lost in operations.

tant industrial and administrative areas had been hit. However, 41 aircraft were lost, including four Manchesters. Although a large number of aircraft, this was still a relatively low 4 per cent of the total force. For the Manchesters, however, the loss was more than double, at 8.7 per cent.

Fortunately for Harris, the raid was deemed a success, and this silenced most of the critics and persuaded the Government to allocate Bomber Command a higher priority for aircraft and, more importantly, for the scientific development of specialist equipment, including navigation aids and radar, which were vital for the accurate delivery of bombs on target. The 'Thousand Bomber' force was again assembled just two nights later, on the night of 1/2 June, with Essen being the chosen target. Again the Manchesters were involved, 33 aircraft taking part in the raid with the loss of just one aircraft. The raid did not prove particularly successful as the bombing was scattered owing to haze and low cloud over the target.

The number of new Lancasters taking part in operations was continuing to grow,

Flying Officer Leslie Manser, of No 50 Squadron based at Skellingthorpe, was the only member of a Manchester crew to be awarded the Victoria Cross, for outstanding courage during the first 'Thousand Bomber' raid against Cologne on the night of 30/31 May 1942. (No 50 Sqn records)

therefore bringing to a close the operational life of the Manchester. The last Manchester operations were flown on the night of 25/26 June when aircraft from the remaining squadrons took part in the third of the 'Thousand Bomber' raids. The target was Bremen and the total force just exceeded that of the Cologne raid with 1,067 aircraft. The Manchesters of No 5 Group were detailed to attack the Focke-Wulf factory. The raid proved partially successful, although the attack on the factory did not result in its destruction as planned, merely that of a few buildings. Of the three 'Thousand Bomber' raids, it could be argued that the only successful effort was the first against Cologne. Nevertheless, they had represented a serious attempt at streaming and concentrating a bomber force to overwhelm enemy defences and, therefore, reduce the overall losses. But it was impossible to keep such a large force together for any period of time: it had, after all, used up every available asset and the training units needed to get back to their primary role. Other contributors, such as the Coastal Command aircraft and crews, equally could not afford the diversion away from the priority of their own tasks.

The operational life of the Manchester was now over, but the aircraft remained in service with the RAF for some considerable time. With the increasing number of Lancasters required for the operational squadrons, the Manchester served as an ideal heavy training aircraft for crews about to join Lancaster squadrons. For

Table 3. Manchester Squadrons and Operating Bases		
Squadron/Unit	*Operating Base*	*Dates*
49 Sqn	Scampton	Apr.–July 1942
50 Sqn	Skellingthorpe	Apr.–June 1942
61 Sqn	North Luffenham, Syerston	July 1941–June 1942
83 Sqn	Scampton	Dec. 1941–May 1942
97 Sqn	Coningsby	Mar. 1941–Feb. 1942
106 Sqn	Coningsby	Feb.–June 1942
207 Sqn	Waddington, Bottesford	Nov. 1940–Mar. 1942
1653 HCU	Lindholme, Colerne	Oct. 1942–Mid-1943
1654 HCU	Swinderby, Wigsley	May 1942–July 1943
1656 HCU	Lindholme	Nov. 1942–Mid-1943
1660 HCU	Swinderby	Oct. 1942–Mid-1943
1661 HCU	Waddington, Scampton, Winthorpe	Mid-1942–Feb. 1943
1662 HCU	Blyton	Feb.–Mar. 1943

example, Manchesters were used for conversion training with No 1654 Heavy Conversion Unit (HCU) at Swinderby from 19 May 1942, and the unit continued with them at Wigsley from June 1942 before eventually being withdrawn in July 1943.

The build-up of the 'heavy' squadrons continued throughout 1942 and Manchesters continued to support the training task. Two more HCUs formed with Manchesters in October 1942, No 1653 at Lindholme and No 1660 at Swinderby. Manchesters were also allocated to other HCUs as they became available, and it was not uncommon for one HCU to operate two or even three different types of heavy bomber. An example of this was No 1656, which formed at Lindholme in November 1942 and by the following February was operating Lancasters, Manchesters and Halifaxes. As well as the training of

Bomber Command aircrews, Manchesters were involved with specialist tasks such as those undertaken by the Bomber Development Unit when it formed at Gransden Lodge in July 1942.

Manchester production totalled two prototypes and 200 Mk Is and Mk IAs, which served with seven Bomber Command squadrons as well as with HCUs and other smaller units. Of those Manchesters that survived, the majority were struck off charge by the end of 1943, thus bringing to an end the career of an aircraft without which the subsequent success of the Lancaster might never have occurred. Although much has been written about the failures of the Manchester, the aircraft enjoyed some success and this was due to the professionalism and determination of the crews which flew and maintained it through a very difficult period of the war. Many lessons had been learned by the Manchester crews, and these enabled the Lancaster to enjoy almost immediate success. As with any new aircraft, there is always a period of uncertainty when finding out the best way to operate it in order 'to get the job done'. For the Lancaster, that period was effectively served by the Manchester.

The first Lancaster prototype (BT308) pictured at Boscombe Down in January 1941. This aircraft was truly a four-engine Manchester, very few changes to the original airframe having taken place. Unlike later aircraft, BT308 was powered by Merlin X engines.

2. Development and Production

For some considerable time before the war Roy Chadwick had been working on the possibility of adapting the Manchester airframe to accommodate four engines, as it had soon become obvious that the Manchester was going to be underpowered. Chadwick also felt that the new four-engine bombers being developed, the Stirling and Halifax, were more likely to offer improved range and maximum bomb load and, therefore, offered greater potential for long-term development. The Stirling had originated as a result of Specification B.12/36 and it became the first of the new four-engine heavy bombers to enter RAF service. Like the Manchester, the Halifax had been developed as a result of Specification P.13/36 and had at first been designed to be powered by two Rolls-Royce Vultures but was later fitted with four Rolls-Royce Merlins instead. Ironically, this significant change in engine type was initially brought about by the likely shortage of Vulture engines because of the increasingly high demand at the time.

Although the future of all the new heavy bomber designs was uncertain during the period leading up to the war, the Manchester did offer one advantage over the other types in that it had been designed with a relatively large bomb bay, and although at that time there were no plans to carry any weapon as large as a 4,000lb bomb, this advantage would prove to be significant. Various powerplant options, such as the Bristol Taurus and Bristol Pegasus, were discussed, although the most realistic and sensible choice available to Chadwick was for the Manchester to be re-engined with either four Merlins (various early marks of Merlin were considered), as fitted to the Halifax, or four Bristol Hercules VI radials, as fitted to the

Stirling. An immediate and obvious penalty arising from the installation of two extra engines was the increased weight of the aircraft: for the option of installing four Merlins, the unladen weight of the Manchester would be increased by 12.5 per cent to approximately 27,000lb, with an additional 1,000lb for the aircraft to be powered by four Hercules. Although planning to install four engines into the Manchester wing, Chadwick did not initially reckon on increasing the length of the wing to accommodate the change, although he did consider changes to the tail and improving the strength of the undercarriage.

The new proposal for a four-engine Manchester, initially designated the Avro Type 680, was discussed although it was not until a new specification was issued by the Air Ministry that the design was considered as a serious contender to the other four-engine bombers already under development. Specification B.1/39 of 6 March 1939 called for a four-engine bomber with a maximum all-up weight of 50,000lb, including a bomb load of 10,000lb, two cannon-armed gun turrets and a crew of seven. The specification also stated that the aircraft should be capable of an operating range of greater than 2,500 miles and of a cruising speed of 280mph at 15,000ft. The idea was that the new bomber would eventually replace all the heavy bombers at that time still under development within five years from the issue of the specification. Several designs were considered, including proposals from A. V. Roe, Armstrong Whitworth, Bristol, Handley Page, Shorts and Vickers.

There had been concern at the Air Ministry that the cost of extending the runways at RAF airfields for the new heavy

bombers to operate was too great, and there was also a strong possibility that airfields would become damaged if attacked. When considering these problems, the Air Ministry suggested that the new heavy bombers should be capable of shorter take-off and landing runs. Amongst other ideas, the Manchester airframe had been strengthened so that the aircraft could be launched by catapult. Trials were carried out and the prototype Manchester was successfully launched, but the project was soon cancelled. The catapult-launch capability no longer a requirement, A. V. Roe could develop an aircraft with a longer and improved wingspan of thinner and lighter (but stronger) material and capable of taking four engines. This resulted in the Avro Type 683 proposal, a design which was to be powered by four Rolls-Royce Merlin X engines and have an increased wingspan and an enlarged tailplane, although this meant that the proposal would slightly exceed the 50,000lb maximum all-up weight stated in the specification. The Type 683 continued at A. V. Roe, separate from the Manchester project, under the guidance of Stuart Davies. However, the outbreak of war in Europe meant that the company's immediate attention was focused on bringing the Manchester into RAF service.

By the summer of 1940 both of the Manchester prototypes had flown and, as will be recalled, it had been found that their early Vulture Mk I engines were boost-limited and lacking in overall power. This had led to Vulture Mk II engines replacing the Mk Is in the second prototype. This early problem in the Manchester prototypes led to a change in the Type 683 design. It was proposed that by increasing the wingspan to 100ft it would be possible

The second Lancaster prototype (DG595) was designed and built as close to the standard of the production airframe as possible.

to achieve a significant improvement in take-off performance; although this would result in a very slight weight penalty, the benefits would be significant. It had also been found that in some areas the proposal exceeded the performance required in the specification, notably in the operating speed and altitude and the maximum bomb load capable of being carried. There continued to be great interest in the proposal although, at that time, Britain was very much up against the daily onslaught from the *Luftwaffe*. Most of the nation's efforts went into the production of fighters, without which Britain would surely have been defeated.

Prototypes

For some time it had been obvious at A. V. Roe that the Manchester would have to be replaced by an improved four-engine heavy bomber. The thought of either the Stirling or Halifax being the ultimate replacement caused concern as neither aircraft had entered operational service and, therefore, each remained an unknown quantity. To the designers at A. V. Roe it seemed more sensible, and perhaps self-evident, that the twin-engine Manchester should be replaced by a four-engine version to ensure maximum commonality. With the introduction of the Manchester into RAF service during the winter of 1940/41, more priority was gradually given by the A. V. Roe designers to the Type 683, although the project nearly suffered a major set-back when the Ministry of Aircraft Production wanted to cancel the development of the Manchester programme after work on improving the Vulture engines ceased in 1940. It appears that the Ministry even suggested that British aircraft designers should go to America to see just how a modern heavy bomber should be built. Furthermore, in the likely event that the Manchester's operational life was going to be short rather than long, there was a campaign by others to suggest that A. V. Roe's production facilities should be made available for the development of the Halifax rather than for the design and development of a four-engine Manchester. Within hours of Dobson receiving notification that this might be the case, he and Chadwick went to the Ministry of Aircraft Production with full performance estimates of the Type 683 and, such were their powers of persuasion, the pair managed to secure a reprieve by agreeing to produce two prototypes by July 1941.

By the end of 1940 A. V. Roe had been awarded a contract to build four prototypes of the new four-engine bomber to replace the existing Manchester. However, no specific details had been outlined for anything more than the first prototype, and only a general outline for the second and third prototypes. The contract stated that the first prototype was to employ a modified Manchester airframe to be powered by four Roll-Royce Merlin X engines. It went on to state that the second prototype should be representative of the initial production airframe and the third prototype should be powered by Bristol Hercules VI radial engines. Authority to go ahead with manufacture of the four prototypes was issued to A. V. Roe on 19 November 1940. In order to save as much time as possible, a standard Manchester Mk I airframe, BT308, was taken from the production line and fitted with four Merlin X engines and became the prototype for the Manchester Mk III. Although the Air Ministry was determined that all available Merlin engines should be kept for fighter production, Chadwick and Dobson somehow managed to 'acquire' four Merlins for BT308 through a close friend at Rolls-Royce. Installation of the new Merlin engines into the airframe appeared to prove little problem to the engineers as the majority of engineering components were interchangeable. The assembly jigs also appeared interchangeable, with the exception of the outer wings, tailplane, fin and rudder which required a relatively small amount of adjustment.

The agreement between Roy Chadwick and Stuart Davies was that the first prototype should have the standard Manchester fuselage sections with new outer wing and powerplant assemblies, although it would retain the Manchester's undercarriage. The prototype would also have an increased 33ft tailplane, as previously tested on the Manchester, with the standard fins and rudders plus a central fin. It was also planned for the prototype to have the standard Manchester electrical system with just two engine-driven generators fitted on the inboard engines. The hydraulic and pneumatic services were the standard Manchester design, although the fuel system had to be modified for the four engines. The two inboard engines remained in the same position as on the original Manchester but were fitted in a reshaped nacelle, whilst the positions of the two outboard engines were determined by propeller diameter (although the design meant that they were positioned as far inboard as possible). The cockpit layout remained similar to that of the original Manchester, although the centre console was widened to accommodate the four throttles side by side. This meant that the propeller controls had to be situated below the throttles

instead of alongside, as in the Manchester, and although there was double the engine instrumentation the remainder of the basic flight instruments remained unchanged.

The first prototype looked like, and quite simply was, a four-engine Manchester with very few changes to the original Mk I airframe having taken place. BT308 was transported to Ringway for its first flight; this was originally scheduled for 31 December 1940, but changes to the hydraulic system meant that it was delayed until the New Year. Engine runs took place during the week over the New Year, and there followed a few days of fog, further delaying the date of the first flight until 9 January. With 'Sam' Brown and Bill Thorn at the controls, BT308 took off from Ringway, now the site of Manchester International Airport. The flight proved successful, and during the following two weeks BT308 made nine more before being delivered to A&AEE at Boscombe Down on 27 January for further intensive flight trials.

It had been decided at A. V. Roe that the four-engine Manchester should adopt a new name. The name 'Lancaster' had been used informally by the company for several months when referring to the Type 683 project, although it had not been officially recognised by the Air Ministry. However, by 28 February the name had been formally approved, and so the new Lancaster arrived to take its own special place in the history of air warfare.

Following the trials at Boscombe Down, BT308 arrived back at A. V. Roe to be fitted with a new tail section and to have

the central fin removed. The results of the trials had proved most successful, particularly regarding the overall performance of the aircraft. As anticipated, the aircraft did suffer slightly in directional stability but it was expected that the fitting of the new tail section would ensure a significant improvement. Having been fitted with its new tail section, BT308 returned to A&AEE for preliminary service evaluation before, once again, returning back to A. V. Roe. BT308 continued to visit A&AEE during the year to undergo more handling trials, with its last visit and trial taking place in August 1941. The following month the aircraft was delivered to Waddington for familiarization and preliminary crew training. From then on the aircraft was removed from the trials programme and delivered to other squadrons for similar training before being transferred to Rolls-Royce at the end of February 1942. Later it took part in further experimental work at Metropolitan-Vickers before finally being struck off charge in May 1944.

The second Lancaster prototype, DG595, made its 20-minute maiden flight on the afternoon of 13 May 1941. It had been built close to the standard production airframe and was stressed to a maximum all-up weight of 60,000lb. It was also capable of carrying a full warload, including the addition of the Nash & Thompson FN50 dorsal and FN64 ventral gun turrets. Unlike the first prototype, DG595 was powered by four Merlin XX engines. The Merlin had come into being around 1933 and reached the production stage some four years later. However, it was not until February 1940 that the engine became a

The second prototype was fitted with both dorsal and ventral gun turrets and made its maiden flight on 13 May 1941.

real option when performance issues relating to an aircraft powered by four Merlins were discussed with the Air Ministry. In terms of man-hours, the cost of the Merlin was about half that of the Vulture and the Air Ministry instructed Rolls-Royce and A. V. Roe that the Merlin XX programme had a higher priority than any solution of the problems with the Vulture. The Merlin XX series engine was a twelve-cylinder, 60-degree upright vee, liquid-cooled inline engine with single-stage centrifugal supercharger and was to become the standard powerplant for the Lancaster. Although the aircraft was then ready for delivery to A&AEE there was some delay owing to congestion in the general trials programme of new types at that time. The aircraft was instead flown to Woodford, where it underwent some modifications to the aircraft systems, including the hydraulics, and had its engine-driven generators uprated to 1,500W in anticipation of the increased electrical services required on the aircraft. DG595 was eventually delivered to Boscombe Down in August, and it carried out service evaluation trials during the following two months before returning back to A. V. Roe for further modifications. It was later delivered to the RAE at Farnborough for further trials and eventually went to the Torpedo Development Unit at Gosport before finally being struck off charge in February 1944.

It was several months before the third Lancaster prototype, DT810, made its first

Left, top: DG595 pictured in August 1941 when it was delivered to Boscombe Down for service evaluation trials.

Left, centre: The third Lancaster (DT810) was powered by four Bristol Hercules VI engines and served as the prototype for the Mk II production aircraft.

Left, bottom: Initially built as a Mk I, W4114 was fitted with Packard-built Merlin 28s at A. V. Roe and became the Mk III prototype. It is seen here in September 1942, just prior to delivery to Boscombe Down.

flight on 26 November 1941. In fact, the first production Lancaster Mk I had already made its first flight because the initial order had stated that the third aircraft was to be the Lancaster Mk II prototype, powered by four Bristol Hercules VI engines. The Hercules VI was a two-row, fourteen-cylinder, sleeve-valve, air-cooled radial engine with two-speed centrifugal supercharger and delivered 1,615hp. The reason for the change in powerplant was the likely shortage of Merlin engines. The Merlin was by far the most utilised engine and powered, amongst others, the Spitfire and Hurricane fighters and the Halifax bomber. Like the previous two prototypes, DT810 carried out service evaluation trials at A&AEE from the spring of 1942, including extensive climb and performance trials, before eventually being delivered to the RAE. It was struck off charge in 1944. The fourth prototype ordered under the contract, intended to be DT812, was never built.

Production

All three Lancaster prototypes were built at A. V. Roe's factory at Newton Heath in Manchester. The factory had been constructed during the First World War and was specifically designed for large-scale aircraft production, providing much better conditions for the company's workers than had been previously experienced. It became the company's head office in August 1920 and throughout the 1920s and 1930s the production lines had always remained busy, culminating in several expansion programmes during the build-up to war. About fifteen miles from the New-

ton Heath factory was the airfield of Woodford, on the outskirts of Stockport, which had been developed on land purchased by A. V. Roe in 1924, and the site also included the company's final assembly factory.

The Government had announced in August 1938 that money was available for a new aircraft factory for A. V. Roe and, almost immediately after the statement had been made, work began to develop a new site at Greengate in Chadderton, near Oldham. By early 1939 workers started to move in, many of them having transferred from the factory at Newton Heath. At approximately one million square feet, Chadderton was bigger than anything which had preceded it, and, like Newton Heath, it was developed to manufacture main aircraft components which would then be transported by road to Woodford for final assembly and air testing. It was soon obvious that even more aircraft would need to be manufactured as the RAF's expansion continued during the final build-up to war. This resulted in A. V. Roe developing a site on the Leeds & Bradford aerodrome at Yeadon in Yorkshire. The factory was completed in February 1941 and, covering approximately one and a half million square feet, was the largest of its type in Europe.

In anticipation of the Lancaster trials proving successful, the original production order for 1,200 Manchesters was amended. The contract awarded to A. V. Roe at Newton Heath for 200 Manchesters (to Air Ministry Specification B.19/37 under Contract No B648770/ 37) was modified so that the first 157 aircraft would be completed as Manchester I/IAs and the remaining 43 as Lancasters. Amendments to a similar contract awarded to Metropolitan-Vickers for 100 Manchesters (also to Air Ministry Specification B.19/37 but under Contract No B.108750/40) required the first 43 aircraft to be completed as Manchester MkI/IAs with the remaining 57 as Lancasters. The initial production orders placed in September 1939 for 300 Manchester MkI/ IAs to be built by the Fairey Aviation Co. and Sir W. G. Armstrong Whitworth & Co. were cancelled.

With production of the Lancaster being spread across different factories and different companies, it was important that the total production programme was coordinated. As a result, the Lancaster Production Group was formed in September 1941, based on experiences gained by the earlier Manchester Group. The Lancaster Group originally consisted of three members of the Manchester Group, A. V. Roe, Metropolitan-Vickers and Armstrong Whitworth, and was later joined by Vickers-Armstrong at Castle Bromwich. The Group was, however, later expanded to meet the increase in demand for Lancasters and included the addition of the Austin Motor Company (Austin Aero) at Birmingham and Vickers at Chester. As there were no airfields at the Metropolitan-Vickers and Austin Motor plants, aircraft would be built here as sub-assemblies and transferred by road to Woodford or Castle Bromwich respectively, where they were to be completed before being air tested.

The first production Lancaster, L7527, had commenced construction as a Manchester airframe at Newton Heath before being modified to a Lancaster Mk I under the amended contract. The aircraft made its maiden flight from Woodford on 31 October 1941 and this proved successful. Although the aircraft suffered damage because of a wheels-up landing during its early trials, the trials programme generally wenrt well. Various recommendations and modifications were made. One significant change was the removal of the Nash & Thompson FN64 ventral turret as it was considered to be of little or no use, particularly for night operations. L7527 went on to serve as a development aircraft before joining No 1654 HCU. In March 1944 it was delivered to No 15 Squadron at Mildenhall and, soon afterwards, was one of six Lancasters which failed to return from a raid against Essen on the night of 26/27 March.

As expected, initial production rates were slow, about two aircraft per week being completed at both the A. V. Roe plant at Newton Heath and the Metropolitan-Vickers plant at Trafford Park. By the end of November a handful of airframes had been completed at Newton Heath and these carried out service evaluation trials during the following month. Finally, on 24 December 1941 the A&AEE declared that the Lancaster was ready for service with Bomber Command and the first three airframes were delivered to No 44 Squadron at Waddington, followed by four more just four days later. Already a veteran unit of many operational sorties, No 44 Squadron had been re-formed in March 1937 as part of the RAF's Expansion Scheme. Since June 1937 it had been based at Waddington as part of Bomber Command, and it had been operating the Hampden since the outbreak of war. Known as No 44 (Rhodesia) Squadron in recognition of that country's contribution to the war effort (25 per cent of the Squadron's aircrews were from Rhodesia or South Africa), it had been selected as the first unit to be equipped with the Lancaster. The decision had been made to re-equip one of the Hampden squadrons first, as part of that aircraft's phasing out from operational service, rather than to re-equip a squadron already operating the Manchester. This may have come as a surprise to some, but it would ensure that there would be a period of time when both Manchesters and Lancasters operated together.

When the first Lancasters arrived, No 44 Squadron was commanded by Wing Commander Rod Learoyd VC although, at that particular time, he was attached to Bomber Command Headquarters. Learoyd was already a veteran of bomber operations, having been the first Bomber Command recipient of the Victoria Cross whilst serving with No 49 Squadron at Scampton. He had only just been appointed Officer Commanding No 44 Squadron and his attachment to Headquarters meant that the task of seeing the Lancaster into RAF operational service went to one of the Flight Commanders, Squadron Leader John Nettleton. Changes in squadron personnel and facilities meant that the Squadron was relatively well prepared to receive its first Lancasters. Nevertheless, it was a difficult time over the Christmas of 1941 for all concerned. The period immediately after the arrival of the first Lancasters required particularly hard work: the Lincolnshire weather during early 1942, with much snow and ice, made conditions extremely difficult and occasionally hazardous. To help with training and to make the transition as efficient as possible, some experienced Manchester aircrews and ground-crews were posted to the Squadron. Several changes also had to be made at Waddington in preparation for receiving twice the previous number of aircrew and groundcrew.

Meanwhile, No 97 Squadron at Coningsby had also been told to prepare for the arrival of its Lancasters early in the New Year. This time the decision had been made to re-equip a squadron which was already operating the Manchester in the heavy bomber role. Now under the command of Wing Commander John Kynoch DFC, the Squadron had been the second Manchester unit to form a year earlier. The first Lancaster arrived on 14 January 1942, followed by two more three days later, and the Squadron began its work-up with the new aircraft. The third Lancaster squadron was No 207, which took delivery of its first aircraft on 25 January. Based at Bottesford, No 207 had been the first to be equipped with the Manchester in November 1940 and had already gained valuable experience in the heavy bomber role.

During the first weeks of 1942 the squadrons worked long and hard, often sharing each other's expertise of aircrew and groundcrew alike, to help make the Lancaster's entry into service as successful as possible: the first weeks of any aircraft's service life, particularly in wartime, are vital to its future prospects. First opinions, amongst both aircrews and ground-crews, were to be of such importance as the rumours about the new Lancaster started to 'flow' around Bomber Command. However, for Chadwick, Dobson and all at A. V. Roe involved with the development of the Lancaster for RAF service, there need not have been any worries as the aircraft immediately proved popular and successful. Even so, very few could have imagined what the Lancaster would go on to achieve.

Production Contracts

The first operational sorties carried out by Lancasters took place on the night of 3/4 March 1942 when four aircraft of No 44 Squadron participated in minelaying operations in the Heligoland approaches. All four aircraft returned safely. The speed at which the Lancaster had entered operational service was quite remarkable, considering that it had been only twelve months since the Manchester had made its operational début. The introduction into operational service had not entirely passed without incident. The work carried out by the A&AEE at Boscombe Down was vital and at times extremely dangerous. Even in wartime, the flight trials carried out on new aircraft about to enter operational service were rigorous and occasionally resulted in accidents, some of which were fatal. One involved R5539, one of the second production batch of Lancaster Mk Is built by A. V. Roe, which suffered structural failure and crashed near Malmesbury, Wiltshire, on 18 April 1942 with the loss of the entire crew.

During early 1942 Lancaster production at the A. V. Roe and Metropolitan-Vickers plants continued to be relatively slow, with approximately four aircraft per week coming from both production lines. However, this figure inevitably started to increase as the workforces became more familiar with machinery and aircraft components. Such was the steady increase in production that by the end of March 1942 a total of 54 Lancasters had been delivered to the three squadrons. The contracts awarded to the various aircraft manufacturers for the production of the Lancaster were often lengthy and complicated. To produce a large and complex aircraft in quantity would require more than one manufacturer, and so work had to go out to a number of aircraft companies. Equally, each manufacturer could not carry out all the work at one plant. Not only would production be quicker by distributing work out to a number of subcontractors; the system was also safer because of the risk of German air attack or, indeed, fire or sabotage.

Many early production contracts ordered aircraft in batches to be delivered

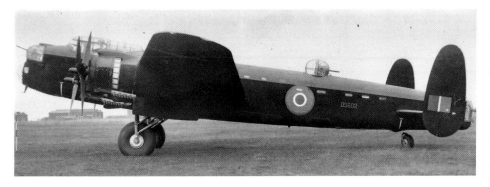

DS602 was the first of the production Lancaster Mk IIs. Delivered to Boscombe Down in September 1942, it remained a trials aircraft and never saw operational service.

during a specific period. Numbers were ordered according to the needs at the time: it was uncertain just how long the war would last and what the aircraft loss rate would be. So, typically, instead of receiving a new contract, an aircraft manufacturer would have an existing contract amended for a further batch of airframes to be completed and delivered at a later date. However, the early, hastily amended contracts for the first Lancasters were followed by new and specifically detailed ones. A new contract (No B.69274/40) was awarded to A. V. Roe which originally ordered 650 more Lancaster Mk Is to be built at Newton Heath, but this was later revised to 407 aircraft, to be delivered in two batches, 200 between February and July 1942 and the balance between July and November 1942. A similar contract (No B.69275/40) was awarded to Metropolitan-Vickers, for a batch of 170 Lancaster Mk Is and 30 Mk IIIs, to be built at the Mosley Road works and delivered between September 1942 and May 1943. Lancaster production by A. V. Roe was at first carried out at the Newton Heath factory in Manchester but was later also carried out at Yeadon in Yorkshire, and these two plants eventually produced nearly half of the total number of Lancasters built. The work by Metropolitan-Vickers was in fact carried out at both Trafford Park and Mosley Road in Manchester. These two companies were responsible for the production of all the early Lancaster Mk Is.

The Lancaster Mk III differed from the Mk I in being fitted with Merlin engines which were built under licence by the Packard Motor Corporation in the United States and sent to Britain from the end of 1942. The differences between the Packard-built Merlins and the Rolls-Royce

Merlins were minor—the former featured a different carburettor and magnetos, and they were slightly more powerful (typically 1,300hp for the Merlin 28)—and therefore did not affect the production lines.

The build-up of Lancaster squadrons continued throughout 1942 as more aircraft came off the production line. The fourth unit to equip with the aircraft was No 83 Squadron at Scampton, which began to receive its first examples in April, followed soon afterwards by No 106 Squadron at Coningsby, No 50 Squadron at Skellingthorpe and No 61 Squadron at Syerston. The last Manchester operations took place on 25/26 June, by which time the number of Lancaster squadrons had reached seven. The rapid build-up of Lancaster squadrons in Bomber Command during the first half of 1942 slowed down slightly as the year progressed. One of the most important objectives had been to replace the Manchester squadrons with the new Lancasters as quickly as possible. Having achieved that, it was time for the squadrons to consolidate—not only for the aircrew but also for the groundcrew.

For everyone involved with the entering into service of the Lancaster, the first half of the year had proved hard work, a point being reflected in the increasing number of unserviceabilities. The problem with aircraft becoming unserviceable was inevitable, first because any new aircraft entering service was likely to suffer from early technical problems, and secondly because the Lancaster was a more complex aircraft than others and often required specialist mechanics to fix certain faults. The mechanics could only gain the right knowledge of the Lancaster's systems and equipment with training and experience, and that could only come with time.

To add to the problem, as aircrew and groundcrew gained experience with the Lancaster, they were then required to train others, and so the problem continued. This problem was unavoidable and there was inevitably going to be a period of consolidation, but it seemed to come at a time when the Lancaster squadrons were being asked to do more and more. For example, at the end of October 1942 Bomber Command had a total of more than 150 Lancasters, of which one-third were unserviceable at any one time. One particular problem about that time was failures in the fuel pumps, which were caused as a result of airlocks at medium-high altitudes. Although the problem could be solved with modifications to the system, it took a long time to service four engines per Lancaster across the fleet of 150 aircraft.

In addition to the production contracts awarded to A. V. Roe and Metropolitan-Vickers, a contract was awarded to Sir W. G. Armstrong Whitworth at Baginton and Bitteswell. With the United States entering the war, and the need for that country to turn its attention to the build-up of its own forces, it was quite possible that the production of Packard-built Merlins would be drastically reduced (this, in fact, never proved to be the case). However, there was also concern that airframe production would exceed engine production due to the increasing demand for Merlins. In anticipation, the contract to Armstrong Whitworth ordered a first production batch of 200 Hercules-powered Lancaster Mk IIs to be built at the company's plant at Whitley. Contract No 239/SAS/C4(C) required the aircraft to be delivered between September 1942 and October 1943. The contract was later amended to include a second batch of 100 Lancaster Mk IIs, to be delivered from October 1943 and completed by March 1944.

The first of the Lancaster Mk IIs, DS601 and DS602, were delivered to

Lancaster production peaked following the Allied invasion of Europe during the summer of 1944, at which time 300 aircraft a month were coming off the various lines.

Boscombe Down in September 1942 for service evaluation trials. The Bristol Hercules VI radial engines proved to be more powerful than the early Rolls-Royce Merlins, although engine handling proved slightly more critical and the engine installation and components produced more drag and, therefore, increased fuel consumption. The effects of this were slightly reduced with the later Mk IIs, which were powered by the improved Hercules XVI engines. The first Lancaster Mk II unit was No 61 Squadron based at Syerston, which received its first aircraft at the end of 1942 and began operations with the type in January 1943. However, it appears that the shortage of Merlins never materialised; if it did, it was a very short-term problem and does not appear to have affected the overall rate of Lancaster production. Because the number of Merlins continued to increase throughout 1943, no further orders were placed for Mk IIs and only 300 were ever produced.

At the same time that the Lancaster Mk II was carrying out service evaluation trials, the prototype Mk III was also delivered to A&AEE. Initially built as a Mk I, W4114 had been fitted with Packard-Merlin 28s by A. V. Roe and was delivered to Boscombe Down in October 1942. As part of Contract No B.69274/40 awarded to A. V. Roe, a fourth production batch of 620 Lancaster Mk Is and Mk IIIs was

ordered for completion and delivery between November 1942 and June 1943. At Metropolitan-Vickers, Contract No B.69275/40 had also been amended to include a further 200 Mk Is and Mk IIIs for delivery between May and November 1943. A new contract awarded to A. V. Roe (No 1807) proved to be the largest of all the Lancaster production orders, although it was issued in several parts. The first two parts ordered 900 Lancaster Mk IIIs, 550 of which were to be built at Newton Heath and 350 at Yeadon, for delivery commencing in June 1943 and November 1942 respectively. The reason for the differences in delivery date for this contract was that Lancasters were still being built at Newton Heath to meet an earlier contract, although it would have made little difference to the production line workers.

Throughout 1942 production rates at the various plants continued to increase. By the time that the second production batch of Lancasters was being completed at Newton Heath, output had risen to ten aircraft per week at that plant alone, and by the time that work was being completed for the latest contract, production there had increased to over twenty aircraft per week. By the end of the year twelve operational squadrons had been equipped, with more than 200 aircraft on strength. Furthermore, serviceabilities had im-

proved by the end of the year such that between 75 and 80 per cent of the total number of Lancasters were now available for operations at any one time. However, the number of aborted sorties for various reasons remained relatively high. The increase in the number of engine unserviceabilities led to a close examination of the Merlins to see if there was a design or manufacturing fault. This was not the case, and the problem seemed more a result of increased wear and tear due to age. Whenever possible, aircraft with problems were returned to the maintenance units for the installation of new engines, often Packard-built Merlins, thus creating Lancaster Mk IIIs. There were even cases when an airframe began life as a Mk I and was then fitted with Packard-Merlins whilst still on the production line. These 'instant' conversions from Mk I to Mk III often lead to slight differences in final Mk I/Mk III production figures, depending on the source.

The installation of the Packard-Merlins into the Mk IIIs certainly reduced the number of aborts caused by problems with the fuel system. One difficulty which could not be readily solved, however, was the increasing number of losses amongst the Lancaster squadrons. By the end of 1942 operational losses, including those aircraft written off while landing back at base following an operational sortie, were averaging more than 25 aircraft per month. This statistic is made worse when considering accidents and losses on training flights. Losses in the Lancaster's early operational life were unavoidable, but, fortunately, production rates continued to increase and so, therefore, did the expansion of the Lancaster squadrons. By March 1943 the Lancaster reached the end of its first operational year, by which time eighteen squadrons in four Bomber Command Groups had been equipped. With the increasing number of Packard-Merlins arriving from the United States, the number of Lancasters built as Mk IIIs was rapidly increasing. The newer Mk IIIs leaving the production lines were, generally, delivered straight to the squadrons and the older Mk Is were returned either to the conversion units or the maintenance units.

As the Bomber Command effort increased, so did the rate of Lancaster production. By the middle of 1943 there were 23 Lancaster squadrons serving with the Command, the establishment of each squadron having been increased to 26 aircraft. By the end of the year this number had increased to 32 operational squadrons. To meet the increasing demand more amendments were made to existing contracts with A. V. Roe, Metropolitan-Vickers and Armstrong Whitworth; in addition, new production orders were placed with other aircraft manufacturing companies—Vickers-Armstrong at Castle Bromwich, Vickers at Chester, Austin Motors at Longbridge and Victory Aircraft in Ontario, Canada.

Peak Production

During the winter of 1943/44 the number of Lancasters taking part in operations was averaging about 500 per raid. Although in terms of percentage losses the number of Lancasters failing to return from operations was relatively low (averaging about 5 per cent), this still represented a large number of aircraft lost throughout the campaign. Statistics in terms of aircraft losses can be straightforward but they do not always take into account the number of aircraft which returned to base severely damaged and therefore unable to take any further part in operations.

The rate of Lancaster production did continue to increase throughout this period, and, when comparing the number of Lancasters delivered to squadrons to those lost on operations, the statistics prove just about favourable: for every three Lancasters delivered to squadrons, two were failing to return from operations. However, when taking into account the

number of aircraft severely damaged during operations or lost on training flights, the rate of Lancaster replacement was probably averaging just about parity. Nevertheless, this fact was significant in that it meant that Bomber Command could keep up a sustained effort.

The anticipated Allied invasion of Europe in 1944 brought a peak in Lancaster production. Further amendments to existing contracts, and to earlier orders placed with other companies, now produced even more aircraft as Lancasters were turned out in their hundreds. During the most productive period, between August and October 1944, the combined factories of the Lancaster Group produced more than 300 aircraft a month—A. V. Roe more than 150 per month, Armstrong Whitworth about 75, Metropolitan-Vickers nearly 50 and other companies the rest, including aircraft delivered from Canada. As an amendment to Contract No 1807, a further 600 Lancaster Mk IIIs were ordered from A. V. Roe, to be delivered between December 1943 and May 1944. The same contract was later increased, for a further 723 Mk Is and Mk IIIs to be built at Newton Heath and 87 Mk IIIs at Yeadon, to be delivered from May 1944. The final part of the contract ordered 47 Mk IIIs, to be built at Yeadon and delivered from June 1944. This was followed by another contract (No 2019) for 200 Mk Is and Mk IIIs from Yeadon, for delivery between October 1944 and March 1945.

The development of the 22,000lb 'Grand Slam' bomb meant that considerable modification to the basic Lancaster airframe was necessary for some aircraft

to be able to carry such a weapon. Because of the vast weight of the 'Grand Slam', certain components of the aircraft had to be omitted in order for it to get off the ground. The nose and dorsal turrets were removed, as were the bomb doors, and the undercarriage was strengthened. The prototype, PB592/G, was one of the batch of 723 Lancasters being built at Newton Heath as part of Contract No 1807, was modified to a B Mk I (Special) during the winter of 1944/45 and began trials in February 1945. An order was placed with A. V. Roe for a production batch of 32 B Mk I (Special)s, to be built at Newton Heath and delivered by March 1945. The final order placed with A. V. Roe was for eleven Mk IIIs, to be built at Yeadon and delivered during September and October 1945.

As the third part of Contract No 239/SAS/C4(C) to Armstrong Whitworth, a further 350 Mk Is were delivered between November 1943 and August 1944, followed by a further 400 Mk Is between July 1944 and February 1945. The final part of the contract ordered a further 170 Lancasters, to be delivered between February and May 1945. Finally, three small orders were placed towards the end of the war for a total of 84 more Mk Is and Mk IIIs, to be delivered between May 1945 and March 1946. In addition, an order was placed for 25 Lancaster Mk I(FE)s, for operations in the Far East, to be delivered between June and July 1945.

At Metropolitan-Vickers, Contract No 2221 ordered a total of 450 Mk Is to be built at Mosley Road and delivered between November 1943 and December 1944. This contract was later increased

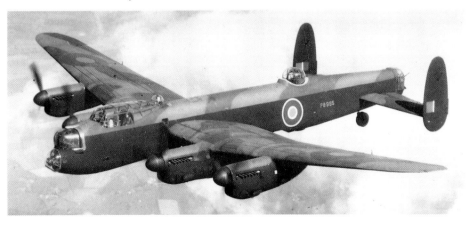

This aircraft, PB995, was one of 32 Mk Is built at Newton Heath and adapted to carry the 22,000lb 'Grand Slam' bomb. Designated Mk I (Special), these aircraft were completed and delivered during early 1945.

Built by Sir W. G. Armstrong Whitworth, TW655 was completed during the summer of 1945 as a Mk I(FE) for service in the Far East. It was put into storage before being sold to the *Aéronavale* in March 1952.

twice, for 158 more Mk Is, to be delivered from November 1944. A final order was placed for fifteen Mk Is to be manufactured by Metropolitan-Vickers and assembled by Vickers at Chester. The first contract awarded to the Vickers-Armstrong plant at Castle Bromwich (No 1336) was made as early as September 1941 and was originally for a first production batch of 200 Lancaster Mk IIs for delivery from December 1943. This was later changed to Mk IIIs and then changed again to Mk Is in April 1943. An amendment to this contract ordered a further 100 Mk Is, to be built at Castle Bromwich for delivery from February 1945. A further contract (No 2791) had been awarded to Vickers which ordered 235 more Mk Is, to be built at Chester and delivered from June 1944. Most of this work was subcontracted to smaller companies, although final assembly was carried out at Chester.

The contract awarded to Austin Motors at Longbridge (No 2827) was in three parts. The first two ordered a total of 150 Mk Is for delivery between March 1944 and April 1945 and the third ordered 150 Lancaster Mk VII(FE)s, for service in the Far East, for delivery from April 1945 and to be completed by September 1945. A

further batch of 30 Mk VII(FE)s was ordered, for delivery between November 1945 and January 1946.

At the Newton Heath factory the rate of production continued to increase throughout 1944 and eventually peaked at about 25 aircraft per week. The production rates achieved at Newton Heath were not quite matched at any other plant, although the Metropolitan-Vickers plant at Mosley Road did peak at about 20 aircraft per week. Although production rates at Armstrong Whitworth at Whitley could never quite match those at Newton Heath or Mosley Road, they did show a significant increase throughout 1944 and eventually peaked at about fourteen aircraft per week. The fact that other plants did not match the rates achieved at Newton Heath is in no way disrespectful to any other factory or its workforce: Newton Heath had, after all, been building Lancasters since the very first day and therefore had all the facilities and expertise required for the large-scale production of aircraft. By contrast, the smaller subcontractors often had to improvise, with poorer facilities available to help make some of the smaller components.

It is estimated that each Lancaster consisted of over 50,000 parts and required some half a million separate manufacturing processes, taking about 35,000 man-hours, at a cost of about £60,000 (excluding weapons, radar and specialist equipment). It was not unusual for bus garages

or even shops to be turned into small factories, such was the demand and effort at that time. The production of Lancasters could not have been possible without the contribution of many smaller and lesser-known firms. Although often unable to build larger parts for the Lancaster, these concerns often manufactured many of the smaller components which were then transported to the assembly factories. It is estimated that over one million people were involved in the manufacturing of parts for the Lancaster, although many of these would at the same time be producing the same parts for other aircraft (for example, engine components). It was a magnificent effort by all involved and it resulted in Woodford's assembly lines turning out up to seven Lancasters a day for flight testing.

Right, top: Originally built as a Mk I by Austin Motors, NN801 was converted to become the Mk VII prototype, pictured here in May 1945.

Right, centre: RT684 was built by Austin Motors at Longbridge and was one of 180 Mk VII(FE) aircraft ordered for service in the Far East. Completed after the cessation of hostilities, it served in the training role instead.

Right, bottom: JA918, a Lancaster Mk III, was built by A. V. Roe and served with No 550 Squadron before it failed to return from operations on the night of 9/10 May 1944.

It is estimated that each Lancaster consisted of more than 50,000 parts, required some half a million separate manufacturing processes and took about 35,000 man-hours to complete.

Amazingly, work proceeded relatively unhindered at many of the factories and workshops. Despite the great importance of the larger plants, they were seldom, if ever, subjected to enemy attack. In the early days production had suffered a blow when thirteen airframes were destroyed at the Metropolitan-Vickers plant at Trafford Park, including its first Manchester, when the factory was bombed on 23 December 1940. Occasionally work was disrupted slightly when bombs fell around the factory (Trafford Park was reasonably close to the city of Manchester). Chadderton was attacked on 23 April 1941 by a lone Junkers 88 which caused only slight damage and no injuries, and Woodford was never attacked. The main disruption occurred when air raid sirens caused a temporary halt in production, although even these warnings were sometimes ignored by the workforce. The largest workforce was that of A. V. Roe, which during the peak period employed about 40,000 people, about 18,000 of them women. Over half of A. V. Roe's total workforce were employed at the Chadderton and Yeadon

plants, which each employed about 11,000 men and women. All the major factories adopted a shift system for their workers, with both day and night shifts running seven days a week, and 60-hour weeks were not uncommon.

A. V. Roe's Chadderton factory was the company's main plant and general office, under managing director Roy Dobson. It also carried out design and experimental work and manufactured tools, as well as building the centre-section of the fuselage and wing spars. Many of the small companies around the Manchester area supplied components to Chadderton for assembly before the main sections were transported by road to Woodford for final assembly. Newton Heath was also responsible for manufacturing parts of the fuselage as well as the wing assemblies. Yeadon manufactured the fuselage, bulkheads, bomb doors and fuel tanks. Other larger A. V. Roe factories, with examples of the work carried out at each, were Ashton (wings and tail section), the Laurel Works at Royton (undercarriage, hydraulic and oxygen systems), the Ivy Works and Empire Works at Failsworth (flaps, elevators, cabin heating and undercarriage doors) and the Wythenshawe Works (fuel tanks). In addition, there were many smaller factories used for, amongst other things, stores and repairs. For example, the A. V. Roe Repair Organisation was set up at Bracebridge Heath near Lincoln in 1940 and expanded to Langar in Nottinghamshire in September 1942 to cope with the rebuilding of badly damaged Manchesters

and Lancasters. Another organisation, known as the Avro Contractors Working Parties, repaired damaged aircraft and helped to put them back into operational service. It is estimated that these organisations helped put back into service some 4,000 aircraft which might otherwise have been written off.

The final assembly of the A. V. Roe and Metropolitan-Vickers Lancasters took place in the huge assembly sheds at Woodford. During the peak period of 1944 there were four production lines at Woodford working at the same time to cope with the increasing demand for airframes and assembly. During the final assembly the Merlin engines were installed, after which the aircraft left the assembly sheds and were towed to the flight line where they were prepared for flight. There were up to seven air test crews at Woodford and each would fly, typically, up to six air tests a day. During the peak period these air tests took part from dawn to dusk every day of the week, and one test pilot at A. V. Roe, Jimmy Orrell, personally tested more than 900 different Lancasters. Such was the excellent design and manufacture of the Lancaster, it was rare for any individual aircraft to need more than two air tests before the aircraft was passed fit for delivery to the RAF. When considering the vast number of

The Lancaster main sections left the various production plants and were transported by road to Woodford for final assembly.

A Canadian-built Lancaster Mk X, manufactured by Victory Aircraft at Malton in Ontario.

Lancaster air tests, it is remarkable that there was only one fatal accident during this period. On 11 September 1944, PB579 crashed into open ground during an air test from Woodford with the loss of the test pilot, Sid Gleave, and the flight engineer, Harry Barnes. This incident was a sad event for all concerned with air testing the Lancaster at Woodford, but fortunately it was an isolated case. The Lancaster proved excellent in design and reliable in the air. After leaving Woodford the aircraft were usually delivered to one of the RAF's maintenance units for final painting before being ferried to an operating base, usually by an Air Transport Auxiliary pilot (many of whom were women).

Canadian Lancasters

Lancasters were built in Canada by Victory Aircraft at Malton, Ontario. The company was owned by the Canadian Government and had already produced a significant number of Avro Ansons. Specialist jigs and parts were shipped out, along with detailed drawings and plans, and a Lancaster was even flown out to Canada to familiarise the engineers and workers. The Canadian aircraft was known as the Lancaster Mk X, and manufacture commenced under the guidance of a young A. V. Roe engineer, Alfred Stewart. The first production order for completion by Victory Aircraft was for 300

airframes, of which the first 75 were to be powered by Packard-built Merlin 38s and the rest by Merlin 224s. The order stated that the first aircraft were to be delivered to Britain from September 1943 and the last by March 1945. The second production order, also to be powered by Packard-built Merlins, was initially for 200 aircraft although the end of hostilities in Europe meant that only 130 were in fact completed.

The first batch of 300 Lancaster Mk Xs was built at an average rate of four aircraft per week. Although a handful were retained in Canada, the majority were either shipped or flown to Britain during 1944 and early 1945 and then delivered to the Royal Canadian Air Force (RCAF) squadrons operating from bases throughout eastern England. A typical example was No 419 ('Moose') Squadron of the RCAF, which operated from Middleton St George (now Teeside Airport) and converted from the Halifax to the new aircraft in March 1944. The Squadron first flew the type operationally on 27 April and at the end of the war was transferred back to Canada before disbanding. The majority of the first batch of aircraft flew on operations with the eight RCAF bomber squadrons eventually equipped with the Lancaster Mk X—Nos 419 and 428 Squadrons at Middleton St George, Nos 405 and 408 at Linton-on-Ouse, Nos 420 and 425 at Tholthorpe and Nos 431 and

434 at Croft. Of those aircraft that flew to Britain, not all made it. One example was KB828, which crashed on landing at Gander in Newfoundland. Of those that did complete the long journey, by air or by sea, some played no significant part in the war, particularly later arrivals in 1945 which were held in storage awaiting a decision on their future. The same applied to the second batch of 130 Lancaster Mk Xs, the majority of which were shipped to Britain between March and June 1945: because hostilities in Europe were coming to an end, most were delivered to various maintenance units and then stored, typically at Aston Down, St Athan, Llandow, Colerne or Silloth. Some were, however, delivered to squadrons, although it is extremely unlikely that many, if any at all, flew on operations. After the war in Europe some Mk Xs were flown back to Canada but the majority were either sold in Britain as scrap or struck off charge; one typical example was FM175, which was shipped to Britain in June 1945 and stored at No 20 MU until it was sold for scrap in May 1947, having probably never got airborne. Some survived, for example FM206, which arrived in Britain in August 1945, returned to Canada the following month and then served with the RCAF's Central Flying

School. The last Lancaster Mk X delivered to Britain was FM207, which arrived in August 1945 and returned to Canada in November. The remaining Lancaster Mk Xs (FM208–FM229) stayed in Canada and were then modified to carry out other duties.

Most of the 430 Lancaster Mk Xs built were delivered to Britain towards the end of the war, but, despite their late arrival, the contribution made by those aircraft and their crews which did serve on operations with the Canadian squadrons was most significant. However, nearly 100 Lancaster Mk Xs were either lost on operations or crashed during training flights in the United Kingdom. The fate of many of these crews remains unknown.

The Total Effort

As the war came to an end, Bomber Command was about to introduce two new Lancaster variants, the Mk IV and the Mk V, although these were later renamed to become the Avro Lincoln Mk I and Mk II respectively. One variant not often referred to was the Lancaster Mk VI, which was modified from the Mk III, powered by uprated Merlin 85/87 engines and saw limited service in 1944. The first two

airframes to be affected were DV170 and DV199, which were built by Metropolitan-Vickers at Trafford Park and delivered to Rolls-Royce in June and July 1943 for modification. The third airframe to be converted was JB675, which was built by A. V. Roe at Newton Heath and delivered to Rolls-Royce in November 1943. This third aircraft became the 'prototype' and, following modification, was delivered to the A&AEE at Boscombe Down for further trials. It later served with four different squadrons—though only ever flew one operational sortie—before being transferred to the RAE at Farnborough and then back to Rolls-Royce. Only a handful of Lancasters were ever converted to Mk VIs, these serving mainly with No 7 Squadron at Oakington and No 635 Squadron at Downham Market in the Pathfinder role. Although the engines did prove to be more powerful, there was concern about their reliability and this was probably the reason why the Mk VIs were withdrawn from operations in November 1944. Experience gained with the type, however, helped the later development of the Avro Lincoln.

During the war the Lancaster flew with 60 Bomber Command squadrons and towards the end of hostilities there were about 2,000 aircraft taking part in operations. With the end of the war in Europe in sight, Lancaster production began to 'wind down'. By the time that the war in the Far East had come to an end, production had ceased altogether, the last Lancasters coming off the various production

lines between August and October 1945; many of these aircraft were only ever stored at maintenance units before being struck off charge.

The three companies A. V. Roe, Metropolitan-Vickers and Armstrong Whitworth eventually built over 6,000 Lancasters, representing 82 per cent of total production. A. V. Roe had produced 3,673 Lancasters and Metropolitan-Vickers a further 1,080, all of which had been finally assembled at Woodford. Production from other plants, including the 430 from Canada, totalled 2,624, making a grand total of 7,377 Lancasters built. In addition, it is estimated that there were enough main components and spares produced throughout the war for at least another 600 aircraft. Some Lancasters were built as one variant and then modified to another (a description of all the Lancaster variants is given in the Appendices). Of all the Lancasters built, over 3,800 were either lost on operations or otherwise destroyed or damaged beyond repair. Of those that survived, many were modified for peacetime duties (see Chapter 8); otherwise most were sold for scrap or struck off charge.

The end of the war also brought a reduction in the Lancaster Group, with Vickers Armstrong, Vickers at Chester and Austin Aero completing their last Lancaster production before leaving the Group. At the end of 1945 Metropolitan-Vickers also left the Group, but A. V. Roe and Armstrong Whitworth remained to continue work and plan for future derivatives of the aircraft (see Chapter 9).

The Lancaster Mk VI was modified from the Mk III and powered by uprated Merlin 85/87 engines. This example, JB675, became the Mk VI prototype and later served with four different squadrons before being returned to Rolls-Royce.

3. Design and Cockpit Environment

Airframe

The Lancaster airframe was, basically, of all-metal construction. It was 69ft in length, had a wingspan of 102ft and was 20ft high. The fuselage was constructed of light alloy monocoque and accommodated the crew and equipment, the bomb bay and the aircraft's defensive armament. The fuselage was of roughly oval cross-section and divided into five sections, the nose, the front fuselage and the intermediate-centre, rear-centre and rear fuselage, each one being fully equipped before they were finally assembled together. The basic empty weight of the aircraft was about 36,000lb.

The nose section included a hemispherical transparent perspex dome (not initially fitted to all early aircraft) which incorporated a flat glass vision panel for bomb-aiming. The forward escape hatch was situated in the floor of the nose section, which also included various perspex windows for the bomb aimer. The front fuselage section housed the main cockpit and the bomb bay. The pilot's position was situated on a raised platform on the forward port side of the cabin. The cabin also accommodated the remainder of the forward crew and associated equipment which, in the earlier development stage, consisted of a second pilot, a navigator and a wireless operator. Below the floor of the main cockpit was the forward part of the bomb bay, which extended back about 33ft to just aft of the wing. The nose and front fuselage sections were just over 20ft in length, and for transportation purposes the nose section remained connected to the front fuselage.

The intermediate-centre section of the aircraft was nearly 8ft in length and was constructed on the front and rear main spars of the wing. An emergency exit was located in the roof which could be used in the event of the aircraft having to ditch in water. Underneath the floor was the bomb bay. The wing was a dihedral cantilever structure and built around the front and rear main spars in the centre section of the fuselage. For construction and transportation purposes the wing was divided into five sub-assemblies from the centre-section to the wing tip. The wing centre-section had a span of 28ft, was integral with the centre-section of the fuselage and included the inboard engine nacelle which housed the main undercarriage when retracted. The outer wing sections and the wing tip sections spanned a total of 74ft. The total wing area, including ailerons, was 1,300 sq ft. Towards the tip of each wing, housed in the front of the outer wing section, was the outboard engine nacelle. Hydraulically operated split trailing-edge flaps were mounted under the wing, with ailerons mounted in the trailing edge of the outer part of the wing. In an emergency, the flaps could be lowered by compressed air. Initially four fuel tanks were

Above: The nose section included a hemispherical transparent perspex dome which incorporated a flat glass vision panel for bomb-aiming.

Below: The last production Lancaster leaves the Yeadon plant in late 1945.

The Lancaster airframe was 69ft in length with a wingspan of 102ft and incorporated a bomb bay 33ft long which extended to just aft of the wing.

incorporated in the wings although this was soon increased to six (more details are included below, in the description of the fuel system).

The rear-centre section of the fuselage was over 20ft in length and extended from the back of the wing towards the tail. The section accommodated the Nash & Thompson FN50 dorsal turret and, on the early aircraft, the FN64 ventral turret. Another small emergency escape hatch was located in the roof. The floor of the section consisted of a walkway towards the rear of the aircraft. Underneath the floor was the rearmost part of the bomb bay.

The main crew entrance and exit doorway situated on the starboard side of the rear fuselage.

The rear fuselage was 21ft in length and the tailplane spars passed through the rear of the section. Below this structure was the tail wheel. The main crew entrance and exit doorway was situated on the starboard side of the section. The tail unit consisted of a tailplane and elevators, with a total span of just over 33ft, with fins and rudders situated on the outboard ends. The total area of the tailplane, including elevators, was 237 sq ft and the height of each fin was just over 12ft.

The main undercarriage was a retracting Dowty oleo-pneumatic system. The undercarriage lever in the cockpit was locked in the down position by a safety bolt which had to be held aside to raise the undercarriage after take-off. The undercarriage indicators in the cockpit showed two green lights when the undercarriage was locked down, two red lights when the undercarriage was unlocked and no lights when the undercarriage was locked up. On the Mk X a pictorial type of indicator was fitted. An undercarriage warning horn sounded if either of the inboard throttles was closed when the undercarriage was not locked down. The undercarriage could be lowered by compressed air in an emergency. The tail wheel was a non-retracting Dowty oleo-pneumatic assembly.

Engines

The standard powerplant for the Lancaster was the Rolls-Royce Merlin XX series engine which for the Mk I was either the XX, 22 or 24 engine with SU carburettors. The Merlin XX was a twelve-cylinder, 60-degree upright-vee, liquid-cooled inline engine with single-stage centrifugal supercharger. The crankshaft was a single-piece, six-throw unit, each crank pin driving two connecting rods. A single cam shaft passed across the top of each cylinder block, operating two pairs of inlet and exhaust valves per cylinder. Engine lubrication was of the dry sump type with one pressure pump and two scavenge pumps driven from the wheel case. The basic weight of each engine was 1,450lb and the propeller reduction gear was a straight spur of 0.42 to 1. The Merlin 22 and 24

Table 4. Airframe Limitations: Maximum Weights and Speeds.

Take-off	63,000–65,000lb (depending on aircraft mod. state)
Landing	55,000lb
Maximum speed	360kt IAS
Maximum speed (bomb doors open)	360kt IAS
Maximum speed (undercarriage down)	200kt IAS
Maximum speed (flaps lowered)	200kt IAS
Maximum climbing speed	160kt IAS to 12,000ft
	155kt IAS from 12,000ft to 18,000ft
	150kt IAS from 18,000ft to 22,000ft
	145kt IAS above 22,000ft
Speed for climbing for maximum range	160kt IAS at +7psi boost
Speed for cruising for maximum range	170kt IAS up to 15,000ft (fully loaded)
	160kt IAS at 20,000ft (fully loaded)

Above left: The main undercarriage was a retracting Dowty oleo-pneumatic system.

Above right: The tail wheel was a non-retracting Dowty oleo-pneumatic assembly.

produced 1,280bhp and 1,620bhp respectively.

The Lancaster Mk II was powered by four 1,735bhp Bristol Hercules VI or XVI fourteen-cylinder, air-cooled radial engines. The Hercules was a heavier engine than the Merlin XX with a basic weight of 1,930lb. The later production variant of the aircraft, the Lancaster Mk III, was powered by four Packard-built Merlin 28, 38 or 224 engines with Bendix Stromberg pressure-injection carburettors, which produced 1,300bhp (Merlin 28) or 1,390bhp (Merlin 38). A modified variant of the Mk III was the Lancaster Mk VI, which was powered by the uprated Merlin 85/87 engines and, as noted, saw limited operational service during 1944.

The Merlin was started by an electrical starter motor situated on the starboard side of the engine and there was also an auxiliary facility for hand-turning the engine. Each engine provided drives to the propeller units as well as individual drives to various other services, including the hydraulic pumps to power each of the aircraft's gun turrets. Two twelve-cylinder magnetos were situated at the front of each engine, of which only the starting magneto was boosted. Engine fire extinguishers were situated within each engine nacelle and could be operated in one of several ways, including pilot activation by push-buttons on the pilot's panel and overheat or impact sensors.

The engine controls consisted of throttle controls and mixture controls, which varied depending on the type of engines fitted. Engine supercharger controls were initially operated mechanically by one lever but were later operated electro-pneumatically. The radiator shutter controls were automatically controlled in flight and a single lever for the hydraulic operation of all four carburettor hot air intakes was provided next to the pilot's seat. A twin-choke carburettor supplied the correct fuel/air mixture to the supercharger on each engine. Fuel was pumped to the carburettor and air was delivered through an intake situated on the lower rear left of the lower engine cowling. An air intake for the engine radiator and oil cooler was situated on the underside of the front cowling. An exhaust flame shroud was situated, externally, on the upper left of the engine assembly.

A single oil tank, with a capacity of 37.5 gallons and 4.5 gallons air space, was provided for each engine and was situated behind each engine bulkhead. The four oil dilution push-buttons were situated on the flight engineer's panel. Oil was circu-lated to the engine by a single pressure pump and returned to the oil tank by two scavenge pumps. The engine was liquid-cooled with a mixture of 30 per cent ethylene glycol and 70 per cent water, the coolant being circulated by a centrifugal pump from a small tank. The engine oil filler cap was situated at the rear port side of the engine nacelle and the tank was topped up from an oil bowser prior to each sortie. When starting the engines it was the duty of the flight engineer to monitor the oil pressures, and should the oil pressure in the engine not rise to more than 90psi during start then the engine had to be stopped immediately. Normal oil consumption during flight was between eight and sixteen pints per hour, sixteen pints

---

Table 5. Merlin 28 Engine-Start Checks

Brake pressure: Minimum of 150psi
ICO: Idle Cut Off
Ground/Flight switch: 'Ground'
Boost cut-out lever: Up
Undercarriage warning lights and flap indicators: Switched on
Supercharger in 'M' gear
Throttles: Three-quarters open (1,000–1,200rpm)
Undercarriage locked down, bomb doors closed, flaps neutral
Propeller levers: Maximum rpm position
Air intakes: Cold
Master cocks: All off
Pumps in No 2 tanks: On; No 2 tanks selected
Select master cock for the appropriate engine
Ignition and booster coil: Switched on
Prime the engine
Starter button: Pressed
ICO: Engine on position when engine fires
If engine fails to run, return to Idle Cut Off position immediately

After-Start Checks
Check engine temperatures and pressures.
Ground/Flight switch: 'Flight'
Switch off booster coil
Test hydraulic services by operating bomb doors and flaps
When coolant temperatures reaches 90°C or oil temperature reaches 80°C, place radiator override switches down

per hour being the maximum permissible. Even if the engine was using the maximum amount, the oil tank could provide enough oil for the duration of any flight.

Controls for the Hydromatic propellers varied the governed rpm from 1,800 to 3,000 with feathering buttons provided on the instrument panel. The propellers for the Lancaster Mk I were, generally, three-blade De Havilland Type 5/40, although three-blade Nash Kelvinator/Hamilton A5/138 propellers, as generally fitted to the Lancaster Mk III, were interchangeable. Both designs were regulated by a propeller constant-speed unit, which maintained the selected rpm, and were variable-pitch, with only slight differences between the two in pitch limits and feathering settings. Each propeller weighed about 500lb and had to be very finely balanced. Feathering pumps for each propeller unit were located on each engine subframe assembly and each propeller was fed with de-icing fluid. The Lancaster Mk II was fitted with Rotol REC fully feathering propellers which were of the left-hand tractor variety as opposed to the right-hand rotation on the other marks of Lancaster. Four switches were provided on the pilot's

Left, top: A close-up view of the starboard inner Merlin engine, showing the three-blade propeller, the air intake below the propeller cowling with the carburettor intake just aft, and the exhaust flame shroud.

Left, centre: The panel showing the main engine instruments, with boost gauges above the rpm indicators. Instruments for No 1 engine are on the left, working across from left to right to No 4 engine. In this photograph No 1 engine is running at 1,150rpm and Nos 2 and 3 at 2,000rpm; No 4 engine is not running.

Left, bottom: The fire warning lamps and feathering switches were monitored and operated by the flight engineer. These are shown in the centre, and below them can be seen the four engine fire extinguisher buttons.

Right, upper: Diagram of oil system (inboard engine).

Right, lower: Diagram of oil system (outboard engine).

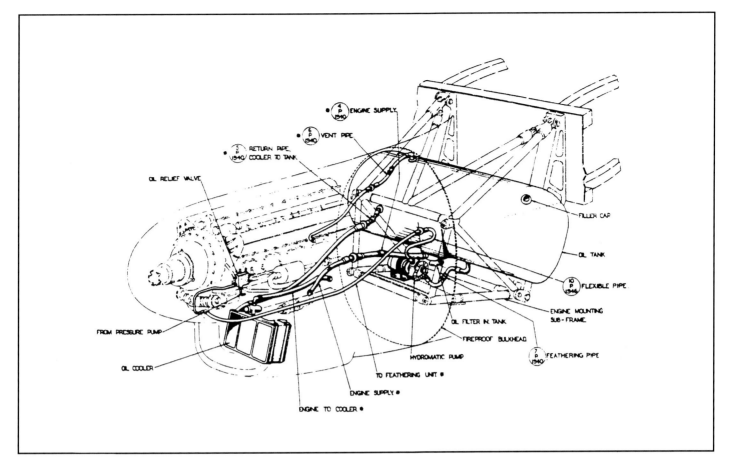

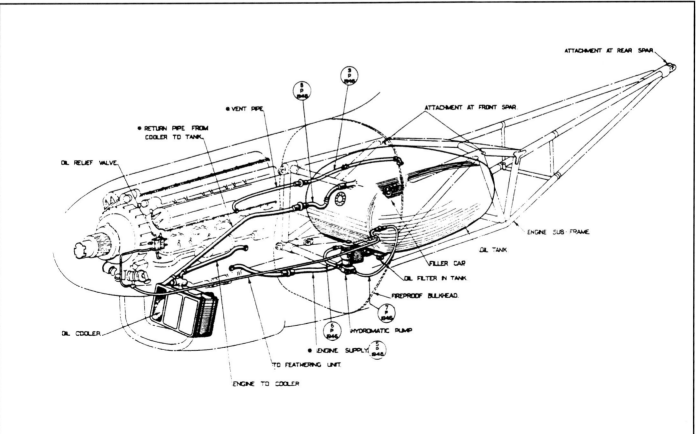

Table 6. Engine Operating Data (Merlin XX)

	rpm	Boost (psi)	Temperatures (°C)	
			Coolant	Oil
Max. take-off to 1,000ft	3,000	+12		
Max. climbing power (1hr limit)	2,850	+9	125	90
Max. rich continuous	2,650	+7	105	90
Max. weak continuous	2,650	+4	105	90
Combat power (5min limit)	3,000	+15	135	105
Oil pressure normal		60–80psi		
Oil pressure minimum		45psi		
Min. oil temperature for take-off		15°C		
Min. coolant temperature for take-off		60°C		

Table 7. Electrical System: Services Provided by Engine-Driven Generators

Engine starting
Propeller-feathering pumps
Radio equipment
Bomb gear and bomb sight
Fuel booster pumps, contents gauges and pressure warning lights/gauges
Controls for radiator flaps and supercharger rams
Flap and undercarriage indicators
Landing lights
DR compass
Heated clothing
Fire extinguishers
Camera

panel for feathering and unfeathering the propellers. Feathering was carried out by pressing the associated button and the circuit remained energised until the action was completed and the button automatically released. To unfeather, the button had to be held in manually. If both inboard propellers were feathered then the aircraft's electrical generators were inoperative; feathering of any one propeller would cause equipment powered from that engine also to become inoperative (for example, the Gee navigation equipment in the case of the port outer engine). The most notable of the propellers was the 'paddle-blade' Nash Kelvinator. No mat-

ter what the mark of Lancaster, or its engine, this propeller improved the cruising speed of the aircraft by about 8mph and the service ceiling by 1,500ft. This meant that the Nash Kelvinator became the standard propeller for the Lancaster, even though it required more regular maintenance.

Flying over enemy territory was not the only hazard to a Lancaster crew, particularly during the winter months. One of the main problems was that the altitudes at which Lancasters operated were often in conditions which led to icing. This can cause tremendous problems for any aircraft, and the Lancaster was no exception. If at all possible, the best option for the crew was to climb out of the icing range but with a full bomb load and full tanks of fuel this was not always possible. To help combat the menace, methods such as the application of anti-ice paste were employed. The engines were protected against icing by the use of hot air and later Lancasters also included glycol protection for the propellers. Icing on the carburettor intakes' protective guards meant a loss

Diagram showing the Lancaster's fuel system.

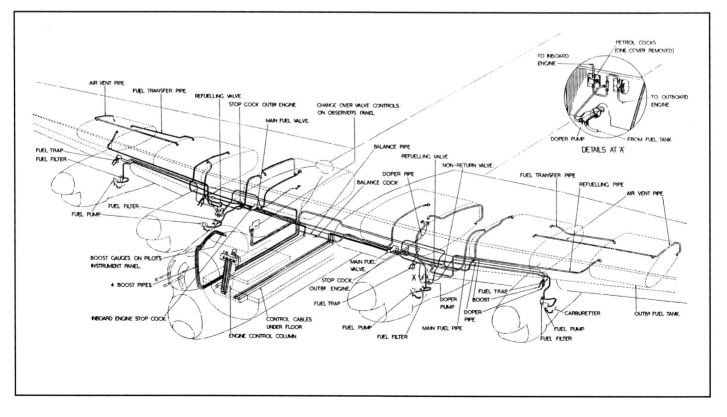

of engine boost if the aircraft were above full-throttle height.

If an engine failed in flight it was possible for air to be drawn into the fuel system through the carburettor of the failed engine. To prevent this, the master fuel cock had to be turned off before feathering. With an outer engine failed the aircraft could be trimmed to fly hands- and feet-off until down to about 130mph as the Lancaster's autopilot had sufficient power to maintain a straight course. If two engines had failed, mechanically or otherwise, the bomb load had to be jettisoned and the aircraft returned to base. Even with both engines failed on one side, the aircraft could be trimmed to fly feet-off down to about 145mph. Lower speeds were possible for landing by use of the rudder.

Aircraft systems

The aircraft's electrical system was based on electrical power being provided by two engine-driven 24V, 1,500W DC generators mounted on each inboard engine, connected in parallel and charging the aircraft batteries, which provided power to over 50 circuits connecting the various aircraft services. Two generator switches were provided on the electrical control panel and a Ground/Flight switch on the starboard side of the fuselage, immediately aft of the front spar, which isolated the aircraft batteries when the aircraft was parked (a list of aircraft services provided by the generators is shown in the accompanying table). All the electrical services obtained a supply from the main control panel and inside the panel were the fuses controlling the main circuits of the general electrical services, with voltmeters and ammeters being situated on the front.

For engine starting, an external battery was used because of the high current consumption of the starter motor. This was achieved by moving the Ground/Flight switch to 'Ground' prior to starting. If the starter button was pressed for too long a period the starter motor would almost certainly burn out. The turning period was, therefore, limited to fifteen seconds, with a 30-second interval before the next attempt should the engine have failed to

Table 8. Weak Mixture Fuel Consumption for Merlin XX, 22 and 24 Engines (gal/hr)			
Boost (psi)	2,650rpm	2,300rpm	2,000rpm
+7	260	225	212
+4	228	204	188
+2	212	188	172
0	192	172	150
–2	172	156	140
–4	152	136	124

Table 9. Weak Mixture Fuel Consumption for Merlin 28 and 38 Engines (gal/hr)					
Boost (psi)	2,650rpm	2,400rpm	2,200rpm	2,000rpm	1,800rpm
+7	240	235	217	200	–
+4	216	204	196	180	–
+2	196	184	176	164	–
0	172	164	156	144	128
–2	148	140	128	124	112
–4	124	120	108	104	96

Table 10. Rich Mixture Fuel Consumption (gal/hr)	
+14psi boost at 3,000rpm (XX, 22 & 24)	500
+12psi boost at 3,000rpm (XX, 22 & 24)	460
+9psi boost at 2,850rpm (XX, 22 & 24)	380
+9psi boost at 2,850rpm (28 & 38)	420
+7psi boost at 2,650rpm (XX only)	320

start; only one further attempt was permitted. Finally, a detonator circuit was also provided and this enabled the pilot, navigator or wireless operator to destroy the aircraft's secret equipment. Three pairs of push-buttons were provided for each of the three crew members and any one of them needed only to push both buttons simultaneously to operate the detonators.

The Lancaster's fuel system was fed from six self-sealing fuel tanks, three in each wing, numbered 1 to 3 outboard of the fuselage between the front and rear spars; in the very early prototypes and production airframes only four tanks were fitted, two in each wing. The total amount of fuel normally carried by the Lancaster was 2,154 Imperial gallons, 580 gallons in each inboard wing tank, 383 in each intermediate wing tank and 114 in each outboard wing tank. Originally, on Mk I aircraft, immersed electric fuel booster pumps were fitted in all tanks but Mod (Modification No) 594 temporarily removed the immersed pumps from the No

1 tanks and fitted stack pipes in their places. The later Mod 512 put back the immersed pumps and incorporated suction by-pass lines to allow fuel to be drawn from the tanks when the pumps were not in use. In aircraft incorporating Mod 539, including all Lancaster Mk IIIs, a Pulsometer pump was fitted in each tank and by-pass lines were incorporated in Nos 1 and 2 tanks. On Mk Xs, Thompson pumps similar to the Pulsometer pumps were fitted. No 3 tank was used to replenish No 2 tank by switching on the No 3 tank fuel booster pump.

The pilot controlled the four master engine fuel cocks, which provided fuel to the engines, and fuel tank selection of either No 1 or No 2 tank on each side was made by the flight engineer. A cross-feed cock was provided to connect the port and starboard fuel supply systems in the case of an emergency when, for example, fuel was available in one side of the aircraft and needed to be fed to an engine on the other side. Normal management of the

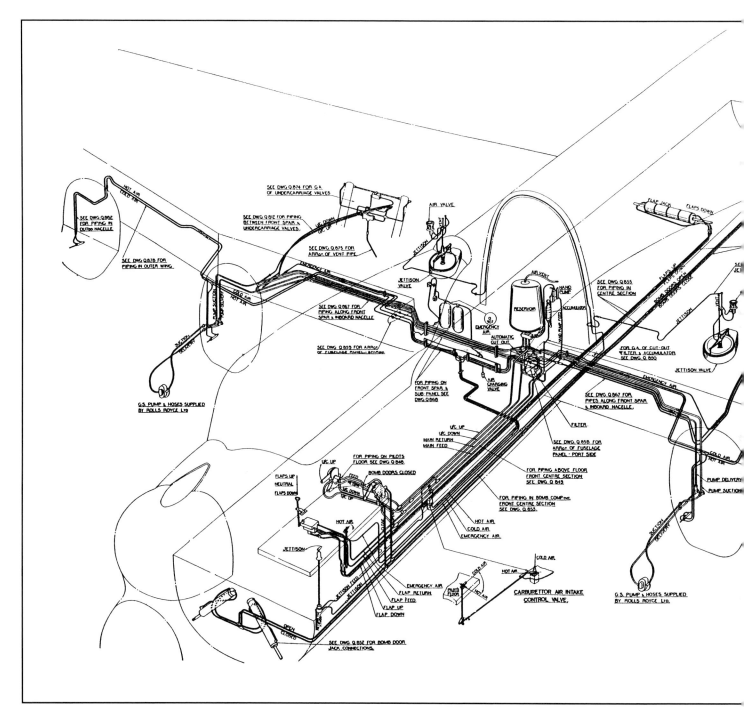

Diagrammatic arrangement of hydraulic general services.

fuel system in flight was to select either No 1 or No 2 tank, the latter being supplied by No 3 tank on selection of the appropriate electrical pump. However, as only the contents of No 1 tank could be jettisoned in an emergency, it was recommended that fuel from the No 2 tanks was used first. The fuel contents gauges and fuel pressure warning lights were on the flight engineer's panel. In the Lancaster Mk I the warning light would come on if the fuel pressure at the carburettor fell below 6psi and in the Mk III at 10psi; on the Mk X, fuel pressure warning gauges were fitted on the flight engineer's panel. Fuel consumption figures for weak and rich mixtures for different marks of Merlin engines are given in the accompanying tables. It was possible to fit an additional one or two tanks, of 400 gallons each, in the bomb compartment for extra long range. The total contents of the two inboard wing tanks (No 1 tanks) could be jettisoned. Fuel jettisoning was carried out by reducing speed, when possible, to 150mph and lowering the flaps to 15 degrees. The jettisoning control, situated on the left of the pilot's seat, was then operated by lifting and turning before returning it to the original position after jettisoning was complete.

The fuel filler caps were located on the upper side of each wing above the inner

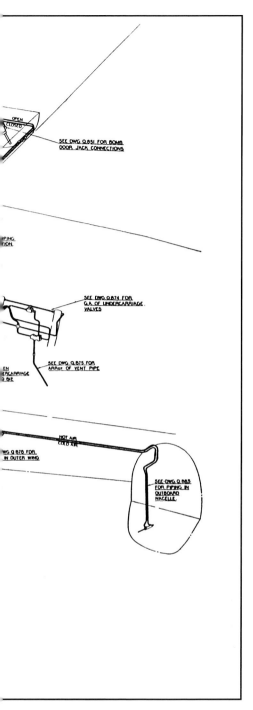

OPEN
CLOSED

SEE DWG. Q.851 FOR BOMB
DOOR JACK CONNECTIONS

PIPING
TION.

SEE DWG. Q.874 FOR
G.A OF UNDERCARRIAGE
VALVES

SEE DWG. Q.875 FOR
ARR. OF VENT PIPE

UNDERCARRIAGE

HOT AIR
COLD AIR

WG Q.878 FOR
IN OUTER WING

SEE DWG Q.883
FOR PIPING IN
OUTBOARD
NACELLE.

end of the outboard fuel tanks, with transfer pumps and transfer pipes between the tanks. Refuelling the Lancaster took the ground crew some time; for example, the Matador petrol bowser could hold 2,500 gallons of fuel which was just enough to refuel one Lancaster for a long sortie. To refuel a squadron for night operations could take the airframe fitters all afternoon; the amount of fuel per aircraft often gave an early indication of 'the target for tonight'.

The hydraulic system operated the main landing gear, bomb doors, flaps, engine air intake shutters and fuel jettison system. The main hydraulic reservoir was situated in the centre section of the fuselage and there was an ancillary hydraulic reservoir located by the mid-upper turret. A later modification included the installation of a smaller reservoir in the nose section. The fluids used in the Lancaster's hydraulic system were mineral oil and therefore required synthetic rubber to be employed for all gland materials. Four different oils could be used, all of which could be mixed if necessary. The system accumulators were pressurized to 220psi by two engine-driven pumps. In the event of a failure of both pumps, the landing gear and flaps could be lowered by compressed air. A hand pump was also provided for emergency operation of the other hydraulic services.

The gun turrets were also hydraulically operated. An engine-driven pump supplied hydraulic pressure to each turret, with each engine driving a different turret. This ensured that the loss of one engine would not make the aircraft completely defenceless. For example, if either of the outboard engines were completely lost (i.e. seized), then hydraulic power was lost to either the rear turret or the mid-upper turret (port and starboard engines respectively). If it was still possible to keep the propeller windmilling, then a limited operation of the services fed from that engine could be retained.

The pneumatic system consisted of a Heywood compressor, driven by the starboard inner engine, charging an air bottle at 300psi. The system provided compressed air to the wheel brakes and for operation of the radiator flaps and supercharger. In the original system four pressure maintaining valves set at 120psi were situated, one on each engine, on the engine bulkhead. In later systems the four pressure maintaining valves were replaced by a single one at a four-way union. A pressure maintaining valve in the supply line from the air bottle allowed pressure to be supplied to the radiator flaps and supercharger only if the pressure in the air bottle exceeded 120psi. This was to ensure

that sufficient pressure was always available to the brakes, which operated at 80psi. A pneumatic triple-pressure gauge was situated in the cockpit. Finally, the crew's oxygen system was supplied from fifteen cylinders which were located in a stowage compartment in the centre section of the fuselage.

The Lancaster Crew
The crew was the heart of the Lancaster, a close-knit team of experts who relied upon each other not only for the success of a mission but also for their lives. When Bomber Command entered the war it had been badly equipped with aircraft and poorly trained for the roles it was called on to perform. The hard lessons of war taught that much had to be changed, including the composition of the bomber crews and the responsibilities of each man. An early rule had been: 'It is a guiding principle in laying down the composition of crews of large bombers that there must be at least two men capable of carrying out each major task. Thus, if any one crew member should become a casualty there is always another man available to take on his work and play his part in carrying out the task allotted and bringing the aircraft safely back to its base.'

As aircraft and equipment became more complex, and in the light of experience, changes were made. The Lancaster's second pilot was removed when a shortage of pilots became apparent and the luxury of two pilots per aircraft could no longer be afforded; instead, one of the other crew members was given training as the pilot's assistant. With the increased specialisation of both navigation and bomb-aiming requirements, the two tasks were split and an 'air bombardier' was added to the crew. Likewise, the increased complexity of the four-engine bombers called for a specialist and so the task of 'flight engineer' was created. Hence the standard crew of the Lancaster comprised seven specialists—pilot, navigator, flight engineer, bomb aimer, wireless operator, mid-upper gunner and rear gunner. Each was an expert in his own field, and each a vital cog in the overall crew wheel. Rank played no part in the airborne life of the crew;

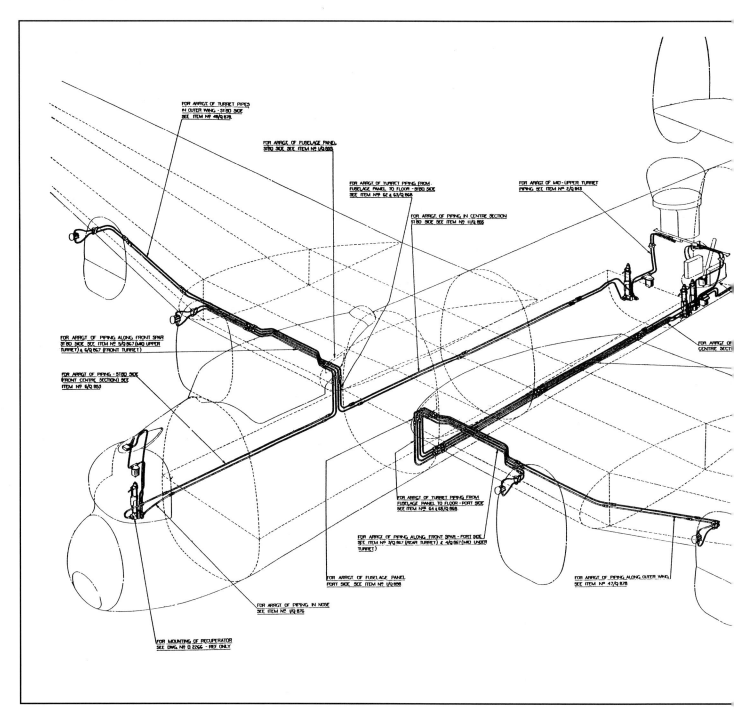

Diagrammatic arrangement of turret hydraulic system. The port outer engine supplied the rear turret, the port inner the mid-under turret (if fitted), the starboard inner the front turret and the starboard outer the mid-upper turret.

for example, a sergeant pilot would have command over his officer navigator. There were cases when the command of the aircraft went to a member of the crew other than the pilot, but these were exception-

ally rare. Every Lancaster captain, regardless of his rank, often had an individual responsibility higher than his equivalent in almost any other sphere of military operations. Once he was airborne from base he was the sole arbiter of the destiny of his share of the attack. It was vital that the individuals worked as part of a team; there was no room for personal friction.

In essence, the Lancaster crew was formed during the time spent training at the Operational Training Unit (OTU),

where training was carried out on Wellingtons and Whitleys. This was when all of the aircrew disciplines first met up. The OTU was, of course, the culmination of a much longer training process. A trainee pilot, for example, first arrived at the Initial Training Wing (ITW) from the Aircrew Reception Centre. ITW comprised about twelve weeks of ground training and consisted of drill and physical training, as well as lectures on meteorology, navigation, gunnery, morse code and aircraft recog-

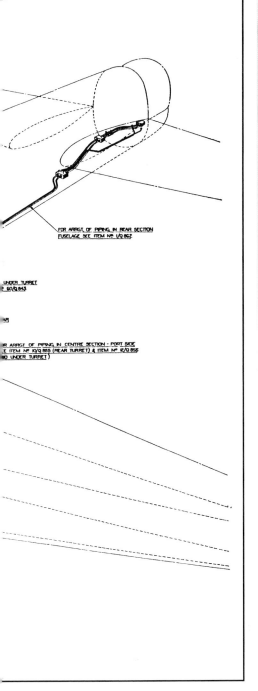

FOR ARRGT OF PIPING IN REAR SECTION
FUSELAGE SEE ITEM Nº 1/Q 862

UNDER TURRET
60/Q 843

R ARRGT OF PIPING IN CENTRE SECTION - PORT SIDE
E ITEM Nº 10/Q 855 (REAR TURRET) & ITEM Nº 12/Q 855
HO UNDER TURRET)

nition. On completion the pilot went to an Elementary Flying Training School (EFTS) to begin flying training. The standard EFTS basic trainer was the De Havilland Tiger Moth, although the Miles Magister was also used. If a potential bomber pilot, the student was then sent to the Service Flying Training School, where he learnt to fly twin-engine Ansons or Oxfords. Typically, at the end of SFTS a student pilot would have between 100 and 130 flying hours, of which about half

would be solo. If he was fortunate there would be some well-earned leave before starting the OTU for what was to become the foundation for his future tour.

One of the most important purposes of the OTU was to try to find the right mix of individuals who would make a good operational crew. Some naturally gravitated towards each other, perhaps having met at various stages of training; others were recommended by colleagues. The duties of all members of the crew were carefully defined as far as the principal tasks were concerned, but the captain of each aircraft maintained responsibility for arranging the duties of his crew and for ensuring that those tasks were carried out punctually and efficiently. A new pilot at the OTU would start the 'trawl' to find the rest of his crew, the decision being left to the individuals as far as possible rather than allowing the training system to put names together. It appeared to work remarkably well and gradually the crew would come together. The OTU was indeed a different world after EFTS and SFTS. Almost all the instructors were on rest tours from operations and, therefore, many OTUs functioned along the same lines as operational squadrons. The syllabus was intended to provide the crew with basic handling and operational skills, the instructors being able to pass on the bene-

From many different backgrounds, and often from many different parts of the world, the crew were the heart of the Lancaster—a close-knit team of experts who relied upon each other, not only for the success of a sortie but for each other's lives. Here Flt Lt Mike Beetham and crew, No 50 Squadron, are pictured at Skellingthorpe in 1944. (Les Bartlett)

fits of their experience. Incidentally, crews from the OTU also occasionally took part in operational sorties, usually on such tasks as leaflet-dropping over France, as a way of introducing new crews to operational requirements. Even such raids as the 'Thousand Bomber' operations of mid-1942 included both staff and student crews from the OTUs.

The introduction into service of the four-engine 'heavies' brought many problems in that these aircraft were quite different from the Whitleys and the Wellingtons being flown at the OTUs. Initially, therefore, an additional four aircraft per squadron were provided to act as a Conversion Flight, but this solution was far from ideal as the squadrons were not established as training units and the level of instruction was variable. The next stage was to combine these extra aircraft into Conversion Flights for each Bomber Command Group. Again, this was not an ideal solution, and so the Heavy Conversion

Left: The bomb aimer's position in the nose of the aircraft. The bomb sight can be seen centrally mounted and the bomb aimer's control panel is to the right.

Below left: The main cockpit, looking forward. The pilot's seat is raised on the left side, the main engine instruments and throttle quadrant are in the centre, and forward (lower right) is the bomb aimer's area.

Below right: The cockpit canopy had wide-view blisters on either side which gave the pilot and flight engineer good all-round visibility.

Bottom right: A view along the port wing and engines from the pilot's position.

Units (HCUs) were formed. The idea was quite simple in that the crew could convert to type, for example the Lancaster, before being posted to a squadron. Initially there was a difficulty in that all the early Lancasters were needed by the squadrons, and so a limited number of aircraft were made available at Lancaster Finishing Schools (LFSs). However, once Lancaster production was established, crews were trained at the HCUs, where the syllabus provided an essential link between the OTU and the squadron. Not only did it cover aspects such as aircraft handling, it provided the crew with more, and extremely vital, hours airborne to 'gel' together before joining a squadron. It also gave the crew training in fighter affiliation and how to handle the Lancaster in the face of fighter opposition. This gave the air gunners precious experience in tracking fighters and calling evasive manoeuvres.

As the war progressed and more operational experience was gained, a wide variety of specialist training units were established within Bomber Command. These generally involved no more than a week's training. An example was the Night Vision Schools, which were often incorporated into the HCU training and specialised in teaching aspects of identifying targets at night.

Once formed and trained, the crew would fly together on the squadron whenever possible, although individuals were 'borrowed' from time to time to make up numbers for a particular sortie. This procedure was not generally popular as it meant that the crew would become 'out of step' with the number of operations that each individual had to perform: the hope amongst crews was that they would all complete their tour of 'ops' together. It was equally bad luck to go sick and miss a few operations with one's crew as that meant catching up flying with another crew for a while. In the highly superstitious world of bomber aircrews this was seen as a great hazard.

Cockpit Environment

Describing the Lancaster's main cockpit from the front, the bomb aimer's position was situated in the nose of the aircraft and he had the additional task of manning the front turret during the long transits to and from the target area. The bomb aimer's equipment and details of the Nash & Thompson FN5A hydraulically operated front turret are covered in detail in Chapter 5. During the take-off and landing phase of the flight the bomb aimer was supposed to be in the main cockpit but many stayed in the nose of the aircraft throughout the sortie. When a larger and improved blister was fitted to the Lancaster from 1943, the bomb aimer's view from the front was probably better than from any other bomber in service at the time. A late modification to the blister was the inclusion of the Identification Friend or Foe (IFF) 'Z' equipment. The lower part of the perspex blister incorporated an optically flat vision panel which prevented any distortion for final bomb-aiming. Situated externally on the lower port side of the nose was the pitot static head. The bomb aimer's parachute was stowed on the left side of the nose compartment and his escape hatch was in the floor directly below his normal operating position. Aft of the bomb aimer's panel was a cockpit fire extinguisher and beneath the main panel was an additional small panel for the release of photo-flares. On the port side of the nose compartment, looking downwards, was the F.24 camera installation (more details about target photography are provided in Chapter 5).

The Lancaster's main cockpit was spacious and the large canopy generally gave the front crew good all-round visibility. The pilot's seat was located on the port side on a raised floor and the back of the seat was armour-plated. In front of the pilot was his main instrument panel which included the basic flight instruments common to most aircraft—artificial horizon, altimeter, airspeed indicator, turn and slip and rate of climb and descent indicators. The pilot's compass was situated by his left knee with a distant-reading (DR) compass repeater on top of the front panel in the central position. The main radio installation and a cockpit fire extinguisher were located to the pilot's left on the side of the cockpit.

The engine instruments and aircraft systems were monitored in the early days by the two pilots, although the introduction of the flight engineer (replacing the second pilot) meant that many of these responsibilities became the flight engineer's and the pilot was left with the important task of flying the aircraft. The flight engineer sat on a hinged seat on the starboard side of the main cockpit, where the second pilot used to sit. Between the pilot and the flight engineer was a central pedestal which housed the engine throttles and propeller controls, within easy reach of the two men. The engine boost gauges and engine rpm indicators were located above the pedestal and behind it were the undercarriage and flaps controls.

To aid the all-round visibility, the canopy had wide-view blisters on either side which meant that the pilot and the flight engineer could both see downwards. The pilot's forward vision was kept free from any icing by windscreen de-icing spray nozzles which were located on the upper surface of the fuselage immediately in front of the canopy. On top of the canopy were the direction finding (DF) loop aerial and the aerial mast for the main radio. A canopy escape hatch was also fitted into the top of the main canopy, although this could only be used for abandoning the aircraft on the ground or in water.

To assist with monitoring the performance of each engine, the flight engineer's panel, which was located on the starboard side of the aircraft, included engine oil temperature and pressure gauges and engine coolant temperature gauges. One of the flight engineer's main tasks was the management of the fuel system, and the panel also included fuel gauges, fuel booster pumps and fuel tank selector cocks. The management of the fuel system was critical and special attention was given to the transfer of fuel between tanks which would minimise fuel loss in the event that the aircraft was hit. The flight engineer generally assisted the pilot from engine start through to final shut-down at the end of the sortie and would operate the aircraft's services such as flaps, undercarriage, throttle and propeller settings. He

Top left: The panel with the basic flight instruments, showing (from top left to right) the airspeed indicator, artificial horizon and rate of climb and descent indicator and (lower left to right) the altimeter, direction indicator and turn and slip indicator.

Top right: The DF indicator (left) and DR compass repeater (right), shown located

on the upper coaming in front of the pilot's position.

Above left: The navigator's plotting table, located on the port side of the main cockpit aft of the pilot's position.

Above right: The wireless operator's position, looking forward. The small window can be seen on the left side.

was also responsible for monitoring the performance of the engines during the sortie, for managing the aircraft's fuel system and for monitoring the other aircraft systems. When not carrying out any of these tasks the flight engineer was a valuable extra pair of eyes in the cockpit. Finally, he was capable also of flying the aircraft in an emergency, at least long enough for the crew to bail out if necessary.

The responsibility of the communications equipment, the electronic warfare equipment and the authentication of

codes and messages belonged to the wireless operator. His station in the aircraft was situated at the back of the main cockpit and adjacent to the leading edge of the wing. The equipment varied according to the mark and batch number of the Lancaster and also depended on what additional modifications, particularly electronic warfare equipment, had been added to the aircraft; for example, the wireless operator was responsible for the operation of the aircraft's tail warning devices. Quite often the wireless operator's specialist

equipment would often be different for aircraft belonging to squadrons with specific roles. Essentially, his equipment included the radios, the electronic warfare equipment, the direction-finding equipment, the IFF equipment and the electrical services panel. The main radio installation and radio receiver was the ARI.5033, which was situated in the main cockpit, for which the aerial mast was, as noted, located on the top of the main canopy. The high-frequency (HF) radio aerial trailed from the front of the aircraft to the starboard fin.

Safety and Survival Equipment

The wireless operator was also generally responsible for checking the safety and survival equipment—a fire extinguisher, axe and signal pistol with cartridges—mainly because he was the crew member nearest to where the equipment was stowed in the centre section of the fuselage. Slightly further aft was the stowage for parachute and emergency packs and the manual release cable for the crew dinghy, which was large enough for the entire crew and was located in the root of the starboard wing. The dinghy was a Type J which could be released and inflated in one of three ways: first, by pulling a release cord running along the fuselage roof aft of the rear spar; secondly, from outside by pulling a loop on the starboard side aft of the tailplane leading edge; and thirdly, automatically by an immersion switch.

There was also a rest bunk for the crew (not that the crew would get much rest on operations!). Further down the fuselage, towards the mid-upper turret, was a walk-round oxygen set, which could be used by one of the crew in an emergency; a second set was situated by the mid-upper turret next to another fire extinguisher. There were also various distress and location markers should the aircraft ditch in the sea. Between the mid-upper turret and tail section was another manual release cable for the dinghy, an emergency kit and parachute stowage, an axe, a first aid kit, distress flares and a toilet. In the tail section, by the rear gunner's access door, was a parachute stowage point for the rear gunner and a fire extinguisher. Generally, the safety and survival equipment supplied for the crew in the case of an emergency was very good—and it needed to be. There were several instances of the rear crew having to fight fires in the fuselage and there were several occasions when the aircraft crash-landed or ditched in the sea.

During the first three years of the war every Bomber Command aircraft carried at least one pigeon. It was part of the wireless operator's pre-flight routine to go and pick up the container with the pigeon. The idea was that if the aircraft came down in the sea, then the crew would send the pigeon back to base with a message of where they were; the Air–Sea Rescue service would then go out and attempt to rescue the crew. The birds were given a thorough training at the regional training centres, such as Finningley, including being released from an aircraft. The message container was made of bakelite and included a partially completed message—station,

aircraft number and date of issue. In the event of an emergency the crew would then complete the rest of the form, giving their location, time, etc. If there was no time to take the container apart and carry out this procedure, then they could simply write on the white strip on the outside of the container. Each station with a pigeon service also had a trained staff to look after the birds, usually one corporal and two airmen. There seems to be no record of Bomber Command pigeons being released operationally, although, presumably, they must have been so used on occasions. It appears that the practice of carrying pigeons had been discontinued by the end of 1943.

Despite the survival equipment provided in the aircraft, the problem of abandoning a stricken Lancaster remained. If the aircraft was hit by flak or shot down by a night fighter, the crew faced the unenviable task of having to vacate the aircraft, usually at night. An analysis of bomber losses shows that of all the Lancasters lost on operations, less than 20 per cent of their crews survived to become prisoners of war. This figure is less favourable than that for the Halifax, for example, which had a survival rate nearly twice that of the Lancaster. When looking at the individual crew positions, it is also possible to assess the chances of each individual crew member. Those at the front of the Lancaster, particularly the bomb aimer, appear to have had a greater chance of

escape owing to their being close to the forward escape hatch, whilst those towards the rear of the aircraft had less chance. Statistically, just over 10 per cent of rear gunners in the Lancaster escaped to become prisoners of war (compared to 30 per cent of Halifax rear gunners) and nearly 20 per cent of wireless operators (compared to 40 per cent of Halifax wireless operators). It is also interesting to note that the statistics of survival rates amongst US B-17 Flying Fortresses and B-24 Liberators, operating over Europe by day, were more favourable—approximately 50 per cent overall.

When trying to determine why these statistics should be different, it is worth looking in more detail at the escape exits for the Lancaster. From the Lancaster's *Flight Engineer's Notes*, it is stated that there was only one official escape hatch for abandoning the aircraft by parachute, this being the forward escape hatch. The notes state that the use of the rear door was not recommended because of the close proximity of the tail section of the aircraft, and it should only be used in cases of extreme emergency. There were, of course, the additional three push-out panel escape hatches on the upper surface of the Lancaster for egress from the aircraft while on the ground or in the water. However, it must be presumed that any crew member towards the rear of the Lancaster having

Lancaster escape exits.

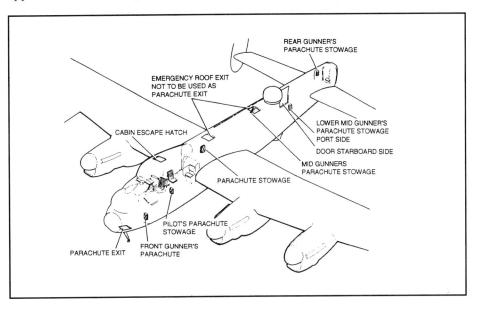

53

Right, top: A crew demonstrating an emergency egress procedure on the ground or having ditched in water. The pilot is using the canopy escape hatch and the wireless operator is using the forward of the two emergency roof exits. (V. Beal via Steve Barker)

Right, centre: Vacating the aircraft by means of the two emergency roof exits. (V. Beal via Steve Barker)

Right, bottom: With the aircraft abandoned, vital survival equipment is passed through the roof exit to a crew member standing on the mainplane. (V. Beal via Steve Barker)

to abandon the aircraft by parachute would opt to vacate by the exit nearest to him: the chances of successfully making his way forward, in the dark and in an aircraft perhaps out of control and on fire, were very slim. This problem was not exactly the same in the Halifax, where the rear door was situated further forward. The design of the Lancaster cannot be held to blame for the low success rate among abandoning crews. There could have been no way that the designers could have appreciated the exact conditions which aircrews would have to escape from: prewar doctrine held that a heavy bomber would be able to defend itself against attacking enemy fighters (see Chapter 5).

Statistics can, of course, be made to suggest almost anything, depending on how they are interpreted. Having accepted the statistics on survival rates, one should then consider the likelihood of crews having to abandon an aircraft in the first place. There were many occasions when Lancaster losses were proportionately fewer than Halifax losses; moreover, losses among the RAF's heavy night bombers were considerably fewer than among the American day bombers. It should also be noted that there were many occasions when rear crewmen survived and front crewmen did not, purely because of where the aircraft had been hit—and there were also instances when the rear gunner was the only member of the crew to survive, having literally been thrown clear of the aircraft. There was an element of luck associated with aircrew survival!

4. Specialist Equipment

The equipment and techniques used for the Lancaster's primary task of flying to and attacking targets can be considered together, since the various items of equipment fitted to the aircraft were usually designed and developed with both tasks in mind. To develop accurate equipment to help the crew deliver a bomb load on target took time. As soon as one piece of equipment or technique was perfected, a German counter to the system made the system either unreliable or unusable, such was the scientific battle of the war.

During the early part of the war the main form of navigation was visual. The problem of navigating to a target in bad weather or at night, and then to deliver a bomb load accurately on target, caused great concern. The traditional method of night navigation or navigating above cloud was known as 'astro', that is, using a sextant and the sun or stars to obtain a fix. In the Lancaster this method was theoretically possible and a navigator's astrodome was situated at the back of the main canopy. However, in practice the method proved cumbersome and time-consuming, while clear conditions were necessary in order to 'shoot a fix'. Furthermore, over enemy territory it was not always possible for the pilot to fly straight and level for any length of time. Nevertheless, it should be mentioned that there were many occasions when crews had to rely on their basic knowledge of the solar system to find their way home when all other methods had failed.

The absence of sophisticated navigation equipment often meant that aircrew had to find their way from one point to another by dead reckoning, that is, by working from a known point, taking the aircraft heading and speed, then accounting for the effect of wind to give a position. It sounds simple, except that errors crept in to every part of the calculation—compass errors, the calculation of the aircraft's true air speed and problems in knowing the exact wind speed and direction. When also taking into account the fact that an aircraft might be forced off heading for a number of reasons, particularly in wartime, then navigating by dead reckoning proved a very difficult task. To emphasise the problem, an error of just one degree over a distance of 60 miles results in a navigation error of one mile. If a compass could be in error by 2 or 3 degrees, and the wind calculation by several degrees, then the result was a bomber several miles off course and unable to find the target area, let alone hit a specific point.

The navigation equipment in the Lancaster varied according to the mark of the aircraft and the layout even varied with batch number. Essentially, the navigator had at his station repeaters of the main aircraft instruments—compass, altimeter and airspeed indicator. Next to these he would have an air position indicator (API) which displayed in latitude and longitude the position of the aircraft in still-air conditions, that is, not taking into account the wind velocity. The API was fed information from the aircraft's compass, the airspeed indicator and the altimeter, which meant that any deviation from the aircraft's course was fed into the system. The aircraft's position was displayed to the navigator in four windows, giving the north, south, east and west position. However, in later aircraft the API was positioned over the navigator's table. With the navigation chart aligned, the aircraft's position was displayed by a pinpoint of light on the chart. Like any piece of navigation equipment, the API suffered various errors and needed to be updated periodically. This meant that the navigator had to take a 'fix' from some other source, after which the API could be re-set to a new and correct position. However, this would not always be possible, particularly over enemy territory when several deviations were taking place or when good fix points were difficult to obtain.

An attachment to the API meant that the equipment could be used as a ground position indicator (GPI). By calculating the wind velocity, a navigator could feed this value into the equipment and the aircraft's position over the ground was then displayed. It was then possible for the navigator to observe the aircraft's track across the ground—particularly important during approaches to targets. Although it sounds a good and easy technique, it did rely totally on the accuracy of the wind velocity data fed into the API. Obviously, any errors of calculation in the wind velocity led to subsequent errors in the aircraft's ground position. Generally, the navigator was always busy keeping aware of the aircraft's position and, in particular, keeping a check on the wind.

Gee

The search for an electronic aid to assist navigation and permit 'blind' bombing, i.e., accurate bombing even when the target was not visible (because it was night or because cloud obscured it), was of critical importance to Bomber Command. The earliest and partially successful device was the radio navigational aid TR.1355, otherwise known as 'Gee'. The concept was fairly simple and relied on the reception of signals from a series of ground stations. The ground organisation comprised three

The task of the navigator was continually improved with the introduction of such equipment as Gee and H2S.

synchronised stations, a Master (A) and two Slaves (B and C), set along a 200-mile baseline, each Slave station being locked to the Master. The time difference for signals A–B and B–C to reach the aircraft was measured and pulses were displayed visually on a display unit (a cathode ray tube) in the aircraft. In essence, this gave the navigator two position lines, the Gee coordinates, and by using a special Gee chart he could plot the intersection of the lines and at any time obtain a fix of the ground position. The theoretical accuracy was 0.5 to 5 miles—far better than any other navigation aid then in service. A series of experimental flights was planned to determine the accuracy and potential range of the system. These trials, carried out by No 1418 Experimental Flight, were promising and so the system went into development. In July 1941 Wellingtons were fitted with Gee sets to conduct operational trials and the following month the system was used operationally for the first time.

When the Lancaster first entered operational service with Nos 44 and 97 Squadrons in early 1942 only a few of the aircraft were fitted with Gee. It was origi-

nally intended that the Gee-equipped Lancasters would lead any of the raids within the operating range of the equipment, although the limitation of Gee's range restricted the choice of targets for which it could be used. It was appreciated that Gee would not be available in all bombers and that to take advantage of it meant developing new tactics. The Air Staff suggested the use of an initial wave of Gee-equipped aircraft to drop incendiaries as a guide for the rest of the bomber force. The question of how best to employ Gee was one which taxed many of the most experienced personnel in Bomber Command.

The initial tactical solution was to adopt what became known as the 'Shaker' technique, the basis of which was to try and make the best use of Gee whilst overcoming some of the known shortcomings of night bombing such as seeing the target at night. The tactical plan of the 'Shaker' technique involved three waves of aircraft, the first two of which included Gee-equipped aircraft. The first wave dropped triple flares to illuminate the target, the second dropped incendiaries and the third—the majority of the bomber force, fifteen minutes behind the first wave—dropped high-explosive bombs.

Gee's main advantages were its ease of operation and the rapidity of obtaining a fix (less than one minute). However, the system also had severe limitations. For example, range (limited by line of sight) depended on aircraft altitude and reliability. With favourable circumstances a maximum range of 400 miles was possible, but more typically strong signals were received out to about 150 miles, after which signal strength would reduce. The Eastern Gee Chain was probably the most popular with the crews owing to its location and signal strength.

Although Gee meant that most crews had little difficulty in finding the approximate target area, the equipment was still generally used just for this purpose: the light of the flares was relied upon to make a visual acquisition of the aiming point. Various reports show that Gee went part of the way towards solving the problem of an accurate navigation and bombing

technique, but it was soon decided that better techniques were necessary and ultimately a trained 'target finding force' would be required. By August 1942 the Germans had also proved capable of jamming Gee, which effectively reduced the range of the system, and although anti-jamming features were later added to the system it remained of limited use once an aircraft had crossed the enemy coastline. However, the navigator was able to get an accurate fix of the aircraft's position before crossing the enemy coast—and, despite its limitations when operating over enemy territory, Gee did offer bomber crews the tremendous advantage of being able to find their way back to base. The benefits of its assistance to crews around the United Kingdom more than compensated for its operational limitations. Statistics show that after the introduction into service of the system, the number of aircraft landing away from base decreased. At the very least, a bomber crew could find its way back over land, if necessary to make a force-landing at a suitable airfield, rather than run out of fuel over the North Sea unable to find its way home. In the event that an aircraft needed to ditch in the North Sea the navigator also had the opportunity to transmit an accurate position prior to ditching so that the search and rescue service stood a good chance of locating the crew.

Oboe

The fact that Gee could be electronically jammed meant that new techniques were required, although the system would remain in service and was probably the most reliable electronic aid developed during the war. However, the most *accurate* of the electronic aids to enter service during the war was undoubtedly 'Oboe'. It was developed by the Telecommunications Research Establishment (TRE) as a result of research into German beacons. Early trials of blind-bombing used a Chain Home Low (CHL) ground station plus an IFF set in the aircraft. The name 'Oboe' appears to have come from the apparent sound of the signal. The system was devised in 1941 and consisted of two ground stations each with a different role. One, a tracking station called the 'Cat', sent out a dot–dash signal and the second ground station, the 'Mouse', sent the release signal. Both stations operated on the same wavelength but used different pulse frequencies, and a pulse repeater in the aircraft responded to both frequencies so that each station could measure the aircraft's range independently. After much development the first Oboe attack was carried out by six Mosquitos of No 109 Squadron against the power station at Lutterade in Holland on the night of 20/21 December 1942. Oboe was mainly fitted to Pathfinder Mosquitos but was also installed in some Lancasters. The first Lancaster-equipped Oboe attack was carried out on 11 July 1944 against Gapennes by an aircraft of No 582 Squadron, Wing Commander G. F. Grant from No 109 Squadron flying with the crew and directing the attack.

For the system to be used during an attack, strict coordination was required in order to ensure adequate separation between aircraft. At the pre-flight briefing the navigator was given a position, height and time at which to be prior to his attack. This was known as the Waiting Point, from where the navigator would also be given a heading, height and speed to carry out his

Improvements in blind-bombing techniques assisted the bomb aimer in delivering bombs accurately on target. (Les Bartlett)

bombing run. During the sortie the navigator would generally use Gee to navigate the aircraft to the Waiting Point and arrive there at the correct time, which corresponded to ten minutes prior to his time-on-target. On reaching the Waiting Point the navigator switched on the Oboe equipment with the exception of the repeater. Each aircraft had its own call-sign, and when it was transmitted the navigator switched on the repeater and the pilot would immediately start receiving a series of dots and dashes. The idea was that the bomber would fly to the target along the arc of a circle with the pilot listening to the dots and dashes to indicate which side of the planned approach track the aircraft was, 'on-track' being indicated by a steady tone. The 'Mouse' measured the ground speed of the aircraft and sent signals to the navigator indicating time to go to the bomb release signal—'A' for ten minutes, 'B' for eight, 'C' for six and 'D' for three, with the release signal being five 'dits' and a long 'dah'. At the moment of bomb release the aircraft's transmitter would cease, thus indicating to the ground stations the point and time of release. The navigator would then switch off the equipment, allowing the next aircraft to use the system.

The fact that the procedure took ten minutes was the system's single major drawback: only one aircraft could use it during that time frame, allowing just six aircraft per hour to use the system during

the raid. Part of the answer to the problem was to build more pairs of ground stations, operating on different wavelengths, although the system was still limited to just three pairs of these stations. Because of the way Oboe had been designed, each aircraft using the system had to follow the same approach path to the target, and it was some time before this problem was solved. Additional limitations with the Mk I version of Oboe were typical of those of any electronic aid: it was limited in range and it could be electronically jammed. Two ground stations were built, at Hawkeshill Down, near Dover, and at Trimingham, near Cromer, which gave adequate coverage of the Ruhr area. However, the problem of range meant that the aircraft typically had to operate at about 26,000ft over the target area, at ranges of about 250 miles from the ground stations. Intermittent interference also caused trouble, and this led to aircraft being fitted with two receivers, tuned to different frequencies, the pulses being transmitted coincidentally from the stations on the two frequencies. This meant that if the aircraft did not receive both pulses then the aircraft transmitter would not work; thus spurious pulses were prevented from being transmitted to the ground stations. This modification was known as 'K Oboe', the 'K' standing for 'coincidence' (!), although even this system had problems with breakthrough when more than one pair of ground stations were operating at the same time. Further modifications, incorporating time delays from the ground stations to the receiver, had been incorporated into the system by June 1943.

More improvements to the system led to the development of Oboe Mk II, of which four versions were produced. The first, known as 'Penwiper', used the klystron tunable valve but proved unsuccessful. The second development was 'Pepperbox', which was a modified version of 'Penwiper' and also proved unsuccessful; it was cancelled by the end of 1943. The first successful development was the Mk IIF known as 'Fountain Pen' (otherwise 'Aspen'), which used the magnetron, a more powerful valve than the klystron, and entered service at the beginning of 1944.

This was followed by the Mk IIM, known as 'Album Leaf', which was a more sophisticated version of 'Fountain Pen' and became the standard variant with a theoretical accuracy of 0.01 mile!

The earlier problem of each aircraft having to fly the same approach path to the target was solved by a technique known as the Delta Approach, which allowed several aircraft to make runs at the target at the same time. Moreover, an increased number of pulse frequencies and the use of more than one wavelength meant that up to 40 aircraft could be in the target area at any one time. These improvements led to the Mk III system, which entered service during mid-1944 and used different ground stations but relied on airborne equipment almost identical to 'Album Leaf'. By that time there were thirteen ground stations and a further ten mobile stations which provided cover across most of Bomber Command's target areas.

The use of Oboe was generally limited for target-marking, although once 'Album Leaf' was in service most Bomber Command raids included Oboe-equipped aircraft. With the use of Oboe the overall bombing results showed a threefold improvement. Numerous modifications were made to the system; for example, it had been shown that Oboe's range could technically be improved by the use of a repeater system. However, many of the technical developments were curtailed in the trials stage by an unfounded confidence in the accuracy of a new system known as H2S.

H2S

The desire to equip Bomber Command with accurate navigation aids had been given great impetus by the findings of the Butt Report of 1941. Among the many devices considered was the use of an airborne radar system, the principle of which had been proved by ASV (Air to Surface Vessel) and AI (Airborne Intercept) devices. There was no technical reason why a reasonable ground image should not be possible from such systems. In October 1941 a meeting held at the TRE put forward the advantages of an AI-type system: it would be independent of ground stations and thus have unlimited range, and it would be impossible to jam. These two points were major considerations and offered significant advantages over Gee and Oboe, although the latter benefit would prove not to materialise.

Trials with a 9cm AI set in a Blenheim proved the principles of ground mapping: all that was needed now was a better set to give a greater definition of ground features. The theory of H2S was relatively straightforward. Pulses from the aircraft transmitter travelled in straight lines and were reflected back from suitable surfaces. By displaying the returned pulses on a cathode ray tube, known as a plan position indicator (PPI), the returned pulses appeared in their relative position from the aircraft. TRE conducted further trials using Halifaxes equipped with a rotating scanner to give 360 degrees of cover. Development continued with the magnetron being used instead of the klystron, giving

To assist in blind-bombing, the bomb aimers were given detailed target maps with target returns highlighted in various colours. (Les Bartlett)

greater range. There were many problems to overcome, including the stabilization of the picture during manoeuvres, the discrimination of pertinent features from the general clutter, and reliability. By December 1942 a number of sets had been delivered and fitted to Stirlings of No 7 Squadron at Oakington and Halifaxes of No 35 Squadron at Graveley, and the system was first used operationally by both squadrons on the night of 30/31 January 1943 during a raid on Hamburg.

Fitted to the Lancaster, the H2S scanner fairing can be easily identified as a large blister situated on the underside of the rear fuselage, directly beneath the position of the mid-upper turret. The H2S set inside the aircraft was situated at the navigator's station and, depending on the production batch, could be hinge-mounted or shelf-mounted next to his working table. It soon became obvious that H2S was an excellent navigation aid: it provided good contrast between land and water, coastal features, lakes and rivers were therefore easy to identify and so general navigation (hence aircraft position) proved fairly straightforward. Quite sim-

ply, it gave the navigator a picture of the ground ahead of and beneath the aircraft, even at night or in cloudy weather (although particularly bad weather limited its use).

Using H2S, the navigator could identify a point on the ground and by plotting the reciprocal relative bearing and distance from that point he could obtain a fix. By maintaining an air plot, he could always keep an accurate assessment of the wind velocity. There were four different range-scales for the navigator to choose from—radii of 100, 50, 30 and 10 miles. The most common method was to use the 30-mile scale for general navigation and then to select the 10-mile scale for the target run. However, the employment of H2S as a bombing aid proved more problematical as it was often difficult to make out an accurate aiming point unless ground features were unique and distinguishable. Using predictions and overlays, the navigator could analyse the picture and interpret what he was seeing, but it took practice to make sense of the often confused series of 'blobs'. Particularly large cities such as Berlin made the identification of

The H2S radar scanner fairing, located on the underside of the fuselage directly beneath the mid-upper turret, is clearly visible on W4963.

exact aiming points more difficult and much was left to the experience of the navigator. Cities near coastlines, such as Hamburg and Bremen, proved easier to cope with. Various modifications to the radar were made to ease the navigator's task, for example improvements to the aerial and to the picture displayed to the navigator, and these modifications resulted in the H2S Mk II. Initially it had been suggested that H2S be used by experienced crews for target-marking, although this suggestion had been countered by reasoning that the Main Force also needed to be at the right place at the right time in order to capitalise on the target-marking. The counter-argument won, and by the end of 1943 approximately 90 per cent of Bomber Command aircraft were equipped with H2S.

The problems of ground clutter and stabilization of the picture were partially solved by using the 3cm band instead of

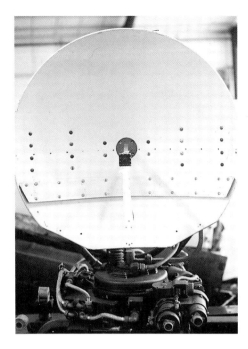

Above: The H2S radar scanner.

Above, right: A close-up view of the H2S blister fitted to NX611.

the 9cm (the shorter the wavelength, the better the horizontal definition) and by using a gyro for stabilization. The first three Lancasters to be equipped with these new sets (H2S Mk III) were Mk IIIs delivered in November 1943, JB352 and JB355 to No 83 Squadron at Wyton and JB356 to No 97 Squadron at Bourn. However, the problem of ground clutter would never be completely solved and much was still dependent on the experience and expertise of the navigator. By the spring of 1944 a number of H2S sets had been modified, and various improvements continued until the end of the war. Experimental systems were also developed, for example H2S Mk IIIF 'Whirligig' (with a larger scanner) and Mk IV 'Lion-Tamer' (using K-band), although these were never employed on operations.

H2S was certainly the most widely used aid to navigation and bomb-aiming throughout the latter half of the war. Despite its limitations as an aid for blind-bombing, due mainly to the problems caused by ground clutter, it would have been very difficult for crews to achieve any degree of accuracy beyond the range of Oboe without it. H2S also allowed

Bomber Command to carry out operations in weather conditions which were unfavourable to normal visual bombing techniques. However, it did not take the Germans long to listen out for the H2S transmissions and thus discover the position of the aircraft responsible. The introduction of Naxos, a device used by the German night fighters for homing in on H2S transmissions, led to crews becoming cautious, and restrictions in the use of H2S over enemy territory were introduced. Nevertheless, H2S was without doubt a superb technical achievement, and it was developed into an excellent radar in the post-war period.

G-H and Loran

Another of the new blind-bombing aids to enter service towards the end of 1943 was AR.5525, known as 'G-H'. The system was not new in that it had been proposed at the same time that Gee was being looked at; this 'H' system would in theory have better accuracy than Gee but would be limited, like Oboe, in the number of aircraft which could use it at any one time. What transpired, therefore, was in effect a 'reverse Oboe' whereby an aircraft transmitted to mobile stations to get its information for fixes. More aircraft could use the system in over given time period, but it depended heavily on the aircrew for accuracy.

G-H made its first large-scale operational début against factories in Düsseldorf on the night of 3/4 November 1943. Of the 344 Lancasters taking part in the raid, 38 were Mk IIs equipped with G-H; five returned early, two were lost and the equipment failed to work properly in sixteen aircraft, leaving fifteen Lancasters to bomb the target using the system. G-H became a useful blind-bombing aid when finally fitted to a large enough number of Bomber Command aircraft. For example, by October 1944 one-third of No 3 Group's Lancasters were fitted with it, giving the Group the capability of operating in overcast conditions. Lancasters fitted with G-H had their fins painted in different colours, making them easy to identify in flight so that aircraft not so equipped could follow them into the target area and release their bomb loads at the same time as the leader.

During the time that Gee was being developed, work on a long-range navigation system was taking place in America. The system, known as Loran (short for 'long range'), was primarily developed for long-range navigation over the sea and therefore its effectiveness over land was reduced. The main difference between Gee and Loran was in the use of the ground stations to obtain a fix: Gee required three stations to obtain a simultaneous fix, whereas Loran used pairs of ground stations which only gave the navigator one position line at a time. After noting the coordinates from the first position line, the navigator would then take a further position line one minute later from another pair of ground stations. Another minute later he would take a further position line from the first pair of ground stations and take an average reading of the two, from which he could combine that position with the second position line to obtain a fix.

The method proved slightly time-consuming and required the navigator to maintain a 'running' fix to keep a plot of the aircraft's position, but it was relatively accurate and could be used beyond the range of Gee—particularly useful when operating deep into Germany. The system was used from 1944 onwards when Loran ground stations were established in Scotland and North Africa. The Gee sets fitted in the Lancaster were modified so that either Gee or Loran could be used.

The Electronic War

The electronic aspects of the Bomber Command offensive were both complex and fascinating. The main period of radio countermeasures (RCM) was from 1943 onwards with the formation of the specialist No 100 Group, but various aspects of the electronic war had been in place from the early months of the conflict. By the end of the war Bomber Command had devoted an entire operational group to the subject and had gone much of the way to reducing the bomber losses to an acceptable minimum. It was very much a game of move and counter-move, and it was new, there being no previous experience to build on.

Until 1941 the major British use of RCM had been to counter German bombing beams, little thought being given to offensive uses of electronic warfare. With the seizing of a Freya radar in the daring Bruneval raid of February 1942, British scientists had more solid data with which to proceed towards a true jamming system to disrupt the German systems. At the same time, Bomber Command was becoming concerned about increasing losses, and any system to reduce these losses would receive its support. During 1942–43 a number of electronic devices were developed, many of which were ground-based systems, although some success had been achieved with airborne jamming systems such as Mandrel, designed to interfere with and saturate the radio frequencies of the German early warning system, and Tinsel, used to jam the frequencies in use between the German night fighter pilots and ground controllers. An important element of RCM was discovering what the enemy was doing, and electronic intelligence requirements expanded.

Throughout the summer of 1943 various new electronic aids, mainly for jamming elements of the German defence network, were introduced. This electronic war had become so complex, and so vital, that the decision was taken to incorporate the main effort within a specialized force. The result was the formation of No 100 (Special Duties) Group on 23 November 1943, under the command of Air Vice-Marshal Addison of No 80 Wing. In addition to giving direct support to night bombing and other operations, the new Group was given three additional, and special, tasks. First, it was to employ airborne and ground RCM equipment to deceive or jam enemy radio navigation aids, enemy radar systems and certain wireless signals. Secondly, it was to examine all intelligence on offensive and defensive radar, radio and signalling systems of the enemy. Finally, it was to provide immediate information, additional to normal intelligence, as to the movements and employment of enemy fighters, to enable the bomber tactics to be modified to meet any changes. The formation of No 100 Group in November 1943 at last provided a coordinated effort that played a significant part in Bomber Command's offensive—although it is a contribution that is hard to quantify, with more systems entering service and the Group acquiring a wider range of tasks and an increasing number of squadrons.

Below, left: H2S radar equipment situated at the navigator's station. It proved to be an excellent navigation aid.

Below, right: A photograph of an H2S radar response for Gelsenkirchen, taken on the night of 29/30 December 1944.

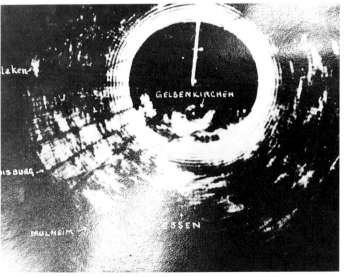

Window

One of the simplest yet most effective devices to be produced during the war was Window. The basic principle involved still forms an essential countermeasure used by current front-line aircraft (it is now known as 'chaff'), and the idea of dropping metallic strips to create spurious radar responses was first outlined in 1938. Development was slow, but by 1941 the TRE was carrying out trials with oblong strips of aluminium foil which, it was thought, would look like an aircraft response, thus presenting more 'targets' to the radar. This had a two-fold benefit: it could confuse the real target response by hiding it among many others, or it could be used to simulate a much larger force of aircraft than was actually present.

By early 1942 the system was ready for use. Fighter Command objected on the grounds that the Germans might employ the same device. The argument continued, Harris claiming that use of Window might reduce bomber losses by some 30 per cent. Agreement came on 23 July and Window went into use with the short offensive against Hamburg. It was an immediate success, throwing the German defences into confusion.

Until early 1944, Window ejected from the Lancaster was dropped through the flare chute. The brown paper parcels of Window were stored in the nose of the aircraft and it was the bomb aimer who was responsible for 'Windowing'. Bundles were thrown out as the bomber crossed a 'line' 60 miles from the target, the rate being one bundle per minute right up to the time that the line was crossed on the return leg. If the bomb aimer was busy over the target area the flight engineer took over the task, which meant that he had to go into the nose of the aircraft. It was hard work but considered well worth the effort if it helped the chances of survival. However, the introduction of the Window dispenser during 1944 eased the crew's task.

The use of Window was extensive and Lancasters were often used as dedicated 'Windowers', tasked with flying ahead of the Main Force to confuse the German radars. No 100 Group, for example, generally operated with Window in one of three ways. First, it could aim to simulate a separate bomber force in an attempt to attract enemy fighters. Secondly, it could split from the Main Force at a predetermined point in order to confuse the defences. Thirdly, it could saturate a large area (such as the Ruhr) with Window in order to disguise the exact target area. The object was to make it almost impossible for the German radar operators to determine the strength of a raid and completely impossible for them to pick out individual aircraft. Three squadrons from No 100 Group contributed to the Special Window Force from July 1944 onwards. A similar spoof was operated during D-Day, but on that occasion the aircraft dropped Window to simulate a fleet of ships!

The German defences soon introduced various counters to the use of Window but they never completely solved the problem, and the system continued to be developed to match the frequencies of other German radars. By 1944 the monthly production of Window was three million bundles for use against Würzburg, one and a half million bundles for use against SN-2, and half a million bundles for use against Freya. The scale of production was enormous, and although the use of Window would perhaps warn the German defences of an imminent raid there was little or nothing they could do about it.

Warning Devices and Electronic Jamming Equipment

As soon as the German ground control organisation had worked out which target a main bomber force might be heading for, the German night fighters were scrambled and vectored towards the bomber stream. On the way to the target the bomber was at a distinct disadvantage in that it was heavier and less agile than a

After the war H2S radar was used to assist in aerial surveys. (V. Beal via Steve Barker)

The wireless operator's position, looking forward.

fighter. Nevertheless, many bomber pilots soon learnt how to fly their aircraft to the limits to evade the ever aggressive night fighters. Any warning a crew might have about the presence of a night fighter, or any notice they might receive that they were about to be located by searchlights followed by the inevitable flak barrage, gave them valuable time to react and take avoiding action. Several warning devices were developed to counter the German defences and help increase the survivability of the bomber. One of the first electronic devices was Boozer, which was fitted to Stirlings of No 7 Squadron based at Oakington during late 1942. Boozer was a piece of equipment designed to pick up enemy radar signals and display their type to the bomber crew. It was a simple system using a series of coloured lights to indicate which type of radar was looking at the bomber: a yellow light warned the crew of an AI radar and a red light warned of a Würzburg ground radar. By early 1943 it was a triple-channel system and the intention was to fit it to all Bomber Command aircraft, but, for various reasons, this did not take place and distribution remained limited.

To improve upon the idea of Boozer the RAE at Farnborough developed a piece of electronic equipment during 1942 which was available for operational service by the spring of 1943. Called Monica, it was a tail-warning device for the rear gunner; it was from this area that most attacks by German night fighters were made. It worked by sending out pulses from an aerial which on the Lancaster was situated at the rear of the aircraft just below the tail turret. If an aircraft was detected behind the Lancaster then signals were returned and converted into 'pips' which were audible to the crew via the intercom circuit; the quicker the 'pips', the closer the aircraft. The Mk III version of Monica first entered operational service in June 1943 and had a minimum range of about 1,000yd and a maximum of about four miles.

Although Monica was initially a good piece of equipment, the crews soon found that it had operational limitations and problems. Apart from occasional spurious indications, there were more intractable difficulties. For example, the equipment could not differentiate between friendly or hostile aircraft, nor did it give the rear gunner any idea about the position of the intruder. Another problem was that when the bomber was flying in a main stream the audible warning would sound continuously and became most annoying to the crew. Finally, it did not take long for the Germans to develop the Flensburg system, which the German night fighters used to home in on the Monica transmissions. A later version, the Mk IIIA, replaced the audible warning with a visual warning, although the problems with the equipment remained. By mid-1944 Monica had been withdrawn from Main Force use but it was retained by the RCM squadrons of No 100 Group. Although a correctly operating piece of equipment would warn the crew of the approach of a night fighter, and it undoubtedly saved many lives, it also helped the *Luftwaffe* pilots find the bomber and many crews considered it more of a hindrance than a help.

Despite the fact that Monica was not as successful as originally hoped, its concept was sound and led to better developments. One such piece of equipment was Fishpond (originally called Mousetrap), which was an improved version of Monica and based on a similar idea. The system used H2S scanner pulses but instead of displaying only the returned pulses from the ground, it also showed any signal between the aircraft and the ground (including, for example, another aircraft) on a separate display. The Fishpond console was located at the wireless operator's desk and the main advantage of the system was that the bearing and distance of the intruding aircraft was displayed. There were several considerations for the crew to wrestle with, particularly the fact that all aircraft returns were displayed, including those of friendly bombers in the main stream. Thus the wireless operator would have to observe the display closely to determine which of the 'blips' was moving faster than any others to suggest that it might be a night fighter closing in and then warn the gunner of its range and bearing. Fishpond did offer a further advantage in that it could be used to reduce the danger from mid-air collisions between bombers. However, all these finer points regarding the use of Fishpond relied very much on the skill and expertise of the operator. The main disadvantage of the system was that it only displayed returns beneath the aircraft, as the H2S scanner was tilted towards the ground for its primary purpose of ground-mapping. Although when flying high this would not cause too much

of a problem, it was, nevertheless, a major factor if the aircraft were flying low for any reason. Further problems occurred later when the German night fighters were fitted with Naxos, a piece of equipment which helped them to find bombers by homing in on either the H2S or the Fishpond transmissions (or, indeed, on Monica). One other tail warning radar introduced into service was Village Inn. This was also used for gun-laying and was first introduced into some Lancasters during late 1944. The equipment was fixed to the rear of the aircraft below the turret.

Since the early days of the war, various jamming techniques had been used against German radars and communications frequencies. Systems such as Tinsel and Special Tinsel were used against night fighter frequencies to cause as much confusion as possible. These relatively simple systems involved equipment, including a microphone, in the engine bay of the aircraft, and a transmitter, resulting in the frequency being 'jammed' by noise. A variation of the same theme was the introduction of Corona, which used higher-powered transmitters in the United Kingdom. To help cause confusion and to counter the German night fighter system, Lancasters from No 101 Squadron at Ludford Magna were equipped with the

highly secret Airborne Cigar (ABC) equipment, which was designed to jam German night fighter communications frequencies. Prior to the employment of ABC most RCM work had been conducted by ground-based stations in Britain with the associated problems of range, the main devices used being Ground Grocer and Ground Cigar. ABC was developed from Ground Cigar, which was used by special ground signals units to jam fighter broadcasts along the French and Dutch coasts. The equipment for ABC consisted of three transmitters and a receiver and was fitted to the Squadron's Lancasters from October 1943. To compensate for the extra equipment the aircraft's bomb load was reduced by about 1,000lb.

These specially equipped Lancasters of No 101 Squadron were first used on the night of 7/8 October 1943 against Stuttgart. The aircraft carried an additional crew member, known as the 'special duties operator', who spoke fluent German. The operator sat at a table fitted in the fuselage above the bomb bay and his task was to listen to the German night fighter frequencies. In the early days of ABC the operator transmitted false information to the night fighter pilots in German and this practice was given the code-word 'Corona'. However, the Germans soon be-

Just visible beneath the rear turret of this aircraft is the Monica aerial, a tail warning device that alerted the crew to any approaching night fighter. (Les Bartlett)

came aware of this spoof and countered it by broadcasting information on several frequencies. Later the procedure required the special duties operator to jam the frequency electronically. The receiver included a cathode ray tube which displayed visually all the radio signals within the waveband covered. As soon as a signal appeared the operator would tune the receiver to it, tune one of the transmitters to the same frequency and switch it on. The jamming signal was a warbling tone, and having jammed that particular frequency the operator could search for other signals. The three transmitters fitted to the modified Lancasters were, simply, three aerials. The ABC aerials were quite distinctive and easily identifiable—two on top of the fuselage and one under the nose. Although not every aircraft of No 101 Squadron was equipped with ABC, the role of these specially equipped aircraft was considered vital and ABC Lancasters flew on every major raid from October 1943 until the end of the war. However, the aircraft became prime targets for the

German night fighters as the latter were able to home in on the jamming frequency being used, and this often led to high losses for the Squadron. This jamming of the VHF control frequencies was very effective and remained an essential element in the RCM conflict. A number of other jamming systems were developed to counter specific German systems, such as Mandrel for jamming the German Freya long-range radar, Airborne Grocer to jam the FuG 202 and 212 airborne radars and Jostle for use against anti-aircraft radars.

The installation of new electronic equipment into the Lancaster was usually carried out at Defford in Worcestershire by the Signals Intelligence Unit (SIU), which was part of the TRE, the flight trials and airborne validation of the equipment being carried out by the Telecommunications Flying Unit. As with any new device which was developed in the 'electronic war', there was soon a counter. The German night fighter's capability to home in on H2S, Monica and Fishpond emissions led the TRE to develop electronic aids which enabled friendly night fighters accompanying the raid to detect German night fighters. Standard AI radars fitted to fighters could not distinguish a hostile aircraft from a friendly one, and so the

introduction of equipment such as Serrate provided a solution to the problem by detecting the emissions from a German night fighter which enabled the friendly fighter to fly towards it and, it was hoped, detect it on its own AI radar. The time and effort spent by so many individuals on the ground in helping to fight the electronic war cannot be overemphasised.

Above: The crew boarding DV267 of No 101 Squadron at Ludford Magna prior to an 'op'. This aircraft was one of many ABC-equipped Lancasters and carried an additional crew member known as the special duties operator.

Below: A Lancaster Mk I of No 50 Squadron, based at Swinderby during the summer of 1942 and later at Skellingthorpe. (No 50 Sqn records)

5. Armament

The theory of heavy bomber operations was quite simple—to get bombs on to the target, as many and as accurately as possible. However, most importantly, the bomber had to be capable of defending itself if and when it came under threat. Yet defensive armament took up space and, more crucially, weight. Every 100lb of defensive armament fitted to the aircraft meant 100lb less in its bomb load. The balance between offensive weapons and self-defence capability in any bomber's design was vital, and the Lancaster was certainly no exception. Trials during the 1930s had proved that the bomber was vulnerable to attack from any quarter, particularly from aft. Therefore the design of the Lancaster, and in particular its defensive armament, had to ensure that the aircraft and crew would be capable of defending themselves from hostile fighters closing at high speed from any direction. The Lancaster was fortunate in that it was not the first of the heavy bombers and, therefore, lessons had already been learned (often the hard way) from the earlier 'heavies' and their defensive capabilities, for example from the Manchester.

It is most important to emphasise that it was the entire defensive system which was crucial to the Lancaster's survivability. A satisfactory and reliable gun turret would have been of little use without good weapons. A good air gunner still required a good gun sight to give him the chance of actually hitting the target and, equally, a good gun sight was of little use without a well-trained gunner. Moreover, if the Lancaster could bring more than one set of guns to bear on to the attacking fighter then this would make the attacking fighter pilot's task very difficult. It is also important to understand the differences between the objectives of the attacking fighter pilot and of the defending bomber's air gunner. The role of the fighter pilot is to shoot down the enemy bomber and, therefore, stop it reaching the target. He must score hits on the bomber to stand a chance of shooting it down or, at least, force it away from the target. But even a damaged bomber could release its bomb load and then be repaired to return another day. And so the pressure was on the fighter pilot to shoot the bomber down. Conversely, the air gunner needed to prevent the bomber from being shot down in order to reach the target; he did not actually need to shoot down the fighter in order to achieve his objective. As it proved extremely difficult to shoot down an attacking fighter, particularly at night, then a good and accurate defensive 'wall of lead and tracer' would often be enough to deter the hardest of *Luftwaffe* fighter pilots. It is true to say that the fighter could also return night after night to harry bombers on their way to the target, but it was the number of bombers on target which would eventually win the war.

Self-Defence

Self-defensive armament for the bomber did not evolve overnight, and it is, therefore, important to understand how the powered turret, armed with capable weapons and good gun sights, came about. Ever since the aeroplane was used as a weapon of war, much thought had been given to the design of its armament. For the bomber this not only involved the carriage of bombs, but also the capability of defending itself against the ever increasing threat of the fighter. Although the bomber would forever be concerned about the threat from the ground, it would be the fighter that would continue to pose the biggest problems. After all, a bomber flying to its target could plan and fly its route to avoid known ground installations. The fighter, however, could be waiting at any point and at any height. And so, ever since the days of aerial warfare began, the greatest game of cat and mouse has taken place with the hunter and the hunted trying to outwit each other.

The bomber's best form of defence has always been to avoid confronting the fighter in the first place. Initially this could be achieved using cloud and the cover of darkness to conceal its position. Equally, the performance of the aircraft compared to its opposite has always been crucial in deciding the outcome of any aerial exchange: even if a fighter can find the bomber, it still has to be able to outperform its opponent in order to make the kill. This reason has always led designers to improve the performance of the bomber without greatly penalising its effectiveness once over its target.

Very early forms of self-defence involved the pilot firing a hand-held weapon at his opponent. Early fighter tactics soon demonstrated that the best way of shooting down an opponent was to 'get in' unseen. This usually meant attacking from the rear quarter. With the introduction of the two-seat aeroplane it was soon realised that the second airman was best suited to the task of protecting the aircraft against attack. This led to British two-seat aircraft being fitted with defensive Lewis guns from mid-1915. The early mountings were somewhat crude and cumbersome in their design and not particularly effective. Problems installing the gun led to restrictions in the aircraft's field of fire such that the gunner would, in some cases, have physically to manhandle the weapon into a mounting socket in order to fire in the direction of the attacking aircraft. However, an effective gun and mounting would only ever solve part of the problem. In the early days the gunner had no assistance whatsoever and his success was down to experience, a 'feeling in the water' and a certain amount of luck!

Life for the air gunner remained largely unchanged following the First World War. It was not until the 1930s that higher air speeds and higher altitudes meant that the air gunners had extreme difficulty operating the guns. It became apparent to the designers that the gunner would need protection if he was to carry out his job effectively. The first fully enclosed gun turret proposed for use by the RAF was designed by the Bristol Aircraft Company for the company's Type 120 biplane. Developed in 1932, the turret was hand-operated and consisted of a dome-shaped cupola with a Lewis gun mounted on a Scarff ring.

The FN5 front turret was the standard fit for all Lancasters.

Trials in 1936 between bombers and attacking fighters highlighted the weakness of aircraft protected by open-cockpit gunners. It was also found that by attacking from the exact line-astern position the gunner's field of fire was limited by the position of the aircraft's tail. With these points in mind, it was decided that new specifications for bombers would include enclosed and, eventually, power-operated, gun turrets. Particular attention would also have to be paid to the problem of fighter attacks from the stern and any future designs would have to incorporate a tail gun installation. One aircraft company leading the way in defensive armament was Armstrong Whitworth, which had been working on a turret for installation in the nose and tail sections of new aircraft, including the Whitley bomber which first flew in 1936. The turret proved successful and was later fitted to Avro Ansons and Airspeed Oxfords for gunnery training. Although very crude, it was probably the most efficient hand-operated aircraft gun turret in service during the mid-1930s.

Although an enclosed turret solved the problem of protecting the gunner from extreme cold, the question of powering the system still remained. Several aircraft designers and manufacturers became involved in the design of power-operated turrets during the mid-1930s. Boulton Paul and Bristol were leading manufacturers during the late 1930s, providing turrets for many of the RAF's front-line and training aircraft. However, it was the work of one specific designer and his company which was to lead the way for the turrets that would eventually be fitted to many of Bomber Command's 'heavies', including the Manchester and Lancaster; other companies would provide experimental, and occasionally operational, turrets for the Lancaster, and these will be covered later.

Frazer-Nash Turrets

Archibald Frazer-Nash had been experimenting with hydraulic gun control for several years. He can only be described as a brilliant engineer. His initial engineering background had been with cars, but he had become more involved with weaponry during the First World War when he had joined the Armaments Branch of the Air Board. It was whilst with the Branch that he had got to know and work with another engineer, Gratton Thompson, and together they had explored the use of hydraulics as a method of gun control. After the war Frazer-Nash returned to his work with sports cars before eventually setting up an engineering consultancy with Thompson in 1928.

Frazer-Nash and Thompson set about working on the idea of again using hydraulics for gun control, but this time for use on aircraft. In June 1932 they submitted a model to the Air Ministry which was received with great enthusiasm. As a result of this they formed the Nash & Thompson Engineering Company based at Tolworth, near Kingston. The following year the company received an order from the Air Ministry for a power-operated turret suitable for the Hawker Demon fighter. Designated the FN1, it was the first operational turret to use the hydraulic control system designed by Nash & Thompson. The turret was not fully enclosed, consisting of a metal cowl to protect the gunner from the aircraft's slipstream and a single 0.303in Lewis gun. The FN1 proved to be most successful and resulted in a large order for turrets being placed by the Air Ministry for Bomber Command. With the increase in orders it was necessary for Nash & Thompson to expand from the limited premises at Tolworth and so the company acquired George Parnall's aircraft business at Yate, near Bristol. It was decided that turret production would take place at Yate, with Frazer-Nash maintaining responsibility for design and development at Tolworth.

The hydraulic design of the FN1 formed the basis upon which so many later variants of Frazer-Nash turrets were founded. The turret hydraulics were kept separate from the main aircraft systems by virtue of an engine-driven pump. A separate pump was required for each turret mounted on the aircraft. The hydraulic oil system was recirculatory and worked at a normal operating pressure of approximately 300psi. The elevation of the guns was also facilitated by hydraulic pressure;

in the event of hydraulic failure most turrets were provided with a system of hand-operation, and the guns could still be elevated by applying manual force. Although new in design, the early power-operated Frazer-Nash turrets proved, generally, most reliable, although problems with the guns did occur.

Built at Yate, the first power-operated turrets were delivered to Handley Page for fitting to the Harrow bomber and to Vickers-Armstrong for the new Wellington. The Harrow was the first heavy bomber in RAF service to be equipped with power-operated turrets, that in the nose being armed with a single Lewis

0.303in machine gun and that at the tail with two Lewis guns. Although the turrets were essentially designed by Handley Page, the power operation systems of both turrets and guns were Nash & Thompson designs, the FN14 (nose) and FN15 (tail).

Despite much development in turret design during the mid to late 1930s, the situation by 1938 was still, generally, that RAF bombers were equipped with early hand-operated turrets. The deteriorating situation in Europe meant that more urgency was required to get Bomber Command's aircraft better equipped. The new Wellington bomber was armed with nose and tail turrets designed by Barnes Wallis.

However, it was decided that the aircraft needed to be more capable of defending itself and so in 1938 Nash & Thompson were given an immediate requirement to design a turret to rearm the Wellington. This resulted in the FN5 nose and tail turrets, equipped with two 0.303in Browning machine guns.

The Armstrong Whitworth Whitley had also been designed with turrets, but again these were considered inadequate. Therefore, it was also decided in 1938 that Nash & Thompson would adapt the FN11 power-operated nose turret (designed for the Sunderland flying boat) to replace the existing Armstrong Whitworth hand-operated turret. Because of a number of installation modifications, the turret was designated FN16 and provided defensive fire up to 60 degrees either side of the aircraft nose with an elevation of 60 degrees and a depression of 45 degrees.

Gunnery trials since 1936 had continued to prove that one of an attacking fighter's best tactics was to approach the bomber from the stern. This led to Parnall receiving a further contract to design a multi-gun tail turret for the Whitley and other new bombers about to enter service with the RAF. The design resulted in a fully powered and enclosed turret armed with four 0.303in Browning machine guns. It provided the bomber with a defensive field of fire of up to 88 degrees to either beam, with 60 degrees in elevation and 45 degrees in depression, and had the staggering rate of fire of 4,800 rounds per minute, making it by far the most heavily armed turret n the world. Designated FN4, the turret proved to be the first real 'tail-end Charlie' in defensive armament and a milestone in the development of the heavy bomber.

With war imminent, the production of guns and turrets accelerated, although the

Left, upper: The FN50 mid-upper turret allowed a full 360 degrees rotation and was standard for all Lancasters.

Left, lower: The only limitation for the mid-upper gunner was the inclusion of a fairing around his turret to protect the aircraft from damage when the guns were deflected downwards.

introduction of better gun turrets and defensive armament for Bomber Command's aircraft was not the immediate success that some might have been so naïve to expect. Although several bombers flying relatively close together concentrated a certain amount of firepower, and sounded in theory to be a reasonable defence against attacking enemy fighters, the fact remained that the RAF's bombers during the early stages of the Second World War were no match for the opposing German fighters. This is in no way a reflection on the efforts of the RAF's gunners but more of a general statement of fact regarding comparisons in aircraft performance. Indeed, the RAF's gunners proved on many occasions most courageous during the opening exchanges of the war, but it was found that the bomber, generally, remained an easy target during daylight operations. It soon became apparent that the best chance for the bomber to survive was for it to operate by night, therefore giving the fighter the vast problem of detection. Although increasing the chances of survival, operating at night had its obvious problems, particularly during the winter months of 1939/40 when severe cold still caused the gunners extreme difficulties. The temperature inside the aircraft often fell to −20°C and the flying clothing (Sidcot suite and sheepskin flying boots, electric Irvin suit and boots for the gunner), mainly from the era of the open cockpit, was bulky and uncomfortable. Crews had to endure hour after hour of freezing cold, with no heating and no real way of alleviating the problem. The unfortunate tail gunner suffered more than most: cooped up in his cramped turret, almost open to the elements, he was both frozen and numb!

During the early months of the war, Bomber Command had attempted a mixture of daylight and night operations and there were few days or nights when no operations took place. The operations were generally small-scale, being in the nature of experimental thrusts to determine capability and tactics. Statistics from the various types of operation flown during the first six months of the war were frequently reviewed. Even with improved defensive armament, daylight losses amongst the Wellingtons had been high—as much as 50 per cent in some instances, a totally insupportable loss rate. The losses amongst the night flying Whitleys were far lower, and this statistic was used by some to prove that the only prospects for the future lay with night bombing. Although Bomber Command never abandoned daylight operations, it is true that from the spring of 1940 onwards the emphasis, especially in the strategic campaign, moved towards night.

With the lessons learnt from earlier developments in gun turrets and defensive armament, particularly the experiences gained from the Manchester, a number of concepts and designs were considered. Most of these ideas were already in an advanced state of development when the Lancaster entered operational service, and so the aircraft was already in good shape to face the daunting task of flying through well-defended enemy territory.

Lancaster Turrets

The FN5 front turret was originally designed for the Wellington in 1938. It was also fitted as the front turret for the Stirling and Manchester bombers. The fact that the turret proved relatively successful for the Manchester ensured that the design was retained for the Lancaster, though it was subsequently designated FN5A. The armament comprised two 0.303in Browning machine guns fed from ammunition boxes (1,000 rounds per gun) either side of the gunner. The field of fire was 190 degrees traversal, 60 degrees in elevation and 45 degrees in depression. Access to the turret was through doors which closed behind the gunner once in position. The gunner was supplied with oxygen and a crew intercom service. The turret was controlled hydraulically through two handles operated by the gunner and could rotate at up to 90 degrees per second. In the event of a hydraulic power failure, the gunner could rotate the turret by hand.

The FN20 was the tail turret most commonly featured on aircraft of Bomber Command. It was developed from the FN4 as fitted to the early heavy bombers (including the Manchester), and became the standard tail turret for the Lancaster. The armament comprised four 0.303in Browning machine guns, and one of the main improvements in the FN20 was that the supporting ammunition boxes were located in the rear fuselage, outside the turret rather than inside, thus allowing the gunner more space. Ammunition (2,500 rounds per gun) was fed from the boxes along ammunition belts. The field of fire was 94 degrees to either beam, 60 degrees in elevation and 45 degrees in depression. The gunner entered the turret from the fuselage through sliding doors which he then closed once in position. He was provided with a clear vision panel, below which he was protected by three armoured plates. Because of the weight of the plates, they were occasionally removed so that more ammunition could be carried. As with other Nash & Thompson designs, the gunner was supplied with oxygen and a crew intercom service into the turret. The powered controls were similar to previous designs and the turret was capable of being hand-operated in the event of hydraulic failure. In the unenviable situation of the gunner having to abandon the aircraft, he first of all had to open the sliding doors to grab his parachute from the stowage position just outside the turret. He would then have to clip on his parachute, traverse the turret to its full-beam position, release himself from his seat harness and fall backwards and away from the aircraft. This procedure cost the gunner precious time and often extreme effort, and, in dark and extremely cold conditions, with the aircraft perhaps out of control and under severe gravity forces, it would often have proved almost impossible to carry out, especially if a gunner were wounded. Yet, amazingly, 'tail-end Charlies' did survive—in some cases when the remainder of the crew perished. A modified FN20 was designed in late 1944 and designated FN120. Apart from being lighter in weight, it had an improved heating system. The FN120 was only ever fitted to the Lancaster. A further variant, the FN121, which included radar tracking, was also developed for the aircraft.

The FN50 mid-upper turret was developed from the FN5 front turret and re-

THE LANCASTER STORY

Armed with four 0.303in Brownings, the FN20 was the standard tail turret fitted to the Lancaster.

placed the FN7 upper turret as fitted to the Manchester and Stirling. The armament was two 0.303in Browning machine guns fed along belts from two ammunition boxes (1,000 rounds per gun) either side of the gunner. The field of fire was a full 360 degrees traversal, 20 degrees in elevation and two degrees in depression. Access to the turret was from the top of the bomb bay on to a step, and up into the turret in a standing position. The gunner then clipped the seat under him. Oxygen and an intercom service were provided. The turret was hydraulically powered through control handles but could also be rotated manually by a handle in the event of a hydraulic failure. There was an armoured apron around the front of the turret which protected the gunner from the waist down. Looking out of the turret, the gunner had an excellent all-around view and a relatively good one vertically down as well. The only limitation for the gunner was the inclusion of a fairing around the turret, to protect the aircraft from damage when the guns were deflected downwards and against the upper fuselage; this limited the full range and rate of movement of the guns. Although the turret was relatively spacious, the method of getting into the turret proved cumbersome, particularly for a large person in full flying clothing. It proved even harder for the gunner to exit rapidly from the turret in an emergency, particularly if the aircraft was out of control. A modified FN50, the FN150, was designed in late 1944; this incorporated a better gun sight and improved controls.

The Nash & Thompson FN64 ventral turret was developed from the FN60 as fitted to the Blenheim but was installed only in the first of the early production Lancasters. It was, however, reintroduced towards the end of the war and fitted to some Lancasters of various units. The armament was two 0.303in Browning machine guns which the gunner sighted using a periscope system and which were fed from ammunition boxes (500 rounds per

gun) fixed either side of him. The field of fire was 180 degrees traversal, zero elevation and up to 60 degrees depression.

Although the Nash & Thompson FN20 was the most common tail turret used by aircraft of Bomber Command during the war, including the Lancaster, new proposals were considered as possible replacements. Developed during the period 1943–44, the Nash & Thompson FN82 was designed as an improved rear turret for the Lancaster. Armed with twin 0.5in Browning machine guns, it included several modifications to the in-service FN20, including radar tracking equipment. However, problems with the design meant that the turret was not available for service use until well into 1944. With the war in Europe reaching its end, the need for the improved turret never really materialised, although it was fitted to some aircraft. Another hydraulically powered rear turret was developed during the same period and fitted to some Lancasters during 1944. This was the Rose Rice Type R, armed with two 0.5in Browning machine guns and giving the gunner a field of fire of 94 degrees to either beam, 49 degrees in elevation and 59 degrees in depression. The design differed from the Nash & Thompson rear turrets in having an open front; many gunners complained that the clear vision panel on the FN20 often frosted up and on occasions they removed the panel

in order to improve the view. Although the open front of the Rose Rice turret provided the gunner with unrestricted vision, it did lead to his having to operate it in extremely cold conditions, particularly when traversing the turret to the beam. However, the turret was generally liked by the 'tail-end Charlies', particularly as it was more spacious and allowed them to keep their parachutes throughout the mission. The gunner could also more easily vacate the aircraft through the open front in an emergency. From mid-1944 over 220 of these turrets were produced and fitted to Lancasters of various units.

In 1944 a Canadian-built Lancaster Mk X (KB805) went to the Emerson Electric factory at St Louis, Missouri, to be fitted with a rear turret as part of a trial. The turret was a Model 3 armed with twin 0.5in Brownings, as fitted to later B-24 Liberators, and it was installed complete with an APG-8 blind tracking radar. The aircraft then flew to the United Kingdom and the system was evaluated at Defford. It was found to be less effective than British turrets at that time and so the project was cancelled.

Right: The improved FN82 tail turret as fitted to later Lancasters from 1944 and armed with twin 0.5in Brownings.

Far right: 'Tail-end Charlie'. (Les Bartlett)

Completed in 1945, this Mk VII (NX612) included the successful Glenn Martin Type 250 mid-upper turret, which became the standard fit for the later Mk VIIs.

Several alternative mid-upper turrets for the Lancaster were proposed during the war; some of these reached the development stage and some were cancelled during the design stage. One turret cancelled before full production could materialise was the Nash & Thompson FN79, designed in 1943 and armed with twin Hispano 20mm cannon. Only twelve turrets were built, but they were never used operationally by the RAF. Another project was the twin-Hispano Bristol Type B.30, designed from the Type B.17 in late 1944, but, with the war in Europe reaching its end, this project was cancelled after just one prototype had been developed.

One company involved in the development of gun turrets throughout the 1930s was Boulton Paul Aircraft. The company had begun a project in 1942 for a twin-Hispano cannon-armed mid-upper turret for the Lancaster, known as the Type H. However, the project was cancelled before any turrets were developed. Boulton Paul also developed a completely new concept in self-defence for the Lancaster during the period 1942–44. Known as the Lancaster Defence System, the concept was for two turrets, or barbettes, to be fitted in the mid-upper and lower positions. The armament for each barbette comprised twin Hispano 20mm cannon which were remotely controlled by one gunner, located in a tail cockpit, aided by a radar-assisted targeting system. However, the need for the new turret never materialised and the project was cancelled in late 1944, although the prototype barbettes were fitted to Lancaster LL780/G and some trials took place.

One more successful design was the Glenn Martin Type 250 CE23 mid-upper turret. Produced in the United States towards the end of the war, the Type 250 would quite probably have replaced the FN50 had hostilities in Europe been prolonged. Fitted to the B-24 Liberator and other American bombers, it became the standard mid-upper turret for the late Lancaster Mk VII and was armed with twin 0.5in Browning machine guns.

Defensive Armament and Gun Sights

Hydraulically powered turrets were essential for air gunners if they were to be able to traverse quickly and accurately towards

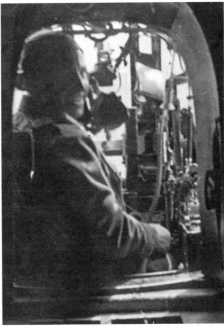

a threat since its defensive armament was vital to the self-protection of the Lancaster. Guns had to be reliable, easy to handle and accurate. Furthermore, the sighting solution presented to the gunner had to be as easy to interpret and as accurate as possible.

Designed by John Browning in America, the 0.303in Browning machine gun became the standard weapon for the RAF from the mid-1930s and was fitted to all Lancaster Nash & Thompson turrets except the FN82. The gun was recoil-operated with a cyclic rate of 1,150rds/min, a muzzle velocity of 2,660fs and a maximum range of 1,000yd. It was mass-produced in Britain and generally proved most reliable, with only the occasional problem being caused by extreme cold or blockages arising as a result of poorly assembled ammunition belts. Any stoppage had to be cleared by the gunner using a special tool, although this became less of a problem with the introduction of improved belt-making machines. Later improvements to the 0.303in Browning included a modified muzzle attachment and the addition of cooling vanes. The ammunition used varied but was most commonly ball rounds or otherwise tracer, incendiary or armour-piercing rounds.

A heavier-calibre version of the Browning, the 0.5in, was fitted to the FN82 and Rose Rice rear turrets and to the Martin 250 mid-upper turret towards the end of the war. It was considerably larger in every way compared to the 0.303in version previously described. It was well over 5ft in length (compared to just over 3ft 6in for the 0.303) and weighed 64lb (compared to nearly 22lb). Like the 0.303in Browning, the gun was recoil-operated, and it had a cyclic rate of 800rds/min, a muzzle velocity of 2,990fs and a most impressive maximum range of 7,000yd (3.5 miles). Generally, all the turrets designed in the latter stages of the war were armed with the larger-calibre 0.5in Browning, which was usually preferred by gunners who had the chance to operate it. The 0.5in Browning was an air-cooled design which suffered occasionally from a short barrel life, although a lack of barrels never appeared to become a problem.

The French-designed Hispano 20mm cannon was built under licence in the United Kingdom and fitted to RAF fighters during the Second World War. Development took place to enable the gun to be fitted to existing and experimental gun turrets but the weapon was only ever used operationally in the Bristol Type B.17 turret, which was not fitted to the Lancaster. Had hostilities in Europe been prolonged, the new Type B.30 turret, developed with the Hispano cannon, would probably have been fitted to the Lancaster. It was also to be fitted to the Boulton Paul Type H mid-upper turret proposal for the Lancaster, but, as noted, this project never materialised. However, Hispano cannon were fitted to the Boulton Paul experimental barbettes as part of the proposed Lancaster Defence System and thus to Lancaster LL780/G for trials.

The introduction of power-operated turrets with better guns and mountings still only solved part of the problem in developing the self-defence capability of the bomber. The gunner still had to hit the attacking fighter or, at least, put up a good enough defence to distract the fighter pilot and make his task equally as difficult. The fighter pilot, after all, still had the problem of achieving his correct firing solution, albeit against a large target, but if the gunner (or gunners) could put up sufficient firepower and tracer this would often be enough to put off the most experienced of night fighter pilots. On a dark night or in bad weather, the latter might be able to make just one attacking pass at the bomber, and an alert gunner with a good system made the difference between the bomber getting through to its target and otherwise. For the bomber crew, it could be the difference between life and death.

Obtaining the correct firing solution from one moving object to another posed (and still poses) problems. One is the closing speed of the attacking aircraft. In addition, the range of the target, the 'lead' required to make sure that the bullets hit the target (and not pass behind) and the amount that the bullet drops due to gravity in that distance, all make the art of air-to-air gunnery a most frustrating affair!

Many of the lessons of air-to-air gunnery learned in the early days of aviation still applied by the time of the Second World War—and still do. Although the gunner was assisted by improved gun sights, his success was still down to experience and that 'feeling in the water'.

The reflector gun sight was the most common type in use with Bomber Command aircraft for most of the war, particularly up until 1944, and that fitted to all the principal turrets in service with the Lancaster (i.e. the FN5, FN20, FN50 and Rose Rice) was the G Mk III reflector sight designed by Barr and Stroud. The design quite simply projected a bright orange aiming reticle, focused at infinity, on to a glass screen mounted at 45 degrees to the gunner's eye. The sight could just as easily be used by day as by night, the brightness of the reticle being controlled by the gunner. The image displayed to the gunner consisted of a full circle and a dot. The diameter of the dot equalled the wing span of a fighter-sized target at a range of 400yd, the diameter of the circle being used to judge the amount of deflection required to hit a crossing target. Air gunners were taught to compare an attacking fighter's wingspan with the graticule of the sight—a technique known as 'stadiametric ranging'. The sight was usually fitted by means of a mounting device at eye level and connecting arms to the framework of the turret. The Mk III reflector sight proved to be one of the most successful gun sights ever designed and was fitted to almost every turret in Bomber Command.

The only ventral turret fitted to the Lancaster was the FN64, which was installed in early production aircraft and reintroduced towards the end of the war. It was aimed using a periscopic sight. The gunner looked down through the sight and was presented with a 20-degree field of view featuring an illuminated reticle similar to that of the G Mk III reflector sight. From 1944 onwards, much improved gyroscopic gun sights were fitted to the later Lancaster turrets, the FN120, FN121 and FN150. The gyroscope allowed for deflection to determine the aiming point for the gunner. Not all attacking fighters would approach on a pure collision course and

The 0.303in Browning was the standard machine gun fitted to the Lancaster's turrets. These are later examples and include the modified muzzle attachment and cooling vanes.

therefore moved relative to the Lancaster, and the gyroscopic gun sight went much of the way towards solving the most difficult problem faced by the air gunner—how much deflection was required to hit a crossing target. The term generally used for this in air-to-air gunnery is 'taking lead' on the target so that the latter flies into the line of fire. Quite simply, the higher the rate at which the target is crossing the more the amount of 'lead' required. Then there was the problem of range: this not only affects the amount of 'lead' required but is also influenced by the gravitational fall of the bullets as they speed towards the target.

Until the gyroscopic sight was developed, the problem of 'lead' had to be addressed by guesswork. The theory of the gyroscopic sight was based on the idea that any attempt by the gunner to follow a crossing target was opposed by a gyroscope and the amount of resistance was dependent on the target's crossing speed. The sight presented the gunner with a sight line held back by the gyroscope, and by keeping to the sight line the gunner's aim would theoretically be correct. The gyroscopic sight was developed and installed in the Lancaster from 1944. The GGS (Gyroscopic Gun Sight) Mk IIC was

more complicated but worked on the same principle. A mirror was fixed to the end of the gyro and reflected an illuminated graticule, consisting of a ring of six small diamonds, on to a reflector plate. The gunner, when possible, would identify the attacking aircraft and manually set the diameter of the diamond ring graticule. The diameter of the ring was then adjusted by the gunner's foot pedals and, having already manually set the target's wingspan, the gunner would operate the left pedal to open the ring to maximum range. As the attacking fighter closed in range, the gunner would track the target in the centre of the ring and use the right pedal to control the ring, keeping the target's wingspan as close to the diamond ring as possible, until the latter was at a minimum diameter, which corresponded to a range of 200yd. The technique appears to rely on total co-ordination by the gunner but reportedly was remarkably accurate.

In even later designs, radar was used so that the gunner could still aim accurately at a target, even at night, which he could not physically see with his eyes. The success of air interception radars in fighters led to the development of a system known as Airborne Gunlaying in Turrets (AGLT). The antenna was fitted to the lower section of the rear turret and gave coverage of 85 degrees either side of the turret and 45 degrees in elevation. In the improved production system, known as Village Inn, the antenna was not linked to turret movement and when a target was located the

antenna 'locked on' to the target return. The rear gunner was provided with a semi-transparent screen on to which a target spot was projected through a collimator and prism. Detection of an enemy fighter was generally quite late (typically 1,000–1,500yd), and the range was given to the rear gunner by the navigator as the fighter approached. The gunner simply lined up his sight graticule with the target spot until the range was within 400yd, when the gunner would open fire—whether he could see anything or not.

The system had the obvious limitation of relying on a second crew member, i.e. the navigator, to provide the ranging information. A later improvement made the target spot look like an aircraft and caused it to grow in size as the fighter approached. The gunner simply had to select what he believed the threat aircraft to be—Messerschmitt 110, Focke-Wulf 190, etc—and the aircraft symbol was correctly shown in shape and size at any given range. An early IFF system was also devised to prevent shooting at friendly aircraft. Two infra-red lamps were fitted into the nose domes of Lancasters, and the AGLT-equipped aircraft were fitted with Z-Type infra-red detectors to the left of the sighting system to detect the emissions.

Trials were carried out by the TRE at Defford using three Lancasters, ND712, JB705 and LL737. The first Lancaster squadron to be equipped with Village Inn was No 101 at Ludford Magna in the autumn of 1944, followed by Nos 49, 159 and 635 Squadrons. Fitted into the FN82 rear turret, the system did have some operating limitations but it nevertheless provided the crew with a further capability and would have certainly given the attacking night fighter pilot one more thing to think about during the final part of his approach.

Offensive Weapons

The question of new and better offensive weapons and bombing techniques had not seriously been addressed until the mid to late 1930s. The reason for this appears to originate in 1932, when the Air Staff stated that there would be no requirement for a bomb heavier than 500lb and that the 250lb GP (general-purpose) bomb would be the RAF's standard offensive weapon. Bombing techniques, too, had remained largely unaltered during the interwar years. Bombing on the ranges was (as peacetime bombing tends to be) rather too easy, undertaken usually in favourable weather conditions and against a fixed, well-known, undefended target. Training and tactics were also unrealistic as exercises 'proved' that the bomber, generally, always got through to its target.

In the early 1930s RAF bombers such as the Virginia were capable of carrying a bomb load of just over 3,000lb. By the mid-1930s, with the development of the Whitley, this figure had been more than doubled to 7,000lb. Within a few more years, with the development of the 'heavies' such as the Stirling and Halifax, this figure had again been doubled to 14,000lb. Just as important was the fact that the newer and more capable bombers had been designed to carry larger

bombs than the earlier 250lb and 500lb types. During the first two years of the Second World War, the small general-purpose bombs were all that were available to Bomber Command, and despite the vast number of bombs dropped there were generally very few notable successes. It must be added, however, that no bombs dropped on any target were ever particularly wasted. Nevertheless, the point remained that the endless risks taken by the Bomber Command crews, and the inevitably high cost in aircraft and lives, were not always well rewarded.

By the time that the Lancaster entered service in 1942 larger bombs were becoming available, although the standard bombs remained the 250lb and 500lb. These general-purpose bombs were either short-finned or long-finned and used for general area bombing of non-hardened targets. Fusing was either instantaneous or delayed. Hardpoints were situated in the Lancaster bomb bay for at least eighteen of these smaller bombs to be carried. The number of 250lb and 500lb bombs dropped on Germany peaked during 1940–41 when a total of nearly 200,000 were deposited by Bomber Command. However, with the development of larger and more capable bombs, the 250lb and 500lb bombs were, generally, only used in addition to larger and more specialised weapons.

With the advent of heavier bombers and increased commitments, the Air Staff recognised the need for larger and more capable bombs. The 1,000lb bomb was a high-explosive weapon, either short-finned or long-finned, and was used for area bombing, for example against industrial

Left, upper: Hardpoints in the Lancaster bomb bay, typically laid out for an area bombing raid with up to fourteen 1,000lb GP bombs.

Left, lower: 500lb GP bombs being loaded up. These and the small 25lb bombs were the standard weapons when the Lancaster first entered operational service in 1942.

Right: Armourers preparing 500lb bombs prior to loading up Lancasters ready for another night of operations.

targets and railyards. Fusing was either nose-armed or tail-armed and either instantaneous or delayed. The delayed fusing could be set for either a few seconds or up to many hours, making target areas extremely hazardous long after the raid had taken place. Up to fourteen 1,000lb bombs could be carried in the Lancaster's bomb bay—a weight limitation rather than a hardpoint limitation.

Although the general-purpose bombs proved adequate for area bombing and against non-hardened targets, there was still a requirement for specialist bombs which could be used against targets such as warships or other hardened areas. This led to the development of the semi-armour-piercing (SAP) and armour-piercing (AP) range of bombs. By the early years of the Second World War examples of the 250lb and 500lb SAP bombs were avail-

able. The idea was not new and the basic design was conceived during the interwar years. The concept of piercing armour was sound but the design had its disadvantages. The main problem was the requirement to design the bomb with a hardened case, to penetrate hardened targets without breaking up, which meant that there was less room within the case for high explosive; so great was the problem that the smaller SAP and AP bombs were unlikely to cause any significant damage to a target.

With the continuing increase in the size of bombs capable of being carried by the larger bombers such as the Lancaster, it was not long before the 2,000lb AP bomb was being used on operations, particularly against targets such as ships and dockyards. Fusing was, generally, tail-armed and slightly delayed for the best effects. Up

to six 2,000lb bombs could be carried in the Lancaster's bomb bay. It is not easy to assess the success of these bombs on operations, particularly as the bigger warships were designed with particularly thick armour plating and in order to penetrate it bombs had to be dropped from high altitudes. Thus the obvious problem with this form of attack concerned the accuracy with which the weapon was delivered. Dropping from lower altitudes increased this accuracy but was unlikely to result in the target being penetrated. Nevertheless, there were successes using the 2,000lb AP bomb, particularly against the German battlecruiser *Gneisenau* docked in Kiel on the night of 26/27 February 1942.

During 1942 the first of the newer and larger blast bombs entered service with the RAF. The 4,000lb HC (high-capacity) bomb, known within the RAF as the

'Cookie', was formally introduced into service in January 1942 although a number had been tried against German targets during the previous year. The first version of the 4,000lb HC 'Cookie' was designed with a cylindrical, mild steel casing filled with high explosive and a conical nose fitted with either an impact or a delayed fuse. There were several developments of this bomb, most notably that in which the conical nose was replaced by a dome-shaped nose. The bomb contained Amatol, Minol or Tritonal and was generally used for area bombing, particularly of tactical targets such as V-weapon sites and of large industrial targets. On the night of 4/5 February 1943 four Pathfinder Lancasters attacked the Italian port of La Spezia using a new type of 4,000lb bomb with a proximity fuse which exploded some 500ft above ground level, making the resulting blast more effective. Progressively more and more 'Cookies' were dropped on operations, and by the final year of the war it was not unusual for the Lancaster Main Force to drop 200 against one target area. A typical individual Lancaster fit for such a raid would be one 4,000lb HC 'Cookie' carried in the central position of the bomb bay and six 1,000lb GP bombs at either end of the bay, with perhaps an extra two 500lb GP bombs carried as well.

The success of the 4,000lb 'Cookie' resulted in a similarly shaped but much larger weapon being brought into service. The 8,000lb HC demolition bomb was, quite simply, two 4,000lb 'Cookies' joined together end to end. This large high-capacity bomb, containing over 5,000lb of Amatex, was used for the demolition of large and heavily industrialised areas. Fusing was either impact or barometric. Several Lancasters were modified with bulged bomb doors so that the bomb could be accommodated. Only one could be carried at a time, although it was possible to

fit other small bombs (for example, six 500lb GP bombs) in the bomb bay with it.

During the early to middle years of the war the Germans began to build hardened U-boat pens; they later also constructed hardened launch sites for their new V-weapons. These hardened areas were built of reinforced concrete and required much larger, specially designed weapons if bombing such targets was to have any effect. At Vickers, Barnes Wallis, the designer of the special 'Upkeep' bouncing

bomb as used in the Dams Raid of May 1943 (see Chapter 7), had spent much time working on a weapon for use against such targets. He calculated that a very strong, streamlined bomb dropped from high altitude would gain a sufficiently high terminal velocity to enable it to penetrate reinforced concrete before detonating. His work led to the first of the really large bombs to be carried by the Lancaster, the 12,000lb HC and the 12,000lb 'Tallboy'. The high-capacity variant was similar in principle to the 4,000lb and 8,000lb HC

Right: A 4,000lb HC impact-fused 'Cookie' surrounded by 500lb GP bombs being finally checked by the groundcrew before take-off. (Les Bartlett)

Far right: Bomb types carried by the Lancaster.

bombs and can, again quite simply, be described as three 4,000lb 'Cookies' joined together end to end, although, because of its size, the 12,000lb version had to have fins fitted. It was intended that the first of the new 12,000lb bombs would be dropped by eight Lancasters of No 617 Squadron against the Dortmund–Ems Canal near Ladbergen on the night of 14/ 15 September 1943. Poor weather led to the raid being cancelled, but it was carried out the following night (although conditions were still poor). One of the Lancasters was lost during the first night and five on the second, among the losses being No 617 Squadron's new Commanding Officer, Squadron Leader Holden, and two of the pilots who had taken part in the famous Dams Raid, Flight Lieutenant Maltby and Pilot Officer Knight. The 'earthquake' weapon known as 'Tallboy' was, when introduced into service, the largest and heaviest bomb ever carried by an aircraft. It was a spin-stabilised bomb with an overall length of 21ft. It contained nearly 6,000lb of Torpex D and was used for penetrating hardened targets such as U-boat pens. Only one 'Tallboy' could be carried at a time, and only by a Lancaster with modified bomb doors; once the 'Tallboy' was clamped into position there was little room to spare. A total of 186 were dropped, almost all by No 617 Squadron based at Woodhall Spa.

An even larger bomb, of similar design and appearance, was developed from the 12,000lb 'Tallboy'. Known as the 'Grand Slam', this huge spin-stabilised bomb, weighing 22,400lb and containing 11,000lb of Torpex D, was used for penetrating exceptionally strong targets. Obviously, only one 'Grand Slam' could be carried at a time. The entire concept of designing and carrying such a large weapon in the Lancaster proved to be a considerable challenge and a specially modified version of the aircraft had to be built. The Mk I (Special) differed from the standard production airframe by having its nose and dorsal turrets removed, the bomb doors removed and the undercarriage strengthened. A total of 32 Mk I (Specials) were built by A. V. Roe at Newton Heath. Trials were carried out by the prototype (PB592) at A&AEE Boscombe Down during the winter of 1944/45 before the first two aircraft were delivered to No 617 Squadron in March 1945 (this unit had largely been employed in pioneering specialist bombing techniques since the Dams Raid of May 1943). The first 'Grand Slam' was dropped by one of the Squadron's aircraft against the Bielefeld viaduct on 14 March, and this was followed five days later by the first squadron effort against the Arnsberg viaduct. The vast weight and drag of the bomb reduced the Lancaster's operational ceiling and bombing was carried out from around 15,000ft (the raids were generally conducted using a mixture of 'Tallboy'-equipped and 'Grand Slam' aircraft). However, the fact that the war in Europe was coming to an end limited the number of raids carried out by 'Grand Slam'-equipped Lancasters.

Throughout the war the Lancaster carried a large number of different bombs, mines and incendiaries as part of its overall arsenal of weapons; its capacity to do

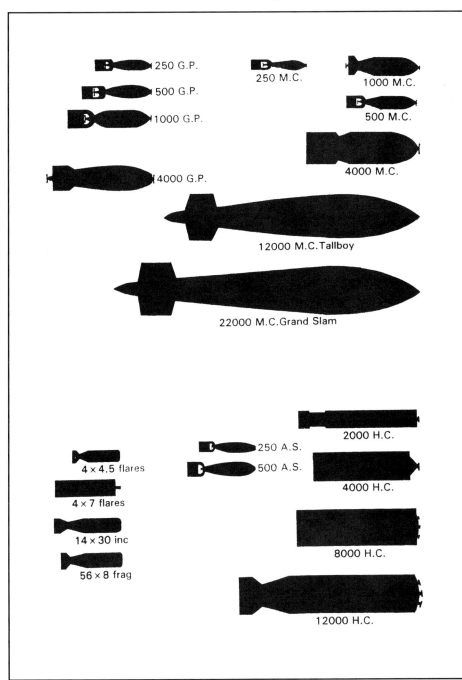

The 8,000lb blast bomb. Note the WAAF driver, engaged in one of many tasks carried out by the ladies at bomber stations. (No 83 Sqn records)

so was one of the main reasons why the aircraft enjoyed so much success when earlier designs had failed. More often than not the aircraft would carry a mixed bomb load. However, the fact that an aircraft could carry a weapon load to the target was only solving part of the problem: its accurate delivery was just as important. The delivery of the bombs was very much a crew effort and not just the responsibility of the bomb aimer. First, the navigator had to get the aircraft to the right part of the target area and had to make an accurate calculation of the wind velocity over the aiming point and pass it to the bomb aimer before the final run-in. Secondly, the pilot had to fly accurately and steadily during the run-in to the target and for the weapon release. If the bomber was being harassed by enemy fighters, it was up to the air gunners to protect the aircraft; and the flight engineer and wireless operator provided an extra pair of eyes or hands to aid the pilot or bomb aimer. Finally, it was up to the bomb aimer to release the weapons at exactly the right point.

Bomb-Aiming Equipment

The bomb-aimer's equipment consisted principally of a bomb sight and a main panel. The standard sight up until mid-1943 was the Course-Setting Bomb Sight (CSBS) which had been designed for daylight bombing and required a straight and level approach to the target prior to weapon release. Its effectiveness at night was extremely limited and its use was impracticable over heavily defended targets. For some time it had been obvious that a more suitable bomb sight was required for night operations which, preferably, would not rely on the pilot having to fly straight and level for any length of time over the target area. With an increase in the number of bombers over the target at any one time it was important for the aircraft to be as quick and as unpredictable as possible. A more accurate sight was also desirable, as, although the CSBS was adequate for bombing cities and towns, it was not accurate enough for smaller targets such as railway junctions and individual buildings.

The replacement for the CSBS was the Mk XIV bomb sight, which, because it was a more automated, stabilised sight and was fitted with a gyro, proved far easier to operate. It did not rely on straight and level flight over the target: povided the aircraft was in steady flight, and not in a hard turn or a rapid descent, the sight was not affected by aircraft manoeuvring. The sighting system actually predicted where the bombs would land on the ground if the bombs were released at a precise moment.

To use the sight, the bomb aimer looked through a reflector and could see the graticule which appeared to him to be on the ground. The graticule was in fact projected on to the reflector, and the target would move along the graticule until it passed through the bomb-release line. The Mk XIV sight still relied on inputs from the bomb aimer prior to weapons release to make sure that it displayed the correct bombing solution after taking into account all the relevant factors involved with bombing from altitude. Some of these factors were fixed and could be preset prior to, or during, the sortie: for example, the target height above sea level, the regional air pressure in the target area, the weight of the aircraft at weapon release and the terminal velocity of the bombs could all be put into the computer by the bomb aimer prior to the run-in. The only real variable about the final bombing solution—and it was one of the most important—was the wind velocity, which was calculated and passed by the navigator. With all this information entered manually into the computer, and with the height and air speed fed automatically into it, the final bombing solution was displayed. Of course, any errors manually inserted into the computer, for example an inaccurate wind velocity, led to errors in the solution.

The computer was also designed to be used with the H2S radar for blind-bombing attacks, which meant that the target had to be identified on radar and a target marker placed over the target's radar return. The normal H2S PPI showed the position of the aircraft in the centre, but for this bombing method the radar picture was 'frozen', with the target shown in the centre of the display and the aircraft offset. The aircraft's heading and track were also displayed and, with the computer using the same information as required for visual bombing, a bombing marker was displayed on the PPI. The aircraft was then manoeuvred to keep the target marker under the track marker, and the bomb aimer would release the bombs when the bombing marker, track marker and target marker all met together. This method was modified slightly if the target was not easily identified on radar. In this case an identifiable point close to the target was used as an offset, with its range and bearing from the target measured, and the aircraft would then be flown to the target marker using the same procedure as before.

The bomb aimer's panel was situated on the forward starboard side of the nose and contained all the equipment he needed to carry out his task. In the top left-hand corner of the panel were sixteen bomb selector switches. Below these switches was the timing device used for stick bombing, with a dial which was set for the interval between bombs. The bomb aimer could also select the order in which the bombs were released, to ensure that the aircraft's centre of gravity remained reasonably balanced as the bomb bay emptied: with several thousands of pounds of bombs spread along the bay, which was 33 feet in length, it was essential that there was no great imbalance during the most vital part of the sortie. The panel also included the master switch, camera controls and heater switch to ensure that there was no hang-up of bombs at the point of release due to icing or freezing of the mechanism. Finally, the bomb release 'tit' which was held by the bomb-aimer during the final run-in had a stowed position on the panel with a guard to prevent inadvertent operation.

Target Indicators

Bombing a target at night, perhaps in bad weather, was a difficult task. In order to achieve the best bombing results from a Main Force, it was necessary that the aiming point for the target was correctly identified. Obviously, the experience of bomb aimers varied, and, generally, the most experienced would be tasked with 'mark-ing' the target, with the intention of saturating that point with bombs. The specialist equipment fitted to some Lancasters also made those aircraft more suited to identifying the correct aiming point. Combining the most experienced crews with and best equipment meant that the chances of a successful mission were increased. Successfully 'marking' an aiming point meant developing an indicator which was clearly visible and stood out against the lights, fires and flak over the target area.

Target indicators (TIs) were developed during 1943 to help identify the specific aiming point for the bomb aimers of the Main Force. Targets such as towns and cities were large, and would have seemed even larger to the bomb aimers of the Main Force after several aircraft had attacked and fires were burning. Decoy fires were often started by the enemy in order to attract the bombers, and the possibility of 'creepback', where bombs were successively dropped early, all added to the general confusion over the target area. It was therefore important that TIs were clear and colourful.

There were, essentially, two methods of marking a target; ground marking and sky marking. The early TIs were first used for ground marking in January 1943. They were basically 250lb bomb cases filled with 60 candles (green, red or yellow) which were dropped by the aircraft marking the aiming point. When the TI reached 3,000ft above the ground, a barometric fuse caused the candles to be ejected; they then ignited and fell to the ground, cover-ing an area approximately 100yd in diameter. The early TIs burnt for only a few minutes, which was not long enough when several hundred bombers flew over a target for perhaps an hour.

Developed from the early TIs were longer burning candles which ignited at different time intervals in three groups of twenty, with approximately two and a half minutes between each group. This meant that each TI was burning for several minutes, and by changing the time interval and the number of candles burning in each group, the length of time the aiming point was marked could be varied. However, this method had the problem of there being fewer candles burning at any one time, making the aiming point less obvious. One solution was to drop several TIs at once; another was the introduction of larger TIs, for example a 1,000lb bomb case filled with 200 candles. Again, by igniting the candles at different time intervals, and by varying the time delays, the larger TIs marked a much larger area and could burn for up to twenty minutes.

The Germans soon learned to use ground-launched decoy TIs which, to the bomb aimers in the Main Force, looked exactly like ordinary TIs. Moreover, if the German services were quick, the ground marking fires could be put out. To coun-

Below left: The bomb aimer's panel, situated at the forward starboard side of the nose compartment.

Below right: The bomb sight was vital in assisting the bomb aimer to deliver bombs accurately on target. (Les Bartlett)

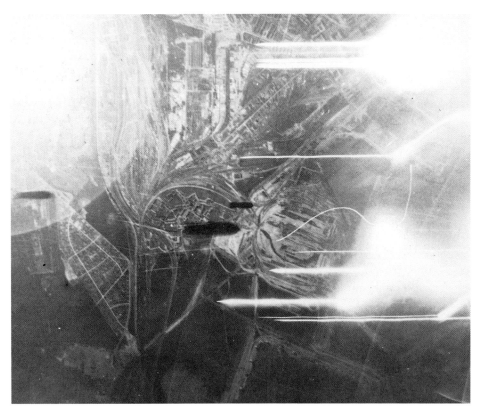

Searchlights, TIs and bombs are all caught in this photograph taken by a member of No 97 Squadron over Nuremberg on the night of 27/28 August 1943.

it burnt for about three minutes. Later modifications to the flares ejected stars of different colours (red, green and orange) at twenty-second intervals, each star burning for only a few seconds. By using 500lb or 1,000lb bomb cases, a group of flares could be more easily dropped from the bomb bay; ejecting them from the container at intervals had the effect of producing a 'ladder' of flares. Two types of fuse were used in sky markers, nose or tail fuses, and these could be delayed if required. The first was a barometric fuse which operated at a pre-set height; its main advantage being that the aircraft's altitude at release did not matter. The second was a combustion fuse, which operated at a pre-set time after release.

After the success of Operation 'Overlord' (the D-Day landings), Bomber Command resumed daylight operations and, although different sky markers were developed, the flares and candles were on occasions difficult to see. To solve this particular problem the Smoke Puff sky marker was developed. This was a 250lb bomb case filled with colour pigment. Once ejected, the pigment burnt as coloured smoke which lasted for about three minutes. A larger version was developed using, again, the 1,000lb bomb case. Although a good method in near still-air conditions, the Smoke Puff marker suffered in stronger winds because the smoke soon dispersed. Other methods of TI were developed and introduced operationally during 1944, including the Photoflash, which enabled the crew to photograph the target at the same time.

The method of sky marking was known as Wanganui and involved flares or Smoke Puff being dropped by the markers; the Main Force bomb aimers, assuming zero wind, literally bombed the flares or smoke above the cloud. Because there were few background distractions through the bomb sight, and because of the fact that the flares and smoke stood out well against the cloud, the results were often better than

ter this, exploding candles were often dropped; some of these even had delayed fuses in order to make the German services think twice about trying to put out the fires. Thus the TI/counter-TI war began. Several varieties of TI were developed, although the problem of decoys was never completely solved. Of course, ground markers relied on clear weather over the target area and, therefore, were of limited use.

Ground-marking a target was carried out either visually or blind. Visual ground marking was known as Newhaven, and this involved flares being dropped by aircraft (Illuminators) at regular intervals over the target area, followed soon afterwards by the Visual Markers with the task of using the light of the flares to identify the aiming point visually. Provided that the aiming point was correctly identified, the Visual Markers then dropped the TIs. This method was further developed during 1944 when particularly accurate marking was required against specific targets. Known as Musical Newhaven or Controlled Visual, the method included a Master Bomber who assessed the best-placed TIs and then broadcast the information to the Main Force.

If the aiming point could not be visually identified, then TIs were dropped 'blind', and this method was known as Parramatta. With Lancasters using H2S to identify the target and aiming point, TIs were dropped blindly on the target. To safeguard the method, more Lancasters followed soon afterwards and dropped further TIs using a different colour, the idea being that the Main Force would only bomb on the first TIs if there were no secondary markers. When Oboe was used instead of H2S for marking the target the method was known as Musical Parramatta.

The introduction of blind-bombing aids brought a change in ideas regarding the employment of TIs. As it was no longer necessary to see the target visually, and quite often cloud would obscure the aiming point, a method of sky marking was developed. Sky markers were generally flares—although candles were still used on occasions—which could be dropped either singly or in groups. Flares were originally dropped through a flare chute by hand. An air-burst fuse ejected the flare from its container and it would then ignite, a deploying parachute enabling it to drop slowly to the ground, where when using other methods. As with all methods of employing TIs, the first marking aircraft were backed up as often as necessary to keep the aiming point marked.

Target Photography

To help assess the success (or failure) of a bombing raid, good photographs were vital for the intelligence experts. During the first six months of the war Bomber Command acquired only 150 usable night photographs from bombing missions (the term 'usable' applying to a photograph showing ground detail that could be plotted to discover where the bomber was at the time of exposure). The ability to photograph the target area was deemed important: thus could each crew determine exactly where their bombs were dropped and the level of success of any raid be assessed. This importance was highlighted in an issue of the *Bomber Command Quarterly Review*: 'Night photography has contributed no small part of the knowledge available about the progress of our bomber offensive, permitting comparisons of the success of different tactics and methods of attack. Thus a night photograph taken with bombing gives the crew positive evidence of where their bombs were dropped. If this proves not to be the intended target, then all the relevant factors can be checked and the necessary corrections in procedure made the next time. Night photography is thus playing an important part in getting more bombs on to the target.'

One of the limitations early in the war was the paucity of cameras: in 1941, for example, the establishment was only four night cameras per squadron. It is easy to see why so few photographs were obtained. In September 1941 a memorandum was sent to all Group Commanders stating the purpose of night photography in Bomber Command—first to confirm

the location of the bomber at the time of attack, secondly to pinpoint the bomb bursts and thirdly to provide general information. Photographs were not intended to be a means of damage assessment, although a crew's photographs were compared to post-raid photographic reconnaissance, whose primary function *was* damage assessment.

There were obvious problems with night photography. For example, a target covered by cloud or thick haze revealed no ground detail. As far as the crews were concerned, an even bigger problem was having to fly straight and level over the target in order to obtain accurate photographs. In the Lancaster the camera controls were located on the bomb aimer's panel in the nose of the aircraft. The camera started operating when the bomb aimer released the bombs and continued making exposures until the calculated moment of bomb impact. The open-plate camera took a series of pictures during the

time that it was being exposed, light being provided by the photoflash and also by other sources such as TIs, searchlights and flak. This often meant flying straight and level for a further 30 seconds after bomb release—something which most bomber crews were reluctant to do! Any evasion by the bomber during this period often made the detail of the photograph unplottable. The films were examined at the bomber stations to see if ground detail had been recorded and then at Group HQ as part of the Group raid analysis. The Command Photographic Interpretation Section carried out more detailed analysis, as did the Central Interpretation Unit. Various changes in equipment were made during the course of the war, including the use of automatic cameras and, from October 1943, the use of colour film. Although colour film did show up the target indicators quite well, it was slow and thus its use resulted in some loss of ground detail.

A classic night photograph taken over Toulouse on the night of 5/6 April 1944. The information includes the captain's name, Flt Lt Mike Beetham of No 50 Squadron at Skellingthorpe, the bombing height of 9,500ft on a heading of 090°, the time of attack (0020 hours) and the bomb load. (Les Bartlett)

6. The First Year at War

The first operational sorties carried out by Lancasters took place on the night of 3/4 March 1942 when four aircraft of No 44 Squadron, based at Waddington, participated in minelaying operations in the Heligoland approaches off the north-west German coast. The sorties were led by Squadron Leader John Nettleton (in L7546) and both he and Flight Lieutenant 'Nick' Sandford (L7568) planted their 'vegetables' (mines) in the 'Yams' area to the south, the other two crews, captained by Warrant Officers Lamb (L7547) and Crum (L7549), planting theirs in the 'Rosemary' area to the north. Each aircraft dropped four mines from 600ft and all four aircraft returned safely. It proved an uneventful introduction to operations, but it marked a significant night in the Lancaster's history.

A week later, on the night of the 10/11 March, the Squadron sent two Lancasters on the type's first bombing mission, flown by Flying Officers Ball and Wilkins, as part of a force of 126 aircraft detailed to attack Essen. The first Lancaster over the target was flown by Ball (L7536) at 2148 hours. His report reads: 'Height 18,000ft, bombs 14 SBCs each 90 x 4lb dropped in area believed to be south-east of "blitz" area. Sixteen bundles of Nickels G.1 dropped over target area. At this height not worried much by searchlights and flak activities, but on leaving target area flak was very accurate both for height and direction.'

The raid was disappointing as cloud over the target area resulted in difficult bombing and only slight damage. Both Lancasters returned safely, although four other aircraft were lost. Again, however, the night was significant as it marked the Lancaster's first bombing mission.

The second Lancaster squadron to commence operations was No 97, based at Woodhall Spa, which had taken delivery of its first Lancasters during January whilst based at nearby Coningsby. On 20 March the Squadron dispatched six aircraft to join thirteen Manchesters detailed to plant 'vegetables' at 'Willow'. Although a mining sortie, it was a potentially hazardous operation as 'Willow' stretched from Arcona to the River Dievenow in the Baltic and involved the Lancasters taking off in daylight, flying across the North Sea and Denmark to the area and dropping their mines at dusk, before returning across the North Sea under cover of darkness. However, although an enemy aircraft was spotted in the target area, the operation proved successful. This was the Lancaster's first daylight operation.

It was inevitable that a Lancaster would eventually be lost on operations and this happened for the first time on the night of 24/25 March when one of No 44 Squadron's aircraft failed to return from a minelaying operation. The South African pilot, Flight Sergeant Lyster Warren-Smith, and his crew of eight (including two Rhodesians and an Australian) were all killed. The following night saw the first joint effort by the two Lancaster squadrons when between them they dispatched seven aircraft as part of a force of 254 detailed to attack Essen. This was the largest force sent by Bomber Command to one target and proved relatively successful thanks to reasonable visibility, although there was slight haze over the target area and decoy fires resulted in not all bombers attacking the target. One of the No 44 Squadron aircraft had to return early. The remaining six Lancasters all returned safely, although nine other aircraft were

lost, including five of the twenty Manchesters taking part in the raid.

March 1942 had been a historic month for the Lancaster: it had seen the aircraft's first operations, by day and by night, and had seen the first bombs dropped on Germany by Lancasters. It had also witnessed the Lancaster's first loss of type—and, sadly, its first casualties. The first weeks of April saw similar activity by the two squadrons, including the night of 8/9 April when seven Lancasters joined a force of 272 aircraft detailed to attack Hamburg— another record number of bombers taking part in a raid against a single target.

Some of the early Lancasters which had arrived on the two squadrons were equipped with Gee navigation aids. Targets in the Ruhr were within Gee range and these aircraft were, therefore, used whenever possible. One of Bomber Command's priority targets was Essen, which was believed to be the heart of the German armaments industry, particularly the Krupps factory. However, during the first years of the offensive the factory was often difficult to bomb owing to the industrial haze so often present in the Ruhr valley. The introduction of aircraft equipped with Gee, although a navigation aid and not specifically designed for blind-bombing, meant that better results should theoretically be possible. Lancasters from both squadrons took part in further raids against Essen on the nights of 10/11 and 12/13 April, bringing to an end the campaign against the city that had seen eight raids during the past month. The campaign did not prove particularly successful, partly because of insufficient photographic evidence to assess any likely damage. It appears that only slight damage was ever caused to the Krupps factory.

Augsburg, 17 April 1942

With the entry into service of the Lancaster, Air Marshal Sir Arthur Harris, CinC Bomber Command, had immediately realised the potential of the aircraft to enable his Command to strike targets almost anywhere in Germany at almost any time. By the middle of April both squadrons were often flying together at low level and rumours of a special operation started to circulate. A special training flight took place on 14 April with the No 44 Squadron crews led by John Nettleton and the No 97 Squadron crews led by Squadron Leader John Sherwood. The training flight involved both squadrons flying independently to the south coast, then joining up for a long transit north to carry out a low-level simulated 'attack' on Inverness before returning to base. By now, the strongest belief amongst some of the crews was that they were to take part in a raid against one of the German warships, and the fact that the training flight had involved coastal features merely added strength to the rumour.

Lancaster Mk Is of No 83 Squadron at Scampton during the spring of 1942. The aircraft at the front, R5620 'OL-H', was lost soon after this photograph was taken when it failed to return from Bremen on the night of 25/26 June.

On the morning of 17 April the crews were briefed at their respective bases for the special operation. There was a certain amount of surprise when the target was finally revealed. It was not to be the German warships, as expected, but a factory at Augsburg in southern Germany. The choice of the Maschinenfabrik Augsburg-Nürnberg Aktiengesellschaft factory was an interesting one. Although the factory was one of the anti-U-boat targets, as a manufacturer of diesel engines, it was also 1,000 miles away, deep in southern Germany, and had up to that point not been considered as one of Bomber Command's primary targets.

The plan was a particularly daring one. Six aircraft from each squadron, flying in two sections of three, would cross the Channel west of Le Havre. With the squadrons just two miles apart, the formations would then transit south at low level before turning east to pass south of Paris. The squadrons would then head towards Munich, as if to carry out an attack, and then turn north towards Augsburg. The factory area was quite small and so pinpoint accuracy was needed for the attack to be successful. It was decided that the attack would be carried out at low level in the last minutes of daylight so that the bombers could then return under cover of darkness. Each Lancaster was to carry just four 1,000lb GP bombs, each with a delayed fuse. In support of the raid, diversionary attacks and fighter sorties over northern France were planned in an attempt to keep the *Luftwaffe* fighters occupied.

At 1500 hours on 17 April the twelve Lancasters took off and set course. As they crossed the enemy coast the diversionary raids brought up the enemy fighters but also led to near disaster: one group of fighters returning to base spotted the rear section of the No 44 Squadron Lancasters and gave chase. Almost immediately the first Lancaster, flown by Warrant Officer 'Joe' Beckett DFM, was shot down and then the fighters turned on the second. Flown by Warrant Officer 'Bert' Crum DFM, this aircraft was attacked by six Messerschmitt Bf 109 fighters. Both port engines were soon hit and set on fire and the bomber crashed into a wheatfield. Fortunately the second pilot, Sergeant Alan Dedman, had managed to jettison the bombs 'safe' before the aircraft crash-landed into the field. The third Lancaster of the rear section, flown by Flight Lieutenant 'Nick' Sandford DFC, was also shot down before the fighters turned on Nettleton's lead section. Quite remarkably, the action had taken only a matter of minutes and all three Lancasters of the rear section of the No 44 Squadron forma-

Table 11. Squadron Crews, Augsburg Raid, 17 April 1942

No 44 Squadron

KM-B (R5508)	KM-A (R5510)	KM-H (L7536)	KM-P (R5506)	KM-T (L7548)	KM-V (L7565)
S/L Nettleton	F/O Garwell DFM	Sgt Rhodes	F/L Sandford	WO Crum DFM	WO Beckett DFM
P/O Dorehill	Sgt Dando	Sgt Baxter	P/O Peall	Sgt Dedman	Sgt Moss
P/O Sands	F/S Kirke DFM	Sgt Daly	F/O Gerrie	Sgt Birkett	F/S Ross
Sgt Churchill	F/S Flux DFM	Sgt Merricks	Sgt Hadgraft	F/S Saunderson	Sgt Seagoe
Sgt Huntly	Sgt Watson	Sgt Wynton	Sgt Venter	Sgt Dowty	Sgt Hackett
F/S Mutter	Sgt Edwards	F/S Edwards	Sgt Law	Sgt Miller	Sgt Harrison
F/S Harrison	F/S McAlpine	F/S Gill	Sgt Wing	Sgt Cobb	Sgt Trustram
F/L McClure					

No 97 Squadron

OF-K (L7573)	OF-B (R5537)	OF-F (R5488)	OF-U (R5496)	OF-Y (L7575)	OF-P (R5513)
S/L Sherwood DFC*	F/L Hallows	F/O Rodley	F/L Penman DFC	F/O Deverill DFM	WO Mycock DFC
P/O Webb	P/O Friend	P/O Colquhoun	P/O Hooey	Sgt Cooper	Sgt Hayes
F/O Hepburn	P/O Cutting	Sgt Henley	P/O Ifould	P/O Butler	WO Harrison
Sgt Page	F/S Louch	Sgt Merrals	F/S Elwood	Sgt Irons	Sgt Eades
Sgt Cox	Sgt Jones	Sgt Cummings	Sgt Tales	Sgt MacKay	Sgt MacDonald
F/S Harrington	Sgt Broomfield	Sgt Ratcliffe	Sgt Overton	Sgt Devine	Sgt Shelly
F/S Wilding	Sgt Goacher	Sgt Crisp	Sgt Hebdon	F/S Keane	Sgt Donoghue

tion had crashed within just two miles of each other, Beckett's and Crum's Lancasters just 500yd apart.

In Nettleton's section his number three, flown by Sergeant 'Dusty' Rhodes, was soon shot down before the fighters turned on Nettleton and his number two, Flying Officer 'Ginger' Garwell DFM. Both of the surviving No 44 Squadron aircraft were hit time and time again. Just at the time that the end seemed likely, the fighters turned for base, short of fuel. Surprisingly, the No 97 Squadron formation, just two miles away, had not been seen and had carried on.

The two remaining Lancasters of No 44 Squadron and the No 97 Squadron formation continued to Augsburg without further incident. The two No 44 Squadron aircraft, with Nettleton leading, pressed home a most determined attack on the factory. However, Garwell's aircraft was hit during the run-in to the target and crashed just after releasing its bombs. Nettleton, now the sole survivor of the six Lancasters from No 44 Squadron, turned for home. The two sections of No 97 Squadron Lancasters were over the target minutes later. By the time the No 97 Squadron aircraft were making their attack, every anti-aircraft gun was in full action and the crews were met with an almost unavoidable barrage of fire. Sherwood led the attack and made a straight

and very low approach and the two other aircraft in his section, flown by Flying Officers 'Darky' Hallows and 'Rod' Rodley, followed him in to attack. Having released their bombs, both pilots then witnessed their leader's aircraft explode on impact with the ground.

The rear section was led by Flight Lieutenant 'Jock' Penman DFC. By now the German gunners had established the exact line and height of the run-in to the target and all three aircraft of the section were hit. The number two of the rear section, flown by Flying Officer Ernest Deverill DFM, received hits in the hydraulic pipes, which put the gun turrets out of action, and hydraulic oil caught fire under the mid-upper turret. At the same time the starboard inner engine was hit and set on fire. The third aircraft of the section, flown by Warrant Officer Tommy Mycock DFC, also caught fire during the run-in. He managed to hold the aircraft steady just long enough to release his bombs on target before the aircraft was seen to blow up. The two remaining Lancasters in the section turned for home. Deverill's aircraft, now on just three engines, faced a long and hazardous flight.

The five surviving Lancasters, from the twelve that had originally set out, returned without further incident although Nettleton's problems were far from over. Having suffered navigational problems

during the return flight, and desperately short of fuel, Nettleton eventually landed at Squire's Gate airfield, near Blackpool, at 0100 hours on 18 April, ten hours after first leaving Waddington. The four surviving No 97 Squadron aircraft had landed back at Woodhall Spa by midnight, with Deverill's aircraft immediately being declared a total write-off.

Of the 85 men who had taken part in the Augsburg raid, 49 were missing, although it was later discovered that twelve had survived to become prisoners of war. All of Crum's crew survived, as did four members of Garwell's. One of the twelve airmen who did not return, but survived the ordeal to become a prisoner of war, was nineteen-year-old air gunner Sergeant Bert Dowty, whose story after being shot down en route to Augsburg is fascinating and, perhaps, typical of so many others. He managed to hear about the result of the Augsburg raid on the BBC whilst evading in France. Having been in the second aircraft to be shot down and crash-land at Folleville, he was caught on a train sixteen days later near Limoges and was eventually repatriated at the end of the war.

For his outstanding leadership of the raid, John Nettleton was awarded the Victoria Cross. His citation concludes: 'Squadron Leader Nettleton displayed unflinching determination as well as leadership and valour of the highest order.'

There were also awards for the rest of Nettleton's crew—a Distinguished Flying Cross (DFC) each to Dorehill, Sands and McClure and Distinguished Flying Medals (DFMs) to Churchill, Huntley, Mutter and Harrison. It was also later announced that the survivors of Garwell's crew were to be decorated: a DFC was awarded to Garwell, a bar to the DFM for Kirke and DFMs to Watson and Dando. Amazingly, John Sherwood survived the crash at Augsburg and, although initially recommended for a Victoria Cross, he was later awarded the Distinguished Service Order (DSO). Four of the No 97 Squadron captains were also decorated for their part in the raid, a DSO going to Penman and DFCs to Hallows, Deverill and Rodley. In addition there were DFCs to Hooey and Ifould and DFMs to Overton, Ratcliff, Louch, Goacher, Irons and Mackay.

The eight Lancasters that reached the target had caused sufficient damage to hold up production for several weeks. In the aftermath of the Augsburg raid there was much discussion as to its value. However, the determination of the crews in carrying out such an attack must rank amongst the highest achievements in the history of Bomber Command.

The Offensive Continues

The night after Augsburg Bomber Command attacked Hamburg, although no part was played by Lancasters as both squadrons were given a few days' well-earned rest. The following week saw the third Lancaster squadron declared operational when No 207 Squadron, based at Bottesford, joined Bomber Command's strength ready for a series of raids against Rostock. This old Baltic coastal city was only lightly defended and one of the main target areas of interest was the Heinkel aircraft factory on its southern edge. The first raid was carried out on the night of 23/24 April, although just one Lancaster, from No 97 Squadron, joined the force of 161 aircraft. The following night five Lancasters took part, including three from No 207 Squadron, which brought the unit into action for the first time with its new aircraft. Two more raids took place on consecutive nights, each with over 100 aircraft. The results of the raids against Rostock proved better each night, extensive damage being caused to the city and its industries, including the Heinkel factory. However, the contribution by the Lancaster squadrons was small: they flew just 3 per cent of the total number of over 500 sorties.

The raids against Rostock were among the few occasions that the new Lancasters joined Bomber Command's Main Force during its early operational life. It was going to take time for squadrons to re-equip with the Lancaster, and each squadron was involved in training aircrew. This was initially carried out at squadron level by a Conversion Flight, made up of experienced crews who had the task of retraining crews from previous types or working up crews posted to the squadron from the training bases. Eventually, however, as we have seen, this task would be undertaken by the HCUs at different bases.

Although the Lancaster was far from ready to make a large contribution in

Not all landings were perfect!

terms of numbers of aircraft, it was still used for selected operations such as Augsburg and Rostock. Within a few days of the raids against Rostock, Lancasters of Nos 44 and 97 Squadrons had deployed to Lossiemouth in Scotland and had taken part in two attempts to sink the German battleship *Tirpitz* lying in Trondheim Fjord. Between 27 and 29 April a total of 23 Lancaster and 54 Halifax sorties were flown, and these resulted in unconfirmed hits on the ship. Seven aircraft were lost in the two raids, one of these a Lancaster.

During the first week of May, Harris received a modified directive which stressed the importance of attacking the German aircraft industry and listed five towns containing vital aircraft factories—Augsburg, Regensburg, Leipzig, Wiener-Neustadt and Warnemünde. Such attacks would, it was hoped, support the effort on the Eastern Front and eventually support any Allied invasion of mainland Europe. Industrial targets in France were later added to the list, to 'discourage the nationals of enemy-occupied countries from working in German controlled factories'. However, the directive went on to state that the targets should only be attacked by the

best crews and in good weather, to ease identification and minimise casualties.

Although not one of the five suggested targets, Stuttgart was raided during the first week of May and Lancasters from Nos 44 and 97 Squadrons took part. One of the main targets was the Bosch factory, which manufactured major mechanical components and was considered to be one of the more important industrial premises. A total of 28 Lancaster sorties were flown without loss, although the raid did not prove particularly successful.

The first raid against one of the five priority targets was on the night of 8/9 May when 21 Lancasters were included in a force of 193 aircraft detailed to attack the Baltic town of Warnemünde, just north of Rostock, and the nearby Heinkel aircraft factory. Although the raid was assessed to be moderately successful, it proved costly as nineteen of the aircraft, including four Lancasters from No 44 Squadron, failed to return. This brought No 44's total losses to ten aircraft in three weeks and would have, no doubt, served as a reminder to the crews that the introduction of the Lancaster into service would not necessarily provide the answer to all problems. Tactics, for example, would still contribute to the success of a particular mission. Navigational and bombing techniques would need to be

improved so that a crew could follow a route to the target accurately and not stray into more heavily defended areas before delivering bombs on the target. Getting it right first time would reduce the number of times that bombers would have to return to a particular target and, therefore, reduce overall losses. With Harris having assumed command, the never-ending line of 'experts' was still plying its opinions on how to win the bombing war. The War Cabinet decided to seek arbitration and established an inquiry under Mr Justice Singleton with the remit: 'What results are we likely to achieve from our air attacks on Germany at the greatest possible strength during the next six, twelve and eighteen months respectively?'

On 20 May Mr Justice Singleton presented his report. His conclusions were that overall accuracy had been low, except for a few exceptions, and that TR.1355 (Gee) did not as yet appear to be having a significant effect. He considered that a trained target-finding force would greatly increase the efficiency of the bombing and that, until greater accuracy had been assured, Bomber Command should confine itself to easily located targets. However, he considered that 'The bombing strength of the RAF is increasing rapidly, and I have no doubt that, if the best use is made of it, the effect on German war production

Lancasters of No 50 Squadron at Swinderby in the summer of 1942. (No 50 Sqn records)

The Lancaster crew: a team of specialists who spent night after night penetrating deep into the heart of Germany.

and effort will be very heavy over a period of twelve to eighteen months, and such as to have a real effect on the war position.'

The 'Thousand Bomber' Raids, May and June 1942

The report by Mr Justice Singleton had given new heart to the proponents of strategic bombing and Harris knew that the best way to prove his belief in how to win the bombing war was to carry out a demonstration of the devastating power of a large bomber force. To prove his point he planned a 'Thousand Bomber' raid against Cologne, the third largest city in Germany, on the night of 30/31 May. By the night of the Cologne raid, the number of Lancaster squadrons taking part in operations had risen to four, with No 83 Squadron, based at Scampton, having taken part in its first sorties just two nights earlier. The Cologne raid was also to in-

clude the first Lancaster operations of the fifth squadron to be re-equipped, No 106 Squadron, based at Coningsby under the command of Wing Commander Guy Gibson DFC.

The plan was to put up a stream of bombers flying the same route and speed, at different heights, to and from the target. The effects of the German night fighters would be reduced because the number of aircraft flying through the air defence areas would saturate them. It was also intended that the amount of time spent over the target area would be reduced to approximately 90 minutes, which again would saturate the German ground defences although, of course, this would also increase the chances of mid-air collisions over the target area. This risk was considered worthwhile: it was imperative to get the bombers over the target and away as quickly as possible. Every conceivable as-

set was made available, including aircraft and crews from training units, and eventually a force of 1,047 aircraft, including 73 Lancasters from No 5 Group, was dispatched. It was by far the largest single effort to date by the Lancaster squadrons. Although just under 900 of the force claimed to have bombed the target, damage was lighter than had been hoped. Nevertheless, the city was turned into a sea of fire with extensive damage to industrial and commercial buildings. There were also a large number of civilian casualties, and one result of the raid was that approximately a quarter of the population fled the city over the ensuing days.

Almost inevitably, with such a large number of aircraft taking part, losses to

Bomber Command were a record 41 aircraft, of which it is estimated that about half occurred over the target area. However, this figure represents less than 4 per cent of the total force. In fact, the concern about the increased risk of mid-air collisions over the target area was ill-founded as only two aircraft were lost in such circumstances. Only one of the aircraft which failed to return was a Lancaster—1.4 per cent of the Lancaster force dispatched.

The force was assembled again just 48 hours later on the night of 1/2 June, when 74 Lancasters were included in a force of 956 aircraft detailed to attack the city of Essen. This particular city had often proved a jinx target and, again, difficulty in locating it through thick ground haze meant that the results did not come up to expectations. A total of 31 aircraft were lost, including four Lancasters—5 per cent of the Lancaster force dispatched. A much smaller force of 195 aircraft, including 27 Lancasters, returned to Essen the following night with no more success. Over the next two weeks Essen was attacked three

more times, bringing the total effort against the city to five raids in fifteen days, during which time over 1,600 sorties had been flown. In addition to the raids against Essen, four were carried out on a smaller scale against the town of Emden. Although taking part in larger numbers, the Lancaster contribution was still relatively light: in the the short campaign against Essen it represented less than 9 per cent of the total effort, while against Emden it was under 5 per cent.

The 'Thousand Bomber' force was called to action again on the night of 25/26 June when 1,067 aircraft, including over 100 from Coastal Command, were detailed to attack the city and port of Bremen. The number of Lancaster squadrons available for operations had now risen to seven, with the addition of No 50 Squadron based at Skellingthorpe and No 61 at Syerston. Again, a maximum effort was ordered for No 5 Group, and from the seven squadrons 96 Lancasters were made available. These were to attack the Focke-Wulf aircraft factory. The tactics were similar to those of the previous large

raids, although the time over the target area was reduced to about one hour. Unfortunately, the target was covered by cloud, making accurate bombing difficult, although Gee-equipped aircraft helped to ensure that the raid proved moderately successful, with damage being caused to numerous industrial works, including the Focke-Wulf factory. However, the fact that 48 aircraft failed to return represented a new record loss for Bomber Command, although just one was a Lancaster, from No 83 Squadron. Although 48 aircraft, again, represents a small percentage loss it was nevertheless a large number of aircraft and crews. During the next few days three more raids against Bremen were carried out, bringing the total effort for the week to 1,789 sorties, of which 237 (13 per cent) were flown by Lancasters. This

shows an increase in the overall effort by the Lancaster squadrons; in fact, on the three smaller raids against Bremen the Lancaster contribution had risen to 20 per cent of the total effort.

Of the three 'Thousand Bomber' raids, it could be argued that only the first against Cologne was successful. Nevertheless, they had witnessed the first serious attempts at streaming and concentrating aircraft to overwhelm the enemy's defences and so reduce overall losses. However, it was impossible to keep such a large force together for any period of time: the training units needed to return to their main task and other contributors, such as Coastal Command, could equally not afford the diversion away from their own duties.

Harris had hoped to prove that, given a sufficient number of bombers, the power of the bombing offensive would be enormous. The arguments continued almost without pause, some calling the whole concept of mass bombing into question. Harris was undaunted by the opposition and in a letter to Winston Churchill summarised his thoughts and anger: 'An ex-

traordinary lack of sense of proportion affects outside appreciation of the meaning, extent and results of Bomber Command's operations. What shouts of victory would arise if a Commando unit wrecked the entire Renault factory in a night, with a loss of seven men! What credible assumptions of an early end to the war would follow upon the destruction of one-third of Cologne in an hour and a half by some swift-moving mechanized force which with 200 casualties withdrew and was ready to repeat the operation 24 hours later! What acclaim would greet the virtual destruction of Rostock and the Heinkel main and subsidiary factories by a Naval bombardment! All this and far more has been achieved by Bomber Command; yet there are many who still avert their gaze, pass on the other side, and question whether the 30 squadrons of night bombers make any worthwhile contribution to the war.'

It was typical Harris material, making references to the other Services and what comments would be passed had they achieved similar results. However, there

By the end of 1942 twelve squadrons of Bomber Command were equipped with the Lancaster.

was still much to do with regard to increasing bombing accuracy and reducing losses. With the exception of the Lancaster, the RAF's heavy bombers, which had been operating for some time, all seemed to be lacking in various important respects. Of the three, the Manchester had suffered particularly badly, with a loss rate averaging about 4.4 per cent (almost double that of the Stirling) as it appeared more vulnerable to flak than the other types. The introduction of the Halifax into service had also proved costly: this aircraft was, up to June 1942, also averaging losses of around 5 per cent, mainly due to night fighter activity (and possibly not helped by the fact that unsatisfactory exhaust shrouds on its engines made the Halifax easier for the night fighters to pick out).

Although the advent of radio aids made the Lancaster more independent of the weather, the latter was still the major consideration on a daily basis—not only over the target area but also during the transit to and from the target and, just as importantly, at base during recovery. By mid-1942 the meteorological briefing system was well established, the Central Forecast Station at Dunstable providing information, as did the Group Met Officers, which resulted in a daily forecast for Britain and Germany. With the approach of summer Bomber Command had a more limited arc of targets within its reach because of fewer hours of darkness—essentially just the coast and towns and cities in the Ruhr.

At about this time Harris was forced to transfer one of his Lancaster squadrons for duties with Coastal Command to help combat U-boats operating in the Atlantic. The first squadron to provide a detachment of aircraft in support of these operations was No 44 Squadron, which deployed five aircraft to Nutts Corner in County Antrim and commenced convoy patrols off the Irish coast during June. Harris was keen to ensure that the crews assigned these duties were not kept away from the bomber offensive for any period of time and so a rotation of crews and squadrons was established.

By the beginning of July the older and less capable bombers—the Manchester, Hampden and Whitley—had been withdrawn from Bomber Command operations and the number of Lancasters available each night was averaging more than 50. On 11 July 44 Lancasters were detailed to make a dusk attack on the U-boat construction yards at Danzig, a round trip of 1,500 miles, of which the first half was to be in daylight. The route to the target was carefully planned, the idea being that the aircraft would split up over Denmark and then use cloud cover to make individual approaches to the target area. The route to the target managed to avoid German fighters and in general the plan worked well, only two aircraft being shot down by flak over the target area. Throughout the remainder of July Lancasters continued the bombing offensive with a series of raids against Duisburg and Hamburg. By the end of the month the Lancaster effort for one target exceeded 100 aircraft for the first time when 113 were included in a force of 630 aircraft detailed to at-tack Düsseldorf on the night of 31 July/1 August.

The Pathfinders

For some time it had been considered that a special target finding organisation was required in order to improve the overall bombing results. Many discussions and debates had taken place and it was eventually accepted that a separate force with special equipment and experienced crews should be formed. Harris was personally more in favour of extending current tactics rather than creating an élite force, as the loss of experienced crews would be hard to accept, particularly by squadron commanders. Again after much debate, Harris reluctantly agreed to form a specialist Pathfinder Force (PFF) for target-finding and marking and he chose one of his best leaders, Donald Bennett, to command it.

Donald Clifford Tyndal Bennett was born in Queensland, Australia, on 14 September 1910. He joined the Royal Australian Air Force (RAAF) in 1930 and was sent to England to complete his pilot training. Having qualified, Bennett was posted to No 29 Squadron at North Weald to fly Siskin fighters, although shortly afterwards he moved to No 210 Squadron at Pembroke Dock on Supermarine Southampton flying boats. He quickly established a reputation for skills in navigation and in 1935 he joined Imperial Airways and operated flying boats around the Mediterranean. When war broke out, Bennett was the captain of a mail-carrying flying boat operating between Southampton and New York. He re-joined the RAF in the summer of 1941 and was given command of No 77 Squadron at Leeming, equipped with Whitleys; the following April he was given command of No 10 Squadron, also at Leeming and equipped with Halifaxes. He led the second of the raids against the *Tirpitz* on 28/29 April as she lay hidden in Trondheim Fjord, during which his aircraft was hit several times and his crew forced to bail out. With Norwegian help they evaded capture and returned to England via Sweden. As a result of the raid, Bennett was awarded a DSO.

Air Vice-Marshal Donald Bennett, who formed the Pathfinder Force (PFF) on 11 August 1942.

Soon after his return to England Bennett was called to see Harris at Bomber Command Headquarters. Promoted to Group Captain, he set about the task of creating the PFF from scratch. The Force was officially formed on 11 August with its headquarters at Wyton, elements at Oakington and other operating bases at Graveley and Warboys. Initially the force was made up of squadrons from each of the bomber Groups—No 7 Squadron (Stirlings) from No 3 Group, No 156 Squadron (Wellingtons) from No 1 Group, No 35 Squadron (Halifaxes) from No 4 Group, No 83 Squadron (Lancasters) from No 5 Group and No 109 Squadron (initially Wellingtons and Lancasters but later Mosquitos). Group commanders were reluctant to release personnel and equipment and Bennett had an uphill struggle. Fortunately he had a fierce determination and much experience and knowledge, and even Harris, although at first not in favour of creating this new force, offered Bennett his full support.

Immediately Bennett and his crews worked hard to make sure that the PFF was going to succeed. The standards set by the crews were extremely high and any crewman who did not meet the required standard was sent back to his squadron and replaced by another volunteer. There was no doubt about it—the PFF was going to be an élite force, and seen as such by the crews of Bomber Command. Such was the determination and pride within the Command that there was no shortage of volunteer crews ready to lead the way. One week after its formation, the PFF took part in its first operation when 31 Pathfinder aircraft were included in a force of 118 bombers detailed to attack the town of Flensburg on the night of 18/19 August. It was not a good beginning: forecast winds were in error and sixteen of the Pathfinders bombed well to the north of the target. Among the four aircraft lost was one Halifax of No 35 Squadron, the first PFF casualty.

The second PFF-led raid, against Frankfurt on the night of 24/25 August, was no more successful as cloud obscured the target. However, three nights later the third raid proved more effective when good weather over the target, Kassel, enabled the Pathfinders to illuminate the area and bomb the aiming points accurately. The fact that two of the first three raids had proved relatively unsuccessful was hardly any great surprise as the equipment used by the Pathfinder crews was no different from that of the Main Force squadrons. It was still early days, and it would

be a while before tactics could be developed to suit the targets and conditions at the time. Bennett had identified many of the difficulties and it was just a matter of time before equipment and tactics could come together to produce the best results. However, it was not until the end of the year that equipment such as H2S and Oboe would enter service with the Pathfinders. Moreover, the fact that two new Lancaster squadrons were being equipped in No 5 Group, No 49 Squadron at Scampton and No 9 Squadron at Waddington, meant that there were no new aircraft available for delivery to No 83 Squadron at Wyton.

There were also problems operating four different types of aircraft. Operating altitudes and aircraft ground speeds differed, and these factors had to be taken into account. The loss rate amongst Pathfinder crews was also expected to be higher as by flying ahead of the Main Force they were exposed to the night fighters and ground defences first. If the German ground control system guessed the target correctly, then night fighters would be waiting and ground defences well alerted, although in the event this was less of a problem to the Lancaster crews of the PFF than it was for crews of other aircraft types. On the first PFF raid, against Flensburg, there were no Lancaster losses, but on the second, against Frankfurt, six Lancasters

were lost, of which two were from the Pathfinders of No 83 Squadron.

The fact that No 83 Squadron were the PFF's only Lancaster squadron put much pressure on the groundcrews at Wyton. There was undoubtedly tremendous pride among the Squadron's personnel in terms of their contribution to the overall effort, and among them there was always the determination to make available the maximum number of aircraft for every raid. This was at a time when many of the Squadron's Lancasters were getting old and could not be replaced. This determination was also evident among the aircrew, who would often fly an aircraft which was, perhaps, not strictly serviceable. This 'pressing on regardless' attitude was typical of many squadrons and crews at that time.

On the night of 27/28 August nine Lancasters of No 106 Squadron, based at Coningsby, took part in a special raid against the new German aircraft carrier *Graf Zeppelin*, which was understood to be almost ready to put to sea at Gdynia. Each aircraft was carrying a special bomb which

A Lancaster Mk I of No 156 Squadron during early 1943. This particular aircraft, W4113, was first delivered to No 49 Squadron during the summer of 1942 and later served with No 5 LFS and No 1668 HCU.

had been developed for attacks against large ships. Poor visibility made it impossible for the crews to locate the ship and so the general harbour area was bombed instead. It is uncertain if any damage was caused to the ship, or what damage was caused to the harbour, but the Germans never did commission the *Graf Zeppelin*.

The first real PFF success came on the night of 28/29 August with a raid on Nuremberg. It was by recent standards a small raid with only 159 aircraft, of which 71 were Lancasters. The PFF was able to mark the aiming point well with a new device known as the 'Red Blob Fire', a converted 250lb incendiary filled with a benzol-rubber-phosphorous mixture which had the advantage that it burned brightly for a long time. The bombers claimed good results, the markers being easy to see and aim at. By the end of the month the PFF had flown 175 sorties and lost sixteen aircraft.

A small but accurate attack on Karlsruhe on the night of 2/3 September was followed two nights later by an equally effective raid on Bremen when 251 PFF-led bombers caused heavy damage. Attacks on Duisburg (6/7 September) and Frankfurt (8/9 September) were not so successful owing to bad weather. The basic PFF tactics had been modified from the 'Shaker' technique and now involved a force of Illuminators dropping flares from

The introduction of newer and heavier weapons brought a fresh dimension to the Lancaster's capability as a bomber.

which the Visual Markers could identify and mark the aiming point. A second force of Backers-Up would then follow and drop incendiaries on the markers. The tactic generally proved successful and became a technique often used by the PFF. Further modifications were introduced during an attack on Düsseldorf on the night of 10/11 September when the PFF employed a new improvised marker, the Pink Pansy (modified from a 4,000lb incendiary and ignited with a pink flash), the most complex marking system to date. PFF aircraft dropped red flares to mark the western edge of the town and green flares to mark the eastern edge. Pink Pansies were then dropped to mark the actual aiming point. The idea was that the Main Force would then fly between the two sets of flares and bomb the markers. Taking part in the Main Force were four Lancasters of No 9 Squadron, marking the Squadron's operational début with the type and bringing the number of operational Lancaster squadrons to nine. It proved to be a good, but costly, raid, with 33 of the 479 aircraft failing to return, five of them Lancasters.

Two nights later a heavy raid caused severe damage to Bremen, and this was followed the next night by a raid against Wilhelmshaven and on the night of 16/17 September by one against Essen. Eleven Lancasters failed to return from these three raids. The continuing build-up of the Lancaster squadrons meant that Harris was reluctant to overwork both the aircrew and groundcrew throughout this

phase. He had, after all, lost two of his Main Force squadrons, one to the PFF and one to Coastal Command to help in the war against the U-boats. There now followed a period of consolidation (not helped by a prolonged period of bad weather), although there were two raids by Lancasters of No 5 Group against the Baltic coastal town of Wismar: 83 Lancasters took part on the night of 23/24 September and a further 78 Lancasters on the night of 1/2 October, with a total of six aircraft lost. By the middle of October 1942 the number of operational Lancaster squadrons had increased to ten, No 57 Squadron at Scampton having made its operational début against Wismar on the night of 12/13 October.

Le Creusot, 17 October 1942

A number of locations in France had been identified earlier in the year as potential Bomber Command targets, one of which was the Schneider factory at Le Creusot situated 150 miles south-east of Paris and more than 300 miles inside the country. The factory was responsible for producing heavy guns, railway engines and, it was believed, tanks and armoured cars. It was decided that the only way to achieve success, and to minimise French casualties, was to attack in daylight at low level. The task of bombing Le Creusot was given to the Lancasters of No 5 Group, and low-level practice flights around the United Kingdom gave crews a chance to get used to some of the problems they might encounter. A few days' rest meant that the nine Lancaster squadrons that were to take part in the raid, code-named Operation 'Robinson', could make available the maximum number of aircraft.

On the afternoon of 17 October the force of 94 Lancasters, led by Wing Commander Leonard Slee (OC No 49 Squadron), took off from their respective bases and joined up before heading south-west across Cornwall and then south for the Brest peninsula. The Lancasters crossed the French coast between La Rochelle and St Nazaire and continued for 300 miles at very low level to avoid detection and German fighters. In the event, the Lancasters met no opposition and arrived over the

DS604, one of the first Mk IIs to be delivered to the RAF, pictured in January 1943 after arriving at No 61 Squadron at Syerston. The Squadron was the first to fly the new mark in service, commencing operations the same month.

target area just after 1800 hours, where they encountered light flak. The Lancasters carried out their attacks from various heights up to 7,500ft. Crews reported accurate bombing and dropped nearly 140 tons of bombs; the individual aircraft bomb loads varied but included 1,000lb bombs, 4,000lb 'Cookies' and incendiaries.

Six aircraft of the force, led by Wing Commander Guy Gibson (OC No 106 Squadron) had been tasked to accompany the Main Force to Le Creusot and then break off to attack the nearby Henri Paul transformer and power station at Montchanin. Each carrying ten 500lb bombs, the Lancasters pressed home a most determined attack from low level, although one aircraft from No 61 Squadron attacked from such a low altitude that it either caught the blast of its own bombs or flew into a building. All the remaining air-

craft made their escape under cover of darkness and landed back at their bases some ten hours after taking off. The only other casualty of the raid was an aircraft of No 207 Squadron which had turned back with an engine failure. As it was flying at a height of just 40ft over Brest it was attacked by three Arado Ar 196 seaplanes. In the ensuing battle the Lancaster shot down two of the attacking aircraft but was hit by at least one burst of fire, which killed the flight engineer, although the bomber returned safely. Four other Lancasters had to abort the mission for various reasons.

The attack proved successful in that only one aircraft was lost; a large number of bombs were dropped and the crews' reports were most optimistic. However, some post-raid reconnaissance photographs suggested that some bombs had not hit the target and that damage was not as extensive as had been hoped, although it was several months before repairs were completed.

Taking the Offensive to Italy

A raid on Genoa by 112 Lancasters of No 5 Group and the PFF on the night of

22/23 October opened a week of Main Force operations against targets in Italy to coincide with the Eighth Army offensive at El Alamein. For the Lancaster crews, this initial raid was followed by a daring daylight raid by 88 Lancasters of No 5 Group against Milan on 24 October. The aircraft flew individual routes across France to rendezvous at Lake Annecy before crossing the Alps. The raid came as a total surprise to the Italian defences and only one aircraft was shot down, although two more were lost on the way home and another crashed back in Britain. Extensive damage was caused to commercial and industrial buildings, including damage to the Caproni aircraft factory.

The Lancasters of No 5 Group and the PFF returned to Genoa on the night of 6/7 November when 72 aircraft carried out an attack on the residential area with the loss of two bombers. The raid was repeated the following night when 85 Lancasters were included in a force of 175 aircraft which carried out a successful raid. The campaign against Italy continued until the end of the month with two further attacks against Genoa (13/14 and 15/16 November) and four against Turin beginning on the night of 18/19 November. The largest of the raids against Italian targets took place on the night of 20/21 November when a force of 232 aircraft, including 86 Lancasters, carried out a successful attack against the Fiat works at Turin.

The short bombing campaign by the Main Force against Italy lasted until 12 December, by which time nearly 1,000 Lancaster sorties had been flown during thirteen raids, seven against Turin, five against Genoa and one against Milan. This represents only part of the total effort when taking into account a further 800 sorties by other aircraft types.

As the Italian campaign was brought to a close, Bomber Command returned to Germany. It should be noted, however, that even during the campaign against Italy the Lancasters had carried out attacks against various German targets. The year ended with the introduction of Oboe and on the last night of 1942 eight Lancasters of the PFF and two Oboe-equipped Mosquitos took part in a small raid against Düsseldorf. Only one of the Mosquitos was able to use the equipment and both aircraft marked the target for the Lancasters to bomb. One Lancaster failed to return.

At the end of 1942, the *Bomber Command Quarterly Review* carried an analysis of the effect of the bombing campaign upon the Ruhr during the year. The main message was that, although a great deal had been achieved, there still remained much to do. The statistics showed a huge increase in effort from the previous years and the Lancaster, no doubt, had much to do with that. The Lancaster force was still expanding, although of the 32 heavy bomber squadrons, only twelve were equipped with the aircraft. However, with more bombers coming off the production lines each day, and with the introduction of new and specialised equipment, the future looked promising.

Into the New Year: 1943

The first days of 1943 saw Lancasters assisting the Oboe-equipped Mosquitos of the Pathfinder Force in more experimental raids against German targets. One such raid against Essen on the night of 3/4 January marked the beginning of a series of smaller raids. During the first two weeks of the year seven were carried out against Essen, all involving Oboe-equipped Mosquitos from the PFF. There were a total of 310 Lancaster sorties, from which fourteen aircraft failed to return.

After the relatively small-scale effort against Essen, Harris was keen to return to the heavy pounding of German towns which had rounded off 1942. Instead he received a directive from the Air Ministry, dated 14 January, which called for a renewed offensive against the U-boat bases in France. The War Cabinet, after considerable pressure from the Air Staff, had agreed to the area-bombing of these installations 'with the object of effectively devastating the whole area in which are located the submarines, their maintenance facilities and other resources upon which their operation depends'. Bomber Command was ordered to attack Lorient at the earliest opportunity and then to analyse the results of the attack before proceeding with the destruction of St Nazaire, Brest and La Pallice. The directive did, however, state that these attacks were not to prejudice concentrated raids on Berlin or other significant targets in Germany or Italy.

The first attack on Lorient took place on the night of 14/15 January, just hours after the directive was issued. Lorient was hit a total of seven times during the first two weeks of the offensive against the U-boat bases, by a bomber force generally made up of Wellingtons, Halifaxes and Stirlings, with only a handful of Lancasters taking part during the early stages of the offensive. The reason for this was that, in accordance with the directive, Harris wanted to renew the offensive against the German capital and also keep the momentum going against other important cities.

On the night of 16/17 January 190 Lancasters and eleven Halifaxes carried out the first attack against Berlin for fourteen months, providing the first opportunity to make use of purpose-designed target indicators. The modified incendiaries which had previously been used as TIs had severe limitations and Bennett had fought

for many months to get improvements. However, despite the TIs, bad weather resulted in scattered bombing and poor results; one Lancaster failed to return. The following night 170 Lancasters and 17 Halifaxes returned to Berlin, and although the weather had improved only unconfirmed damage to industrial buildings was reported. The fact that nineteen of the Lancasters (11 per cent) failed to return brought an end to these attacks against the capital until better bombing aids became available.

On the last night of January the H2S radar system made its operational début during an attack against Hamburg. A total of thirteen Halifaxes and Stirlings of the PFF were equipped with H2S for locating and marking the target and were followed up by the Main Force of 135 Lancasters. It was not a particularly successful night for H2S and bombing was scattered, although it was obviously very early days; five of the Lancasters failed to return. Two nights later a similar-sized force carried out an H2S attack against Cologne, again with disappointing results. The following night a larger mixed force of 263 aircraft, including 62 Lancasters, returned to Hamburg, but, despite the increased numbers, the overall bombing was no more successful. However, at long last Bomber Command had a piece of equipment which did not rely on ground stations and could be used anywhere with no limitations. Although the theory was sound, the practice would take a little longer to perfect—it was only a matter of time.

By early February there was a plethora of new ideas and tactical concepts. Almost monthly someone came up with a new way to attack a particular type of target, the best way to use TIs and so on. The PFF was often in the forefront of invention, although the Groups were never short of ideas. February brought a call from the Air Staff for Bomber Command to attack Berlin again, although it would be the following month before the next attack against the 'Big City' would take place. The main effort throughout February was a renewed offensive against Italian targets, more intensive attacks against Lorient and the continuation of visits to lesser German targets.

The renewed offensive against Italy began on the night of 4/5 February when 77 Lancasters were part of a force which bombed Turin. On the same night, four Lancasters from the PFF were dispatched to the Italian port of La Spezia to try a new type of 4,000lb bomb which exploded some 500ft above the ground to increase the effects of the blast. Three of the aircraft successfully bombed and all four aircraft returned safely. The increased effort against the U-boats at Lorient began on the night of 7/8 February when a force of 323 aircraft carried out a devastating attack. There were two more large raids against Lorient during the month, 466 aircraft on the night of 13/14 February and 377 aircraft on the night of 16/17 February. The total Lancaster effort during these three raids against Lorient was 375 sorties, resulting in the loss of six aircraft. Having progressively destroyed Lorient since the beginning of the year, the bombers turned to St Nazaire on the last night of the month when a force of 437 aircraft, including 152 Lancasters, caused widespread destruction in the port. By the beginning of March, Lancasters had continued the offensive against German targets with four raids against Wilhelmshaven (the total Lancaster effort was 316 sorties) and additional raids against Bremen (130 sorties), Nuremberg (169) and Cologne (145).

On the night of 1/2 March 156 Lancasters were part of a force of 302 aircraft dispatched once more to Berlin. The raid was not particularly successful; damage was caused to parts of the city but there was not the concentration of bombs expected, mainly because of the difficulty in identifying features using the H2S: a large city produced a large area of radar responses, which made the identification of individual features confusing and difficult, even for the most experienced operators. An attack on Hamburg two nights later was the last raid before Harris changed his strategy.

The Battle of the Ruhr

Harris marked the end of his first year of command by making a series of changes throughout Bomber Command, including the appointment of Air Marshal Sir Robert Saundby as his deputy, and it was the continuity of this team that would see the Command through the main bomber offensive over the next two years. Air Vice-Marshal Donald Bennett retained command of No 8 (Pathfinder) Group, and command of No 5 Group, including command of the Lancaster Main Force, was given to Air Vice-Marshal the Hon. Ralph Cochrane. Born in 1895, the third son of Baron Cochrane of Cults in Fifeshire, Cochrane had served with the RNAS during the First World War. In 1918 he transferred to the newly formed RAF and during the early 1920s served in Egypt and

Iraq. Following a tour in Aden, he returned to England in 1930 and later became the Director of the Staff College. Following appointments at the Air Ministry and the Imperial Defence College, Cochrane became defence adviser to the New Zealand Government and Chief of the Air Staff of the Royal New Zealand Air Force (RNZAF). In 1939 he became aide-de-camp to King George VI, after which he assumed command of RAF Abingdon. In February 1942 he was promoted to Air Vice-Marshal and appointed Air Officer Commanding (AOC) No 3 Group before his appointment as AOC No 5 Group. Cochrane was described as a strict but fair man and went on to command No 5 Group until January 1945. Harris himself described him as a 'most brilliant, enthusiastic and hard working leader of men'.

The possibility of attacking industrial targets in the Ruhr had been addressed as early as 1937 as Britain began its preparations for war against Germany. Under the Western Air Plans, drawn up by the Air Staff, it was decided to attack the German war effort at the heart of its industrial areas, including the Ruhr valley. At the end of his first year in command Harris felt that aircraft, equipment and tactics had developed sufficiently and that the time was right to increase the momen-

Lancasters of No 57 Squadron lining up for take-off during the winter of 1942/43.

tum in his main bomber offensive. In March Harris launched a sustained attack on Germany, the first part aimed at destroying the vital war industries of the Ruhr. The opening move of this new offensive was made on the night of 5/6 March when 442 aircraft, including 157 Lancasters, carried out an attack against the industrial city of Essen. The Main Force Lancasters formed the third wave of the attack and successfully bombed targets such as the Krupps factory. Three nights later the target was Nuremberg, followed the next night by Munich, two nights later Stuttgart and then Essen again on the night of 12/13 March. The first week generally proved successful with the Lancasters totalling 777 sorties (43 per cent of the total Command effort) for the loss of 21 aircraft.

With this new offensive under way Harris was reluctant to divert any of his forces, but the fact that the U-boats were still causing major problems in the Atlantic meant that further large-scale attacks against St Nazaire were necessary. Two raids were carried out during the week beginning 22 March, totalling 239 Lancaster sorties. Harris continued to argue against this diversion of effort and remarked that sustaining these attacks would mean a 25 per cent reduction for at least two months in his efforts against the industrial targets in the Ruhr. Reluctantly the Admiralty agreed to suspend its request: in a directive dated 6 April the Air Staff instructed Harris to discontinue these area attacks in order to concentrate on the offensive over Germany.

Two large minelaying operations involving Lancasters took place during the last days of April, against the Biscay and Brittany ports on the night of 27/28 and off Heligoland the following night. However, it was German industry which remained at the forefront of operations. In the period from the start of the Battle of the Ruhr to mid-May, some 60 per cent of Bomber Command's Main Force effort was tasked against industrial targets in the Ruhr, Duisburg having been the most frequently visited (five raids between 26 March and 13 May), and a total of 870 Lancaster sorties were flown. Other large raids were dispatched against Essen (four raids), Bochum, Dortmund, Nuremberg, Munich, Stuttgart (two), Berlin (two), Frankfurt, Stettin, Kiel and, farther afield, the Skoda works at Pilsen (two raids). During this period of 22 raids, more than 3,750 Lancaster sorties were flown, at a cost of more than 130 aircraft lost, although this figure represents less than 4 per cent of the sorties.

Throughout the period of the first two months of the campaign, the range of success varied enormously. There was an unsuccessful attempt by a Main Force including 197 Lancasters against the Skoda works at Pilsen on the night of 16/17 April which resulted in the loss of eighteen Lancasters, but a most successful effort four nights later when a similar number of Lancasters took part in a raid against Stettin. The latter proved to be the most successful raid to date beyond the operating range of Oboe, good visibility and good marking by the PFF leading to the complete destruction of many industrial buildings.

The German Defences

There were four elements in the active German defence organization, early warning and Ground-Controlled Interception (GCI), searchlights, anti-aircraft artillery (flak) and fighters. All were inter-connected at various levels and, from 1942, formed an effective system that caused heavy casualties among Allied bombers.

The standard German radar was the Freya, which had a maximum detection range of 180 miles. It was an excellent system and at 60 miles' range had an accuracy of one degree in bearing and 1,000 yards in range, but, like most other early radars, it had no true height-finding capability. Two long-range radars were developed, Chimney and Mammut, both with maximum detection ranges of about 250 miles. Long-range detection, of course, depended on the height of the target; Mammut, for example, had a maximum range of 187 miles for a target at 26,000ft. The other ground radar elements were those connected with the control of fighters and guns. The Freya system had many variants, some of which

The German night fighter, with its sophisticated array of aerials, was the worst nightmare for any Lancaster crew.

were used for GCI. The other GCI radar was Giant Würzburg. With its 24ft aerial this radar was very accurate, having a bearing accuracy of one-tenth of a degree at 25 miles' range and height information to within 200ft. The primary purpose of the original Würzburg radar was the control of heavy flak batteries.

The principal role of the searchlights was to assist the guns and fighters in the destruction of enemy aircraft. Many of the major targets in Germany had extensive searchlight defences, dozens of beams lighting up the sky and turning night into day. In a coordinated system, tied in with sound locators, optical devices and radar, the master beam (usually distinguishable by its blue/mauve tinge) would latch on to a target, to be followed by many others forming a cone of light which then became the focus for the flak barrage. Three main searchlight types were in use: 60cm for light flak and 150cm and 200cm for heavy batteries and general use. It was essential for the bombers to get out of the beam as soon as possible, twisting and turning, diving and climbing. One of the accepted techniques was to dive down the beam, making prediction for tracking and gunlaying more difficult, and then breaking away to one side. If it looked as if a beam was going to pass through the aircraft, the best technique was to turn into it so that it crossed the aircraft as rapidly as possible. Unfortunately, the target had still to be bombed straight and level to give the bomb aimer a chance. The total number of searchlights in Germany doubled between 1941 and late 1944, and almost 5,000 were in position by early 1945.

Anti-aircraft guns or flak (from *Flieger-abwehrkanonen*) were an important part of the *Luftwaffe*; they also proved to be a heavy drain on German resources. Divided into light and heavy types, the former were used both as a mobile defence for the Army and in a point-defence role for important targets, to counter low level attacks. For the heavy guns, usually in batteries of four or six, the standard tactics were either aimed fire, relying on data fed into a predictor, or unaimed box barrage. The main heavy weapons varied from 88mm to 128mm and had rates of fire up to twenty rounds a minute, maximum ranges varying from 1,600 to 22,000yd, with a maximum ceiling of some 40,000ft.

The heavy flak batteries were only one part of the system. The light flak weapons were far more numerous, and deadly to low flying aircraft (although some of the weapons were effective to heights of

An example of the damage caused by the German defences. This aircraft was lucky enough to return to base.

more than 10,000ft). They varied from 20mm to 50mm and were all optically laid, rapid-fire weapons, relying for their effect on the sheer quantity of shells being 'thrown' into an area. The maximum rate per gun was over 200 rounds per minute. The combined defences could be quite extensive. The Ruhr, or 'Happy Valley' as it was called by some aircrew, was very heavily defended by searchlights and guns. By late 1943 typical figures were: for Berlin, 600 flak guns (of which 350 were heavy) and 200 searchlights; for Bremen, 600 guns (230 heavy) and 100 searchlights; and for Munich, 220 guns (130 heavy) and 60 searchlights. By the end of 1943 the overall figures, in Germany alone, stood at 6,716 heavy guns and 8,484 medium/light guns.

The German night fighter defences evolved from a not particularly effective collection of single-engine fighters, mainly Messerschmitt Bf 109s, to a complex organization that reacted well to the tactical changes made by the bombers and remained potent up until the last weeks of the war. The early single-engine tactics, working with searchlights, made very few kills. With the RAF's general move to a night bombing offensive, however, and the increased numbers and quality of radars, the *Luftwaffe* night defences expanded. The increased use of radar meant that the bombers were picked up at long range and as they entered a box they were 'handed off' to a controller. Both target and fighter were tracked on Giant Würzburg radars and the interception was set up to allow the fighter to pick up the bomber. Following Bomber Command's adoption of stream tactics to swamp a limited number of boxes (from mid-1942), the defensive belt was deepened so that the stream would have to penetrate more boxes.

With the advent of the Lichtenstein AI radar, the German two-seat night fighters had an excellent interception system although the GCI unit still positioned the fighter in the approximate area. Each of the boxes was based on a beacon; the fighters would orbit the beacon until sent off on an interception, and would return to the beacon once the combat was over. With minor modifications the system

worked well until the advent of Window; this device, and the later RCM techniques, made the Germans' GCI task much more difficult and led to many variations of tactics.

In essence the system evolved into two main types: *Wilde Sau* (Wild Boar) and *Zähme Sau* (Tame Boar). *Zähme Sau* was an extension of the existing controlled tactic, the fighter orbiting a beacon and being given control towards the bombers, the variations being those required to counter the use of Window and communications jamming. *Wilde Sau* was a reintroduction of the single-engine fighter to the night fighting role, under the system proposed by *Major* Hans-Joachim Hermann; the specialist unit JG 300 in the Bonn area became the initial exponents of this tactic. It proved successful and so further units were formed at Munich (JG 301) and Berlin (JG 302). These two basic tactical concepts remained valid until the end of the war, with minor changes to incorporate new equipment or to suit developing bombing tactics.

Improved radars, such as the SN-2 (FuG 220) version of Lichtenstein, and the use of homers such as Flensburg (to home on to Monica) and Naxos (to home on to H2S), helped counter the use of RCM by Bomber Command. New weapons were introduced in an attempt to bring down the bombers with fewer hits and thus give a greater chance of a 'first-pass' kill. In August 1943 the night fighters introduced *Schräge Musik* (jazz music), twin upward-firing cannon fitted to Messerschmitt BF110s, the idea being that the night fighter would attack the bomber from below and then fire up into the aircraft's belly and wings, often with devastating success; it was a tactic to which the Lancaster crews had little answer. Despite the increased fighter threat, the basic bomber tactic remained that of avoiding contact, or, if an interception took place, to try and disengage from the combat without being seriously damaged. The advised technique was that of the 'corkscrew', a stomach-churning manoeuvre but one that saved the lives of many aircrews. It was all a battle of wits—new tactics, new counters, revised tactics, revised counters, and so on.

7. From the Dams to Final Victory

From the Western Air Plans, which had laid down that the German war machine should be attacked in the heart of its industrial areas, the dams and reservoirs in the Ruhr valley were studied in great depth as likely targets long before the outbreak of war. However, as early as 1938 it was realised that the main problems lay in designing a suitable weapon and delivering it accurately, and so for the early part of the war the Ruhr dams featured low on the list of priorities. Although the Ruhr did not rely totally on water from the dams for the generation of electricity, it was estimated that it consumed some 25 per cent of Germany's water. The two most important reservoirs, one on the Mohne and the other on the Sorpe, between them held back some 76 per cent of the total water available in the Ruhr valley. A third dam on the Eder was the largest of the three and similar in construction to that on the Mohne. Located in a valley some 60 miles to the south-east of the Mohne, the Eder dam held back over 200 million tons of water. Other dams in the target area were considered for attack, but in the end only three of these were detailed as potential targets, the Ennepe dam to the south-west of the Mohne, the Lister dam to the south of the Sorpe and the Diemel dam to the north-west of the Eder. After discussion it was decided that there was a possibility of attacking the Ruhr dams in the future and, if this was to become the case, the Mohne dam should be the primary target. Not only would its destruction affect hydroelectricity generation: mass destruction would occur through the flooding of vital areas and industrial assets. Any breaches of other dams within the surrounding area would obviously increase such destruction.

For some considerable time a civilian engineer, Barnes Wallis, had worked on the idea that breaching the Ruhr dams would cause the production of industry, oil and coal to be brought to a halt. As the war in Europe began Wallis was the Assistant Chief Designer at the Vickers-Armstrong Aviation Section at Weybridge in Surrey. On his own initiative he had considered the destruction of natural sources of energy, which led him to the study of reservoirs and dams, and a further study of explosives. His initial ideas were along the lines of designing a massive bomb dropped from very high altitude which, by creating shock waves underground, would cause massive destruction to large areas within which a vital target was located. The Air Ministry refused to sanction any such design and so Wallis turned his thoughts to other methods. After countless experiments he considered exploding a weapon against the surface of the dam. He calculated that a charge detonated against the dam would cause a shock-wave capable of weakening the structure and that successive detonations would eventually breach the dam. According to his estimates, an explosive charge of just 6,000lb of RDX would be required.

In April 1942 Wallis commenced trials in his garden using marbles fired from a catapult to ricochet from water in a tub and land on a table, where recordings were made. By the end of April he had collected sufficient data and the following month permission was given for him to go ahead with further trials. These trials, concerned at this stage merely with the delivery of a suitable weapon, began at Teddington on 9 June and lasted over three months. In the meantime tests were carried out at the

Road Research Laboratory where one-tenth scale models of the Nant-y-Gro dam in Wales were constructed and detailed explosions carried out at various distances. Many more tests were carried out during August to determine the amount of explosive required, and the result was the construction of six half-size prototype bombs for dropping from a Wellington bomber. The bomb was initially spherical in shape. It had to be dropped from a very low altitude and designed in such a way that it would bounce across the water to the target. Five dropping tests were carried out off Chesil Bank during December using a modified Wellington bomber. The decision to install the new weapon, code-named 'Upkeep', into a new Lancaster was made in February 1943.

The gross weight of the weapon was 9,250lb, of which 6,600lb was the main explosive charge. The bomb was designed to be carried beneath the Lancaster by two vee-shaped arms. Rotating the weapon backwards meant that on impact with the water it would begin a deceleration process whilst bouncing towards the target. By expertly calculating the rate of deceleration, Wallis was able to determine at what point the weapon should be released. This distance proved to be between 400 and 450yd, and to ensure the vital accuracy the Lancaster would have to fly at an exact height of 60ft and an exact ground speed of 220mph. Through the study of German records it was apparent that the water level in the reservoirs would be at its highest in mid-May, and it was decided that the best moon conditions for a raid to be carried out would occur on the night of the 16th/17th.

It had been decided at Bomber Command Headquarters that a special squad-

Top: As No 617 Squadron was forming at Scampton, work had already begun at A. V. Roe to modify the Lancaster to carry the new 'Upkeep'. The aircraft depicted, ED817, carried out drop tests at Reculver before the weapon was finally cleared for use.

Above: To carry the special weapon, code-named 'Upkeep', the Lancaster modifications basically comprised the removal of the bomb doors and the omission of the dorsal turret. This particular aircraft, ED825/G, was flown by Flt Lt Joe McCarthy and attacked the Sorpe dam before returning safely to Scampton.

ron would be formed for the attack on the dams. Quite clearly, owing to the short time available for any unit to train for such a task, the new squadron would have to be made up of some of the best crews that Bomber Command could spare. This would mean taking experienced pilots and crews from operational squadrons, something that was not always viewed favourably by the squadron commanders. Harris turned to Cochrane at No 5 Group for the formation of the new squadron. One of the first decisions to be made was to appoint Wing Commander Guy Gibson

as its new commanding officer. By that time Gibson had commanded great respect as a leader, he had already completed 174 'ops' and he had been awarded the DSO and bar and the DFC and bar—a Bomber Command veteran at just 24 years of age!

Gibson had completed his tour of operations with No 106 Squadron at Syerston on 15 March. The following day he reported to Cochrane and was asked if he would fly just one more trip. Gibson agreed and was told to form a new squadron, Squadron 'X' as it was then known,

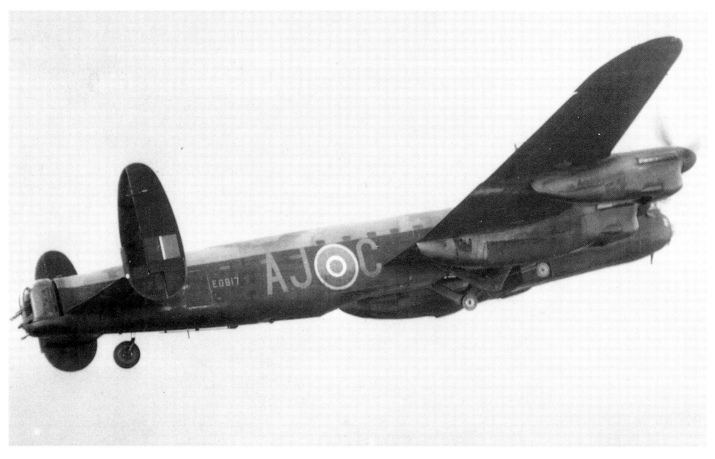

based at Scampton, but all he knew initially was that the 'job' would be done in just two months' time. Untypically for that time, Gibson was allowed to choose his crews and so he set about the task of picking his aircraft captains. Later he was told that the job would involve flying at low level at night, and so he picked some of the best pilots he knew that were capable of carrying out such demanding flying.

Operation 'Chastise', 16/17 May 1943

No 617 Squadron officially formed at Scampton on 21 March. Immediately the crews began to arrive and within hours rumours had started to spread as to why this special squadron, made up of so many of the finest crews in Bomber Command, had been formed. In all, 22 crews (157 aircrew) plus engineers and support personnel made up No 617 Squadron, although this figure was later revised to 21 crews. Initially the Squadron had just ten Lancasters, which were loaned from other squadrons and made available for flying training. One of the first tasks carried out

by the Squadron was to photograph several lakes around the country. The crews were told that this was for the benefit of the OTUs, to give training crews practice in navigation. Within a few days of the Squadron forming, Gibson was called to Weybridge where he was given a general briefing by Barnes Wallis of what the operation would involve. Gibson was shown films of the new weapon during trials and was told that the operation would involve flying very low and very accurately.

As No 617 Squadron was forming at Scampton work had already begun at A. V. Roe to modify the Lancasters to carry the new 'Upkeep'. The modifications included the removal of the bomb doors (to mount the gear for the rotating weapon) and the omission of the dorsal turret to save weight. A small hydraulic motor to drive the rotating gear was installed in the middle section of the cabin. The result of the modifications was an increase in aircraft weight of about 1,000lb, plus the weight of the 'Upkeep' itself. The aircraft was known as the Type 464 Provisioning Lancaster and an order was placed for 30,

The second prototype Type 464 Provisioning Lancaster, ED817 'AJ-C'. The rotating assembly for the 'Upkeep' can clearly be seen in the central area, although this particular aircraft did not take part in the Dams Raid.

although this was later reduced to 23. The first prototype, ED765/G ('G' for Guard, denoting special security), was delivered to the RAE at Farnborough on 8 April. Two days later the aircraft was moved to Manston for dropping trials and the first release was carried out on 16 April, off the north Kent coast at Reculver, using a non-exploding 'Upkeep' which broke up on hitting the water. A second, strengthened weapon was then dropped, with little more success, before it was then decided that the height and speed of the aircraft would have to be exactly 60ft and 220mph.

The normal pressure altimeter of the Lancaster was not accurate enough for these purposes and even the more sensitive radio altimeter was not considered reliable, particularly if the aircraft was turning. The method decided upon to determine the exact height of the aircraft was to fit two Aldis lamps, one in the nose and the other at the rear of the bomb compartment. The lamps were angled in such a way that the beams converged on the water exactly 60 feet below the aircraft. The idea was not new: it had been employed by Coastal Command for some time whilst attacking U-boats at night. Of course, the use of lights at night was undesirable, but there was no alternative.

The first successful release of 'Upkeep' was achieved on 29 April at Reculver. By that time several newly modified Lancasters had arrived at Scampton. By the end of the month training was consolidated at the Uppingham reservoir and a dam on the Colchester reservoir and, from early May, low-level flying was reduced from 150ft to just 60ft. Additional training was carried out at the Wainfleet bombing range on the Wash, where two boards were erected some 700ft apart to simulate towers on the dams. A simple sight was developed using a piece of wood with an eyesight and two nails, the idea being that the bomb aimer would look through the sight and when the two nails were lined up with the two towers the aircraft was at the correct distance from the dam to release the weapon. However, when tried by the crews in the air the new sight proved difficult to use, particularly as one hand was needed for the bomb release, and many of the bomb aimers set about designing their own personal method of sighting. Various ways of simulating night flying were tried, including covering the windscreen with celluloid and the wearing of goggles. Trials using Aldis lamps at night soon followed, first over the airfield runway and later over water. As problems were met they were soon overcome using all resources and individual initiative, and the fact that the Squadron was ready to operate by early May was a tribute to all. On 8 May Gibson made a successful practice drop, followed on the night of 14 May by the crews carrying out yet another night practice on the Uppingham and Colchester reservoirs. This, although the crews did not realise it, was the final 'dress rehearsal' for the attack—now just 48 hours away.

Table 12. No 617 Squadron Complement, April 1943.

	'A' Flight	'B' Flight
Captain	W/C G. P. Gibson DSO* DFC* [1]	
Navigator	P/O H. T. Taerum	
Flight Engineer	Sgt J. Pulford	
Bomb Aimer	P/O F. M. Spafford DFM	
Wireless Operator	F/L R. G. Hutchison DFC [2]	
Front Gunner	F/S G. A. Deering	
Rear Gunner	F/L R. D. Trevor-Roper DFM [3]	
Captain	S/L H. M. Young DFC* [4]	S/L H. E. Maudslay DFC [5]
Navigator	F/S C. W. Roberts	F/O R. A. Urquhart DFC [6]
Flight Engineer	Sgt D. T. Horsfall	Sgt J. Marriott DFM
Bomb Aimer	F/O V. C. MacCausland	P/O M. J. D. Fuller
Wireless Operator	Sgt L. W. Nichols	W/O A. P. Cottam
Front Gunner	Sgt G. A. Yeo	F/O W. J. Tytherleigh DFC [7]
Rear Gunner	Sgt W. Ibbotson	Sgt N. R. Burrows
Captain	F/L W. Astell DFC	F/L J. V. Hopgood DFC*
Navigator	P/O F. A. Wile	F/O K. Earnshaw
Flight Engineer	Sgt J. Kinnear	Sgt C. Brennan
Bomb Aimer	F/O D. Hopkinson	P/O J. W. Fraser DFM
Wireless Operator	W/O A. A. Garshowitz	Sgt J. W. Minchin
Front Gunner	F/S F. A. Garbas	P/O G. H. F. G. Gregory DFM
Rear Gunner	Sgt R. Bolitho	P/O A. F. Burcher DFM
Captain	F/L D. H. Maltby DFC	F/L H. B. Martin DFC
Navigator	Sgt V. Nicholson	F/L J. F. Leggo DFC [8]
Flight Engineer	Sgt W. Hatton	P/O I. Whittaker
Bomb Aimer	P/O J. Fort [9]	F/L R. C. Hay DFC [9]
Wireless Operator	Sgt A. J. B. Stone	F/O L. Chambers
Front Gunner	Sgt V. Hill	P/O T. B. Foxlee DFM
Rear Gunner	Sgt H. T. Simmonds	F/S T. D. Simpson
Captain	F/L D. J. Shannon DFC	F/L J. L. Munro
Navigator	F/O D. R. Walker DFC	F/O F. G. Rumbles
Flight Engineer	Sgt R. J. Henderson	Sgt F. E. Appleby
Bomb Aimer	F/S L. J. Sumpter	Sgt J. H. Clay
Wireless Operator	F/O B. Goodale DFC	W/O P. E. Pigeon
Front Gunner	Sgt B. Jagger	Sgt W. Howarth
Rear Gunner	F/O J. Buckley	F/S H. A. Weeks
Captain	F/L R. N. G. Barlow DFC	F/L J. C. McCarthy DFC
Navigator	F/O P. S. Burgess	F/S D. A. MacLean
Flight Engineer	P/O S. L. Whillis	Sgt W. D. Radcliffe
Bomb Aimer	P/O A. Gillespie DFM	Sgt G. L. Johnson
Wireless Operator	F/O C. R. Williams DFC	F/S L. Eaton
Front Gunner	F/O H. S. Glinz [11]	Sgt R. Batson
Rear Gunner	Sgt J. R. G. Lidell	F/O D. Rodger
Captain	P/O G. Rice	P/O L. Burpee DFM
Navigator	F/O R. McFarlane [12]	Sgt T. Jaye
Flight Engineer	Sgt E. C. Smith	Sgt G. Pegler
Bomb Aimer	W/O J. W. Thrasher	F/S J. L. Arthur
Wireless Operator	W/O C. B. Gowrie	P/O L. G. Weller
Front Gunner	Sgt T. W. Maynard	Sgt W. C. A. Long
Rear Gunner	Sgt S. Burns	W/O J. G. Brady
Captain	P/O V. W. Byers	P/O L. G. Knight
Navigator	F/O J. H. Warner	F/O H. S. Hobday
Flight Engineer	Sgt A. J. Taylor	Sgt R. E. Graystone
Bomb Aimer	P/O A. N. Whittaker	F/O E. C. Johnson [13]
Wireless Operator	Sgt J. Wilkinson	F/S R. G. T. Kellow
Front Gunner	Sgt C. McA. Jarvie	Sgt F. E. Sutherland
Rear Gunner	F/S J. McDowell	Sgt H. E. O'Brien

continued

Table 12 continued			
Captain	P/O W. H. T. Ottley DFC	F/S W. C. Townsend	
Navigator	F/O J. K. Barrett DFC	P/O C. L. Howard	
Flight Engineer	Sgt R. Marsden DFM	Sgt D. J. D. Powell	
Bomb Aimer	F/S T. B. Johnston	Sgt C. E. Franklin DFM	
Wireless Operator	Sgt J. Guterman DFM	F/S G. A. Chalmers	
Front Gunner	Sgt H. J. Strange	Sgt D. E. Webb	
Rear Gunner	Sgt F. Tees	Sgt R. Wilkinson	
Captain	F/S K. W. Brown	F/S C. T. Anderson	
Navigator	Sgt D. P. Heal	Sgt J. P. Nugent	
Flight Engineer	Sgt H. B. Feneron	Sgt R. C. Paterson	
Bomb Aimer	Sgt S. Oancia	Sgt G. J. Green	
Wireless Operator	Sgt H. W. Hewstone	Sgt W. D. Bickle	
Front Gunner	Sgt A. Buntaine	Sgt E. Ewan	
Rear Gunner	F/S G. S. MacDonald	Sgt A. W. Buck	
Captain	P/O W. G. Divall[14]	F/L H. S. Wilson[14]	
Navigator	F/O D. R. Warwick	F/O A. Roger	
Flight Engineer	Sgt E. C. A. Blake	Sgt B. Johnson[15]	
Bomb Aimer	Sgt R. McArthur	P/O B. Coles	
Wireless Operator	Sgt J. S. Simpson	Sgt S. Mieyette	
Front Gunner	Sgt D. Allatson	Sgt E. Payne	
Rear Gunner	Sgt A. Murray	Sgt F. Hornsby	

Notes
1. OC No 617 Squadron
2. Squadron Signals Leader
3. Squadron Gunnery Leader
4. Officer Commanding 'A' Flight
5. Officer Commanding 'B' Flight
6. 'B' Flight Navigation Officer
7. 'B' Flight Gunnery Leader
8. Squadron Navigation Officer
9. 'A' Flight Bombing Leader
10. Squadron Bombing Leader
11. 'A' Flight Gunnery Leader
12. 'A' Flight Navigation Officer
13. 'B' Flight Bombing Leader
14. Did not fly on Operation 'Chastise'
15. Flight Engineer Leader

The plan of the raid, code-named Operation 'Chastise', was that nineteen aircraft would attack in three sections. The first section of nine aircraft, led by Gibson, was to attack the Mohne dam and, if successful, would fly on to attack the Eder. The second section of five aircraft would attack the Sorpe and the third section of five would act as a mobile reserve, briefed to attack last-resort targets or any of the primary targets had the dams not been breached. Soon after 2130 hours on the night of 16/17 May the first wave took off in the three sections. After crossing the Rhine one aircraft in the second section, flown by Flight Lieutenant Bill Astell, was hit by crossfire from two flak positions. The aircraft was seen to fly on for several miles before suddenly becoming engulfed in flames and crashing north-west of Dorsten. There were no survivors.

Gibson's section arrived unscathed over the Mohne soon after midnight. Gibson attacked the dam first and, despite intense ground fire, hit the target although the dam remained intact. Allowing the water to settle, Flight Lieutenant 'Hoppy' Hopgood commenced his attack. During the run-in his aircraft was badly hit by ground fire, causing the weapon to be released late. The aircraft was seen staggering away from the target and then blew up. It was later discovered that two of the crew, Pilot Officers Fraser and Burcher, had, amazingly, survived. Realising that the Lancasters were vulnerable to ground fire, Gibson escorted the third aircraft, flown by Flight Lieutenant Micky Martin, into the attack; his 'Upkeep' exploded short of the dam. Escorted by Gibson and Martin, the next to attack was that by Squadron Leader 'Dinghy' Young. Young's weapon was released with devastating accuracy and the bomb was seen to strike the dam, causing cascades of water over the parapet—but there was still no breach. As the fifth aircraft, flown by Flight Lieutenant Dave Maltby, released its 'Upkeep', the dam began to collapse. The previous attack by Young had caused the vital weakening of the dam. The seven surviving Lancasters circled the target to watch the spectacular sight of thousands of tons of water burst into the valley below. Gibson ordered Maltby and Martin to return home and the remaining five aircraft flew on to the Eder.

Having had difficulty in finding the Eder, the crews discovered the dam undefended. However, the degree of skill required in the approach to and the recovery from the target was somewhat greater than at the Mohne. The first aircraft to

'Upkeep' *in situ* **beneath 'AJ-G', Gibson's aircraft used to attack the Mohne dam.**

Table 13. Type 464 Provisioning Lancasters

Serial	Operation 'Chastise' details	Remarks
ED765/G	–	1st prototype; crashed 5.8.43
ED817/G	–	2nd prototype; SOC 23.9.46
ED825/G	Returned safely	Missing France 10.12.43
ED864/G	Failed to return	
ED865/G	Failed to return	
ED886/G	Returned safely	Missing France 10.12.43
ED887/G	Failed to return	
ED906/G	Returned safely	SOC 29.7.47
ED909/G	Returned safely	SOC 29.7.47
ED910/G	Failed to return	
ED912/G	Returned safely	SOC 26.9.46
ED915/G	–	SOC 8.10.46
ED918/G	Returned safely	Crashed in sea 20 Jan 44
ED921/G	Returned safely	SOC 26.9.46
ED923/G	–	SOC 7.10.46
ED924/G	Returned safely	SOC 23.9.46
ED925/G	Failed to return	
ED927/G	Failed to return	
ED929/G	Returned safely	SOC 7.10.46
ED932/G	Returned safely	SOC 29.7.47
ED934/G	Failed to return	
ED936/G	Returned safely	SOC 28.7.44
ED937/G	Failed to return	

attack was Flight Lieutenant Dave Shannon's. His weapon hit the target, causing a slight breach. Next was Squadron Leader Henry Maudslay; his weapon was seen to fall late, hitting the dam without bouncing, and it exploded, catching the Lancaster in full blast. Several crew members thought that they may have detected a faint transmission from Maudslay's aircraft, but nothing was definitely heard of the crew again. From evidence collated

years later it was found that Maudslay's aircraft had survived the explosion but was in fact shot down by flak near the German-Dutch border on the way home; there were no survivors. The last aircraft to attack the Eder dam was flown by Pilot Officer Les Knight, and his bomb hit the dam accurately. Watched by the remaining crews, the breach rapidly widened and a great tidal wave swept down the Eder valley. The four aircraft then turned for

home. Shannon arrived back at Scampton at 0400 hours, some 45 minutes after Martin and Maltby. Gibson and Knight returned soon afterwards, but Young failed to return. From later evidence it was discovered that a German coastal flak battery had shot down Young's aircraft, with the loss of the entire crew.

Of the second wave, two aircraft were forced to return early. Flight Lieutenant Munro reluctantly returned to Scampton, having been damaged by flak, and the other Lancaster, flown by Pilot Officer Rice, returned having lost its 'Upkeep' after clipping the sea whilst flying too low on the way to the target! The fate of two others is unclear as nothing was heard after take-off. Flight Lieutenant Barlow crashed close to the German-Dutch border but it is uncertain whether his aircraft was shot down or whether it hit power cables. What is certain, unfortunately, is that the entire crew was lost. The other aircraft, flown by Pilot Officer Byers, was shot down by flak off the island of Texel near the Dutch coast with the loss of the entire crew. This left just one aircraft from the wave to press on to the target. All alone, Flight Lieutenant Joe McCarthy attacked the Sorpe dam, and although he hit the target the dam was not breached. McCarthy returned safely to Scampton.

The third wave was led by Pilot Officer Bill Ottley. After crossing the Rhine it appears that his aircraft was hit by flak and blew up. Amazingly, Sergeant Tees survived when the rear turret, with Tees still inside, was thrown clear. The second aircraft, flown by Pilot Officer Burpee, was shot down by flak over Gilze-Rijen airfield; there were no survivors. Flight Sergeant Anderson returned to Scampton with his 'Upkeep' still intact. His rear turret was out of action and, having been the last aircraft to take-off, he had encountered mist, making navigation difficult. Without his rear guns Anderson had had to make large detours to avoid areas of intense flak. This caused him to fall behind schedule, and with daylight just over an hour away

Gibson and his crew boarding ED932 'AJ-G' prior to the Dams Raid on the night of 16/17 May 1943.

Table 14. Aircraft and Crews Taking Part in Operation 'Chastise', 16/17 May 1943

Aircraft	Captain	Details
ED825 'AJ-T'	F/L J. McCarthy	Attacked Sorpe dam; aircraft returned safely
ED864 'AJ-B'	F/L W. Astell	Crashed/shot down outbound, crew killed
ED865 'AJ-S'	P/O L. Burpee	Shot down outbound, crew killed
ED886 'AJ-O'	F/S W. Townsend	Attacked Ennepe Dam; aircraft returned safely
ED887 'AJ-A'	S/L H. Young	Attacked Mohne Dam; aircraft shot down inbound, crew killed
ED906 'AJ-J'	F/L D. Maltby	Attacked Mohne Dam; aircraft returned safely
ED909 'AJ-P'	F/L H. Martin	Attacked Mohne Dam; aircraft returned safely
ED910 'AJ-C'	P/O W. Ottley	Hit by flak outbound, 6 killed + 1 PoW
ED912 'AJ-N'	P/O L. Knight	Attacked Eder Dam; aircraft returned safely
ED918 'AJ-F'	F/S K. Brown	Attacked Sorpe dam; aircraft returned safely
ED921 'AJ-W'	F/L J. Munro	Damaged by flak outbound; aircraft returned to base
ED924 'AJ-Y'	F/S C. Anderson	Aircraft unserviceable; returned to base
ED925 'AJ-M'	F/L J. Hopgood	Hit by flak during attack on Mohne Dam, 5 killed + 2 PoW
ED927 'AJ-E'	F/L R. Barlow	Hit by flak/struck by cables outbound, crew killed
ED929 'AJ-L'	F/L D. Shannon	Attacked Eder Dam; aircraft returned safely
ED932 'AJ-G'	W/C G. Gibson	Attacked Mohne Dam; aircraft returned safely
ED934 'AJ-K'	P/O V. Byers	Shot down by flak outbound, crew killed
ED936 'AJ-H'	P/O G. Rice	'Upkeep' torn off by sea outbound; aircraft returned to base
ED937 'AJ-Z'	S/L H. Maudslay	Crashed after attacking Eder Dam, crew killed

he reluctantly decided to return to Scampton. This left just two aircraft to press on to the dams. Flight Sergeant Ken Brown attacked the Sorpe dam; although his weapon hit the target there was no breach. Brown and his crew returned safely to Scampton. Finally, Flight Sergeant Bill Townsend attacked the Ennepe dam, but without success. With daylight getting dangerously close, Townsend raced for home and landed back at

Guy Gibson signing a photograph of the shattered Mohne dam.

Scampton at 0615 hours, the last of all the aircraft to return.

Operation 'Chastise' was undoubtedly a success. Two of the primary targets had been breached, resulting in widespread damage from flooding. However, the loss of life suffered by No 617 Squadron had been exceptionally heavy. Eight of the nineteen Lancasters failed to return and 53 aircrew died. A total of 34 gallantry awards were made to survivors of the raid. Wing Commander Guy Gibson DSO DFC was awarded the Victoria Cross for his outstanding bravery and leadership

during the raid. The other surviving officer pilots, Knight, McCarthy, Maltby, Martin and Shannon, were each awarded the DSO, with Brown and Townsend both receiving the Conspicuous Gallantry Medal (CGM). In addition, fourteen DFCs and twelve DFMs were awarded to some of the other survivors of the raid.

The King and Queen visited Scampton on 27 May to meet the members of No 617 Squadron. Whilst there they were shown various badges proposed for the Squadron and the Queen herself chose the version that was eventually used. The daring attack on the dams carried out by the crews of No 617 Squadron on the night of 16/17 May 1943 has taken its own special place in the history of air warfare. It is, without doubt, the most famous of all the Lancaster raids.

The Effort Increases

At the height of the Ruhr offensive, yet another directive landed on Harris's desk. One of the plans under consideration was the 'Eaker Plan' (presented by the American bomber commander General Eaker), which argued that 'it is better to cause a high degree of destruction in a few really important industries than to cause a small degree of destruction in many industries'. A list of 76 precise targets was produced, the destruction of which was seen as an essential prerequisite to the Allied invasion of mainland Europe. Eaker stressed that his plan could only work if both the Americans and Bomber Command worked together. A directive emerged from this on 3 June and brought into effect a combined bombing strategy known as 'Pointblank', which was to remain in force for nearly a year. The four primary target systems were U-boat construction and bases, the German aircraft industry, ball-bearing production and oil installations. The overall strategic plan called for the US Eighth Air Force to attack the given targets by day and for RAF Bomber Command to attack the same targets by night—a combined offensive which in the event rarely happened.

After a nine-day break following Operation 'Chastise', the Battle of the Ruhr resumed with an increase in effort. The offensive reopened on the night of 23/24 May when the largest force since the 'Thousand Bomber' raids assembled for an attack on Dortmund. A total of 826 aircraft, including 343 Lancasters, were dispatched to the target in what proved to be an accurate and destructive raid. Throughout the next week similar large-scale raids were carried out against Düsseldorf, Essen and Wuppertal, with the raid on Wuppertal proving to be one of the most successful yet of the Ruhr offensive.

A new directive of 10 June continued the general precepts of 'Pointblank' but with a somewhat different slant on the target systems to be attacked. Much of the wording in the directive was vague, which gave Harris the flexibility he needed in his selection of targets. There was certainly nothing in the directive to deflect Harris from his now well-established campaign of attacks against key industrial cities, all of which contained at least some element covered by the target systems referred to in the directive.

Lancaster production was reaching good levels and the expansion of the force was taking effect. This generally enabled large numbers of aircraft to be available for operations whenever required. In an attempt to keep losses low, Fighter Command instituted offensive patrols ('Flower') against German night fighter airfields to coincide with the period that the bomber force was crossing the enemy coast. These were further developed to include AI-equipped aircraft patrolling around the German airfields (known as 'Mahmoud').

The middle of June saw further large-scale efforts against Düsseldorf and Bochum and smaller-scale raids against Oberhausen and Cologne. One interesting raid was on the night of 11/12 June when 72 bombers of No 8 Group, including 29 Lancasters, were dispatched against Münster as part of an H2S trial. The marking and bombing proved accurate and much damage was done to the railway installations. Two of the Lancasters failed to return.

On the night of 20/21 June a force of 60 Lancasters took part in a highly successful raid against the Zeppelin works at Friedrichshafen. This raid was significant in that it was the first of the 'shuttle' raids, the idea being that the Lancasters were to land in North Africa instead of returning to England. The factory was an important centre for the manufacture of Würzburg radars and the destruction of this target would help the overall Bomber Command offensive by reducing their supply. An account from one of the crew members involved was as follows:

'Approaching the French coast at 19,000ft we encountered heavy cloud and storms up to 24,000ft. We descended down to 5,000ft and were suddenly engaged by the defences of Caen and Le Havre for about four minutes. We altered course and changed our height to avoid the flak. We flew on below cloud at about 3,000ft across France and encountered no further opposition. About 45 minutes from the target area we had to feather our port inner engine, which had been emitting sparks, and so we continued on three engines until we sighted Lake Constance. As the port inner engine is essential for the Mk XIV bomb sight it was unfeathered and allowed to windmill but shortly after the engine caught fire. We were unable to feather it or extinguish the fire, which grew in intensity. We jettisoned our bombs and prepared to abandon the aircraft when the engine seized and the fire went out. By this time we were at 4,000ft but were able to maintain height. We stayed over Lake Constance and had an excellent view of the attack. There were approximately sixteen to twenty heavy flak guns and about the same number of light flak guns with about 25 searchlights, all within a radius of about six miles of the target. As the defences were heavier than expected the attack was eventually delivered between 10–15,000ft. Leaving the target area, we flew over the Alps at about 14,000ft. The 600-mile flight over the Mediterranean was slow, as we were limited to 140mph to prevent overheating. Eventually we sighted the Algerian coast and landed at Maison Blanche at 0752 hours, after a flight of more than ten hours.'

The attack had been in two parts, the first bombs falling on TIs provided by a small number of PFF aircraft and the second attack being a timed run from a visual point on the shores of the Lake (a technique developed by No 5 Group). The factories received numerous hits and were heavily damaged, with no aircraft lost. Three nights later 52 of the Lancasters flew back to England, bombing targets at La Spezia on the way home.

The final four weeks of the Battle of the Ruhr saw attacks on Krefeld, Mülheim, Wuppertal and Gelsenkirchen (twice) and a small campaign of three raids against Cologne between 28 June and 9 July. This period concluded with a return to Turin on the night of 12/13 July. The nights were getting shorter as summer progressed and so only the nearer targets could be attacked. However, increased losses were placing a strain on the resources. The majority of losses could be attributed to the growing strength and efficiency of the German night fighter defences, including the operational début in early July of JG 300 operating single-engine fighters in the *Wilde Sau* tactic.

Operation 'Gormorrah', July–August 1943

After the battle of the Ruhr it was the turn of Hamburg, and during a ten-day period between 24 July and 3 August 1943 the city received four very heavy and accurate attacks. Hamburg was considered a target of major importance as it was Germany's second largest city; more importantly, it was the country's largest port.

Although outside the range of Oboe, the city and port area were considered ideal for H2S and, therefore, for accurate marking.

The offensive opened on the night of 24/25 July when 347 Lancasters were included in a force of 791 aircraft detailed to attack the centre of the city. Although bombing was spread, the raid resulted in much damage to the centre and surrounding districts. The raid marked another significant event in that it was the first occasion on which the main bomber stream used Window. The use of Window against the Würzburg ground radars proved most successful and caused great confusion in the German ground defences. Three nights later the force returned to the city, when weather conditions were such that the concentrated bombing developed into a firestorm lasting several hours. From the results of the first two raids, a third raid took place on the night of 29/30 July when a similar-sized force returned to bomb the remaining areas of the city, causing considerable damage to residential areas. The last of the raids took place on the night of 2/3 August, but bad weather over the target area militated against success and many crews bombed alternative targets.

The total effort of the four raids amounted to over 3,000 Bomber Command sorties, of which nearly half were by Lancasters, and dropped a total of nearly 10,000 tons of bombs on the city. Altogether 39 Lancasters failed to return. The offensive was the subject of a report by the Operational Research Section: 'The very low casualties incurred in the first two raids were largely due to the temporary disorganization of the German fighter defences by a new countermeasure which precluded the vectoring of night fighters. The final attack was ruined by an unexpected deterioration of weather conditions over the target. The loss of aircraft is a high price in itself, but in comparison with the loss sustained by Germany in the almost complete annihilation of her second city, it can only be regarded as minute. The destruction of Hamburg by bombing was thus far the stiffest task yet undertaken in air warfare. It was not until 1 August that smoke from the conflagrations cleared sufficiently to make reconnaissance possible. The heavily damaged areas covered 6,200 out of the 8,380 acres which comprise Hamburg's closely built-up residential areas. All parts of the city and dock were shattered: all four main shipbuilding yards were hit, five floating

A Lancaster Mk II of No 408 Squadron RCAF. This aircraft, D5723 'EQ-B', failed to return from Berlin on the night of 26/27 November 1943 when flown by the Squadron Commander, Wg Cdr A. Mair.

docks were sunk or badly damaged, 150 industrial plants were destroyed or badly damaged, plus massive distortion of communications and power.' German reports were equally candid about the extent of the destruction: 'The port was severely hit, the damage was gigantic. The failing of the water system, and the fighting of the fires which remained from earlier attacks, hampered all work severely. The whole of Hamburg was on fire. Economically, Hamburg was knocked out, as even the undamaged parts had to stop work on account of the destruction of water, gas and electricity supplies.'

Operation 'Hydra': Peenemünde, 17/18 August 1943

Early August brought a large-scale return to Italy, mainly to encourage that country to leave the war. Genoa, Milan and Turin were attacked on a number of nights by Lancasters of the Main Force: 197 Lancasters against all three targets on the night of 7/8 August, 321 to Milan on 12/13

August, a further 140 to Milan two nights later and 199 against the same target the night after that. These raids had a major impact on Italian morale and undoubtedly contributed to the Italian decision to seek an armistice a few weeks later.

On the night of 17/18 August Bomber Command launched Operation 'Hydra', an attack on the German research installation at Peenemünde. There had been increasing evidence that the Germans had been working on rocket weapons and that one of the most important installations was located at Peenemünde on the Baltic coast. The War Cabinet had decided that the site must be destroyed and called on Bomber Command to mount a large-scale attack at the earliest opportunity. Harris had initially insisted on a slight delay so that his bombers could take advantage of the longer nights and, in the interim, time could be spent preparing a suitable plan. In the event the plan was to be one of the most complex yet devised and it was to include a number of novel features, for example the use of a Master Bomber, on this occasion Group Captain John Searby of No 83 Squadron based at Wyton (Searby had been partially successful in a rehearsal of the role against Turin on the night of 7/8 August).

A force of 324 Lancasters was included in a total of 596 aircraft detailed to attack Peenemünde, including the first Mk II

The first of the Lancaster Mk Xs built in Canada and delivered to the United Kingdom. This aircraft, KB700, was issued to No 405 Squadron at Gransden Lodge in October 1943.

Lancasters of No 6 (RCAF) Group. The route was devised to cause confusion to the German defences: it was desirable to try and hide the intention of the Main Force for as long as possible if the raid were to be successful. A diversionary raid managed to keep most of the night fighters away from the Main Force throughout the initial phase of the attack, and the PFF managed to find the target area with relative ease thanks to the clear weather and moonlit conditions. The original markers were a little wide of the aiming point but this was soon corrected and the factory and experimental establishment received the brunt of the attack. One report from a Lancaster Mk II captain of No 426 Squadron RCAF based at Linton-on-Ouse read: 'Excellent visibility and green TIs guided us to the target. Ruden Island turning point was plainly marked with green TIs and bombing was carried out with green TIs in the bomb sight. The whole peninsula wall appeared ablaze and smoke was rising to 4,000ft. We bombed at 0036 hours from 8,000 feet. Diverted to Newmarket on return.'

Of the 324 Lancasters dispatched to the target, 23 failed to return and a further 17 other types were lost, most of the casualties being from the final wave which was hit by night fighters after the initial confusion of the diversion raids. In the weeks following the Peenemünde raid, Lancasters were continuously involved in a renewed effort against German cities and industrial targets, with no fewer than eleven major efforts up until the end of September 1943. During this period there were three raids against Berlin (a total of

nearly 1,000 Lancaster sorties) and further raids against Leverkusen (257 Lancasters), Nuremberg (349) and München-Gladbach/Rheydt (297), two raids against Mannheim/Ludwigshafen (total 611), one against Munich (257) and two against Hanover (total 634). This continuous effort brought an inevitable large number of losses, including 121 Lancasters, of which 22 were lost in one raid against Berlin on the night of 3/4 September. The cost in aircrew lives was devastating, yet the offensive against the German cities continued through October and until the middle of November. In October alone the number of Lancaster sorties on major raids passed 2,500, from which 87 aircraft failed to return; these figures do not include the number of smaller or diversionary raids carried out by Lancasters of Bomber Command.

The Battle of Berlin, 18/19 November 1943–24/25 March 1944

By the last weeks of 1943 Bomber Command was a force capable of carrying out large-scale raids, on a regular basis, deep into the heart of Germany. Harris had believed for some time that the war might be brought to a close by one final onslaught from the air. He felt that if the United States Eighth Air Force were to join with Bomber Command in one major offensive then it would bring about the downfall of Nazi Germany, thus saving a prolonged land offensive. Harris had estimated that it would cost the Allies a total between 400 and 500 aircraft but would cost Germany the war. However, this was

not to prove the case as the Americans were not interested in a prolonged campaign at that time and the losses to Bomber Command proved to be much higher than anticipated.

Although raids had been carried out against the German capital during August and September, the Battle of Berlin began in earnest on the night of 18/19 November 1943. At the beginning of the offensive Bomber Command was divided into six Groups comprising 57 heavy bomber squadrons, over half of which were equipped with the Halifax or Stirling. The limitations of both types in performance and range led to several of these squadrons being withdrawn from the campaign and it was the Lancaster squadrons which would have to bear the brunt of the battle.

The Battle of Berlin can be divided into four phases. The first lasted two weeks and included five raids against the city. Problems with the weather and blind-bombing techniques meant that the opening raid was generally a failure. Near perfect weather conditions for the second raid, on the night of 22/23 November, led to Harris ordering a maximum effort and the total of 764 aircraft (including 469 Lancasters) was a record for the first phase of the offensive. In actual fact, the weather proved worse than expected, although this had the benefit of keeping the German night fighters on the ground. Excellent marking by the Pathfinders and accurate bombing by the Main Force meant that the raid was most successful. Harris immediately ordered another raid. There were problems, however, in preparing a force which had only just returned from the previous night and fewer than 400 aircraft were dispatched although, once again, the bombing proved to be successful. A further raid by 443 Lancasters took place on the night of 26/27 November with mixed results. Although the bombing proved to be successful, the 28 Lancasters lost brought home the fact that

casualties were going to be anything but light. The final raid of Phase 1 took place on the night of 2/3 December. It was, again, a maximum effort. This time, bad weather and a large number of German fighters produced very disappointing results, with only slight damage caused to the city.

There then followed a two-week break until the second phase began on the night

of 16/17 December. For this raid, Harris decided to make the most of a favourable weather forecast which predicted fog over the German night fighter airfields. The fog did in fact keep many of the German fighters on the ground, but not all, and several bombers were shot down en route to the target. Over the target conditions were favourable for the bombers and the attack by the Main Force proved successful, al-

The aircraft's protective covers are evident on this Lancaster pictured at Skellingthorpe during the hard winter of 1943/44.

though a total of 54 aircraft (including 25 Lancasters) were lost out of the 493 dispatched. By the end of the year two more raids against the capital had taken place, neither of which was particularly successful. Although conditions had proved near perfect, bombing was scattered and relatively unproductive for no apparent reason, and there was concern that the continuing campaign against the 'Big City' was having an increasingly adverse effect on the crews.

The New Year began as 1943 had left off, with further concentrated efforts against the capital. Consecutive raids were flown on the nights of 1/2 and 2/3 January, the first being an all-Lancaster effort of over 400 aircraft and the second seeing a dozen Mosquitos and a handful of Halifaxes making up the numbers. There had been no rest for the Lancaster crews and the results achieved were below what had been hoped. For the time being, this brought to an end a series of unsuccessful raids against Berlin. The reasons for the lack of success are not particularly obvious, although the long transits in severe weather conditions in the middle of winter must have been a factor. Moreover, the fact that there was little rest between op-

Table 15. Lancaster Raids in Support of the Battle of Berlin, November 1943–March 1944

Date	Total force	No of Lancasters	Lancaster losses
18/19 November	444	440	9
22/23 November	764	469	11
23/24 November	383	365	20
26/27 November	450	443	28
2/3 December	458	425	37
16/17 December	493	483	25
23/24 December	379	364	16
29/30 December	712	457	11
1/2 January	421	421	28
2/3 January	383	362	27
20/21 January	769	495	13
27/28 January	530	515	33
28/29 January	677	432	20
30/31 January	534	440	32
15/16 February	891	561	26
24/25 March	811	577	44

erations would have pushed the Lancaster crews to the limits of their capabilities. Although German defences proved to be strong on occasion, they were no stronger than during earlier raids on Berlin, so they alone could not have been the dominant factor. The weather over the target area was often unfavourable and made marking difficult. The fact that the Pathfinders suffered heavy casualties had two major effects on the results achieved during this phase of the offensive. First, fewer Pathfinders actually reached the target area and therefore fewer markers were dropped, making the task of the Main Force that much more difficult. Secondly, the experienced crews lost on operations could not always be replaced by crews of the same calibre. It was also noticeable that the number of aircraft dispatched for each raid, apart from one maximum effort, steadily reduced during this phase of operations. Finally, it appears that morale among the crews had begun to suffer in the face of high losses for little positive result.

By the time the Battle of Berlin resumed on the night of 20/21 January, it was estimated from Bomber Command studies that less than 25 per cent of the city had been destroyed. This was a considerably smaller proportion than that pertaining to other major cities at that time of the war— Hamburg and Wuppertal (70 per cent each), Mannheim and Hanover (55 per cent) and Düsseldorf and Essen (40 per cent). To increase the pressure on Berlin, Harris clearly had to bring more aircraft into his plans, including more Mk III H2S-equipped Pathfinder Lancasters. Over the next two weeks four major raids took place against the city, including nearly 1,900 Lancaster sorties. The most successful raid of the phase took place on the night of 28/29 January when, despite fierce air activity, the Pathfinders carried out very accurate marking which brought very good bombing results. Flight Sergeant Les Bartlett, a bomb aimer serving with No 50 Squadron at Skellingthorpe, kept a personal diary during his tour of operations during the winter of 1943/44. He and his crew, captained by Pilot Officer Michael Beetham (later Marshal of the Royal Air Force Sir Michael Beetham GCB CBE DFC AFC), took part in several raids against Berlin and an extract from his diary reads:

'The first opposition we met was crossing the enemy coast not far from Flensburg. Searchlights were more active than usual, showing us through a few very large breaks in the clouds, but the Pathfinders were on top form and put down our route markers very accurately which enabled us to keep out of the most hazardous areas. We were in the fifth wave and as we approached Berlin I could see that the attack was in full swing. With the target in my sight I could see numerous large fires and one particularly vivid explosion which seemed to light up the whole of Berlin with a vivid orange flash for about ten seconds. At the critical moment I called for bomb doors open and then released our bombs bang on target. Just as I was taking my usual checks to ensure that no bombs had hung up we saw a night fighter attacking a Lancaster ahead of us. I jumped straight into the front turret and started blazing away. It did a slow turn to port and then spiralled down to earth. From then on we saw absolutely nothing but occasional short bursts of flak, but no searchlights and no fighters at all.'

Although the raid was a success, losses had once again proved high, another 20 Lancasters failing to return. Despite these losses, the damage to Berlin was now assessed to be significant and the effect on the population must have been devastating. The weather during this period was very cold and the scattered bombing left large areas of Berlin in ruins.

The final phase saw just two raids before the end of March. There had been a long rest for the crews before the penultimate raid because the moon and weather conditions were unfavourable for operations against the city. Harris ordered a maximum effort when the campaign resumed on the night of 15/16 February. Nearly 900 aircraft were dispatched—a record number of aircraft, a record bomb tonnage for the offensive and, as it proved, the heaviest raid on Berlin during the entire war. The route taken was the northerly one across Denmark and then southeast to Berlin. Numerous combats took place, resulting in several bombers being shot down. The target area was covered by cloud, making marking difficult, although the concentration of numbers ensured that the Main Force met with reasonable success. The return journey was flown virtually directly across the North Sea.

There were several more attempts during the following nights to continue the offensive, but these attacks were cancelled on account of the weather. Other raids were made instead against other German cities, but it was more than a month before Harris decided to have one more attempt against the capital. With the planned Allied invasion of Normandy getting closer, he probably realised that this would be the last opportunity for a raid on Berlin before his forces were diverted for other tasks. For the final raid a maximum effort was ordered for the night of 24/25 March. More than 800 aircraft were dispatched to the target, but, unfortunately, inaccurate wind forecasts resulted in the Main Force becoming scattered and the Lancasters arrived over Berlin at different times instead of as one stream. Les Bartlett's diary reads:

'We took off and set course over the North Sea for a point off the German coast; this was where our first problems started. The winds were so variable and instead of passing the northern tip of Sylt we went bang into it and had to fly up the island's west coast and then around the top. Chaps were off course all over the place and some got a real pasting over Flensburg. The next leg took us across Denmark and then down the Baltic coast. Many chaps then got into trouble with the

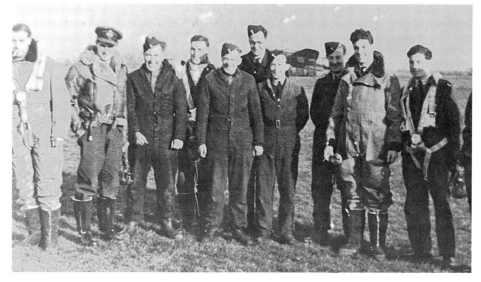

R5546 'VN-T' served with No 50 Squadron from August 1943, taking part in eight raids before being lost on the Nuremberg raid on the night of 30/31 March 1944. (Les Bartlett)

defences of Kiel, Lübeck and Rostock; I saw at least four go down in a very short space of time. We had a near squeak at Rostock as the wind blew us into their defences and we were coned by about four searchlights, but after a few violent manoeuvres we managed to shake them off before the flak got into range; they were very tense moments for us. With a strong wind behind us we were soon approaching Berlin. Luckily, over the target a thin layer of stratus cloud had formed which made it difficult for the searchlights to pick us up, so we had little trouble during the bombing run. Shortly after, however,

Flt Lt Beetham (second from the left) with aircrew and groundcrew at Skellingthorpe in early 1944. (Les Bartlett)

things started to get hot as the enemy fighters were waiting for us. Although we saw fighters we were lucky that none attacked us as we dodged the flak and kept out of the defences of Leipzig, Brunswick, Osnabrück and Hanover. Along this leg we saw several combats with kite after kite going down in flames. Luckily we got through and back home although we had to divert to another base. In the debrief we found

out that it had been a bad night although our squadron had suffered no losses.'

Many of the Main Force managed to bomb the capital but several which had been blown south had no option but to release their bombs and turn for home. However, it was during the return transit that the majority of losses were suffered. This raid proved to be a disaster for Bomber Command: 72 aircraft, including 44 Lancasters, failed to return—a loss rate of 8.9 per cent and the heaviest proportion for the offensive.

So the Battle of Berlin was over. Harris's belief that Germany would be defeated by a sustained bombing offensive against Berlin and other major cities had proved to be inaccurate. A total of over 9,000 sorties, including 7,249 by Lancasters, had been flown against Berlin during the offensive and nearly 30,000 tons of bombs had been dropped on the capital; at no stage of the war was a bombing campaign against a single target carried out with the same intensity. Whether or not the Battle of Berlin was successful has been a source of discussion and argument over the years. It certainly cost Bomber Command heav-

This Lancaster Mk II, LL678, served with No 514 Squadron at Waterbeach and failed to return from Gelsenkirchen during the Allied offensive of June 1944.

ier losses than anticipated, and of the 500 aircraft lost during the offensive, 380 were Lancasters. However, Berlin was in virtual ruins and the effect that the campaign had on local industry and the morale of the German people may never be known. Statistics alone should not determine the success or failure of the campaign; the latter had forced Germany into boosting its anti-aircraft defences at a time when steel was desperately needed for armour and had weakened the *Luftwaffe* in terms of both aircraft and experienced pilots. The disaster of the final raid should not be looked upon as a reason why the offensive came to an end. Nights were becoming shorter and bombing targets at long range was considered too risky; furthermore, Harris knew that his efforts would from then on be required in direct support of preparations for the forthcoming Allied invasion of Normandy.

The Nuremberg Raid, 30/31 March 1944

Throughout the winter of 1943/44, thousands of tons of bombs had been dropped on German cities other than Berlin as the Main Force of Bomber Command continued the offensive. In addition there were smaller and more select raids, such as that which took place on the night of 8/9 February when twelve Lancasters of No 617

Squadron carried out a raid against the Gnome et Rhône aero-engine factory at Limoges. The attack was led by the Squadron's new Commanding Officer, Wing Commander Leonard Cheshire, who marked the target from very low level. The other eleven Lancasters each dropped a 12,000lb bomb, which caused heavy damage to the factory and resulted in production coming to a complete standstill. Four nights later the Squadron carried out another specialist raid against the Anthéor viaduct when ten Lancasters made a most determined attack on this important railway link.

Despite such specialist raids by No 617 Squadron the principal effort was continued by the Main Force against German cities. For the target on the night of 30/31 March Harris chose Nuremberg—an interesting choice since the city was not known as being of major industrial importance. There were, however, several small factories around the city and it was a central link in rail and water communications. The force of 795 aircraft dispatched to the target included 572 Lancasters and the raid proved to be the worst night for Bomber Command. An extract from Les Bartlett's diary reads:

'Everything was quiet during the climb to 20,000ft over the Channel. We crossed the enemy coast and as we drew level with

ED588 'VN-G' of No 50 Squadron. This Lancaster completed at least 126 operational sorties, of which 116 were flown with No 50 Squadron at Skellingthorpe. The aircraft was lost soon after this photograph was taken, during a raid on Königsberg on the night of 29/30 August 1944.

the south of the Ruhr valley things began to happen. Enemy night fighter flares and their familiar red Very signals were all around us and in no time at all combats were taking place with aircraft going down in flames on all sides. So serious was the situation that I remember looking out at the other poor blighters going down and thinking to myself that it must be our turn next; it was just a question of time. We altered course for Nuremberg and I looked down on the starboard beam at the area over which we had just passed. It looked like a battlefield: there were kites burning on the deck all over the place with bombs going off where they had not been jettisoned and incendiaries burning across the whole area—such a picture of aerial disaster I had not seen before and certainly hope never to see again.

'On the way to the target the winds became changeable and we almost ran into the defences of Schweinfurt but altered course in time. The defences of Nuremberg were nothing to speak of—a modest amount of heavy flak which did not prevent us doing a normal approach—and we were able to see the TIs dropped by the Pathfinders and score direct hits with our 4,000lb "Cookie" and our 1,000lb bombs and incendiaries. With our

eyes peeled we were able to successfully get out of the target area, which was always a dodgy business, and set course for home. However, the varying winds continued to cause us a dance and we found ourselves approaching Calais instead of being 80 miles further south so we had a slight detour to avoid their defences. Once near the coast it was nose down for home as fast as possible but even then we saw some poor bloke "buy it" over the Channel. Back in debriefing we heard the full story of our squadron's effort: four aircraft lost with another written off on take-off. It was the worst night for our squadron and for Bomber Command.'

Of the 795 aircraft, 95 failed to return, including 64 Lancasters. A further five Lancasters were written off after returning to base and many more were seriously damaged; overall, the losses represented 12.1 per cent of the Lancaster force dispatched to the target. It appears that the weather forecast had been wrong and several wind-finding errors had been made, causing the Main Force to become so scattered that it is estimated that 20 per cent of the aircraft did not pass within 30 miles of one turning point. This led to a 'straggling' force of more than 100 bombers which then bombed the town of Schwein-

furt by mistake. Finally, the *Luftwaffe* night fighters scored considerable successes. The first fighters had appeared before the bombers reached the Belgian border and constantly harassed the force for the next hour. By the time the Main Force had reached Nuremberg, some 80 bombers had been shot down with a further 55 aircraft having aborted for technical reasons. The main raid at Nuremberg was considered a failure. The city was covered by cloud and little damage was done to the target area. It later appeared, from German sources, that most of the damage done at Nuremberg was to residential areas, with only slight damage to industrial buildings.

Operation 'Overlord', 6 June 1944

The plan for the Allied invasion of Europe, code-named 'Overlord', had rapidly developed from a distant and sometimes even doubtful project to that of an imminent operation. Following the long and strenuous bombing campaign against Berlin, it had become apparent that the war would only finally end with the defeat of Germany in the field. The Nuremberg raid was temporarily the last of Bomber Command's all-out offensives against the German homeland. In preparation for 'Overlord' the emphasis was switched to targets in occupied Europe and the transportation system in western Germany, although occasional raids against cities further east were carried out in an effort to keep the German night fighters as far to the east as possible. As a part of the build-up, Lancasters also took part in deception raids against targets further north from the planned invasion area of Normandy.

The final weeks before 'Overlord' saw the Lancasters of Bomber Command taking part in a campaign different from those previous. During April 1944 less than half the bomb tonnage dropped was directed against targets in Germany and by the following month over three-quarters of sorties were against targets in France and other occupied territory outside Germany. The effort devoted in these weeks to the French railway system and other objectives outside Germany was not part of the strategic air offensive against that country, but it did have a profound bearing on it. During the final weeks before the invasion Lancasters had concentrated much of their effort on destroying the German lines

of communication in France and, in the final two weeks, had attempted to destroy the German coastal batteries covering the approaches to the French channel ports. Only when the invasion was imminent did the attacks switch to the coastal batteries overlooking the planned landing beaches.

The successful Allied invasion of the Normandy beach-heads on 6 June, and the following break-outs, did not permit Bomber Command to resume a full-scale strategic air offensive against Germany. Instead, the first week after the landings saw Lancasters flying many sorties in support of the operations, two-thirds of the total effort being against road and rail communications. Following one such raid against rail yards at Cambrai, on the night of 12/13 June, Pilot Officer Andrew Mynarski of No 419 Squadron RCAF was posthumously awarded the Victoria Cross after he had tried to save the rear gunner in his burning aircraft.

On 14 June Bomber Command was able to resume daylight operations, the first for over a year. Such raids were again possible as the bombers could expect fighter cover for short penetration attacks. The target for the first operation was German naval shipping at Le Havre which had been opposing Allied shipping off the Normandy beaches. An all-Lancaster force of 221 aircraft took part and, despite the protection of fighters, many bombers became exposed to fighter activ-

ity although remarkably only one Lancaster was lost. Poor weather and cloudy conditions around the target area made accurate bombing difficult. A certain amount of success was achieved, however, by Lancasters of No 617 Squadron which dropped 'Tallboys' against the E-boat pens. However, the exposure to fighters in daylight, and the risk to French civilians, led to a reluctance to dispatch more daylight raids than necessary, although many more support operations were flown during the rest of June.

V-Weapon Sites

Although Operation 'Overlord' took much of the attention throughout June, many other operations were carried out by the Lancaster squadrons during the latter half of the month and throughout the summer. The most notable of the efforts, which relied on great courage and determination by the crews involved, was the bombing campaign against the V-weapon sites. These raids, often carried out in daylight, began in earnest on the night of 16/17 June when a force of 400 aircraft, including 236 Lancasters, conducted raids on four sites in the Pas de Calais area. The targets were marked by Oboe Mosquitos and the bombing was assessed to be successful, with no aircraft lost. By the fourth week of the campaign Lancasters had taken part in more than a dozen major efforts against the V-weapon sites, with many more smaller-scale raids. The targets varied from the actual launch sites to their supporting fuel installations and storage facilities.

The bombing effort was immense, such was the fear of Germany's new secret weapons. The largest raid throughout this opening month of the campaign took place on the night of 24/25 June when 535 Lancasters formed part of a force of 739 aircraft detailed to attack seven V-weapon sites. It was a clear night and much damage was caused to the sites, although accurate assessment was difficult due to the continuous destruction now being caused. The clear night also gave the German night fighters successes and 22 Lancasters failed to return. Three nights later a similar-sized force returned: this time 477

Table 16. Major Lancaster Operations in Support of Operation 'Overlord', June 1944

Date	Target	Dispatched	Losses
5/6	Coastal batteries	551	1
6/7	Communications	589	10
7/8	Communications	122	17
8/9	Communications	286	3
9/10	Airfields	206	0
10/11	Railways	323	15
11/12	Railways	225	3
12/13	Communications	285	6
14	Le Havre	221	1
14/15	Troop positions/railways	284	1
15	Boulogne	155	0
15/16	Ammunition dumps/railways	303	11
17/18	Railways	196	1
22/23	Railways	111	4
27/28	Railways	214	4
30	Villiers-Bocage	151	1

Table 17. Major Lancaster Operations Against V-Weapon Sites, June–August 1944

Date	Dispatched	Losses
16/17 June	236	—
23/24 June	226	5
24/25 June	535	22
27/28 June	477	3
29 June	286	3
2 July	374	—
4/5 July	231	13
5/6 July	321	4
6 July	210	—
20 July	174	1
1 August	385	—
2 August	234	2
3 August	601	6
4 August	112	2
5 August	257	—
31 August	418	6

Lancasters were involved and three failed to return.

The offensive continued through July and August with little respite for the crews. The biggest effort of all against the V-weapon sites was a daylight raid on 3 August when a force of more than 1,100 aircraft, including 600 Lancasters, was detailed to attack sites at Trossy St Maximin, Bois de Cassan and Forêt de Nieppe. Clear weather in the target area led to successful results, with just six Lancasters failing to return. Many pilots distinguished themselves during this period of operations, none more than Squadron Leader Ian Bazalgette of No 635 Squadron, who was posthumously awarded the Victoria Cross following a raid against a V-1 storage depot at Trossy St Maximin. Despite the fact that his aircraft had been hit by flak during the run-in to the target, he carried on to release his markers so that the rest of the Main Force could accurately bomb the target. His aircraft eventually became uncontrollable but he managed to recover enough for four members of his crew to parachute to safety. He force-landed the aircraft with two of his crew members still on board, one of whom was wounded, but the Lancaster then suddenly exploded and killed all three men.

Operation 'Pavarane', September–November 1944

The V-weapon launch sites and storage sites took much of Bomber Command's efforts throughout the summer of 1944, as did the continuing attacks against the French railways in support of 'Overlord' and against the plants desperately trying to supply oil and aviation fuel to the German fighter bases. In September 1944 Lancasters from two squadrons were tasked with yet another special operation. The Admiralty believed that the German battleship *Tirpitz*, then anchored in the Kaa Fjord in northern Norway, was about to put to sea. This ship remained a major concern for Churchill, who was determined to achieve her destruction. Unfortunately, when armed with a 12,000 'Tallboy' bomb, the Lancaster did not have the range to reach the fjord from a British base. However, the Russians agreed to allow British aircraft to use an airfield at Yagodnik near Archangel, and so a raid was planned to be carried out by twenty Lancasters of No 617 Squadron, led by Wing Commander 'Willie' Tait, and eight-

ED860 (foreground) and ED588 about to take off from Skellingthorpe in 1944. ED860 flew a total of 130 'ops' before being written off following a crash in October 1944.

een Lancasters of No 9 Squadron, led by Wing Commander James Bazin.

The original plan, code-named Operation 'Pavarane', which was for the Lancasters to take off from Scotland, attack the *Tirpitz* and then fly on to Yagodnik, was abandoned on the morning of 11 September; so the alternative plan, to fly direct to Russia and to operate from there, was adopted. The squadrons were ordered to take off at 1700 hours in order to land at Yagodnik soon after dawn on 12 September, and then carry out the raid later that day.

Weather conditions were as forecast until the aircraft reached the Russo-Finnish frontier. From there on, some 200 miles, conditions became extremely bad: the cloud base was between 150 and 300ft, with visibility in heavy squalls down to 600yd. This was certainly not the weather that had been forecast and, combined with the fact that no navigation aids were available, it meant that the arrival in the vicinity of Archangel was as difficult as one could possibly imagine. The force had become quite scattered, but most managed to land undamaged at various airfields,

although six aircraft did crash. Not all the aircraft that landed undamaged were fit to operate. Many required repairs, the crews were exceptionally tired, and there was no question of operating that day. The immediate aim was to recover all the aircraft to Yagodnik in preparation for the attack, and it was not until 0500 hours on 14 September that all serviceable aircraft were ready.

Weather forecasts for 15 September indicated that there would be the chance of a cloudless sky over Kaa Fjord during the afternoon, and, following a weather reconnaissance by a Mosquito, the decision was made to carry out the attack. Led by Tait, the 28 Lancasters took off from 0630 hours and the force set course at a very low altitude. Twenty-one aircraft were armed with 'Tallboys' and the other seven carried 500lb 'Johnny Walker' mines, specially designed for attacking ships in shallow water.

The operation proceeded as planned until the final run-in to the target. Several 'Tallboy' aircraft did not bomb on the first run because bombs hung up or because the run was not quite good enough. Even-

tually seventeen 'Tallboys' were dropped, two hung up and two were taken back to Yagodnik because, by that time, the target had become obscured under a smokescreen and could not be identified. No fighter opposition was encountered, and the flak, although plentiful, was ineffective. All 'Johnny Walker'-equipped aircraft dropped their mines, and all returned safely to Yagodnik.

It was difficult to assess the result of the attack from the interrogation of the crews, their observations having been hampered by the very effective smokescreen. Many crews saw a large red flash followed by black smoke from the area of the *Tirpitz*, but there was no definite evidence that this represented a hit on the battleship. A Mosquito made an attempt to obtain photographs of the *Tirpitz* two hours after the attack, but by then low cloud covered the fjord. The pilot did manage, however, to sight the *Tirpitz* through a gap in the cloud from 9,000ft, but he could only report that

R5868 flew a total of 137 'ops' and is now preserved in the RAF Museum at Hendon.

A daylight bombing photograph of Heinsburg taken on 16 November 1944 by F/O Rowe's crew of No 115 Squadron. (Alan Rowe)

the battleship was still afloat. It was not until 20 September that photographs were eventually taken by the Mosquito, and from these there was sufficient detail to show that one hit may have been obtained.

After the operation had been completed all efforts were made to return the aircraft to Britain as quickly as possible. Unknown to the crews and the Admiralty at the time, the damage caused by the attack had been sufficient to prevent the Germans returning the *Tirpitz* to full seaworthiness, which resulted in her move south near Tromsø for use as a heavy artillery battery. This move meant that a second attack on the battleship could be carried out from a base in Scotland.

On 29 October Tait led a force of 40 Lancasters, 20 each from Nos 617 and 9 Squadrons, from Lossiemouth to attack the *Tirpitz* once again. Unfortunately they arrived to find the fjord covered by cloud. Thirty-two aircraft released their 'Tallboys' but none hit the battleship. Just one aircraft was damaged by flak, but it managed to land in Sweden.

Finally, on 12 November Tait led a third attack on the *Tirpitz*. Thirty-one Lancasters (eighteen from No 617 Squadron and thirteen from No 9 Squadron) took off from Lossiemouth and, this time, arrived to find clear weather over the ship. Complete surprise was achieved and no smokescreen obscured the target. During the attack several hits were seen by the Lancaster crews, followed by a tremendous explosion as one of the battleship's magazines blew up. At 0952 hours the mighty *Tirpitz* rolled over and capsized. Just one Lancaster was damaged by flak, but again it was able to land in Sweden.

As a result of the attack, messages of congratulation arrived at the two squadrons from the highest of authorities. For his excellent leadership throughout the three raids on the *Tirpitz*, Wing Commander 'Willie' Tait was awarded a third bar to his DSO—the first time an RAF officer had been so honoured.

To Final Victory

During September Lancasters of Bomber Command had been involved in supporting the airborne landings of British and American troops at Arnhem and Nijmegen as part of Operation 'Market Garden'. On the opening night, 16/17 September, a force of 200 Lancasters carried out attacks against various *Luftwaffe* airfields and flak installations. During the following day and night many more supporting operations were flown by Lancasters of Nos 1 and 8 Groups.

More specialist sorties were flown by Lancasters of No 617 Squadron, including a medium- and low-level attack by thirteen aircraft against the Kembs Dam on the Rhine on 7 October. The force dropped 'Tallboys' and the attack proved successful as the gates to the dam were destroyed, although two of the low-level Lancasters were shot down.

Although No 617 Squadron was the leader in specialist raids, it was not the only unit to carry out such attacks. Its friendly rival from such raids as attacks on the *Tirpitz*, No 9 Squadron, carried out an attack the following week on the Sorpe Dam. This dam in the Ruhr area had been one of the targets on the famous Dams Raid some seventeen months before. Eighteen Lancasters carried out the attack and, although hits were observed, no breach was made.

By the end of 1944 the Allied armies were approaching the Rhine and, on their way, had overrun the V-weapon launch sites. This presented the opportunity for a final and overwhelming strategic air offensive against Germany. Thus, beginning early on 14 October, the Allies launched an all-out assault against targets in the densely populated area of the Ruhr with the intention of demonstrating overwhelming air superiority. Codenamed Operation 'Hurricane', the offensive was a joint maximum effort by Bomber Command and the United States Eighth Air

Force. Bomber Command's first raid consisted of over 1,000 bombers (including 519 Lancasters), with fighter escort, detailed to attack the city of Duisburg. This was backed up by the Eighth Air Force dispatching over 1,000 bombers, and nearly as many fighters, to the Cologne area. That night Bomber Command continued the offensive with another raid of more than 1,000 aircraft against Duisburg, the total effort against that city during the twenty-hour period involving 8,500 tons of high-explosive and incendiary bombs.

During October Lancasters continued the offensive against many of the German cities with thousands of sorties throughout the month, Cologne, Essen, Stuttgart and Wilhelmshaven being among the targets. By now the *Luftwaffe* was beginning to experience serious problems and its losses were beginning to tell, although the night fighters continued to achieve suc-

cesses. From German records it is estimated that the total *Luftwaffe* strength towards the end of 1944 stood at about 1,800 aircraft, with about 200 able to take to the air at any one time to meet each attack. However, the increasing shortage of fuel at the night fighter bases meant that aircraft could sometimes be employed only for a matter of a few days or nights during any one month.

The German Ardennes Offensive began on 14 December and the pressure on the Lancaster crews remained high. The Pathfinders continued to lead the way and many gallant airmen distinguished themselves. One such pilot was Squadron Leader Robert Palmer of No 109 Squadron, who was posthumously awarded the Victoria Cross for leading a daylight raid against Cologne on 23 December. It was his 111th 'op'. Palmer typified the gallantry of the Lancaster crews, who con-

Above: A No 61 Squadron crew at Skellingthorpe, pictured in front of RF160, a Lancaster Mk I delivered towards the end of the war.

Right: The ill-fated crew of *Mickey the Moocher* (EE176), who were killed during a raid on Würzburg on the night of 14/15 March 1945 when they left this aircraft behind and took another Lancaster instead.

tinued to press home every attack with the utmost determination and skill. Indeed, on the very first day of the New Year, one of the bravest acts by a young serviceman was witnessed, resulting in the posthumous award of the Victoria Cross to Flight Sergeant George Thompson following a daylight raid against the Dortmund–Ems Canal. Further details of Palmer's and Thompson's heroism are given in Chapter 11.

By the beginning of 1945 the Lancaster force had grown to 51 squadrons with some 1,200 aircraft on operational strength. The previous year had begun with the Lancaster crews locked in a bitter struggle during the Battle of Berlin but had ended with victory in sight. Although the final victory was anticipated in the very near future, the struggle went on as the strong German resistance continued. The German offensive in the Ardennes failed but it had nevertheless held up the Allied advance and it was several weeks before the Allies could cross the Rhine.

The Air Ministry had considered a new phase of raids against German cities and began Operation 'Thunderclap' in February—mass raids against supply and communications targets in Dresden, Chemnitz and Leipzig. The first of these raids took place on the night of 13/14 February when a force of over 800 Lancasters and Mosquitos attacked the city of Dresden with devastating results. Clear

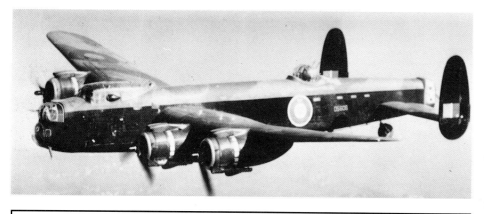

DS606, a Lancaster Mk II built by Sir W. G. Armstrong Whitworth at Whitley, Coventry.

Table 18. Total Lancaster Operational Effort, March 1942–May 1945	
Operational sorties flown	156,308
Total amount of high explosives dropped	608,613 tons
Total number of incendiaries dropped	51,513,106
Total number of mines laid	12,733
Total amount of fuel used	228 million gallons

conditions led to accurate bombing which caused a firestorm across the city and extremely high casualties (often estimated to be in the region of 50,000). The raid was, and still is, the subject of extreme criticism, not because of the size of force dispatched but because of the widespread destruction and the high number of civilian casualties. The counter-argument would be the importance of Dresden as a vital supply route to the German forces in the East facing the advancing Russian army. In terms of RAF losses, six Lancasters failed to return, and it has been suggested that any land offensive through the same area would have produced far more casualties to the Allies. The following night 'Thunderclap' continued with an attack by 500 Lancasters against Chemnitz. This time cloudy conditions over the target area meant that most of the bombing was ineffective.

The last Victoria Cross awarded to a member of a Lancaster crew went posthumously to a South African, Captain Edwin Swales of No 582 Squadron, who was the Master Bomber of a raid against a vital rail junction at Prorzheim on the night of 23/24 February. The month of March began with two large raids against Mannheim and Cologne before 'Thunderclap' was resumed on the night of 5/6 March with a further raid on Chemnitz. Extensive damage to the city was caused by large fires, although fourteen Lancasters were lost.

The following week, within the space of 24 hours, Bomber Command twice established new records for the number of bombers sent to a target. On 11 March 1,079 aircraft (including 750 Lancasters) attacked Essen, followed the next day by 1,108 aircraft (including 748 Lancasters) dispatched to Dortmund. These two raids

resulted in nearly 10,000 tons of bombs being dropped and the raid against Dortmund was to remain a record until the end of the war. The end of March saw the Allies crossing the Rhine in strength and advancing eastwards towards Berlin.

Throughout the following month the major cities of the Ruhr fell into Allied hands. By now there was no more area bombing of cities but more precise attacks against selected military targets. On the night of 9/10 April a force of nearly 600 Lancasters and Mosquitos was dispatched to attack German shipping and U-boats at the Baltic naval base at Kiel, which resulted in the sinking of the German pocket battleship *Admiral Scheer*. In support of the Russian advance in the East, 500 Lancasters were dispatched a few days later against Potsdam, a suburb to the southwest of Berlin. This was the first heavy attack on the capital since the night of 24/25 March and it proved to be the last major raid of the war against a German city. The final major effort of the war took place on 25 April when a force of 375 Lancasters and Mosquitos attacked the Berghof (Hitler's 'Eagle's Nest') and the SS barracks at Berchtesgaden in the Bavarian Alps. The weather made bombing difficult, but considerable damage was caused to the barracks.

The end of the war in Europe brought many disbandment parades as squadrons and stations were gradually withdrawn from operations. (No 50 Sqn records)

8. At Peace Once More

Although the war in Europe had come to an end there was still much to do in preparing Europe for peace once more. A large amount of humanitarian aid was needed to help the European population and there were a large number of prisoners of war still in Europe who obviously wanted to get back home as soon as possible. The Lancaster, although designed and used as a heavy bomber, was able to assist in both of these tasks. Then, of course, there was still the war in the Far East, and many Lancaster squadrons were prepared for service with Tiger Force. However, it was in this new, peaceful world that the Lancaster would see out its operational days both at home and overseas.

Operation 'Manna', 28 April–8 May 1945

As the war was already drawing to a close in Europe, preparations were made to drop vital food supplies to the civilian population of the Netherlands and on 28 April Operation 'Manna' commenced ('manna' being the Israelites' word for food in the Bible). Unfortunately, bad weather meant that the first planned drops on 28 April had to be postponed until the following day. This time, the crews at the Lancaster operating bases were briefed on drop zones instead of targets and had been told that the Germans had agreed to let the aircraft through, in certain corridors, and that there would be no shooting. The

first sortie of 'Manna' involved 242 Lancasters to drop food supplies and eighteen Mosquitos to mark the drop zones. The aircraft to make the first food drop was a Lancaster of No 115 Squadron; aircraft of Nos 186 and 576 Squadrons followed. A total of 239 Lancasters successfully dropped over 500 tons of food at four different locations—the airfields at Waal-

Lancasters were involved in the immediate tasks required in the first days after the war. These included the dropping of food supplies under Operation 'Manna' and the repatriation of British PoWs under Operation 'Exodus'.

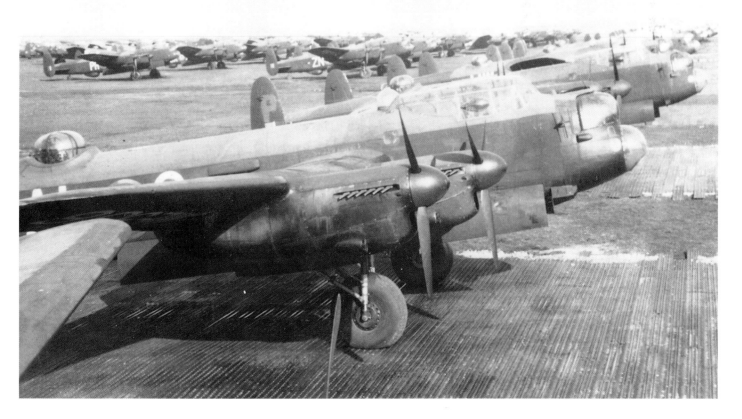

Joy on the faces of repatriated prisoners-of-war during Operation 'Exodus', which commenced on 2 May 1945. Lancasters such as PB422 were converted to carry up to 25 PoWs each back to Britain.

haven, Ypenburg and Valkenburg and a fourth drop zone at Duindigt.

Only certain areas were agreed by the Germans to be 'safe', and it was vital that the dropping force remained within these corridors and areas to avoid being targeted by the Germans—hence the need for the Mosquitos to mark the drop zone accurately. The method used was for either Lancasters or Mosquitos to drop red target indicators to mark the zone, with green flares fired from the ground to indicate that the aircraft were dropping correctly or red flares to indicate that they were straying into a danger area; the centre of the drop zone was also marked by a large white cross. The food parcels were then dropped by the Lancasters following up. To minimise damage to the food parcels and to ensure the accuracy of a drop, the Lancasters had to fly at low level (typically 500ft or less) and at a very slow speed (less than 150kt). The food parcels were dropped in large containers fitted into the Lancaster bomb bay.

Although the weather en route to Holland was poor, the visibility over the drop zone on the first day proved very good and crews could drop visually. On the following day the visibility again proved to be good and a further 1,000 tons of food sup-plies were dropped. Every time the Lancasters approached the drop zones they were greeted by thousands of people as most of the local Dutch population turned out in force. From 1 May the number of drop zones was gradually increased and supply drops took place on a daily basis. The beginning of May also saw the Americans, using B-17G Flying Fortresses from several Bomber Groups, carrying out similar drops as part of Operation 'Chowhound', which lasted the week between 1 and 7 May. Generally, a reduced crew took part in the operation so that more food could be carried on board. It should also be emphasised that men from several nationalities, including Dutch, who were serving with RAF squadrons at the end of the war took part in the food drops and much was made by the media across the world of the joint participation in the operation. After a long tour of operations this period came as one of welcome change and of great reward to the Lancaster crews. Generally, most of the food parcels were dropped accurately within the zone although occasionally some ended up in nearby ditches. There were also isolated cases when damage was caused by fire, due to the Pathfinder TIs, and there were occasional injuries caused by food parcels hitting people, but, generally, the operation proved most successful.

During the next week over 3,000 sorties were flown by Lancasters from 31 squadrons, dropping some 7,000 tons of food. VE-Day on 8 May brought an end to Operation 'Manna' although, of course, the problem of famine in Holland was far from over.

With the end of the war in Europe, plans were made for the repatriation of British and Commonwealth prisoners-of-war under the code-name Operation 'Exodus'. Many Lancasters were converted to carry up to 25 passengers for this purpose. 'Exodus' began on 2 May and the first flight back from Europe with PoWs was made from Brussels two days later. In theory, the evacuation of PoWs from airfields across Germany and France should have been easy enough, but the Lancaster crews often had to operate from damaged airstrips, making take-offs and landings extremely hazardous. Receiving camps and transit camps were set up in the United Kingdom for the thousands of men returning home from Europe, each camp receiving up to 1,000 men a day; fortunately, very few of these required

Table 19. Lancaster Squadrons Taking Part in Operation 'Manna'

Squadron	Operating Base
7 Sqn	Oakington
12 Sqn	Wickenby
15 Sqn	Mildenhall
35 Sqn	Graveley
75 (NZ) Sqn	Mepal
90 Sqn	Tuddenham
100 Sqn	Elsham Wolds
101 Sqn	Ludford Magna
103 Sqn	Elsham Wolds
115 Sqn	Witchford
138 Sqn	Tuddenham
149 Sqn	Methwold
150 Sqn	Hemswell
153 Sqn	Scampton
156 Sqn	Upwood
166 Sqn	Kirmington
170 Sqn	Hemswell
186 Sqn	Stradishall
195 Sqn	Wratting Common
218 Sqn	Chedburgh
300 (Polish) Sqn	Faldingworth
405 (RCAF) Sqn	Gransden Lodge
460 (RAAF) Sqn	Binbrook
514 Sqn	Waterbeach
550 Sqn	North Killingholme
576 Sqn	Fiskerton
582 Sqn	Little Staughton
622 Sqn	Mildenhall
625 Sqn	Scampton
626 Sqn	Wickenby
635 Sqn	Downham Market

Table 20. Lancaster Operations in Support of Operation 'Manna', 29 April–8 May 1945	
Date	*Sorties flown*
29 April	242
30 April	484
1 May	492
2 May	487
3 May	383
4 May	204
5 May	199
7 May	545
8 May	145
Total	**3,181**

hospital treatment, just a clean-up and shave! Although the Lancaster was hardly designed as a comfortable airliner, there were no complaints from the returning PoWs. By the end of the first month following the end of hostilities some 3,000 return trips between Europe and the United Kingdom had been made, returning some 74,000 PoWs. The time interval between repatriation and the return itself was typically one week. Other large aircraft, such as the Stirling, were also used in the operation. Despite the problems, 'Exodus' ran extremely smoothly and there were very few incidents. Finally,

Lancasters were also used for flying home the British Eighth Army from Italy and the Central Mediterranean, in an operation code-named 'Dodge'. However, it was September before all the troops had been returned to Britain

Lancasters for the Far East

Although the war in Europe was over, many Lancaster squadrons prepared for service in the Far East as part of what became known as Tiger Force. With the Americans using the Boeing B-17 Fortress and B-29 Superfortress for long-range strategic bombing, it was decided that an RAF element would be established which would initially consist of ten heavy bomber squadrons. It was originally agreed that Lancasters would be used until the new Lincolns were available. Lancaster Mk Is coming off the production lines at Vickers-Armstrong and Armstrong Whitworth were allocated for tropicalisation and designated Mk I(FE), the 'FE' standing for 'Far East', and stored at No 38 Maintenance Unit, Llandlow, prior to being 'tropicalised' and sent to the squadrons of Tiger Force, arriving in the Far East from November 1945. For the squadrons iden-

tified to form Tiger Force, training involved long-range sorties of up to twelve hours around the United Kingdom.

Many suggestions concerning the necessary increase in range for the Lancaster were made. One idea which actually resulted in flight trials saw two Lancasters (HK541 and SW244) being converted to carry large saddle tanks on the upper central fuselage, situated in large fairings and extending from the cockpit to just aft of the trailing edge of the wing. The saddle tanks increased the aircraft's fuel capacity by 1,500 gallons, which, however, also gave it a much increased all-up weight of 72,000lb. The possibility of increasing the Lancaster's all-up weight had been considered before, for example when it was first decided that the Lancaster would be used to carry newer and much larger weapons such as 'Grand Slam', and the carriage of extra fuel instead of an increased bomb load was simply a variation of the theme (as long as the aircraft's centre of gravity were unaffected).

The first modified Lancaster, HK541, was originally a Mk I which had been fitted with Merlin 24 engines. It had carried out preliminary trials at Boscombe Down before flying out to Mauripor in India during May 1944. The second aircraft, SW244, was a new Mk I built by Metropolitan-Vickers, and this aircraft flew out to Mauripor in August 1945, although the end of the war meant that further trials were unnecessary. The two aircraft conducted their trials with No 1577 Flight, but the aircraft's handling characteristics were poor and the Lancasters were both eventually flown home and later scrapped.

Another idea was for some 600 Lancasters to be further converted to serve as aerial refuelling tankers and for 600 Lincolns to be modified to receive fuel via a pipeline. In-flight refuelling had been demonstrated before the Second World

Left, upper: SW244 was one of two Lancasters fitted with large saddle tanks on the upper fuselage in an attempt to increase the range of the aircraft.

Left, lower: Flight Refuelling carried out trials with Lancasters for several years after the war.

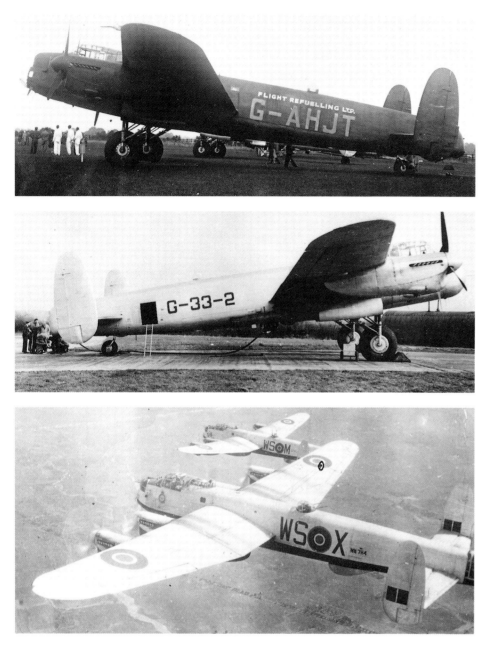

ment, including Gee, Loran, Rebecca and H2S.

It was also intended for Lancasters to provide close air support in Burma, scrambled like fighters and operating in the low-level bombing role, although this idea never came to fruition. There were many other plans and ideas for the Lancaster, including projects overseas and the possible use of the aircraft by the Royal Navy. Lancasters had also carried out glider-towing practice in India during the latter half of the war and had, in general, successfully operated in a much hotter and more humid climate. All the experiences gained from these trials in the Far East led to the various modifications incorporated in the 'FE' variants. The subsequent American atomic bomb attacks on Hiroshima and Nagasaki brought an end to all adventurous ideas and also a swift end to hostilities in the Far East, before Tiger Force had had a chance to deploy in theatre. Following the Japanese surrender the Force disbanded in October 1945 and, since the aircraft affected were no longer required to carry out these long-range missions, the mid-upper turrets were installed again.

The end of the war in Europe brought a considerable reorganisation of the RAF, and in particular of Bomber Command, which was about to introduce into service new variants of the Lancaster, the Mk IV and Mk V (renamed the Lincoln Mk I and Mk II respectively, and covered in more detail in the next chapter). The immediate RAF post-war policy concerning the Lancaster was that the tropicalised (FE) variants would be sent to the Middle East and the Far East while the standard aircraft would continue with Bomber Com-

War, although the military application was still relatively untried. Trials began at the A&AEE from the end of 1944 using LM730, the aircraft having been modified to include flight refuelling couplings. However, the increasing delays in Lincoln production meant that the programme's relevance to Tiger Force became academic, although studies using the Lancaster as a refuelling platform continued during the years following the war. Development work was carried out during the late 1940s by Flight Refuelling at Staverton, and later at Tarrant Rushton, using more than twenty Lancasters (most of which were registered as civilian aircraft) equipped as either tankers or receivers. Later trials included Lancasters refuelling Meteor jet fighters using a simple 'probe and drogue' technique. The technique proved so popular, and became of such vital operational importance, that from then on the capability to refuel in flight was included in every fighter design.

It was decided instead that the aircraft destined for Tiger Force would be standard Mk I, Mk II or Mk VII airframes with the mid-upper turrets removed to allow an extra 400-gallon fuel tank to be installed in the bomb bay. Other modifications saw the 'FE' modified Lancasters equipped with the best navigation equip-

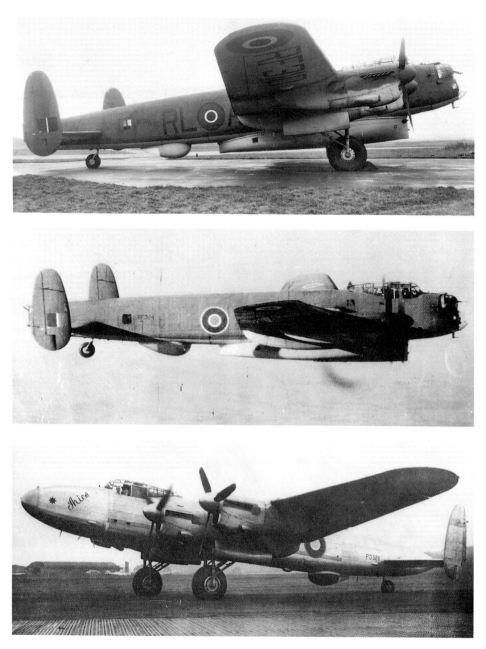

ary 1946. The Squadron was subsequently divided into two, No 179X converting to Lancasters and No 179Y remaining operational with Warwicks. This arrangement was, however, short-lived as in June No 179Y was renumbered No 210 Squadron and No 179X simply dropped the suffix letter. In the absence of a genuine maritime aircraft, the ASR.3s were employed within general reconnaissance squadrons from 1946 and into 1947. The aircraft were were equipped with ASV radar in the H2S radome and had their dorsal turret removed.

Some Lancasters became known for their peacetime service and achievements rather than for wartime operations. One of the most famous post-war Lancasters was PD328, known as *Aries*, which served with the Empire Air Navigation School (EANS) at Shawbury and had been specially modified in May 1945 to carry out flights to the North Geographic and Magnetic Poles. The aircraft was no stranger to long and unusual flights as it had already been modified from a standard Mk I during the war and had completed the first round-the-world flight by a Lancaster at the end of 1944; during the early part of 1945 the aircraft had completed several long-distance flights, visiting, for example, North America and South Africa. However, the journey to the North Pole required extra modifications, including the removal of both front and rear turrets and replacing them with aerodynamic fairings and the addition of extra fuel tanks in the bomb bay. *Aries* was also fitted with the latest navigation equipment, and during May and June 1945 the aircraft completed many successful flights within the

mand at home. However, because of the number of American aircraft which had served with Coastal Command during the war under Lend-Lease arrangements, the RAF were left without a suitable maritime aircraft immediately the conflict ended and the US aircraft were returned. Lancasters had been employed on maritime reconnaissance duties during 1942 and, although the crews then had to rely largely on visual surveillance, the airframe had proved ideal for the stresses of long-range maritime patrol. As a result, a number of Lancaster Mk IIIs were converted by Cunliffe Owen for the air–sea rescue (ASR) role. It had been intended to equip

two squadrons with Lancaster ASR.3 variants for operations in the Far East. Originally equipped with Hudsons, No 279 Squadron had been formed in November 1941 as an air–sea rescue unit and had been the first ASR squadron to employ lifeboats. The Squadron was serving at Beccles when it received its first Lancaster Mk IIIs in September 1945. A detachment of the Squadron was sent to Pegu, Burma, in December and operated from there until the Squadron disbanded in the following March. A second unit, No 179 Squadron, was operating Warwicks from St Eval in Cornwall when it received a number of Lancaster ASR.3s in Febru-

Arctic Circle before later going on to break a number of flight distance records.

Lancasters of Nos 9 and 617 Squadrons were sent to India in early 1946 to take part in a victory fly past at Delhi and also to act as a standby force for emergency operations if necessary during a revolt by parts of the Indian Navy. The detachment was only temporary and both squadrons returned to the United Kingdom later in the year. During the early part of the following year, Lancasters of No 7 Squadron based at Upwood flew to Singapore and for two months carried out live bombing in Perak prior to the emergency in Malaya. Canadian-built Mk Xs which had returned to Canada immediately after the war became involved in mapping and rescue work—other examples of the many tasks carried out by Lancasters overseas.

It was originally planned to retain about 450 Lancasters in service with the RAF after the war but this number was later reduced to under 300. Thus there was a large surplus of Mk Is and Mk IIIs, and from 1946 these began to find their way to the scrap yards. Many of these aircraft had not seen squadron life, let alone taken part in any operations. A number of Lancasters were bought back by A. V. Roe to meet various requirements at home and

Fifteen Lancaster Mk Is were delivered to the Argentine Air Force during 1948–49 and were later converted to the transport role.

abroad. One such commitment abroad was an order placed by Argentina in 1947 for the delivery of fifteen Lancasters over the following two years. These aircraft (B.031–B.045) were ex Mk Is and were delivered to *Grupo 2* of the *Fuerza Aérea Argentina* (Argentine Air Force) at Buenos Aires from mid-1948 until early 1949; three were later converted to the transport role. Of the fifteen aircraft delivered, ten were subsequently written off in flying accidents.

Lancasters in the Middle East

Even with all hostilities over, Lancaster production did not come to a total halt. With the production of the Lincoln suffering delays it became evident that the Lancaster would remain the RAF's principal bomber during the early post-war years. The Lancasters already tropicalised for Tiger Force duties were considered ideal replacements for other aircraft, such as the Liberators, already serving overseas. However, this required more changes to the aircraft as they had already been modified specifically to carry out long-range bombing attacks from Pacific bases against targets in Japan; in particular, equipment such as the mid-upper turret had been removed to enable the aircraft to carry more fuel for these missions. The emphasis on long-range capability is highlighted by the fact that the Lancaster's bomb load was considerably reduced, to a total of less than 10,000lb. Various trade-offs regard-

ing fuel load and bomb load were tried; for example, a Lancaster with a 7,000lb bomb load had a maximum range of more than 3,000 miles.

Three Lancaster squadrons were sent from Italy to Egypt to help protect the Suez Canal—No 104 Squadron to Abu Sueir in October 1945 (Mk VIIs), followed by No 178 Squadron (Mk IIIs) and No 214 Squadron to Fayid (Mk Is) the next month. In January 1946 No 40 Squadron converted from Liberators to Lancaster Mk VII(FE)s at Abu Sueir, bringing the number of Lancaster squadrons in Egypt to four. In April No 214 Squadron at Fayid was renumbered No 37 Squadron, which then converted to Mk VIIs and flew these until the unit was disbanded a year later. Prior to the Second World War relations between Britain and Egypt permitted British forces to be based in Egypt in exchange for defence and security commitments. Following the war it was hoped that peace would allow the arrangement to be resumed and that the security of the Suez Canal would be safeguarded. However, strong nationalist sentiment in Egypt after 1945 resulted in the Egyptian leadership renegotiating the arrangement: Britain reluctantly agreed to withdraw from Egypt on the understanding that she would be invited to return to the Canal Zone should the area be threatened by any neighbouring country.

There were, however, further problems. The withdrawal from Egypt meant that

Right, upper: Built as a Mk I by Sir W. G. Armstrong Whitworth during 1945, this aircraft was re-registered and delivered to the Egyptian Air Force in 1950.

Right, lower: Under the Western Union agreements of 1948, the decision was made to re-equip the French *Aéronavale* with modified Lancasters to carry out maritime reconnaissance duties. The first aircraft was delivered in January 1952.

Palestine had to provide facilities if Britain were to maintain the security of the Canal, and early in 1947 it was clearly stated by the British Government that the defence of Palestine was essential to the security of Egypt, which had been Britain's main base in the Mediterranean. With the war in Europe over, however, many Jews tried to move to Palestine, threatening the British Mandate and also the generally peaceful co-existence, maintained by the British, between Arabs and Jews in a land which both claimed to be theirs. The Mandate was due to expire in May 1948, and increasing resentment, particularly amongst the European Jews who wanted an independent state, led to bitter unrest. The Arabs felt threatened by the ever increasing number of Jewish immigrants and as a result the RAF and Royal Navy stepped up their patrols in the Eastern Mediterranean. Lancasters of Nos 37 and 38 Squadrons operating out of Ein Shemer (south of Haifa) in Palestine assisted the control of Jewish immigration by preventing illegal entry via the Mediterranean. These two squadrons operated in the long-range reconnaissance role and carried out many air–sea searches in the central and eastern Mediterranean. By the end of 1947 many attempts to beat the blockade had taken place and the Lancasters were kept busy trying to spot the growing number of immigrant-laden vessels, many of which approached at night. The role of the RAF in anti-immigration operations brought attacks on the British by active terrorist organisations and the troubles in Palestine reached new heights in early 1948. The result was the evacuation of all service and civilian families in Palestine and the withdrawal of the two Lancaster squadrons to Luqa in Malta

during March, although No 38 Squadron retained a detachment in Palestine operating out of Ramat David in the Haifa enclave until May. With the end of the British involvement in Palestine, Egypt ordered nine Lancaster Mk Is as heavy bombers, although these were not delivered until two years later.

Under the Western Union agreements of 1948 the decision was made to re-equip the French *Aéronavale* (Naval Air Arm) with modified Lancasters to carry out maritime reconnaissance duties. As a result Mk Is and Mk VIIs were converted at the A. V. Roe factories at Woodford and Langar and designated Mk I (Modified). The emphasis was typical of peacetime modifications, when there was no longer the need for gun turrets and the large bomb bay represented space which could be better utilised. Modifications to the airframe were

quite extensive and included the removal of the mid-upper turret and the installation of extra fuel tanks in the bomb bay; additional specialist equipment was fitted inside the aircraft.

An initial order for 58 Lancasters was placed in 1948 although it was some time before the aircraft were ready for delivery. The Lancasters were allocated Western Union (WU) registrations, and the first airframe (WU-01) was handed over at Woodford in January 1952 and then flown to the French Naval Air Station at Les Mureaux. The first of three *Aéronavale* units to be equipped with the Lancaster was *Flotille 2F*, which took delivery from the following month, and by the end of the summer all three units had been equipped. By the mid-1950s the three *Flotilles* had re-equipped with American Lockheed Neptunes and the Lancasters were trans-

▲ 1

▲ 2

▲ 3

▲ 4

▲ 5 ▼ 6

▲ 7

▲ 8

▲ 9

▲ 10

▲ 11 ▼ 12

1. Lancaster Mk I PP689 was fitted with a Lancastrian-type nose, re-registered G-AGUJ and named *Star Pilot*. It was delivered to British South American Airways in December 1945 and operated between London and Montevideo.

2. This Lancaster Mk I (NG465) was fitted with a Rolls-Royce Dart turboprop in the nose and first flew in this configuration in October 1947.

3. Lancaster Mk VI ND784 with an Armstrong Siddeley Mamba turboprop mounted in the nose.

4. Flight trials of the Armstrong Siddeley Python turborpops with TW911, January 1949.

5. A close-up view of the tail section of SW342 in 1953 at Bitteswell when fitted with an Armstrong Siddeley Adder turbojet and reheat installation. (Peter Green)

6. KB976 at Malton, Toronto, in September 1951. This aircraft was modified as a Mk 10AR and used for Arctic survey work with No 408 Squadron RCAF.

7. LL735, a Lancaster Mk II, was used as an engine test-bed and fitted with a Metrovick Beryl turbojet with a long jetpipe fitted in the tail.

8. Built by Vickers-Armstrong at Chester, PA474 was a modified Lancaster Mk I and was used extensively for aerofoil trials. The aircraft later found fame as *City of Lincoln*, and it still serves with the Battle of Britain Memorial Flight at Coningsby. (Via RAF Coningsby)

9. TW911 during ground testing of the Armstrong Siddeley Pythons fitted in the outboard nacelles.

10. SW342 fitted with an Armstrong Siddeley Mamba turboprop in the nose. Around the Mamba is a waterspray rig used for de-icing evaluation.

11. Another of the variety of tasks for which the Lancaster was used post-war, this aircraft being delivered to Sweden as part of the development programme for a Swedish jet fighter.

12. FM128 was converted after the war to Mk 10MR standard and served with No 404 Squadron RCAF in the maritime reconnaissance role.

ferred to various reserve *Flotilles* and *Escadrilles*, with which they carried out a number of maritime duties until the early 1960s.

An additional five aircraft (FCL01–FCL05) were ordered to the same standard by the French *Aviation Civile et Commerciale* (Civil and Commercial Aviation) in 1952 and were delivered to France in early 1954.

A Variety of Tasks

During the latter part of the 1940s and early 1950s several Lancasters were involved in tasks which demonstrated the remarkable versatility of the aircraft. One Lancaster (TW669) was attached to Fighter Command and worked with its Communication Flight carrying out air photographic duties; another (PA427) went on to complete a six-year survey of colonial territories in Africa; yet another, belonging to the Empire Air Armaments School, known as Thor, and equipped with the latest armament, completed a tour of the Far East and Australia.

However, it was inevitable that the Lancaster would slowly be withdrawn from RAF service, and the last aircraft to serve in front-line squadrons were those of Nos 37 and 38 Squadrons which had been withdrawn from Palestine to Malta in 1948. The two units enjoyed several years in the Mediterranean theatre before the last Lancaster to leave the island, RF273, returned to the United Kingdom in 1954. The Lancaster did, however, continue to serve in Coastal Command at St Mawgan, with the School of Maritime Reconnaissance, the last aircraft, RF325, retiring in October 1956.

The increased range of the Lancaster meant not only that it had potential as a long-range bomber but also that it fitted the requirement as a civil aircraft either for a limited number of passengers or as a freighter. As early as the latter stages of the war, a Lancaster Mk I built by Metropolitan-Vickers at Trafford Park, DV379, had been delivered to Hurn airfield at Bournemouth for evaluation by the British Overseas Airways Corporation's Development Flight; it was subsequently re-registered G-AGJI and used for experi-

mental purposes. The aircraft retained its camouflage paint scheme and differed from the standard Mk I in having no gun turrets. For the next three years it carried out various long-range flights worldwide before eventually being scrapped in 1947. A total of twelve Lancasters were delivered to BOAC for development work and it was clear that the aircraft had tremendous potential in the world of civil aviation—as described in the next chapter.

Almost from the time the Lancaster entered service the aircraft was used for trials with more powerful engines. As Rolls-Royce developed an improved Merlin design, so an aircraft was fitted with an example of the new engine for trials and evaluation. This was particularly evident towards the end of the war when improved performance and range became the main objectives because of the requirements of service in the Far East. However, despite a huge effort by the designers at Rolls-Royce developing the Merlin 85 engine, only thirteen aircraft were re-engined as the Lancaster Mk VI.

It was inevitable that, following the design and early trials of the Whittle turbojet, such an engine would be installed in a large aircraft. This proved to be the case in 1943 when BT308, the first Lancaster prototype, was delivered to Armstrong Whitworth and fitted with a Metrovick F.2/1 turbojet in the rear fuselage and with a large dorsal intake and tail pipe. This aircraft was finally struck off charge during May 1944, by which time further trials had taken place using LL735, a Mk II built by Armstrong Whitworth at Whitley and delivered direct to the RAE at Farnborough, where it was employed as a testbed for Metrovick F.2/1 and F.2/4 Beryl engines.

By the end of the war the potential of the jet engine was fully appreciated and several companies became involved in the design and development work on this new form of propulsion. Ironically, despite the fact that Rolls-Royce had provided the Merlin engine, the Lancaster was not used to test Rolls-Royce turbojets. It was used, however, for development trials of the Dart turboprop, an example of which was developed by Rolls-Royce and fitted in the

Above left: A Lancaster Mk 10P (FM207) of No 408 Squadron RCAF, used for photo-reconnaissance duties.

Above right: Originally KB729, this Mk X was retained in Canada and re-registered CF-CMV for operating the transatlantic service from Dorval to Prestwick with Trans Canada Air Lines.

nose of NG465 at Hucknall during 1946–47. The aircraft first flew in this configuration in October 1947 and over the next six years carried out many trials with different Darts before being written off in an accident in January 1954.

The Lancaster was used for a number of different engine trials during the latter half of the 1940s as companies jostled for leadership in the rapidly developing field of powerplants. One of the leading companies was Armstrong Siddeley, who had developed an axial-flow turbojet and installed it into the bomb bay of ND784, a Mk III built by A. V. Roe which had already been modified as a Mk VI and delivered to Armstrong Whitworth before being transferred to Power Jets late in 1945 for further modifications and trials. The successful trials of this axial-flow turbojet led to the development of the Sapphire, by which time ND784 had been fitted with a Mamba turboprop in the nose for further trials. The Mamba led to the larger and more powerful Python turboprop, and a pair of these engines were first fitted in the outboard nacelles of TW911, a Mk I airframe built by Armstrong Whitworth after the war and delivered direct to Armstrong Siddeley. The aircraft first flew in this configuration in January 1949, and it was used for various trials before being struck off charge just four years later.

Lancasters were also used abroad for the development of aero engines during the 1950s, Mk Xs in Canada and a Mk I in Sweden as part of the development programme for a Swedish jet fighter. Closer to home, Lancasters were further used in various civil airliner projects and for aero-dynamic research projects at establishments such as the College of Aeronautics at Cranfield and the RAE at Farnborough. The aircraft proved to be an ideal platform for such studies: engines could be removed and replaced easily and various items of equipment could be added to the front or on top of the airframe. It seemed that the Lancaster could be used for almost any project imaginable at that time, and there was certainly no shortage of aircraft or of people to fly them. However, during the early 1950s many of the surviving aircraft were consigned to the scrap yards.

In Canada the story was slightly different, and the Lancaster remained in service until the mid-1950s and beyond. Many of the Mk Xs which had been built in Canada and flown to the United Kingdom during the latter months of the war returned to Canada soon afterwards whilst a decision on their future was being made. It had been originally intended that many of the aircraft would be made available for the war in the Far East as part of Tiger Force but with hostilities ending in the Pacific their future was now uncertain. Many of the aircraft were relatively new, and it was eventually decided that some of the airframes would be converted for other roles, mainly maritime duties. As a result, many different derivatives of the Mk 10 aircraft were produced and all were given different designations depending on their role. For example, the Mk 10MR was the maritime reconnaissance variant and the Mk 10N was used for navigation training. A list of the Mk 10 variants is included in the Appendices. Lancasters remained in service with the Royal Canadian Air Force until the late 1950s when many were sold for scrap, although some survived for use as transport aircraft by civilian operators.

Its various roles during the days immediately following the Second World War proved that the Lancaster had tremendous potential and that it was only a matter of developing the aircraft. First, a successor would be required for the post-war Royal Air Force in the long-range heavy bomber role. Secondly, the aircraft could be developed for military troop-carrying and transportation duties. Thirdly, there was undoubted potential for a civil version of the Lancaster for passenger carrying until aircraft companies could produce new purpose-built airliners. All these developments are covered in the following chapter. As for the Lancaster itself, of the 7,377 aircraft built, only a handful avoided the scrap yard so that the type could be seen and remembered for all time. Two Lancasters have been maintained as airworthy exhibits, one in the United Kingdom and the other in Canada (see Chapter 12 for details of the British example), whilst further aircraft have been preserved by dedicated individuals for display in museums.

9. Derivatives

In the same way that the Manchester was the Lancaster's predecessor, so the Lancaster preceded a number of aircraft which entered service after the Second World War as derivatives of its airframe, either as a replacement aircraft or using main Lancaster components in the design. No story of the Lancaster would be complete without looking at these derivatives—which carried the Lancaster's basic design in operational service until 1990.

The Avro Lincoln was the actual replacement for the Lancaster and became the RAF's standard heavy bomber for ten years following the end of the Second World War. In 1943 an official Transport Command was formed, which led to the Lancaster's being developed for troop-carrying and later for freight-carrying duties, with the transport development becoming known as the Avro York. The first Lancaster to be 'civilianised' was allocated to BOAC for conversion in November 1943 and re-registered the following year. Later-production Lancaster airframes were assembled and then earmarked for completion to a new standard which became known as the Lancastrian. Finally, the story would not be complete without discussing the development of a maritime reconnaissance variant of the Lincoln which led to the Shackleton. However, with the requirement for a land-based airborne early warning aircraft the Shackleton served well past its proposed time-scale and became a tremendous workhorse for the RAF. It was in this final role that Roy Chadwick's concept and

design lived on until finally being phased out of service in 1990, more than 50 years after the first flight of the Avro Manchester and only just short of 50 years since the Lancaster entered operational service.

The Avro Lincoln

Originally designated the Lancaster Mk IV, and officially renamed in August 1944, the Avro Lincoln was designed to meet Air Ministry Specification B.14/43 which stated a requirement for a large bomber to be powered by two-stage, two-speed Merlins and to be capable of operating at heights up to 35,000ft. To mount the new engines, and to provide the increased lift required for an all-up weight of 70,000lb, Roy Chadwick at A. V. Roe proposed several modifications to the existing Lancaster airframe. These included a lengthened

Three prototypes of the Lincoln Mk I (originally designated Lancaster Mk IV) were built, the first making its maiden flight on 9 June 1944.

Left, top: A production Lincoln Mk I pictured in January 1945. These early examples were powered by Merlin 85 engines.

Left, centre: A Lincoln Mk II of No 57 Squadron. The Mk II was the standard production version for the RAF and No 57 was the first squadron to deploy to Tengah, Singapore, during the Malayan Emergency in 1950.

Left, bottom: RE418 was one of several Lincoln Mk IIs later used for engine testing. This particular aircraft was used by the Bristol Aeroplane Co. for the development of Theseus engines.

fuselage, a new nose design, a new wing of greater span and a modified bomb bay. The lengthened fuselage included a new section over 8ft long inserted into the rear fuselage. The change in nose design came about from an improvement in the bomb aimer's position in the aircraft by fitting a forward seat and new bomb-aiming equipment. The new outer wing sections increased the overall span of the aircraft to 120ft and were necessary for the design to meet the increased range and altitude demands of the specification. It was also planned for the new aircraft to be equipped with a heavier defensive armament, although the number of crew positions was to remain unchanged.

The new design was designated the Avro Type 694 but known amongst the workforce at the company as the Lancaster Mk IV, to be powered by Merlin 85 engines; a second variant, to be powered by Merlin 66 engines, became known as the Lancaster Mk V. The increase in span also enabled more fuel to be carried in the wing tanks, giving the Lincoln a maximum fuel load of 3,500 gallons. There were many other minor design changes, despite which the aircraft was still to be manufactured using many standard Lancaster components.

Flown by Sam Brown, the first of three Lincoln Mk I prototypes (PW925) made its maiden flight from Ringway on 9 June 1944, as Operation 'Overlord' had just got under way. The flight proved successful and the aircraft's handling controls were reported by Brown to be better than those of the standard Lancaster, despite the increased size of the new aircraft. The second prototype (PW929) made its first flight from Ringway in November, followed by the third prototype (PW932) the next year. There appear to have been differences in priorities, which probably explains why the production of the new Lincoln was not immediately put in hand. At that time Lancaster production figures were at a peak and the manufacture of the Lincoln would have had to be carried out at existing plants: despite the fact that the Lincoln was to be built using many existing Lancaster components, it was decided not to risk reducing Lancaster output by introducing the workforce to a new variant. Although the Air Staff favoured production of the Lincoln, it was established that the priority should still remain with the production of the Lancaster, at least for the time being. However, although the war in Europe was coming to an end, it seemed likely that hostilities in the Far East would continue for several months, possibly years, and so the Ministry of Aircraft Production issued contracts for up to 3,000 Lancasters of Mk IV and MkV design to be built by A. V. Roe, Metropolitan-Vickers, Vickers-Armstrong, Sir W. G. Armstrong Whitworth and Austin Motors in Britain as well as by Victory Aircraft in Canada. The first Lincoln completed in Canada (FM300) was designated the Lincoln Mk XV and it was planned for more to be completed, although this did not come to pass. Meanwhile, because of the end of the war in Europe, and the subsequent plans for the RAF to use Lincolns in the continuing war in the Far East, a programme to build Lancasters in Australia was cancelled and the RAAF opted for the Lincoln as its standard long-range heavy bomber.

Although the first Lincolns were completed in early 1945, it was not until August that the first unit, No 57 Squadron based at East Kirkby, received its first aircraft and began the aircraft's introduction into operational service. As part of Bomber Command's post-war shuffle the Squadron moved briefly to Elsham Wolds in November, where it absorbed part of the disbanded No 103 Squadron, and then to Scampton the following month. Over the next year the Squadron moved twice more, to Lindholme and finally to Waddington in October 1946. The second unit to take delivery of the Lincoln was No 44 Squadron at Mildenhall, which received its first aircraft in October 1945. Only a small number of Mk Is were delivered to the RAF as the newer and improved Mk II was soon to enter service. The Mk II differed from the earlier Mk I in being fitted with Packard-built Merlin 60 or 300 series engines. Both Nos 44 and 57 Squadrons re-equipped with the Mk II when the latter entered service; the Mk Is were withdrawn during 1947 and were transferred to the Lincoln Operational Conversion Unit at Lindholme.

There was also interest in the Lincoln from overseas customers, and this led to 30 Mk IIs being sold to Argentina in 1947, some of which were Mk Is modified to Mk II standard. One of these was later further modified to carry passengers, similar in design to the Lancastrian, and became known as the Lincolnian. Three more such aircraft were converted from Mk II standard and operated for commercial purposes in Paraguay for a short period during the late 1940s, although they did not prove particularly successful. A further variant of the Lincoln, the Mk 30, entered service with the Royal Australian Air Force following an order for 50 aircraft powered by either Merlin 102 or Australian-built Merlin 85 engines. Eighteen of these aircraft were modified by having additional radar in an extended nose and were redesignated Mk 30(MR)s. These aircraft operated with the RAAF in the maritime reconnaissance role until 1961.

There were also further developments of the Lincoln, including a Mk III, a maritime reconnaissance design (which later became the Shackleton), and a Mk IV, which was simply a Mk II with the Packard-built Merlins replaced by Merlin 85s. A total of 60 aircraft were converted from Mk II to Mk IV standard to preserve some of the Packard-built Merlins for spares as the number being made available from America shrank. Improvements in the H2S radar and other navigation equipment fitted to the later production Lincolns led to different variations of Mk II entering service.

By the end of 1949 there were twenty RAF squadrons in Bomber Command equipped with the Lincoln, operating from six main bases, and this was the height of the aircraft's operational career. Several more of the bombers operated with schools and establishments within the RAF. Some of these aircraft took part in overseas visits, demonstrating their long-range performance and navigational capability.

During 1950 six Lincolns from No 15 Squadron based at Wyton were modified with larger bomb bay doors to carry 'Tallboy' and flew out to Australia to take part in various trials. By October 1950 the number of Lincoln squadrons had been reduced to fifteen as four squadrons (Nos 15, 90, 115 and 149) all re-equipped with American B-29 Washingtons, two further squadrons (Nos 44 and 57) re-equipping in early 1951. However, the Washington's service career with the RAF did not prove particularly successful and all the aircraft were phased out of service within two years. The last Lincoln Mk II to be built was delivered from Armstrong Whitworth to the RAF in April 1951.

Table 21. RAF Lincoln Operating Bases and Squadrons, January 1950

Binbrook	9 Sqn
	12 Sqn
	101 Sqn
	617 Sqn
Hemswell	83 Sqn
	97 Sqn
	100 Sqn
Mildenhall	35 Sqn
	115 Sqn
	149 Sqn
	207 Sqn
Upwood	7 Sqn
	49 Sqn
Waddington	50 Sqn
	57 Sqn
	61 Sqn
Wyton	15 Sqn
	44 Sqn
	90 Sqn
	138 Sqn

Table 22. Deployment of Avro Lincoln Squadrons to Tengah, Singapore, 1950–51

Squadron	Home base	Deployment dates
57 Sqn	Waddington	20 March–6 July 1950
100 Sqn	Waddington	31 May–8 December 1950
61 Sqn	Waddington	2 December 1950–3 April 1951

Table 23. Deployment of Lincoln Squadrons to Eastleigh, Kenya, 1953–54

Squadron	Home base	Deployment dates
49 Sqn	Wittering	11 November 1953–16 January 1954
100 Sqn	Wittering	4 January–10 March 1954
61 Sqn	Wittering	8 March–11 June 1954
214 Sqn	Upwood	10 June–30 December 1954

Overseas Operations

During the Second World War the British had armed the anti-Japanese communist guerrillas in Malaya. After the war these same guerrillas used their power, and the presence of one million Chinese in Malaya, to try to seize power. As the situation deteriorated a State of Emergency was declared in 1948 and reinforcements were flown in to assist the restoration of law and order. Initial air resources were inadequate for the types of operations proposed and one of the important tasks during the first two years of the Emergency was the provision of new airfields. By early 1950 the communist organisation was well established and the RAF offensive element gradually increased. A major increase in strike capability came when the first heavy Bomber Command aircraft deployed to the Far East under Operation 'Musgrave'.

SX971 was extensively modified to accommodate a Rolls-Royce Derwent engine mounted in a ventral pod fairing under the fuselage, used to further the development of afterburners.

The first Lincoln squadron to deploy to the Far East was No 57, which sent eight aircraft from Waddington to Tengah in Singapore on 20 March 1950. During the following year aircraft and crews rotated every few months in order to keep a Lincoln squadron constantly in-theatre. The RAF Lincolns joined the Singapore-based Lincolns from No 1 Squadron RAAF and were used to carry out bombing attacks against communist guerrilla positions, although this task was made particularly difficult by the dense jungle areas from which the guerrillas operated. Two main types of offensive action were taken: direct bombing of communist positions, generally beyond the reach of ground forces, and selective bombing of communist groups to try and push the latter towards an ambush zone. Various techniques were applied to assist the Lincolns in finding their target, including the employment of Auster light aircraft to use smoke to mark it. A typical 'maximum effort' would consist of Lincolns dropping 1,000lb bombs on the target, followed by further bombing and strafing attacks from

other aircraft such as De Havilland Hornets.

The success of these missions is difficult to estimate because of the problems of establishing mission results, but they kept communist guerrillas constantly on the move, making it difficult for them to set up a permanent base from which to operate. No 100 Squadron took over the commitment during June, No 57 Squadron returning to Waddington the following month. The final rotation took place in December when No 61 Squadron arrived; this unit operated from Tengah until returning to Waddington in April 1951. With the arrival into service of the Canberra the commitment was handed over to new squadrons under Operation 'Mileage'. The RAF bomber campaign lasted until Malaya became independent in 1957, but the conflict continued until the last of the guerrilla groups fled to Thailand and the State of Emergency officially ended in July 1960.

Another of the so-called 'post-colonial' struggles, the Mau Mau uprising in Kenya, was one of the most vicious of small wars although the British were able to use the experience gained in Malaya to contain and then defeat the terrorists. The British presence in Kenya had been disputed by some since the 1930s. After the Second World War there was renewed activity, including the continued growth of the extreme Mau Mau society with its policy of rituals and reform through violence. Various attempts were made to achieve political settlements, but without results, and continued unrest led to the Mau Mau being declared an illegal body in 1950. By 1952 the violence had increased, and a State of Emergency was declared that October.

The air element at this time was limited and it soon became apparent that a heavier offensive would be needed; thus a detachment of six Lincolns was deployed. As with the deployment of Lincolns during the Malayan Emergency, the RAF commenced a rotation system, always maintaining a Lincoln detachment in-theatre, based at Eastleigh in Kenya, during the period of tension. The first unit to deploy was No 49 Squadron which moved

Table 24. Summary of Avro Lincoln Variants

Mk I	Served in limited numbers with RAF from 1945 to 1947
Mk II	Standard RAF variant; served operationally between 1947 and 1955
Mk II/3G	Improved H2S Mk IIIG, Gee and Rebecca
Mk II/4A	Improved H2S Mk IVA, G-H and Rebecca
Mk III	Reconnaissance project; later became Avro Shackleton
Mk IV	Mk II fitted with Merlin 85 engines
B.XV	Built in Canada to Mk II standard, with Merlin 68 engines
B.30	Built in Australia with Merlin 85 or 102 engines
MR.31	Built in Australia with extended nose for radar equipment
Lincolnian	Unofficial designation for Lincoln fitted with faired nose and tail

Table 25. Lincoln Mk II Aircraft and Performance Data

Crew	Seven (2 pilots, navigator/bomb-aimer, 2 wireless operators/air gunners, 2 air gunners)
Length	78ft 3in
Wingspan	120ft
Height (on ground)	17ft
Powerplant	Four 1,750hp Packard-built Merlin 68A engines
Armament	2 x 0.5in Browning guns in Boulton Paul 'F' nose turret; 2 x 20mm Hispano cannon in Bristol 17 mid-upper turret; 2 x 0.5in Browning guns in Boulton Paul 'D' tail turret
All-up weight	75,000lb
Fuel	3,580 gallons
Operational speed	305mph at 19,000ft
Cruising speed	244mph at 22,500ft
Operational range	2,800 miles with 14,000lb bomb load

Table 26. RAF Lincoln Operating Bases and Squadrons, 1945–63

Squadron	Dates	Operating Bases
7 Sqn	Aug. 1949–Dec. 1955	Upwood
9 Sqn	July 1946–May 1952	Binbrook
12 Sqn	Aug. 1946–May 1952	Binbrook, Hemswell
15 Sqn	Feb. 1947–Oct. 1950	Wyton
35 Sqn	Aug. 1949–Feb. 1950	Mildenhall
44 Sqn	Oct. 1945–Jan. 1951	Mildenhall, Wyton
49 Sqn	Nov. 1949–Aug. 1955	Upwood, Waddington, Wittering
50 Sqn	July 1946–Jan. 1951	Waddington, Binbrook
57 Sqn	Aug. 1945–Apr. 1951	East Kirkby, Scampton, Lindholme, Waddington
61 Sqn	May 1946–Aug. 1954	Waddington, Hemswell, Marham, Wittering
83 Sqn	July 1946–Dec. 1955	Hemswell
90 Sqn	May 1947–Sept. 1950	Wyton
97 Sqn	July 1946–Dec. 1955	Hemswell
100 Sqn	May 1946–May 1954	Lindholme, Hemswell, Waddington, Wittering
101 Sqn	Aug. 1946–June 1951	Binbrook
115 Sqn	Sept. 1949–Mar. 1950	Mildenhall
116 Sqn	Aug. 1952–Apr. 1954	Watton
138 Sqn	Sept. 1947–Sept. 1950	Wyton
148 Sqn	Jan. 1950–July 1955	Upwood
149 Sqn	Oct. 1949–Mar. 1950	Mildenhall
151 Sqn	Jan. 1962–May 1963	Watton
192 Sqn	July 1951–Mar. 1953	Watton
199 Sqn	July 1951–June 1957	Watton, Hemswell
207 Sqn	July 1949–Mar. 1950	Mildenhall
214 Sqn	Feb. 1950–Dec. 1954	Upwood
527 Sqn	Aug. 1952–May 1957	Watton
617 Sqn	Sept. 1946–Jan. 1952	Binbrook

from Wittering to Eastleigh on 11 November 1953. Again as in the Malayan Emergency, the Lincolns were used to carry out bombing attacks against the dissidents, generally dropping either 500lb or 1,000lb bombs, although they were also used on occasion to carry out supply drops to friendly forces.

The Wittering-based Lincoln squadrons continued the commitment and No 49 Squadron was soon replaced in January 1954 by No 100 Squadron. This rotation was followed in turn by No 61 Squadron and, finally, No 214 Squadron from Upwood from June until the end of December 1954 after the continued campaign of bombing against tribal positions finally began to take effect. In 1954 the RAF flew a total of more than 5,000 operational sorties in support of the ground forces. The final ground offensive, using air support, and advance towards Mount Kenya and the southern Aberdares broke up the terrorist groups and a number of defections led to the loss of local support. The gradual withdrawal of British forces commenced in 1955, although small-scale operations continued until the Emergency was declared over in 1956.

Into a New Era

As with the other piston-engine aircraft types of this period, the Lincoln was also used for the continuing development of turboprop and turbojet engines. A number of aircraft were delivered to Rolls-Royce and other aero-engine companies during the late 1940s and early 1950s. The Rolls-Royce aircraft were essentially used in the development of the Tyne turboprop engine and the Derwent and Avon turbojets. Similar trials were carried out by Lincolns with the Theseus and Phoebus engines at Bristol, the Naiad and Nomad engines at Napier and the Python engine at Armstrong Siddeley. Lincolns were used in a number of other experimental projects during the 1950s, including flight refuelling and meteorological research.

With the arrival into Bomber Command of the new Canberra jet aircraft, the Avro Lincoln was gradually phased out of service from January 1952; by the end of 1954 seven Bomber Command squadrons

Table 27. Lincoln Engine Test-Beds, 1946–54

Aircraft	Engine(s)	Companies
RA643	Phoebus	Bristol Aeroplane Co.
RA716	Theseus/Avon	Bristol Aeroplane Co./Rolls-Royce
RE339	Python/Theseus	Armstrong Siddeley/Bristol Aeroplane Co.
RE418	Theseus	Bristol Aeroplane Co.
RF402	Naiad	Napier
RF530	Tyne/Naiad	Rolls-Royce/Napier
SX971	Derwent	Rolls-Royce
SX972	Proteus	Bristol Aeroplane Co.
SX973	Nomad	Napier

had been re-equipped and by the end of the following year a further six squadrons had been disbanded in preparation for receiving the first of the new V-bombers, the Valiant and Vulcan. The Avro Lincoln was the last of Bomber Command's piston-engine aircraft before it converted to become an all-jet force. However, the Lincoln did remain in RAF service until 1963, continuing, with other aircraft types, the development of airborne radar, in which capacity it served with No 151 Squadron based at Watton.

The Avro York

Roy Chadwick and the designers at A. V. Roe had been considering a design for a future large civil passenger-carrying aircraft since the early part of the Second World War. To Chadwick it had become clear that, once the war was over, there would be a need for aircraft to be able to cross the North Atlantic on a regular basis, carrying both freight and fare-paying passengers. He also had the foresight to perceive that the world would soon be covered by a network of air routes, and he coinsidered it important that Britain play a major part in their post-war development and not repeat the disinterested attitude which had been evident following the First World War.

Chadwick started designing the future civilian aircraft, based on the Lancaster design, as early as 1941 and his first drawings were passed to the experimental department at Chadderton in early 1942. Although various civil concepts for carrying either passengers or freight were under consideration, the priority was still very much with the continuing development and production of the heavy bomber. However, there was interest in any concept which also had a troop-carrying capability, and it was along these lines that the project progressed. There was an urgent need during the middle war years for a transport aircraft, and future production would be easier, quicker and cheaper if the existing Lancaster jigs were used.

Chadwick's original design led to the Type 685, soon named as the Avro York, which was flown by Sam Brown on its maiden flight from Ringway on 5 July 1942. The first prototype (LV626) was fitted with the Lancaster twin-fin tail arrangement and powered by four Merlin engines. The original concept was very much along the lines of a military transport rather than a passenger-carrying aircraft, with accommodation for up to 40 troops. Although the Lancaster's wings and undercarriage were used, the fuselage was completely redesigned.

The first prototype suffered from directional problems, caused by the twin-fin arrangement and the change in the design of the fuselage area, but there was enough interest at the Ministry of Aircraft Production for an order for four York prototypes to be completed, with the possibility of 200 Yorks being ordered for production. It was further stated that two of these prototypes should be powered by Bristol Hercules engines, as fitted to the Lancaster Mk II, and each of the four aircraft were to be fitted in a different configura-

The first York prototype, LV626, was fitted with the Lancaster's twin fin arrangement and made its maiden flight from Ringway on 5 July 1942.

tion but with interchangeable equipment—a troop-carrier, a paratrooper, a passenger transport and a freighter. However, it was stressed by the Ministry that development of the York was in no way to interfere with Lancaster production.

In the second York, LV629, the engines were replaced by Bristol Hercules VI radials and to improve lateral stability a central fin was added. This aircraft became the prototype for the proposed Mk II and it made its first flight in August 1942, but the engine installation was not considered particularly successful. The third and fourth prototypes (LV633 and LV639) were also fitted with the characteristic central fin. The fourth prototype was fitted as a paratrooper, although disturbance in the airflow around the aircraft exits made the aircraft unsuitable for such purposes.

It was the third of the prototypes which became the most famous York throughout the war—not that it carried out any of the specific roles for which the York had been designed. Named *Ascalon*, LV633 was converted for VIP duties and delivered to No 24 Squadron at Northolt for use by HM King George VI and the Prime Minister, Winston Churchill. The aircraft was used by the Prime Minister for many of his overseas trips to war conferences, including those to Moscow and Yalta, and was also used by the King for his tour of North Africa during 1943. The aircraft served in the Far East after the war before being returned to the United Kingdom and scrapped in 1954.

Following service trials, A. V. Roe was awarded a contract for 200 Yorks to be completed as transport aircraft. Because of the continuing production of the Lancaster, initial York production was very slow and only a handful of airframes were completed in the first year. The first two examples (MW100 and MW101) were also delivered to No 24 Squadron at Northolt for use as VIP transport aircraft. The third production aircraft (MW102) was flown out to India and later used by Lord Louis Mountbatten who, at the time, was Commander-in-Chief of South-East Asia Command. The second unit to be equipped with Yorks was No 511 Squadron based at Lyneham, which received its first aircraft at the end of 1943. By the end of the war No 46 Squadron at Holmsley South and No 242 Squadron at Stoney Cross had also received Yorks. Production at Ringway had increased: some 40 aircraft were completed during the final year of the war, after which production was carried out at Yeadon, where the last batch of the original order was completed.

The York's potential as a civil passenger-carrying aircraft was recognised towards the end of the war when five aircraft capable of carrying twelve passengers were re-registered G-AGJA to G-AGJE and delivered to BOAC. These were later joined by a further 25 aircraft for world-wide travel. A number of Yorks were used as passenger-carrying aircraft with other small airlines and charter companies in places such as South Africa and the Middle East. The York proved an excellent workhorse during the years immediately after the war, until such time as air-

Table 28. Avro York Squadrons and Operating Bases, 1943–51

Squadron	Dates	Operating Bases
24 Sqn	May 1943–Nov. 1951	Northolt, Hendon, Bassingbourn, Waterbeach, Oakington, Lyneham, Topcliffe
40 Sqn	Dec. 1947–Mar. 1950	Abingdon, Bassingbourn
51 Sqn	Jan. 1946–Oct. 1950	Stradishall, Waterbeach, Abingdon, Bassingbourn
59 Sqn	Dec. 1947–Oct. 1950	Abingdon, Bassingbourn
206 Sqn	Nov. 1947–Aug. 1949	Lyneham
242 Sqn	Apr. 1945–Sept. 1949	Stoney Cross, Merryfield, Oakington, Abingdon, Lyneham
246 Sqn	Dec. 1944–Oct. 1946	Holmsley South
511 Sqn	Nov. 1943–Sept. 1949	Lyneham
241 OCU		Dishforth

craft could be designed specifically to meet the needs of the post-war world. Eventually more than 250 Yorks were completed. The last was delivered to the RAF in April 1948, by which time seven squadrons were in service.

The York will probably be best remembered as a freight-carrying transport aircraft, and it was in this role that it excelled during the Berlin Air Lift of 1948–49. After the war Berlin had been divided into sectors by the victorious occupying powers and the city immediately became a source of tension between the Western Allies and the Soviet Union. In the face of growing Soviet intransigence over the use of road and rail links into Berlin during March 1948, the Allies cancelled all movements except those by food trains. This meant that all essential supplies to the British, American and French sectors of Berlin had to be ferried by air. Under Operation 'Plainfare' the 40 Yorks used by the RAF flew nearly 30,000 sorties and delivered 230,000 tons of supplies during the year-long blockade. Six RAF York squadrons (Nos 40, 59 and 242 based at Abingdon, No 51 at Bassingbourn and Nos 206 and 511 at Lyneham) and the York Operational Conversion Unit (No 241 OCU, based at Dishforth) took part in the operation, extra effort being provided by civilian operators. Although a number of other RAF aircraft types, including Lancasters, were involved with carrying relief supplies during the Berlin Airlift, it was the York which carried the bulk of the British contribution.

The York proved to be a perfectly adequate and capable military and civilian transport aircraft. It served the RAF well as a VIP aircraft during the latter stages of the war and formed the mainstay of Transport Command during the immediate post-war years. With the introduction of the new Handley Page Hastings the York was gradually phased out of RAF service during the early 1950s, some being sold overseas and many others being scrapped—the Berlin Airlift had taken its toll! By the end of the decade only a handful were still being operated in the United Kingdom, and not many more worldwide. The aircraft eventually reached retirement in the early 1960s.

The Lancastrian

As part of Roy Chadwick's early plans to develop an airliner capable of crossing the North Atlantic, designers at A. V. Roe had been working on a project which would later lead to the design of the Avro Tudor. With the Avro York proving successful as a freight-carrying transport aircraft, the design team concentrated on an interim project based on adapting the Lancaster airframe to become Britain's first post-war airliner.

The first Lancaster to be converted for civilian use was DV379, a Mk I built by Metropolitan-Vickers, which was delivered to BOAC for conversion on 9 November 1943. It carried out experimental flights with BOAC's Development Flight at Hurn before being re-registered G-AGJI the following year. Although Chadwick personally remained more involved with the design and development of the Avro Tudor, the conversion led to the Avro Lancastrian, which was designed straight from

the early production Lancaster which had flown to Canada to assist Victory Aircraft at Malton, Ontario, in their own production of Lancasters. The aircraft involved was R5727, a Lancaster Mk I built by A. V. Roe at Newton Heath, which was fitted with extra fuel tanks in the bomb bay and stripped of any armament which caused excess weight. The aircraft was flown from Prestwick and delivered to Victory Aircraft in November 1942, where it went through a modification programme during the winter and was then re-registered CF-CMS. The aircraft was fitted with nose and tail fairings, additional fuel tanks in the bomb bay and ten passenger seats and additional windows. There followed a number of experimental flights across the North Atlantic.

Meetings between Chadwick and his designers and the Ministry of Aircraft Production led to the Ministry issuing Specification C.16/44 which called for an aircraft capable of carrying ten passengers up to a maximum range of 4,000 miles. The variation of the Lancaster met the specification and it was decided towards the end of the war that 60 Lancasters under production would be completed as Lancastrian Mk Is for use by the RAF. Half of these were subsequently transferred to BOAC, including the Lancastrian prototype (VB873), which, flown by Jimmy Orrell, made its maiden flight from Woodford on 17 January 1945. This aircraft eventually went to BOAC's Development Flight at Hurn, Bournemouth, and was re-registered G-AGLF. In fact, none of the 60 Lancastrian Mk Is actually entered service with the RAF. The BOAC order was increased to 39, with a further two being ordered by Rolls-Royce; 23 were completed as Mk Is and eighteen were transferred for completion as Mk IIs. These eighteen were amongst a new order of 70 for service with the RAF, although several of these were subsequently transferred to the Mk III and Mk IV programmes.

The result of the changes in Lancastrian programme meant that 33 Mk IIs were eventually delivered to the RAF, designated C.2. The first of these were delivered in October 1945 to No 231 Squad-

Top: Many Yorks were eventually dispersed to smaller operators around the world. Shown here are two aircraft of Trans-Med Airways at Bahrain in June 1961.

Above: The Lancastrian prototype, VB873, which made its maiden flight on 17 January 1945.

ron at Full Sutton in Yorkshire, which became the Lancastrian Training Unit, followed by delivery to No 24 Squadron at Bassingbourn in June 1946. The operation of two Lancastrian squadrons was short-lived as No 231 Squadron disbanded the following month, leaving just No 24 fulfilling the VIP transport role. The remaining Lancastrians were located at Mamby (Air Armament School), Shawbury (Air Navigation School), Hullavington (Central Flying School), Brize Norton and Benson (Transport Command Development Unit). The service life of the Lancastrian was relatively short as by the end of 1949 it had been phased out of the RAF inventory.

The Lancastrian Mk III, known to the RAF as the C.4, was an improved variant with the capability of carrying thirteen passengers. Eighteen aircraft were delivered to various airlines and independent operators during early 1946, including six to BOAC and five to the Italian airline Alitalia. The aircraft did not prove particularly successful on long-range flights with BOAC as by the end of 1947 four of these Mk III aircraft had crashed. Another tragic loss of a Lancastrian during this period was that of a BOAC aircraft on 24 March 1946 which vanished without trace in the sea on its way to Australia. One of the passengers was Jack Dobson, the son of A. V. Roe's Managing Director Roy Dobson. It was a tragic blow to both the company and the Dobson family as it was widely believed that Jack would eventually succeed his father.

The remaining two Lancastrian Mk IIIs were later sold to Flight Refuelling at Tarrant Rushton. These aircraft were employed during the Berlin Airlift for the delivery of fuel and oil. A number of Lan-castrians also operated with minor companies during the Airlift and, like the Avro York, the tremendous strain put on these aircraft during the operation resulted in many aircraft quickly being scrapped. Eight aircraft had previously been converted from the Mk III programme to become Lancastrian Mk IVs. Of these eight, three were delivered to BOAC in 1946 and five to British South American Airways.

Although the Lancastrian provided a useful stop-gap for the airlines until better, purpose-built airliners became available, it could not carry the number of passengers that aircraft were becoming increasingly required to do. It was, however, the only commercial aircraft at that time which was capable of flying the South Atlantic. Nevertheless, as far as A. V. Roe was concerned, it would not be long before the Avro Tudor would enter service with BOAC; an initial order for twenty aircraft had already been placed. But the Tudor programme had suffered major setbacks since the aircraft's first flight in June 1945. Flight testing had not proved suc-

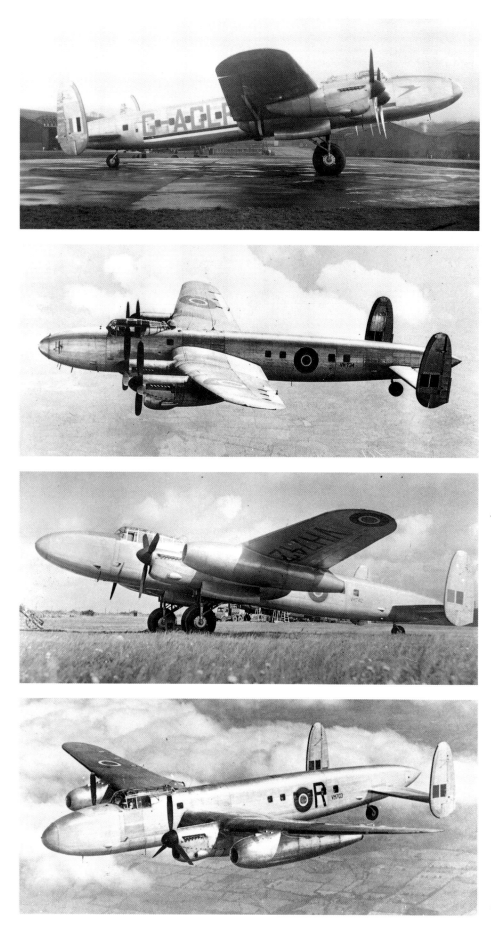

cessful owing mainly to the aircraft's directional and longitudinal instability. The greatest tragedy to hit the programme, however, occurred on 23 August 1947 when the prototype Tudor II crashed on take-off at Woodford. Amongst those killed in the accident was the legendary Roy Chadwick. It was indeed a most tragic blow to the world of aviation. The man who had been at the forefront of design for A. V. Roe since its early days, and particularly instrumental in the design of the Lancaster, was now gone. Also killed in the accident was A. V. Roe's chief test pilot, Bill Thorn—again, a severe blow to the company. Roy Dobson may well have also perished had it not been for a telephone call minutes before take-off which prevented him from boarding the flight. The crash investigation determined that the aircraft's ailerons had been wrongly connected, resulting in their performing in the opposite way from that required. It was a terrible twist of fate, and the effects of Chadwick's loss cannot be overemphasised. William Farren was appointed technical director at A. V. Roe, with Stuart Davies, who had fortunately survived the Tudor crash, remaining as chief designer. Jimmy Orrell was appointed the new chief test pilot to replace Bill Thorn. The loss of the Tudor was, undoubtedly, a major setback for the programme although the aircraft did go on to become Britain's first four-jet transport aircraft.

Left, top to bottom:
The Lancastrian prototype, shown after its delivery to BOAC's Development Flight at Hurn, registered G-AGLF.

A total of 33 Lancastrian C.2s were delivered to the RAF, the first to No 231 Squadron at Full Sutton during October 1945.

Lancastrian VH742, fitted with Rolls-Royce Nene turbojets in the outboard nacelles, was flown in August 1946.

Lancastrian VM703 served with the RAF before being delivered to De Havilland and fitted with Ghost turbojets in the outboard nacelles and flown in this configuration in June 1947. Note that both inboard engines are shut down.

Table 29. Lancastrian Squadrons and Operating Bases, 1946–49

Squadron	Dates	Operating Bases
24 Sqn	June 1946–Oct. 1949	Bassingbourn/Waterbeach
231 Sqn	Jan.–July 1946	Full Sutton

The Lancastrian was used as an engine test-bed during the late 1940s and early 1950s. A number of airframes were modified and fitted with various powerplants, including examples of the new turbojets which would power the airliners of the future. Two Lancastrian Mk Is were operated by Rolls-Royce during the development of the Nene I turbojet, and the same company operated five former RAF Lancastrian Mk IIs during the development of the Avon series of turbojet engines and further developments of the Merlin 600 series piston engines. Two Lancastrian Mk IIs were also operated by the De Havilland Engine Company during the development of the Ghost turbojet.

It was not unusual to see these development Lancastrians with various fits of powerplant. Two turbojets would, perhaps, be fitted in the outboard engine nacelles and two piston engines in the inboard nacelles. As the programmes progressed, or were scrapped, two engines were often replaced by two improved types, or even two completely different types. As in other trials and development programmes, the Lancastrian did not escape misfortune. One example was the crash of Rolls-Royce's VL970 in March 1955 with the loss of the crew. Most of these trials aircraft were scrapped in the early 1950s, although the last type was not eventually retired from flying duties until 1957.

The Avro Shackleton

Although designed as a heavy bomber, the Lancaster had been used since the war in a number of roles, such was the versatility of the aircraft. The first Lancaster employed in the maritime role was the A.S.R.3, which had been converted from the Mk III bomber by the Cunliffe-Owen company for air–sea rescue duties. This variant, along with the General Reconnaissance version (the G.R.3) equipped Coastal Command squadrons at home and in Malta during the late 1940s and early 1950s. By the mid to late 1940s, however, it was apparent that a new long-range aircraft, capable of missions of some eighteen hours or so, was required. Although modifications of the Avro Lincoln were considered it was soon apparent that a brand new design was required, especially considering such aspects as crew comfort. This led to Air Ministry Specification R.5/46 (issued in March 1947) and resulted in the development of the Avro Type 696, a design concept which was essentially that of Roy Chadwick.

The A. V. Roe Company described the Type 696 as 'a four-engined mid-wing monoplane developed from the Avro Lincoln and the Avro Tudor to perform the duties of a maritime reconnaissance aircraft.' The aircraft became known as the Shackleton, after the Arctic explorer. Powered by four Griffon 57 engines, each driving six-blade, contra-rotating propellers, the prototype (WV126) first flew from Woodford on 9 March 1949. The Shackleton Mk I was just over 87ft in length with a wingspan of 120ft, and had an all-up weight of 87,000lb with a bomb bay designed to carry up to 20,000lb of bombs or maritime stores. The ten-man crew consisted of two pilots, two navigators, a flight engineer and five crew members capable of performing various other tasks. The first 29 production aircraft were delivered to the RAF during 1950–51, the first unit to operate the type being No 120 Squadron at Kinloss. One early design modification was the installation of more powerful Griffon 57A engines to produce the Shackleton Mk IA, and all aircraft were modified to this standard. A total of 47 Mk IAs were built in addition to the 29 modified airframes and the aircraft served with eleven RAF squadrons.

VW126 went back to A. V. Roe for modification as a prototype for the Mk 2, with a lengthened nose and tail and a retractable tail wheel. A Mk IA airframe (WB833) was then taken off the production line and completed to the full Mk 2 specification. The first production Mk 2

Although the Lancaster operated in the maritime role at the end of the war, it soon became apparent that a new long-range aircraft was required, and this led to the design of the Shackleton.

Table 30. Shackleton Mk 3 Aircraft and Performance Data

Crew	Ten (2 pilots, 2 navigators, flight engineer, 5 crew members)
Length	87ft 4in
Wingspan	120ft
Height	23ft 4in
Tail span	33ft
Basic weight	64,000lb
All-up weight	100,000lb
Powerplant	4 x Griffon 58 engines
Total fuel capacity	4,700 gallons

Above left: The basic Lancaster design is very apparent in this view of an Avro Shackleton.

Above right: Roy Chadwick's design concept lasted for more than 50 years: the last Shackleton AEW.2s served with No 8 Squadron until May 1990.

went for evaluation and trials at Boscombe Down in September 1952 before entering service with the RAF. The variant went through a number modifications, often just internal differences, but later more significant changes with the introduction of Griffon 58 engines. A total of 70 Mk 2s were built and served with fourteen squadrons before production came to an end in late 1954. A further design change led to the Shackleton Mk 3, the main differences being the addition of wing-tip fuel tanks and the installation of a tricycle undercarriage which increased the all-up weight to 100,000lb. The prototype Mk 3 (WR970) first flew in September 1955 and altogether 34 were built for service with six RAF squadrons, a further eight being delivered to the South African Air Force from 1957. The Mk 3 was built under different phases and included improved ASV radar and a new range of avionics and navigation aids.

The main role of the Shackleton was to seek and attack surface ships and sub-marines and the Mk 2s and Mk 3s were the workhorses of Coastal Command for many years until the introduction into service of the Nimrod. Shackletons also served in the Mediterranean and the Middle East during the 1950s and early 1960s as well as taking part in the United Kingdom's nuclear weapons development programme during the late 1950s. But it was in the role of airborne early warning (AEW) that the Shackleton was to see out its long and distinguished career with the RAF. With the phasing out of service of the Royal Navy's Gannets, there was a de-ficiency in early warning for the Royal Navy. With the long-term solution for a land-based AEW aircraft up for competi-tion, the interim solution was the conver-sion of some maritime reconnaissance Shackleton Mk 2s to the AEW role. As a result, No 8 Squadron was re-formed in January 1972 and later equipped with six Shackleton AEW Mk 2s. The delay in bringing a new land-based AEW aircraft into service with the RAF meant that the AEW Shackletons remained until 1990— a remarkable feat considering that the air-craft had only been an interim solution.

Table 31. Avro Shackleton Squadrons and Operating Bases, 1951–90

Squadron	Mark(s)	Dates	Operating bases
8 Sqn	2/AEW.2	Jan. 1972–May 1990	Kinloss, Lossiemouth
37 Sqn	2	Aug. 1953–Sept. 1967	Luqa, Khormaksar
38 Sqn	2	Sept. 1953–Mar. 1967	Luqa, Hal Far
42 Sqn	I/2/3	June 1952–Sept. 1971	St Eval, St Mawgan
120 Sqn	I/IA/2/3	Apr. 1951–Feb. 1971	Kinloss, Aldergrove, Kinloss
201 Sqn	3	Oct. 1958–Sept. 1970	St Mawgan, Kinloss
203 Sqn	I/IA/2/3	Nov. 1958–Jan. 1972	Ballykelly, Luqa
204 Sqn	I/IA/2	Jan. 1954–Apr. 1972	Ballykelly, Honington
205 Sqn	I/IA/2	May 1958–Oct. 1971	Changi
206 Sqn	I/IA/2/3	Sept. 1952–Oct. 1970	St Eval, St Mawgan, Kinloss
210 Sqn	I/IA/2	Dec. 1958–Nov. 1971	Ballykelly, Sharjah
220 Sqn	I/IA/2/3	Sept. 1951–Oct. 1958	Kinloss, St Eval, St Mawgan
224 Sqn	I/IA/2	Sept. 1951–Oct. 1966	Gibraltar
228 Sqn	2	July 1954–Mar. 1959	St Eval, St Mawgan, St Eval
240 Sqn	I/IA/2	May 1952–Nov. 1958	St Eval, Ballykelly
269 Sqn	I/IA/2	Jan. 1952–Dec. 1958	Gibraltar, Ballykelly
236 OCU	I/IA		Kinloss

Table 32. Comparison of Leading Particulars for Lancaster Derivatives

Type	Engines	Span	Length	Armament	Max. speed	Ceiling
Lincoln II	4 x Merlin 86	120ft	78.3ft	14,000lb bombs	295mph	22,000ft
York C.1	4 x Merlin T24	102ft	78.5ft	–	298mph	26,000ft
Lancastrian C.2	4 x Merlin 24/84/500	102ft	76.9ft	–	310mph	30,000ft
Shackleton MR.2	4 x Griffon 57A	120ft	87.3ft	20,000lb bombs	300mph	25,700ft

10. Flying and Maintenance

No story about the Lancaster could be written without recalling the memories of some of the men who either flew the aircraft or maintained it during the dark days of the Second World War. This chapter recalls the experiences of some of those men whose lives depended on the Lancaster. The experiences include different aspects of flying the Lancaster—the training, the first operational sortie and the quick thinking and reactions called for during flights. Also recalled are the memories of groundcrews, who worked endless hours to ensure that as many aircraft as possible were available for operations every night but who could only stay behind whilst the aircraft and crew were on operations and wait for their safe return.

Flight Sergeant Les Bartlett— Bomb Aimer

Les Bartlett was a bomb aimer serving with No 50 Squadron at Skellingthorpe during the winter of 1943/44. He was later commissioned and awarded the DFM during his tour of operations. He now lives in retirement in Southampton, and his diary, which he kept throughout his tour, reminds him of those dark days of struggle during the Battle of Berlin. Extracts from his diary have already been used earlier in this book, but Berlin was to be his first op.

'I walked up to the aerodrome at 1000 hours and immediately knew that ops were on. Men were dashing in and out of flight offices, crews in flying kit were piling into transport and everyone was generally busy. I got the crew together and we went off to do our night flying test. One or two minor defects were evident: the escape hatch in the floor of the bombing compartment wasn't quite as free as I liked it to be and

the starboard outer engine temperature gauge was unserviceable, but that was the flight engineer's problem.

'Briefing started at 1330 hours and what do you think—it's the "Big City", bags of flak; it's a helluva long trip, at least 1,400 miles the way we were going. First I drew my maps and stuck down the route, then got my bombing "gen", i.e. the bomb load we were taking, route markers to be seen, techniques to be used and which flares to be bombed should the target be obscured by cloud. That over, we all met in the main briefing room where each crew had a good chat about the trip. Needless to say, we were all very excited because, to an experienced crew, Berlin was quite an assignment, so you can imagine what we felt like to be doing it for our first trip. Then came our ops meal at 1445 hours, eaten with much relish as if it was to be our last. Now the great bind of getting dressed. I used to wear ordinary battle dress, two pairs of long wool underpants, white polo sweater, electric waistcoat, electric slippers, electric gloves, flying boots, silk gloves, kapoc flying suit, Mae West, parachute harness and helmet. I also carried two spare pairs of gloves, torch, goggles, six maps, handkerchiefs and escape kit.

'Getting in and out of the aircraft was a bind. To get from the door of the aircraft to the bombing compartment was even harder, getting hooked up on one thing and another and climbing over the main spar used to get me all steamed up. Next, as bomb aimer, I had to check my equipment—check the bomb load and settings of pre-selection switches, look over the camera circuit, check the lens heater, magazine muff and last but not least the photoflash. That I used to think was perhaps the deadliest thing in the aircraft; they

developed over one million candle power and had been known to blow an aircraft to pieces. With everything OK we started the four Merlins and each member of the crew checked his apparatus. The two gunners checked the rotation of the gun turrets, the operation of the guns and the ammunition feed. The wireless operator checked his various transmitters and receivers whilst the navigator checked his compass, the Gee set and other items of equipment. Finally, the flight engineer checked the instruments to ensure that all four Merlins were fit and healthy whilst the pilot checked the flying controls.

'It was still daylight when we lined up for take-off and it was a tremendous sight to see. Waiting to see the aircraft off were a number of ground crew, other aircrew not on "ops", the Wing Commander with the usual visitors and friends and, last but not least, the usual crowd of WAAFs waving goodbye to their boyfriends. At the crucial moment we got a "green" from the control tower and with the mighty roar of the Merlins we gave the crowd a quick wave and roared off down the runway. Dusk was rapidly falling and almost as soon as we set course we were in cloud. For me there was not much to do and so I plugged in my electric suit and made myself as comfortable as possible. It was then that I first thought about what we were about to go off and do and I realised just how frightened I really felt; after all, this was my first operational trip, and in spite of the unsuitable surroundings I said a prayer to ask for a safe flight and to enable us to return safely—to our loved ones, especially my wife.

'We climbed through 9,000ft when we broke cloud and it was almost dark. It was comforting to know that we were not alone.

Again we entered cloud and finally we levelled off at 20,000ft and settled down in the cruise. Already we could see attempts by the enemy to stem the raid: all along the Dutch coast the bright flashes of flak lit up the clouds, although the shells burst below us. I then started to set up the bombing panel—"bombs selected", fusing switches "on", distributor set—and I then started my regular bit of jamming to the German radio direction-finding apparatus (dropping Window). Far away on the port beam the defences of Bremen were in action against some poor "bods" off track. Then Hanover—they shot up all they had got, but to no avail. Our route took us just out of range of their flak, searchlights tried to pick us up, but there was enough cloud to prevent that. On and on we went, passing the occasional track marker put down by the Pathfinders until at last we made a final alteration to heading to take us towards the target.

'Excitement was now at its height—fifteen minutes to zero hour and still no sign of the attack. But time passed by and bang on time down went the first TI. It was a yellow one though, just for the use of the Pathfinders. Then there were reds cascading into greens, gradually descending into the clouds; these were the ones for us to bomb. Already I could see the first wave of aircraft unloading their bombs and at the same time I could see a line of fighter flares go down, brilliant and white, parallel to our track about two miles away, but no panic as it was a decoy laid down by our Mosquito boys. Things were now getting larger and clearer as we approached the target and then the final turn in—this was it! I kept turning my neck in an excited attempt to see everything at once. It was my job to decide in my own mind which of the target indicators were most accurate; this done, I gave the necessary corrections to the skipper so that I could get the TIs lined up in my bomb sight. At last the doors were opened, but I noticed a Halifax beneath us and decided that I didn't want to hit him with our bombs and so we did a quick weave and ended up on a parallel course. With a final quick turn to the left I pressed the bomb release tit and we lurched as the bombs left the air-craft. I quickly threw the jettison bars across to ensure that we had no hang-ups in the bomb bay and then we straightened up while the camera operated to photograph our aiming point. With the camera off and the bomb doors closed, we weaved away from the target area. Now I had time to survey the scene below us. The clouds were not enough to hide the many bright colours around the target, which was almost [light] enough to read by. As far as flak was concerned it was very moderate and all seemed to fall about 3,000ft below us. Across on the port beam I saw an aircraft falling to earth with smoke pouring from it, but no fire, and so I thought at least the crew had a chance of baling out. Another disconcerting sight was seeing a "scarecrow" which burst about 1,000 yards on the starboard side. They were supposed to simulate an aircraft on fire and, having not seen one before, I was certainly fooled. It seemed to hang there, numerous minor explosions followed and clouds of black smoke poured out, after which it just dropped to earth in a mass of flames.

'By now we were leaving the target area and everything ahead looked very black, which was good from a cover point of view. This, we were told, was often a dangerous area where fighters would often be waiting. The red Very signals which they used to attract one another's attention were all around us, so to avoid being "jumped" we continued a steady weave for about five minutes. Time was starting to pass very slowly now, I suppose because we were so keen to get back having accomplished our task. However there was still another 600 miles to go and so there was no need to get over-anxious. Cloud was still to our advantage as we passed close to the defences of many German cities, but the searchlights could not penetrate the cloud which meant that the flak was very dispersed and spasmodic. Finally we passed the last track marker in enemy territory and we altered course for the Dutch coast. Although things were quiet we carried out occasional banking turns to ensure that no enemy fighters were trying to get us from underneath or from behind. There was one final gesture from

Les Bartlett shortly after being commissioned. He was the bomb aimer of the crew skippered by Mike Beetham, a crew whose tour of 'ops' with No 50 Squadron at Skellingthorpe included the Battle of Berlin during the winter of 1943/44. (Les Bartlett)

the enemy as three rounds of flak burst under our nose and we went into a violent evasive manoeuvre and I dropped more Window from the aircraft. Now it was all quiet and our navigator told us that we were crossing the Dutch coast and we began to let down from 25,000ft. Half an hour later we were able to drop our oxygen masks as we passed 8,000ft in the descent—what a wonderful feeling to breathe freely once more! We then passed around flasks of hot coffee which refreshed us no end and we even started to chat over the intercom. By now we could see other kites as they began to switch on their navigation lights and as we approached the English coast I could see hundreds of green and red navigation lights. I realised then that those aircraft must have been there all the time but we could not see them of course.

'Now came the final problem of finding base. We were well below cloud and I could see kites weaving off in all directions to their various bases. Luckily we didn't have too far to go and found base easily enough. We were soon in the circuit and passed the message—"Hello Black Swan this is Pilgrim 'D-Dog', may I land please—over." This was acknowledged and I breathed a sigh of relief as the wheels finally touched down. Safely back, it was a great feeling to just stand on the ground and hear familiar voices all around us. Next stop was the locker room where we returned all our flying kit and I put on my greatcoat and forage cap once more. We then made our way to the debriefing room for our intelligence debrief where we offered as much information as possible— flak, searchlights, fighter opposition, air battles and any kites shot down with any parachutes sighted etc. and generally anything else such as weather conditions which we could think of. There were then the inevitable questions such as "Are all the boys back OK?" Finally we had supper (more like breakfast) and told each other about the events of the night until we were all too tired to talk any more when we just all slipped off quietly to bed. For me there was the final prayer of thanks before finally falling asleep.'

Flight Lieutenant John Chatterton DFC—Pilot

Flight Lieutenant John Chatterton had completed a tour of operations with No 44 Squadron at Dunholme Lodge when he was posted to No 5 Lancaster Finishing School at Syerston. As with so many others, his tour of operations must have seemed never ending, and little thought was given to 'what happens next'. He explains:

'I can't remember much about my last "op" on the Squadron except that it was a long haul to Munich (nearly ten hours) and that the Alps looked a splendid sight in the bright moonlight—a sharp contrast to the murky nights that had made up most of my tour. Although I knew it to be my last trip I had got into the habit of not looking too far ahead in life and it was the following day before I felt the warm feel-

ing of relief and release of tension. Someone asked me, what was I going to do next? I hadn't even thought about it. A friend of mine was about to be posted to No 5 LFS as an instructor and advised me to try for the same, and so off I went.'

John Chatterton now explains the training that each new Lancaster crew was given before joining a squadron:

'Student crews were at Syerston for about two weeks depending on the weather. There was a period of about three days' ground school and up to ten days of flying. There were a few ground school instructors in the navigator, bomb aimer, wireless operator and air gunner trades but the only flying instructors were pilots and flight engineers who worked as a team, usually with three student crews from each course. I remember there being on average about four courses per month. There were seven flying exercises in the course and if the weather and aircraft serviceability were good then the crew could finish in one week.

'The first exercise was a daytime dual sortie and lasted about two hours. The full student crew all flew on the sortie with an instructor pilot and flight engineer. The instructor pilot sat in the right hand seat as the aircraft was fitted with dual controls. The sortie included familiarisation with the Lancaster and general aircraft

Flt Lt John Chatterton DFC. (John Chatterton)

handling, including turns, stalls, circuits and landings. If the student pilot was above the average I would get out after three landings and let him go solo.

'The crew's second exercise was solo by day with the instructor flight engineer stood behind the student engineer in the right-hand seat. This sortie lasted about one hour and included more general handling and landings. The third exercise was dual again and introduced the more operational aspects of flying the Lancaster such as corkscrew manoeuvres, feathering and flying on three engines. The next exercise was a crew solo again and consolidated the lessons learnt in the previous exercise.

Flt Lt John Chatterton and crew.

'By the end of the fourth exercise the crew had had about eight hours on the Lancaster and were getting well used to its handling and performance. The fifth exercise was flown at night and introduced more evasive handling with the following exercise being consolidation for the crew, also at night. The final exercise was a crew solo at night and included a cross country navigation exercise with high-level bombing carried out on the bombing range at Wainfleet. Although the course gave the crew a total of about fifteen hours' flying, there was no time for low flying or fighter affiliation which the crew would have to try and do during their early days on the squadron.'

Flying Officer Bill Spence—Bomb Aimer

Bill Spence joined the RAF as a bomb aimer in August 1942. He carried out flying training in the United Kingdom and Canada and he remembers his first flight in a Lancaster, which took place at No 5 LFS Syerston on 10 August 1944. He recalls:

'It was a familiarisation flight for the pilot and the crew were not obliged to fly. However, I chose to do so and as the mid-upper gunner was not flying I occupied the turret. The sortie involved shutting down engines and to see from the turret the sight of three engines shut down one after the other was a bit worrying. However, when I saw that the aircraft was capable of maintaining height on one engine my faith in the Lancaster was born, and it never wavered after that!'

On completion of training, Bill Spence was posted to No 44 Squadron at Dunholme Lodge. His first 'op' was on the night of 29/30 August 1944 when his aircraft was one of 189 Lancasters detailed to attack Königsberg. Owing to the distance of the target the bomb load was just 8,300lb, which included one 2,000lb bomb and a number of cluster incendiaries. From his log book Bill Spence notes that the aircraft was airborne for just less than twelve hours and when recovering to base the crew noticed that the hydraulics were damaged and the undercarriage had to be lowered by hand. Damage also pre-vented the crew from knowing if the undercarriage was locked down, but thankfully it was!

The versatility of the Lancaster and the variations in bomb loads are well illustrated by the operations flown by Bill Spence and his crew. His next op was a daylight raid against two warships at Brest when the load was eleven 1,000lb and four 500lb bombs. The following day, against an airfield at Deelen, the bomb load was the same except that all the bombs were set with half-hour delays. In a later night attack against industrial targets at Düsseldorf on 2/3 November, the aircraft carried a mix of one 4,000lb, six 1,000lb and six 500lb bombs. Later that month, against Harburg, the aircraft carried the same bomb load although two of the 500lb bombs were set with six-hour delays. And so the 'mix and match' of bombs, with or without delays, continued.

If for any reason the crew were unable to release their bombs or mines, there were drills to be carried out. Bill Spence recalls:

'If we were unable to bomb the target then we had to bring the bombs back to base. If we were unable to drop mines then the brief was to jettison the mines "safe" in deep water. If we had any bombs or mines "hung up" then attempts were to be made to get rid of them over the sea. This would be done manually if all other attempts failed. I remember we had a mine "hung up" over the Kattegat east of Denmark. I was using H2S to drop them with the flight engineer operating the bomb release. When he examined the bomb bay immediately after the drop had been made he reported that one was still in position. A quick assessment on the H2S, and I told the pilot to maintain his course and to re-open the bomb doors. I instructed the flight engineer to keep pressing and releasing the bomb release tit and judged that the mine may be frozen on and that the repeated surge of current may release it. This is what happened, and the navigator recorded the release time and distance flown from the designated dropping zone. With this information base assessed that this mine had dropped between the mainland and an island, and we later learned that a ferry carrying German troops be-tween the two had gone down due to a mine!'

Bill Spence, who now lives in York, has nothing but praise for the Lancaster, his groundcrew and the work of other support personnel, such as the WAAFs in the air traffic control tower. One such memory will live with him for ever:

'Returning from a raid, we were in the circuit down-wind to land when two aircraft collided in mid-air. At the spilt moment before the collision there was a shout of "look out" over the radio, then flaming wreckage falling to the ground. We had to fly just above the flames in order to land. My lasting impression was of the calmness of the WAAFs in the control tower who continued to talk the Squadron down, even though they must have been horrified by the accident that they had just witnessed before their very eyes.'

Sergeant Frank Cornett—Flight Engineer

At the age of just eighteen, Frank Cornett joined the RAF as a flight engineer in January 1943. Promoted to Sergeant in June 1944, he carried out his Lancaster flying training at No 1651 HCU at Wratting Common and No 3 LFS at Feltwell before joining No 115 Squadron at Witchford in September 1944.

The duties of the flight engineer started with the initial walk out to the aircraft. He would carry out the walk-round checks, removing the pitot head cover and static vent plugs. He would then examine the various inspection hatches and check for any oil or coolant leaks. Following a close inspection of the wheels and tyres, he would inspect the aircraft for any damage and check that all the control surface locks had been removed. Having boarded the aircraft, the flight engineer, and/or the wireless operator, then checked the first aid kits, fire extinguishers, portable oxygen sets, escape hatches and pyrotechnics. He then checked the pressures in the emergency air bottles and hydraulic accumulators before preparing the aircraft for starting the engines. Once all four engines were running, the flight engineer then operated the bomb doors and flaps before cross-checking instruments with the pilot

Sgt Frank Cornett and crew, of No 115 Squadron, at Witchford during late 1944. (Alan Rowe)

prior to taxying. During taxy there were further checks to be carried out before a final check of the engines, temperatures and pressures prior to take-off. During the take-off the flight engineer opened the throttles to zero boost against the brakes, then released the brakes and opened the throttles fully, with the port throttles slightly ahead to check the aircraft's tendency to swing to port. As the speed increased, the pilot used the rudders to control the aircraft and raised the tail as quickly as possible, easing off the ground at between 95 and 105mph, depending on the weight of the aircraft. At a safety speed of 135mph the undercarriage was selected 'up', followed by the flaps being raised at about

800ft. During the climb, the flight engineer set the revs and monitored the fuel pumps feeding the engines. Frank Cornett explains the routines of the flight engineer once the aircraft was established in the transit:

'During the flight I kept an engine log and a separate fuel log, monitored instruments, revs and boost settings, which involved synchronising engines after any change to lessen vibration and undue sound annoyance for the other crew members. I also helped with the dropping of Window whenever necessary and generally keeping a look-out, initially for friendly aircraft to avoid collisions (particularly at dusk and dark) and later for enemy aircraft. During the target run I would generally assist with the run-in, help with the observation of the target, and offer any assistance during the bombing and run-

out from the target. Throughout all of this I would keep an eye on the instruments and warning lights whilst listening out for changes in either engine or airframe sounds.

'As flight engineers we were trained to be "tuned in" to the aircraft environment and rapidly became aware of any minor alteration affecting the "norm". It seems a lot, but one seemed to have time in hand without "flapping" and still had time for the odd remark over the intercom.'

On the recovery to base, the flight engineer carried out his final checks before landing. Speed was reduced to below 200mph, the undercarriage was selected 'down', the flaps were lowered, the fuel mixture and propeller controls were set and all four fuel booster pumps were switched on. Approach speeds varied between 110 and 130mph, depending on weight, and engines were monitored during the landing. After landing the bomb doors were opened and the engines shut down. After carrying out more checks the flight engineer finally vacated the aircraft and his work was done for another day or night, although there was still the debrief!

Frank Cornett completed his tour of 'ops' in February 1945 and now lives in Winsford, Cheshire. He recalls:

'On most ops we were hit by shrapnel from flak, but only once was an engine taken out, although nothing approaching major damage. Fighters were encountered on a number of daylight raids but luckily we weren't the target. Returning one night from an op, a Ju 88 formated on our port wingtip and stayed there for a couple of minutes in a position impossible for our guns to bear on him. He then flashed his navigation and cockpit lights before scarpering; we never saw him again and assumed that he was out of ammo. This event, for me, demonstrated a somewhat less than hostile attitude by the night fighter pilot!'

Finally, Frank Cornett has always kept his A. V. Roe Engineer's Manual. He recalls some advice passed to the new flight engineer from the Lancaster's manufacturers:

'"We, the makers of your aircraft, believe that aircraft can inflict more damage on the enemy than can any other weapon produced by the same expenditure of man hours and material, and that the aircraft we have given you is the best in the world for its purpose—*you* can prove the truth of both these statements."'

In the same manual, the flight engineers were reminded that they 'were the technical brains of the crew'. Statements such as these would see that the new flight engineers were given the best possible advice. Frank Cornett explains:

' I believed implicitly in these statements and tried to adhere to them, both for the Lancaster and later the Lincoln and York. I admit to being completely sold on Avro aircraft. During an early engineer's training course we visited A. V. Roe's factory at Woodford, where we were virtually given a free run of the factory from material input production lines for Lancasters

through to roll-out and run-up. The course lasted only two weeks but we learned more about the aircraft handling than we did on later type training at St Athan—the "hands on" approach paying dividends.'

Sergeant Ron Irons—Wireless Operator

The responsibility for the Lancaster's communications equipment, the electronic warfare equipment and the authentication of codes and messages was that of the wireless operator. His equipment varied very much with the mark and batch number of the Lancaster in which he was flying and also depended on what modifications, particularly regarding the electronic warfare equipment, had been made to the aircraft (for example, he was responsible for the operation of the aircraft's tail warning devices). Quite often the wireless operator's equipment would also differ depending on which squadron he served, particularly if the squadron had a specific role. Essentially, his equipment consisted of the radios, electronic warfare equipment, direction-finding equipment, IFF equipment and electrical services panel.

Apart from his routine duties, the wireless operator was always a useful additional pair of eyes for the crew and an assistant to any crew member in difficulty. His position in the aircraft was further aft than that of the other members in the main cockpit and he was, therefore, the closest man to the two air gunners. Sergeant Ron Irons was a wireless operator serving with No 97 Squadron at Woodhall Spa during the Lancaster's early operational days and he took part in the famous daylight raid against Augsburg on 17 April 1942. As the Lancaster approached the target area, it was met by an unavoidable barrage of enemy fire. Ron Irons recalls:

'We were flying as number two of the rear section and by the time that we arrived over the target area the element of surprise had completely gone. The German defences were very alert and were firing everything imaginable at us, including heavy gunfire. We were hit during the run-in to the target. Flak had hit the hydraulic pipes, which had put the gun tur-

A propeller is changed by a groundcrew. Men and women worked endless hours to ensure that as many aircraft as possible were available for operations.

rets out of action, and hydraulic oil had caught fire under the mid-upper turret. I left my position to help the gunner extinguish the fire. At the same time our starboard inner engine had been hit and was on fire. Having eventually extinguished the engine fire, we faced a long and hazardous journey back to base on just three engines.'

Being the wireless operator, Ron Irons was the first to react and, together with the mid-upper gunner, was able to extinguish the fire and save the aircraft—an act which brought both men the award of a DFM.

Sergeant John 'Buck' Rogers—Fitter II

'Buck' Rogers joined the RAF just before his seventeenth birthday as an aircraft apprentice at Halton in September 1936. Following three years of training, he qualified as a Fitter II and served at home and in Africa before being promoted to Sergeant and posted to No 100 Squadron at Grimsby (Waltham) in April 1943:

'I worked on all marks of the Lancaster which were on active service with No

1 Bomber Group. I was proud of my ground-crew and their effort. When necessary I flew on air tests to check work done, but had no desire to become a pilot—although I did fly at the controls of the gentle giant on one of the air tests for ten minutes or so. We had deadlines to meet which put pressure on us all and we "signed up" only when we would have been happy to fly aboard ourselves; anything less would have been letting our aircrew down. They simply had to trust us.

'Ultimately, of course, I came unstuck when my attitude earned me a severe reprimand for insubordination. It was probably the way I described the need for a powerplant (starboard inner engine) replacement and our daily routine which had been the secret of our success up until then. The kite was towed to the hangar where, overnight, working high on the servicing platforms in chilling sub-zero wind, we struggled with spanners and hand torches. Our eyes watered and our noses ran. Our frozen fingers fumbled and we also told the world to get lost! After what seemed to be a lifetime we reached the stage for a test-run, only to find the MT Section duty driver flatly refusing to "turn out". I gave the matter careful thought. Firstly, the kite had to be serviceable by dawn; secondly, the hangar doors were immovably frozen open at both ends; and thirdly, the kite was standing fair and square just inside the west end doors.

'I discussed with my crew the idea of taxying out of the hangar. The wingtip clearance at each side was about a foot or so and with a couple of "bods" on the towing arm we could keep her straight until clear of the hangar doors. But outside the apron was smothered with frozen, rutted snow and glazed ice on a falling gradient. I would also have to blast her round to port towards the perimeter track. I had visions of losing her in a colossal broadside. There were no volunteers so I decided to run-up in the hangar. If I had to be court-martialled for insubordination then my epitaph must be a sort of "Moses in the Temple", if you know what I mean. The noise in the hangar was shattering and in moments the watchers stationed at critical positions around the aircraft had

stepped outside. I need not have worried. The air pressure and brakes held; the tail arm kept the tail wheel straight and the chocks did not move whilst I feathered and unfeathered the prop, checked the magnetos and finally went through to full power as the exhaust glowed cherry red. All indicated serviceable and OK. However, any loose equipment or pendant lights in the hangar which happened to be in the slipstream were soon removed to a safe place some 50 yards outside the hangar to the east! As a result I was offered a severe reprimand, with no further questions asked, or a court martial!'

Whilst serving with No 100 Squadron, 'Buck' Rogers was responsible for the servicing of ED750 'HW-M', which was captained by Lieutenant 'Tommy' Morgan of the United States Air Force, serving as a volunteer with the RAF. On the subject of amusing memories, he recalls:

'The specifications of the Lancaster in battle order would not be concentrating on such luxuries as a toilet. It is possible that the "war lords" thought of it as just dead weight. So designers were only allowed to make token improvements. What was really needed was a holding tank fitted with a non-return valve or trap. The tank in turn could then be emptied and flushed through an external skin fitting and into a sanitary truck so as not to smother the operator in the process. Such a toilet bowl would have, thereby, a double seal against spillage (the valve and the lid). At the time our problem was where to dispose of the effluent. We were lucky to have a nearby agricultural ditch which soon became stripped of vegetation by the "burn-off". We had no water laid on to our dispersal so we rinsed with water carried in a bucket, perhaps for up to half a mile, on a bicycle. We were not instructed in the clean-up process and few of us appreciated the strength of Elsan fluid and/or urine on the airframe. Any "splashes" could eventually corrode and perhaps cause a failure, such as a tail dropping off during hard manoeuvres.'

This somewhat light-hearted look at the problem of toilet facilities in the Lancaster leads to the much more serious problem of corrosion, and 'Buck' Roger's last

suggestion of such corrosion causing a tail to drop off is made in reference to the loss of his pilot and flight engineer. Sadly, it was in another Lancaster (ED583, 'HW-K') that Tommy Morgan and Jimmy Giles were killed on 4 October 1943 when their aircraft crashed whilst demonstrating the manoeuvrability of the Lancaster to nine new aircrew during a fighter affiliation training sortie. Buck Rogers adds:

'The aircraft had completed 58 ops and had been "bent" on the previous op. She had just come out of the maintenance hangar after a "thorough" symmetry and other safety checks, and had been passed serviceable. Tommy Morgan had just completed his tour of operations with the Squadron and I am unsure exactly why he was flying this sortie—what a tragic end.'

Buck Rogers went on to serve with No 550 Squadron at Grimsby and North Killingholme before eventually leaving the RAF in 1949. He now lives in Victoria, Australia, and from his memoirs he summarises matters in the most fitting of ways:

'I now ask you to lift your glasses of champagne in a toast to Tommy Morgan and Jimmy Giles, who for more than half a century have remained in orbit asking for permission to land. One corkscrew too many—they gave us their all.'

LAC Eric Howell—Flight Mechanic (Engines)

Eric Howell joined the RAF in August 1941. Having completed training as a flight mechanic at Locking, he was posted to No 44 Squadron at Waddington in February 1942. As an engine mechanic, Eric Howell worked on most marks of Lancaster engines until the end of the war. Like other groundcrew, he worked very long hours at the aircraft dispersal areas. He explains:

'The vast majority of the time there were only two engine mechanics and one airframe mechanic (rigger) on duty to service one Lancaster over a 24-hour period in the dispersal area. We would be on duty from 0800 hours. If the aircraft was serviceable and the Form 700 (aircraft servicing record) was signed by the three of us, the two on night duty for operations or training flights would go to eat at the cookhouse at about 1600 hours. We would then return at about 1730 hours to relieve the third member, who would be off duty until 0800 hours the next morning.

'After take-off one member would then be off duty until 0800 hours the following morning and the remaining member would wait for the return of the aircraft. When the aircraft returned from its sortie, he would marshall the aircraft to the pan stand. He would collect any "snags" from the pilot and flight engineer and then refuel the aircraft to a minimum load (about 1,200 gallons) and check the engine oil for excessive use. He would then be off duty until about 1300 hours that day.

'This cycle of duty for one team of three men would be repeated every three days as long as there were operations or training flights. Other tradesmen (armourers, electricians, radar and wireless technicians, etc.) were constantly in and out of the flight dispersal areas. When on operations there was usually one electrician and instrument basher on duty with the groundcrew.

'The most distressful time of all was the all night duty. After the pre-flight ground test, the aircrew would debark from the Lancaster for about half an hour to smoke and talk to try and relieve the tensions. After months and years of seeing the aircrew off on operations the groundcrew had a feeling for the emotions of the aircrew even though there was an effort on their part to conceal their feelings. When the time came to re-board the aircraft for take-off it was all business again and the groundcrew could finally retire to the safety and warmth of their billets.

'To depict the loneliness and apprehensions of one of those groundcrew waiting in the black of night for his aircraft to return from operations, I can offer the following. Thirteen of my Lancasters failed to return from operations over enemy territory. I was not on duty every time this happened, as there were three of us sharing the duties, but the loss was always felt by us all. We would get a hollow feeling in our stomachs and wonder if we had ever missed something in our inspections, which always made us all the more determined to be more diligent.'

The vast effort of the groundcrews often passes unrecognised except by aircrews, who, almost without exception, have always paid tribute to the men and women left back at base whilst the Lancaster and its crew flew deep into enemy territory. No matter what the time of day or night, or the weather, servicings had to continue. In the summer months the hours spent out at dispersal would often be most pleasant, but in winter it could be completely different. Eric Howell explains:

'The winter servicing of the Lancaster was more difficult than servicings during the summer. A typical day started with removing the engine, canopy and turret covers. The bows and everything else would be frozen solid and would be hard to undo with gloved hands. We would then remove the escape hatches to gain access to the mainplane so that we could clean off the snow and ice with brooms or any other tool at hand.

'If the temperature was very low we would ground-test the engines first to warm them up ready for a daily inspection. Starting the engines on a bitterly cold morning demanded an intimate knowledge of each engine's starting ability. Every engine was different, and only practice gave us the ability to start each engine with little trouble. One engine might take a dozen or more pumps on the Kygas priming pump, and others much less. After the ground test we moved the trestle to each engine in turn to look for any one of a thousand things—check the coolant levels and look for any leaks from the pump and pipes, check for oil leaks, check the exhaust stubs, etc., etc. Any snags found during the ground test would be taken care of there and then.

'By now the two engine fitters and the rigger would be frozen to the bone and we would retire to our "mansion" that we had built close to our Lancaster. It was usually built of tree branches with a spare canopy and engine covers thrown over the top. A five-gallon can supported a wood fire, fed with old engine oil, which would be very close outside the entrance. We had to be very careful not to touch any metal such as the trestles with our bare hands. It was almost impossible to service a Lancaster with gloved hands. Although removing the cowling was no problem, the problem was in working on a cold engine with bare hands to service the individual component parts. It was particularly miserable to service the Lancaster in the incessant rain. We would throw an engine cover over the engine and work underneath the cover whilst sitting on the wet trestle platform. Shovelling snow, helping to pull the aircraft out of mud with the help of a tractor, and all sorts of other odds and ends, were all part of our job working out at the dispersal area!'

Like father, like son! Flt Lt Mike Chatterton (right), the present-day captain of PA474, with his father Flt Lt John Chatterton DFC, the former wartime Lancaster pilot. (Mike Chatterton)

11. For Valour

There were undoubtedly many stories of extreme courage amongst the thousands of men who flew the Lancaster on operations; many were decorated for their action, but many were not. This chapter is a tribute to those who did receive awards—although there were too many by far to cover them all. All the Victoria Cross recipients are detailed, and there are examples of the various other awards, selected to include all types of Lancaster crew members and the nationalities of those who fought with the RAF during the war.

The Victoria Cross

Britain's highest military decoration for valour, the Victoria Cross (VC), could be awarded to anyone, of any rank, who distinguished himself in the face of the enemy. It was awarded on just 32 occasions to aircrew of the RAF and Commonwealth air forces during the Second World War; nineteen were awarded to members of Bomber Command, of which ten were awarded to Lancaster aircrew. This number seems surprisingly low when considering the thousands of aircrew involved in Lancaster operations throughout the war. One simple explanation for this is that a heroic act had to be witnessed and reported for an individual to be decorated for his courage: how many similar acts would have gone untold because the crew had perished? This chapter gives brief accounts of those ten men who distinguished themselves above all others to be awarded the supreme symbol of courage; many, however, never lived to receive their award, and of those who did receive the VC in person, some would not survive the war. Some became household names, through films, television and books, whilst others remain generally little known.

Squadron Leader Ian Bazalgette VC DFC (No 635 Squadron)

Ian Willoughby Bazalgette was born in Alberta, Canada, in October 1918. Following the outbreak of the war, he was initially commissioned as a Second Lieutenant in the Royal Artillery before transferring to the RAF Volunteer Reserve as a pilot in 1941. His first operational tour was flying Wellingtons with No 115 Squadron based at Mildenhall and he later converted with the Squadron to the Lancaster in early 1943. He was awarded the DFC in July before completing his tour of operations in August. Following a tour as an instructor with No 20 OTU at Lossiemouth, Bazalgette returned to operational flying with No 635 Squadron 'Pathfinders' at Downham Market in April 1944. On 4 August that year Bazalgette was the captain of Lancaster ND811 as part of the PFF marking for an attack against a V-1 storage site at Trossy St Maximin. His citation reads:

'When nearing the target his Lancaster came under heavy anti-aircraft fire; both starboard engines were put out of action and serious fires broke out in the fuselage, and the starboard main plane, and the bomb aimer was badly wounded. Despite the appalling conditions in his burning aircraft, he pressed on gallantly to the target, marking and bombing it accurately. After the bombs had been dropped the Lancaster dived, practically out of control. By expert airmanship and great exertion Bazalgette regained control. However, the port inner engine then failed and the whole of the starboard main plane became a mass of flames. Bazalgette fought bravely to bring his aircraft and crew to safety; the mid-upper gunner was overcome by fumes. Bazalgette then or-dered those of his crew who were able to leave by parachute to do so. He remained at the controls and attempted the almost hopeless task of landing the crippled and blazing aircraft in a last effort to save the wounded bomb aimer and helpless gunner. With superb skill, and taking great care to avoid a small French village nearby, he brought the aircraft down safely. Unfortunately, it then exploded and Bazalgette and his two comrades perished.'

After the war was over, the survivors of Bazalgette's crew returned to the United Kingdom and the full account of the captain's heroic deeds was told. Soon afterwards came the announcement of a posthumous Victoria Cross to Squadron Leader Ian Bazalgette (LG 17 August 1945); he was just 25 years old. His citation concludes: 'His heroic sacrifice marked the climax of a long career of operations against the enemy. He always chose the more dangerous and exacting roles. His courage and devotion to duty were beyond praise.'

*Wing Commander Leonard Cheshire VC DSO** DFC (No 617 Squadron)*

Geoffrey Leonard Cheshire was born in Chester on 7 September 1917. He was commissioned as a pilot in the RAFVR in 1937 and following the outbreak of war joined No 102 Squadron, equipped with Whitleys, at Driffield in June 1940. Cheshire was awarded the DSO in November 1940 before completing his first tour of operations in January 1941, after which he volunteered for a second tour of operations and was posted to No 35 Squadron, equipped with Halifaxes, at Linton-on-Ouse. In March 1941 he was awarded the DFC, followed soon afterwards by the award of a bar to his DSO for outstand-

Gp Capt. Leonard Cheshire VC DSO DFC.

ing leadership on operations. Having completed his second tour of operations, Cheshire was posted as an instructor to No 1652 HCU at Marston Moor in January 1942 before returning to operations in September as the Officer Commanding No 76 Squadron, another Halifax squadron based at Linton-on-Ouse, having already been awarded a second bar to his DSO. At just 25 years old, Cheshire was promoted to the rank of Group Captain in April 1943 and posted as the Station Commander of Marston Moor. By September he was desperate to return to operational flying and, accepting reversion back to the rank of Wing Commander, he was appointed as the Officer Commanding No 617 Squadron at Woodhall Spa, where his squadron flew the Lancaster in the specific role of precision bombing. Having flown his 100th operational sortie on 6 July 1944, Cheshire was withdrawn from operations, having by far exceeded what could be reasonably expected from any one man in his contribution to the war. Soon after this came the announcement of the award of the Victoria Cross to Cheshire (LG 8 September 1944). His citation reads:

'This officer began his operational career in June 1940. Against strongly defended targets, he soon displayed the cour-

age and determination of an exceptional leader. He was always ready to accept extra risks to ensure success. At the end of his first tour of operational duty he immediately volunteered for a second. Again, he pressed home his attacks with the utmost gallantry. When he was posted for instructional duties in January 1942 he undertook four more operational missions. He started a third tour in August 1942 when he was given command of a squadron. He led the Squadron with outstanding skill on a number of missions before being appointed as a station commander. In October 1943 he undertook a fourth operational tour, relinquishing the rank of Group Captain at his own request so that he could again take part in operations. He immediately set to work as the pioneer of a new method of marking enemy targets involving very low flying. During his fourth tour Wing Commander Cheshire led his squadron personally on every occasion, always undertaking the most dangerous and difficult task of marking the target alone from a low level in the face of strong defences. Cheshire's cold and calculated acceptance of risks is exemplified by his conduct in an attack on Munich in April 1944. This was an experimental attack to test out the new method of target marking at low level against a heavily-defended target situated deep in enemy territory. He was obliged to follow, in bad weather, a direct route which took him over the defences of Augsburg and thereafter he was continuously under fire. As he reached the target, flares were being released by our high-flying aircraft and he was illuminated from above and below. All guns within range opened fire on him. Diving to 700 feet he dropped his markers with great precision and began to climb away. So blinding were the searchlights that he almost lost control. He then flew over the city at 1,000 feet to assess the accuracy of his work and direct other aircraft. His own was badly hit by shell fragments but he continued to fly over the target area until he was satisfied that he had done all in his power to ensure success. Eventually when he set course for base the task of disengaging himself from the defences proved even more hazardous than his approach.

For a full twelve minutes after leaving the target area he was under withering fire, but he came safely through.

'Wing Commander Cheshire has now completed a total of 100 missions. In four years of fighting against the bitterest opposition he has maintained a record of outstanding personal achievement, placing himself invariably in the forefront of the battle. What he did in the Munich operation was typical of the careful planning, brilliant execution and contempt for danger which has established for Wing Commander Cheshire a reputation second to none in Bomber Command.'

Wing Commander Guy Gibson VC DSO* DFC* (No 617 Squadron)

Guy Penrose Gibson was born at Simla, India, on 12 August 1918. He was commissioned into the RAF as a pilot in 1937 and following training was posted to No 83 Squadron, equipped with Hinds and then Hampdens, based at Scampton. Gibson took part in operations from the very first day of the war and completed his first tour in September 1940, having already been awarded the DFC in July. Following a short tour as an instructor with Nos 14 and 16 OTUs, he was posted to No 29 Squadron based at Digby, where he flew Beaufighters as a night-fighter pilot until December 1941; during this period he flew 100 operational sorties and was credited with three enemy aircraft destroyed, bringing him a bar to his DFC in September.

Following a short period as an instructor with No 51 OTU at Cranfield, Gibson returned to operational flying in April 1942 as the Officer Commanding No 106 Squadron at Coningsby, where he first flew heavy bombers, initially the Manchester and then the Lancaster. He completed a further year of operational flying and was awarded the DSO in November and a bar to the DSO in March 1943. Having completed his tour of operations with No 106 Squadron, Gibson was posted as Officer Commanding No 617 Squadron, a newly formed unit at Scampton, where he planned and led the famous Dams Raid on the night of 16/17 May 1943. His citation reads:

Wg Cdr Guy Gibson VC DSO DFC.

'Under his inspiring leadership, this squadron has now executed one of the most devastating attacks of the war—the breaching of the Mohne and Eder dams. The task was fraught with danger and difficulty. Gibson personally made the initial attack on the Mohne Dam. Descending to within a few feet of the water and taking the full brunt of the anti-aircraft defences, he delivered his attack with great accuracy. Afterwards he circled very low for thirty minutes, drawing the enemy fire on himself in order to leave as free a run as possible to the following aircraft which were attacking the dam in turn. Gibson then led the remainder of his force to the Eder Dam where, with complete disregard for his own safety, he repeated his tactics, and once more drew on himself the enemy fire so that the attack would be successfully developed. Wing Commander Gibson has completed 170 sorties. Throughout his operational career, prolonged exceptionally at his own request, he has shown leadership, determination and valour of the highest order.'

Following the Dams Raid, Gibson carried out various staff appointments, occasionally managing to escape the office to take part in further operational raids. On one such raid, on the night of 19 September 1944, Gibson failed to return after flying a Mosquito of No 627 Squad-

ron as Master Bomber of a raid against rail and industrial targets at Rheydt and München-Gladbach. His aircraft was seen in flames and crashed at Steenbergen in Holland. Gibson was just 26 years old.

Sergeant Norman Jackson VC (No 106 Squadron)

Norman Cyril Jackson was born in Ealing on 8 April 1919. On the outbreak of war he joined the RAF as an engine fitter before becoming a flight engineer and being posted to No 106 Squadron, equipped with Lancasters, at Syerston in July 1943. In November the Squadron moved to Metheringham. His citation reads:

'This airman was the flight engineer in a Lancaster detailed to attack Schweinfurt on the night of 26 April 1944. Bombs were dropped successfully and the aircraft was climbing out of the target area. Suddenly it was attacked by a fighter at about 20,000 feet. The captain took evading action at once, but the enemy secured many hits. A fire started near a petrol tank on the upper surface of the starboard wing, between the fuselage and the inner engine. Sergeant Jackson was thrown to the floor during the engagement. Wounds which he received from shell splinters in the right leg and shoulder were probably sustained at that time. Recovering himself, he remarked that he could deal with the fire on the wing and obtained his captain's permission to try to put out the flames. Pushing a hand fire extinguisher into the top of his life-saving jacket, and clipping on his parachute pack, Jackson jettisoned the escape hatch above the pilot's head and started to climb out of the cockpit and back along the top of the fuselage to the starboard wing. Before he could leave the fuselage his parachute pack opened and the whole canopy and rigging lines spilled into the cockpit. Undeterred, Jackson continued. The pilot, bomb aimer and navigator gathered the parachute together and held on to the rigging lines, paying them out as the airman crawled aft. Eventually he slipped and, falling from the fuselage to the starboard wing, grasped an air intake on the leading edge of the wing. He succeeded in clinging on but lost the extinguisher which was blown away.

'By this time the fire had spread rapidly. Jackson's face, hands and clothing were severely burnt. Unable to retain his hold he was swept through the flames and over the trailing edge of the wing, dragging his parachute behind. When last seen it was only partially inflated and was burning in a number of places. Realising that the fire could not be controlled, the captain gave the order to abandon the aircraft. Four of the remaining members of the crew landed safely; the captain and the rear gunner have not been accounted for. Sergeant Jackson was unable to control his descent and landed heavily. He sustained a broken ankle, his right eye was closed through burns and his hands were useless. These injuries, together with the wounds received earlier, reduced him to a pitiable state. At daybreak he crawled to the nearest village where he was taken prisoner. After ten months in hospital he made a good recovery, though his hands require further treatment and are only of limited use.

'This airman's attempts to extinguish the fire and save the aircraft and crew from falling into enemy hands was an act of outstanding gallantry. To venture outside, when travelling at 200 miles an hour at a great height and in intense cold, was an almost incredible feat. Had he succeeded in subduing the flames, there was little or no prospect of his regaining the cockpit. The spilling of his parachute and the risk of grave damage to its canopy reduced his chances of survival to a minimum. By his ready willingness to face these dangers he set an example of self-sacrifice which will ever be remembered.'

Pilot Officer Andrew Mynarski VC (No 419 Squadron)

Andrew Charles Mynarski was born in Winnipeg, Canada, on 14 October 1916. He joined the RCAF as a wireless operator/air gunner and was posted to No 9 Squadron based at Bardney in October 1943. In April 1944 Mynarski was posted to No 419 Squadron RCAF at Middleton St George. His citation reads:

'Pilot Officer Mynarski was the mid-upper gunner of a Lancaster aircraft detailed to attack a target at Cambrai, France, on the night of 12 June 1944. The aircraft was attacked from below and astern by an enemy fighter and ultimately came down in flames. As an immediate result of the attack, both port engines failed. Fire broke out between the mid-upper turret and the rear turret, as well as in the port wing. The flames soon became fierce and the captain ordered the crew to abandon the aircraft.

'Mynarski left his turret and went towards the escape hatch. He then saw the rear gunner was still in his turret and apparently unable to leave it. The turret was, in fact, immovable since the hydraulic gear had been put out of action when the port engines failed, and the manual gear had been broken by the gunner in an attempt to escape. Without hesitation, Mynarski made his way through the flames in an endeavour to reach the turret and release the rear gunner. Whilst doing so, his parachute and his clothing, up to the waist, were set on fire. All his efforts to move the turret and free the gunner were in vain. Eventually the rear gunner clearly indicated to him that there was nothing more he could do and that he should try and save his own life. Mynarski reluctantly went back through the flames to the escape hatch. There, as a last gesture to the trapped gunner, he turned towards him, stood to attention in his flaming clothing and saluted, before he jumped out of the aircraft. Mynarski's descent was seen by French people on the ground. Both his parachute and clothing were on fire. He was found eventually by the French, but was so severely burnt that he died from his injuries.

'The rear gunner had a miraculous escape when the aircraft crashed. He subsequently testified that, had Mynarski not attempted to save his comrade's life, he could have left the aircraft in safety and would, doubtless, have escaped death. Mynarski must have been fully aware that in trying to free the rear gunner he was almost certain to lose his own life. Despite this, with outstanding courage and complete disregard for his own safety, he went to the rescue. Willingly accepting the danger, Mynarski lost his life by a most conspicuous act of heroism which called for valour of the highest order.'

Squadron Leader John Nettleton VC (No 44 Squadron)

John Dering Nettleton was born in Natal, South Africa, on 28 June 1917. He was commissioned into the RAF in December 1938 and following pilot training was posted to No 207 Squadron at Cottesmore and then No 98 Squadron at Hucknall. He then spent time with No 185 Squadron at Cottesmore, where he served as an instructor on Hampdens until June 1941, when he was posted to No 44 Squadron at Waddington. His citation reads:

'Squadron Leader Nettleton was the leader of one of two formations of six Lancasters detailed to deliver a low-level attack in daylight on the diesel engine factory at Augsburg in southern Germany on 17 April 1942. The enterprise was daring, the target of high military importance. To reach it and get back, some 1,000 miles had to be flown over hostile territory. Soon after crossing into enemy territory his formation was engaged by 25 to 30 fighters. A running fight ensued. His rear guns were out of action. One by one the aircraft of his formation were shot down until in the end only his and one other remained. The fighters were shaken off but the target was still far distant. There was formidable resistance to be faced. With great spirit and almost defenceless, he held his two remaining aircraft on their perilous course and after a long and arduous flight, mostly at only 50 feet above the ground, he brought them to Augsburg. Here anti-aircraft fire of great intensity and accuracy was encountered. The two aircraft came low over the roof tops. Though fired at from point-blank range, they stayed the course to drop their bombs true on the target. The second aircraft, hit by flak, burst into flames and crash-landed. The leading aircraft, though riddled with holes, flew safely back to base, the only one of the six to return. Squadron Leader Nettleton, who has successfully undertaken many other hazardous operations, displayed unflinching determination as well as leadership and valour of the highest order.'

The announcement of the award of the Victoria Cross to John Nettleton came in the *London Gazette* on 28 April 1942. He spent time serving with No 1661 HCU before returning to No 44 Squadron as the Officer Commanding in January 1943. Sadly, John Nettleton failed to return from a raid against Turin on the night of 12/13 July 1943. He was just 26 years old.

Squadron Leader Robert Palmer VC DFC* (No 109 Squadron)

Robert Anthony Maurice Palmer was born in Gillingham on 7 July 1920. He joined the RAF as a sergeant pilot in 1939 and was initially posted to No 75 Squadron, based at Feltwell, and then to No 149 Squadron at Mildenhall. Having completed his first tour of operations on Wellingtons, Palmer was posted to No 20 OTU at Lossiemouth as an instructor. Having been commissioned in January 1942, he finally got his wish to return to operational flying and was posted to No 109 Squadron at Warboys in January 1944. As part of the PFF he flew Mosquitos operationally throughout the rest of the year and was awarded the DFC in June and a bar to the DFC in December 1944, by which time the Squadron had moved to Little Staughton. Having completed 100 operational sorties, he could have easily asked to be rested but instead elected to stay with the Squadron.

On 23 December Palmer flew in a Lancaster belonging to No 582 Squadron, another Pathfinder unit at Little Staughton, as Master Bomber for a raid against marshalling yards at Cologne. His citation reads:

'This officer has completed 110 bombing missions. Most of them involved deep penetration of heavily-defended territory; many were low-level "marking" operations against vital targets; all were executed with tenacity, high courage and great accuracy. The finest example of his courage and determination was on 23 December 1944 when he led a formation of Lancasters to attack the marshalling yards at Cologne in daylight. He had the task of marking the target, and his formation had been ordered to bomb as soon as the bombs had gone from his, the leading aircraft. The leader's duties during the final bombing run were exacting and demanded coolness and resolution. To achieve accuracy he would have to fly at an exact height and airspeed on a steady course, regardless of opposition. Some minutes before the target was reached, his aircraft came under heavy anti-aircraft fire, shells burst all around, two engines were set on fire and there were flames and smoke in the nose and the bomb bay. Enemy fighters now attacked in force. Palmer disdained the possibility of taking avoiding action. He knew that if he diverged the least bit from his course, he would be unable to utilise the special equipment to the best advantage. He was determined to complete the run and provide an accurate and easily seen aiming point for the other bombers. He ignored the double risk of fire and explosion in his aircraft and kept on. With his engines developing unequal power, an immense effort was needed to keep the damaged aircraft on a straight course. Nevertheless, he made a perfect approach and his bombs hit the target. His aircraft was last seen spiralling to earth in flames. Such was the strength of the opposition that more than half of the formation failed to return.'

Robert Palmer was posthumously awarded the Victoria Cross (LG 23 March 1945); at the time of his death he was just 24 years old. His citation concludes:

'Squadron Leader Palmer was an outstanding pilot. He displayed conspicuous bravery. His record of prolonged and heroic endeavour is beyond praise.'

Flight Lieutenant William Reid VC (No 61 Squadron)
William Reid was born in Glasgow on 21 December 1921. He joined the RAFVR in April 1941 and, following pilot training, was posted to No 61 Squadron at Syerston in September 1943. His citation reads:

'On the night of 3 November 1943, Flight Lieutenant Reid was pilot and captain of a Lancaster aircraft detailed to attack Düsseldorf. Shortly after crossing the Dutch coast, the pilot's windscreen was shattered by fire from a Messerschmitt 110. Owing to a failure in the heating circuit, the rear gunner's hands were too cold for him to open fire immediately or to operate his microphone and so give warning of danger; but after a brief delay he managed to return the Messerschmitt's fire and it was driven off.

'During the fight with the Messerschmitt, Reid was wounded in the head, shoulders and hands. The elevator trimming tabs of the aircraft were damaged and it became difficult to control. The rear turret, too, was badly damaged and the communications system and compasses were put out of action. Reid ascertained that his crew were unscathed and, saying nothing about his own injuries, he continued his mission.

'Soon afterwards, the Lancaster was attacked by a Focke-Wulf 190. This time, the enemy's fire raked the bomber from stem to stern. The rear gunner replied with his only serviceable gun, but the state of his turret made accurate aiming impossible. The navigator was killed and the wireless operator fatally injured. The mid-upper turret was hit and the oxygen system put out of action. Reid was again wounded and the flight engineer, though hit in the forearm, supplied him with oxygen from a portable supply.

'Flight Lieutenant Reid refused to be turned from his objective and Düsseldorf was reached some 50 minutes later. He had memorised his course to the target and had continued in such a normal manner that the bomb aimer, who was cut off by the failure of the communications system, knew nothing of his captain's injuries or of the casualties to his comrades. Photographs show that when the bombs were released the aircraft was right over the centre of the target. Steering by the pole star and the moon, Reid then set course for home. He was growing weak from loss of blood. The emergency oxygen supply had given out. With the windscreen shattered, the cold was intense. He lapsed into semi-consciousness. The flight engineer, with some help from the bomb aimer, kept the Lancaster in the air despite heavy anti-aircraft fire over the Dutch coast.

'The North Sea crossing was accomplished. An airfield was sighted. The captain revived, resumed control and made ready to land. Ground mist partially obscured the runway lights. The captain was also much bothered by blood from his head wound getting into his eyes. But he made a safe landing although the leg of the damaged undercarriage collapsed when the load came on.

'Wounded in two attacks, without oxygen, suffering severely from cold, his navigator dead, his wireless operator fatally wounded, his aircraft crippled and defenceless, Flight Lieutenant Reid showed superb courage and leadership in penetrating a further 200 miles into enemy territory to attack one of the most strongly defended targets in Germany, every additional mile increasing the hazards of the long and perilous journey home. His tenacity and devotion to duty were beyond praise.'

Captain Edwin Swales VC DFC (No 582 Squadron)
Edwin Swales was born in Natal on 3 July 1915. He trained as a pilot in the SAAF and was officially seconded to the RAF in August 1943, joining No 582 Squadron at Little Staughton in July 1944. He was awarded the DFC following a raid against Cologne on 23 December, the same raid for which Squadron Leader Robert Palmer was posthumously awarded the Victoria Cross. On 23 February 1945 Swales was chosen as Master Bomber for a raid against a vital rail junction at Pforzheim. His citation reads:

'As "Master Bomber", he had the task of locating the target area with precision and of giving aiming instructions to the main force of bombers following in his wake. Soon after he had reached the target area he was engaged by an enemy fighter and one of his engines was put out of action. His rear guns failed. His crippled aircraft was an easy prey to further attacks. Unperturbed, he carried on with his allotted task; clearly and precisely he issued aiming instructions to the main force. Meanwhile the enemy fighter closed the range and fired again. A second engine of Swale's aircraft was put out of action. Almost defenceless, he stayed over the target area issuing his aiming instructions until he was satisfied that the attack had achieved its purpose.

'It is now known that the attack was one of the most concentrated and successful of the war. Captain Swales did not, however, regard his mission as completed. His aircraft was damaged. Its speed had been so much reduced that it could only with difficulty be kept in the air. The blind flying instruments were no longer working. Determined at all costs to prevent his aircraft and crew from falling into enemy hands, he set course for home. After an hour he flew into thin-layered cloud. He kept his course by skilful flying between the layers, but later heavy cloud and turbulent air conditions were met. The aircraft, by now over friendly territory, became more and more difficult to control; it was losing height steadily. Realising that the situation was desperate, Swales ordered his crew to bale out. Time was very short and it required all his exertions to keep the aircraft steady while each of his crew moved in turn to the escape hatch and parachuted to safety. Hardly had the last crew member jumped when the aircraft plunged to earth. Captain Swales was found dead at the controls. Intrepid in the attack, courageous in the face of danger, he did his duty to the last, giving his life that his comrades might live.'

Flight Sergeant George Thompson VC (No 9 Squadron)
George Thompson was born in Trinity Gask, Perthshire, on 23 October 1920. Having joined the RAF as a wireless tradesman, he transferred to flying duties as a sergeant wireless operator in 1943. He was posted to No 9 Squadron at Bardney in September 1944. His citation reads:

'This airman was the wireless operator in a Lancaster aircraft which attacked the Dortmund–Ems Canal in daylight on 1 January 1945. The bombs had just been released when a heavy shell hit the aircraft in front of the mid-upper turret. Fire broke out and dense smoke filled the fuselage. The nose of the aircraft was then hit and an inrush of air, clearing the smoke, revealed a scene of utter devastation. Most of the perspex screen of the nose compartment had been shot away, gaping holes had been torn in the canopy above the pilot's head, the inter-communications wiring had been severed, and there was a large hole in the floor of the aircraft. Bed-

ding and other equipment were badly damaged or alight; one engine was on fire.

'Thompson saw that the gunner was unconscious in the blazing mid-upper turret. Without hesitation he went down the fuselage into the fire and exploding ammunition. He pulled the gunner from his turret and, edging his way round the hole in the floor, carried him away from the flames. With his bare hands, he extinguished the gunner's burning clothing. Thompson himself sustained serious burns on his face, hands and legs. Thompson then noticed that the rear turret was also on fire. Despite his own severe injuries he moved painfully to the rear of the fuselage where he found the rear gunner with his clothing alight, overcome by flames and fumes. A second time Thompson braved the flames. With great difficulty he extricated the helpless gunner and carried him clear. Again, he used his bare hands, already burnt, to beat out flames on a comrade's clothing.

'Flight Sergeant Thompson, by now almost exhausted, felt that his duty was not yet done. He must report the fate of the crew to the captain. He made the perilous journey back through the burning fuselage, clinging to the sides with his burnt hands to get across the hole in the floor. The flow of cold air caused him intense pain and frost-bite developed. So pitiful was his condition that his captain failed to recognise him. Still, his only concern was for the two gunners he had left in the rear of the aircraft. He was given such attention as was possible until a crash-landing was made some forty minutes later.

'When the aircraft was hit, Flight Sergeant Thompson might have devoted his efforts to quelling the fire and so have contributed to his own safety. He preferred to go through the fire to succour his comrades. He knew that he would then be in no position to hear or heed any order which might be given to abandon the aircraft. He hazarded his own life in order to save the lives of others. Young in years (24 years old) and experience, his actions were those of a veteran.

'Three weeks later Flight Sergeant Thompson died of his injuries. One of the gunners unfortunately also died, but the

other owes his life to the superb gallantry of Flight Sergeant Thompson, whose courage and self-sacrifice will ever be an inspiration to the Service.'

Commissioned Officers' Awards
For the officer aircrew, there were two further awards for outstanding gallantry and devotion to duty in the face of the enemy, the Distinguished Service Order (DSO) and the Distinguished Flying Cross (DFC), further acts of bravery being denoted by a bar, or bars, awarded to the decoration. During the Second World War a total of 870 DSOs were awarded to officers of the RAF. Amongst the more famous recipients were Wing Commander Guy Gibson, who received a DSO and bar, Wing Commander Leonard Cheshire who received a DSO with two bars and Wing Commander 'Willie' Tait who was one of only two RAF officers to receive a DSO and three bars. The DFC was awarded in much larger numbers, more than 20,000 during the Second World War alone, and could be awarded 'immediate' or 'non-immediate' depending on circumstances. For example, an aircrew officer may have been awarded the DFC for a sustained period at the end of his tour of operations, and thus would have merited a 'non-immediate' award. Otherwise he may have carried out a particular act of bravery which merited an 'immediate' award. Thus the reasons for which Lancaster aircrew may have received the award are very varied. Recommendations for awards were generally made by the Station Commander of the recipient's unit and then passed up the chain of command for final approval by the Commander-in-Chief. The recommendation consisted of a narrative including details of the individual, the number of operations and hours flown, and which award was recommended.

Squadron Leader J. Starky DSO RNZAF (No 115 Squadron)
'One night in September 1943, Squadron Leader Starky was captain of an aircraft detailed to attack Mannheim. When nearing the target area, the aircraft was attacked by a fighter. The bomber was badly

hit and sustained much damage. It became filled with smoke and dived earthwards out of control. By a tremendous effort, Squadron Leader Starky succeeded in regaining control as the fighter came in to resume the attack. The situation was critical as the bomber had been badly crippled while the second pilot and the flight engineer had been wounded. Nevertheless, Squadron Leader Starky battled his way over enemy territory, often under fire from the ground defences. Displaying superb airmanship and unconquerable spirit, he finally reached an airfield near the coast and effected a safe landing. In most harassing circumstances, Squadron Leader Starky discharged his duty in an exemplary manner, setting an example worthy of the highest praise.'

Pilot Officer F. W. Gates DSO (No 101 Squadron)

'Pilot Officer Gates was a member of a Lancaster crew detailed to attack Milan on the night of 14/15 February 1943. Whilst over the target area, the aircraft was attacked by an enemy fighter at close range; its gunfire exploded some incendiary bombs which had failed to release and a fire quickly developed in the aircraft. The fuselage became a mass of flames reaching the mid-upper turret. Ammunition in the turret boxes and ducts commenced to explode in all directions. The situation had become extremely critical and the captain ordered the crew to abandon the aircraft. When informed that one of the crew was helpless, the captain decided to attempt a forced landing. Meanwhile, Pilot Officer Gates bravely tackled the fire and succeeded in getting it under control. The aircraft was now down to 800 feet but, as the fire had subsided, the captain decided to attempt to fly the badly damaged aircraft home. For the remainder of the journey, Pilot Officer Gates rendered valuable assistance to his captain and frequently ministered to his wounded comrades. In circumstances of the greatest danger, Pilot Officer Gates displayed courage, fortitude and devotion to duty in keeping with the highest traditions of the RAF.'

Incidentally, this brave action by the entire crew brought not only the award of a DSO to Gates, but, uniquely, the award of five CGMs to the remainder of the crew.

Warrant Officer A. A. L. Andersen DFC RAAF (No 582 Squadron)

'Warrant Officer Andersen was the wireless operator in an aircraft detailed to attack Cologne in December 1944. When approaching the target, the aircraft was hit by anti-aircraft fire and sustained some damage. On leaving the area the bomber was engaged by ten fighters. In the face of persistent attacks, the rear gunner's turret was hit by cannon shell. The windscreen was shattered and the intercommunications system was smashed. The turret doors became firmly jammed and the rear gunner was trapped. Warrant Officer Andersen had seen his comrade's plight and went to render assistance. It was a dangerous task as the pilot was taking violent evading action and the fuselage had suffered considerable damage. Nevertheless, he negotiated a safe passage to the rear turret and extricated his comrade after forcing the turret doors with an axe. Soon afterwards, it became necessary to leave the crippled aircraft by parachute. Had Warrant Officer Andersen not been successful, the rear gunner would have had no hope of success. In most distressing circumstances, Warrant Officer Andersen displayed cool courage and great determination.'

Non-Commissioned Officers' Awards

For the non-commissioned aircrew, the two awards for gallantry were the Conspicuous Gallantry Medal (CGM), arguably the non-commissioned equivalent to the DSO, and the Distinguished Flying Medal (DFM), awarded for similar reasons to the DFC. Until 1942 the only gallantry medal available to other ranks for flying duties was the DFM. To make good this deficiency the CGM (previously only awarded to the Royal Navy) was extended to airmen of the RAF for gallantry 'whilst flying in active operations against the enemy'. The first award of the CGM for flying was to Flight Sergeant Leslie Wallace, a Lancaster wireless operator serving with

No 83 Squadron, for his action whilst wounded in fighting a fire on board his aircraft during a raid against Munich in December 1942. A total of just 110 CGMs (flying) were awarded. Two of the better-known recipients were Flight Sergeants Bill Townsend and Ken Brown of No 617 Squadron for their part in the Dams Raid on the night of 16/17 May 1943. A total of just over 6,600 DFMs were awarded during the Second World War, a figure which represents just one-third of the number of DFCs awarded. One possible explanation for the large difference in numbers is that some aircrew were commissioned towards the end of their tour of operations and therefore would receive the DFC rather than the DFM. Recommendations for awards were again generally made by the Station Commander of the recipient's unit and then passed up the chain of command for final approval by the Commander-in-Chief and consisted of a narrative including details of the individual, the number of operations and hours flown, and which award was recommended. Warrant Officers, incidentally, qualified for the DFC rather than the DFM.

Sergeant D. J. Allen CGM RAF (No 467 RAAF Squadron)

'Derek Allen was the mid-upper gunner of a Lancaster detailed to attack Düsseldorf in November 1944. His aircraft was attacked by a fighter; Allen opened fire but the bomber was struck, causing much damage. A second attack followed and the Lancaster was again hit, resulting in the port engine catching fire. All efforts to extinguish the fire were unavailing, the aircraft lost height and began to lose control, and so the captain ordered the crew to bale out. The rear gunner was unable to open the turret doors and was trapped. With complete disregard for his own safety, Allen promptly went to assist his comrade. The aircraft was now on fire and falling rapidly. Nevertheless he hacked away at the turret doors with an axe and finally succeeded in freeing his comrade. Just as Allen was about to jump the aircraft broke in two. However, he fell clear and pulled his ripcord and descended safely. In the face of extreme danger, this airman displayed conduct in keeping with the best traditions of the Royal Air Force.'

Flight Sergeant W. E. Crabe CGM RCAF (No 170 Squadron)

'This airman was the mid-upper gunner detailed for a sortie one night in February 1945. Soon after leaving the target, the aircraft sustained severe damage. The rear turret was wrecked. Flight Sergeant Crabe went back at once to attend to the trapped rear gunner. Assisted by another member of the crew he cut away the side of the turret. Then, tying a rope round himself, Flight Sergeant Crabe climbed into the wrecked turret. He was completely exposed to the slipstream and in danger of falling and not wearing his parachute. Heedless of this and despite the intense cold, this valiant airman toiled until he had succeeded in freeing the gunner and getting him back into the fuselage. Unfortunately, his comrade was dead. Although his efforts were in vain, Flight Sergeant Crabe's brave and determined bid to save his co-gunner were worthy of the greatest praise.'

Flight Sergeant G. C. C. Smith CGM RAAF (No 156 Squadron)

'This airman was the rear gunner of an aircraft detailed to attack Berlin one night in February 1944. When nearing the target, Flight Sergeant Smith reported a fighter coming in to attack. As evading action was being taken, the aircraft was hit by a bullet which shattered the lower part of his right leg and foot. The hydrau-lic gear had been damaged and his turret was rendered unserviceable. Although suffering intensely and in a dazed condition, Flight Sergeant Smith refused assistance and insisted on remaining at his post to manipulate the turret manually until the enemy coast was crossed. In most distressing circumstances, this gallant airman, whose leg has since been amputated, displayed courage and fortitude of a high order. His determination to defend his aircraft until the enemy coast was crossed set a magnificent example.'

Flight Sergeant W. D. Coates DFM RAFVR (No 97 Squadron)

'This airman was the pilot of an aircraft detailed to attack Berlin one night in December 1943. It was his first operational sortie. Whilst over the target, his aircraft was damaged, the front turret and amidships of the bomber being set on fire. Flight Sergeant Coates immediately dived in an effort to put out the flames. These were eventually extinguished and height was regained. Some time later, the aircraft was hit by shrapnel which broke off the propeller tips of the starboard inner engine. One of the flying fragments pierced the fuselage and severed the hydraulic pipe lines and another portion hit and damaged the tail plane; the engine had to be feathered. A second engine was also damaged and had to be feathered. The aircraft was losing height rapidly as the enemy coast was neared and the situation became serious. Flight Sergeant Coates succeeded in maintaining height at 5,000 feet, however, and eventually reached this country, effect-ing a masterly landing at an airfield. In harassing circumstances, this airman displayed great skill, coolness and resolution.'

Second World War Campaign Stars and Medals

For the majority of Lancaster aircrew there were no gallantry awards. However, all Second World War service was recognised by the issue of campaign stars and medals. Lancaster aircrew and groundcrew qualified for the award of the 1939-45 Star which was issued for service between 3 September 1939 and 2 September 1945, the only difference between aircrew and groundcrew being the qualification period for the award. Lancaster aircrew involved on operations from United Kingdom bases over Europe during the period 3 September 1939 to 5 June 1944 also qualified for the Air Crew Europe Star. After this period—that is, after D-Day until 8 May 1945—aircrew qualified for the France and Germany Star instead. Aircrew who additionally took part in other areas of operations, such as the Battle of the Atlantic or operations over Italy, also qualified for the Atlantic Star (or 'Atlantic' clasp if already awarded the Air Crew Europe or France and Germany Stars) or the Italy Star. Lancaster groundcrew serving at UK bases could not qualify for these other campaign stars.

In addition to the campaign stars, all aircrew and groundcrew could be eligible for the award of the War Medal and the Defence Medal. The War Medal was awarded for all service of more than 28 days and if a recipient was subsequently awarded a Mention in Despatches then he or she wore an oak leaf on the ribbon. The Defence Medal was generally awarded to all who served in non-operational areas subject to air attack, or closely threatened, provided such service lasted for three or more years.

The medals belonging to Bill Reid VC. From left to right are the Victoria Cross; the 1939–45 Star; the Air Crew Europe Star with Clasp 'France and Germany'; the 1939–45 War Medal; the Coronation Medal 1953; and the Queen's Silver Jubilee Medal.

12. In Memory

There can be no better tributes to the Lancaster than those to be found in the county of Lincolnshire. Bearing in mind the importance of the county's airfields to the Lancaster story, it is fitting that Lincolnshire is still home to two Lancasters, both of which are available for the public to see. Some of the airfields from which the Lancaster used to fly remain operational with the RAF, some are home to flying or gliding clubs, and others have long been returned to agriculture. It difficult to drive around the county without passing or driving through the site of a famous airfield, and Lincolnshire contains many memorials to those who served with the Lancaster during the Second World War.

There are, of course, Lancasters to be seen at museums such as the RAF Museum at Hendon and the Imperial War Museum in London. These are magnificent examples and are well preserved.

However, to see the Lancaster at its best the enthusiast should travel to the only airworthy example in the country at RAF Coningsby. Within a few minutes of Con-

PA474, *City of Lincoln,* **of the Battle of Britain Memorial Flight, photographed while flying over its namesake. The aircraft carries the code 'KM-B', used by Sqn Ldr John Nettleton during the Augsburg raid of 17 April 1942. (Steve Barker)**

Left, top: **PA474 earlier in its career, when it was used by the College of Aeronautics at Cranfield for testing aerofoil designs. (Via RAF Coningsby)**

Left, centre: **PA474 pictured during the 1995 display season, carrying the code 'WS-J' after an aircraft of No 9 Squadron which took part in the first attack on the German battleship** *Tirpitz.* **(Steve Barker)**

Left, bottom: **Out of the display season, PA474 receives an extensive overhaul at St Athan. (Steve Barker)**

Above: **PA474 during ground running at its home base of RAF Coningsby in Lincolnshire. (Via Steve Barker)**

ingsby is another superb example, which, although not airworthy, is privately maintained and still carries out ground runs so that the public can witness the sound of its Merlins. Elsewhere there are visitors' centres and memorials, maintained either privately or by associations to ensure that the history of the Lancaster, its squadrons and its personnel shall never be forgotten.

PA474 of the Battle of Britain Memorial Flight

Each year thousands of enthusiasts see the Battle of Britain Memorial Flight either performing at air displays or at its home at RAF Coningsby. It continues to serve as a living memorial to those airmen who gave their lives in the defence of their country. Initially known as the Historic Aircraft Flight, the organisation was formed at Biggin Hill in 1957. Lancaster

PA474 joined the Flight in 1973. Three years later, in 1976, the BBMF moved to RAF Coningsby in Lincolnshire, where it has remained ever since.

Of the 7,377 Lancasters built, PA474 is just one of two surviving airworthy examples, the other being in Canada. Built in 1945, PA474 was intended for operations in the Far East. However, the war with Japan ended before it could take part in hostilities and it was later assigned to No 82 Squadron for photographic reconnaissance duties in East and South Africa. Having later served with Flight Refuelling and the College of Aeronautics at Cranfield, PA474 was adopted by the Air Historical Branch and moved to RAF Henlow in preparation for display at the RAF Museum at Hendon. However, it was the Commanding Officer of No 44 Squadron who gained permission for the aircraft to be transferred to Waddington. Following a lengthy restoration period at Waddington, permission to fly PA474 regularly was granted in 1967 and the aircraft joined the Flight in November 1973.

Known as *City of Lincoln*, PA474 carries the Lincoln coat of arms on the forward fuselage in recognition of the long and deep association of the Lancaster and Bomber Command with the city. During a display the Lancaster is crewed by two pilots, one navigator and an air engineer. The Officer Commanding BBMF captains the Lancaster during the display. There are, generally, two pilots at RAF Coningsby who are qualified as co-pilots for the display, and each takes his turn dur-

ing the season. The Flight, generally, has three navigators qualified on the Lancaster during the season and these are selected from instructors serving with No 56 Squadron at Coningsby. The task of the navigator can be very demanding: it is his responsibility to make sure that the Lancaster (and fighters if in formation) are at the right place exactly at the right time. The fourth member of the crew is the air engineer, three of which are selected from the instructors at the Air Engineer School.

The Lancaster is maintained in display condition by a small number of dedicated engineers. Led by a warrant officer, the engineering team are all full-time members of the Flight and all volunteers; most are able to serve with the Flight for several years. Only the engine fitters have to carry out specialist training (a short course at Kidlington on piston engines and propellers); otherwise the tradesmen are left to develop their skills with experience over the years. PA474 is maintained to an extremely high standard and all the lengthy maintenance schedules are carried out during the winter months, ensuring that the aircraft is available for the display season; even during the display season it does not escape further inspections and routine servicing. Fortunately, and perhaps surprisingly, there tend to be few problems maintaining the Lancaster in terms of spares. Some components have to be made at the manufacturers either from original drawings or, if these are not available, from the original piece. The other source of spares is the general public, who very kindly donate parts to the Flight. Often, these parts have been lying around in lofts or garages for many years.

The Lancaster is limited in the number of hours it may fly during the year (currently 85) to ensure that it can continue flying for as long into the future as possible. Time taken during transit to and from air displays has to be taken into consideration and, when possible, the aircraft flies directly to a venue. For the same reason, the Flight will try to coordinate more than one display to ensure maximum benefit for a given number of flying hours. Each year 'bids' for the Lancaster to display are sent in writing to a Participation Committee in London. It is the task of the Committee to gather all the 'bids' and to decide which events will be attended. The Committee meets in the January preceding the display season and forwards a proposed programme to the Flight. It is then up to the Flight's staff and the Lancaster's aircrew to make the final plans.

Flight Lieutenant Mike Chatterton is one of two display captains for PA474. His father flew Lancasters during the war. He graduated from the RAF College Cranwell in 1976 and flew the Shackleton with No 8 Squadron before converting to the Nimrod. Having completed two tours, he

PA474 during a pan wash at Coningsby. The aircraft is always kept in superb display condition. (Steve Barker)

was posted as an 'ops' officer at Coningsby, where he was given the opportunity to fly the Memorial Flight's Lancaster. It was an opportunity not to be missed, as he explains:

'The dropping of one million poppies over the VJ Remembrance Service at Buckingham Palace in August 1995 was yet another tremendous honour amongst the many I have enjoyed since I have been flying PA474. In the far off days, as a schoolboy, I used to watch and listen in awe to *the* Lancaster at any air display my father and I could get to. I knew that he had flown Lancasters in the last war, and he would often talk about their fine flying qualities, but like many of his contemporaries he was reticent in discussing the war and so I was unaware of the horrors he had been through on his operational tour or of the magnificent war record of this amazing machine. Now, years later, having realised an ambition beyond my wildest dreams of becoming captain of the best aircraft ever built, I have learnt of the suffering and hardships endured by the bomber crews. I am delighted that I have the privilege of flying the Lanc in memory of the many thousands of aircrew who were killed or injured so that we may live in freedom today. We on BBMF always feel very humbled when we meet the men who flew these aircraft "in anger" and I am personally very proud that my father is amongst their number.

'I am now twice the age that my father and his colleagues were when they set out, night after night, for Germany or occupied Europe and two thoughts are uppermost in my mind when I contemplate our unique father/son achievement. The first thought is the vast responsibility he had to shoulder at such an early age and the second is the concept that he never dared think about "the future" because the odds were that he would not live to have one. After his operational tour he went on to become an instructor on Lancs until the end of the war, so we often compare notes on handling techniques, although, over the years, some of the challenges have changed. He used to frequently operate at max. all-up weight but had a choice of six runway directions, whereas we always fly at the minimum weight but often have to battle with a crosswind as most of today's airfields only have one runway.

'We are often asked how closely PA474 resembles a wartime Lanc. The authenticity actually improves every year as the BBMF groundcrew acquire and fit the proper internal equipment. These parts are manufactured, usually by the School of Technical Training at RAF St Athan, using old drawings and photographs. Recently, components and piping for the turrets' hydraulic system and ammunition tracking rails have been added. We have to admit to having Lincoln undercarriage legs and Shackleton mainwheels, although both are very similar to the original Lancaster design, and the tailwheel is from a Hastings. The four Merlins that are installed at any one time come from a pool which includes American-built Packards and Rolls-Royce versions built for either civilian or military use. A 24-volt electrical system is installed in place of the original 12-volt one and we now have to use a more up to date intercom, modern radios and a radar transponder (IFF) to smooth our passage through today's highly congested lower airspace.

'On the day of a display I like to arrive at the Met Office at Coningsby two hours before the planned take-off time. Because of the altitude we operate at I'm particularly interested in the low-level visibility and height of the lowest cloudbase, and

The spectacular nose art on PA474 during the 1995 display season, the figure of Johnny Walker with bombs recording the 106 operational sorties flown by W4964, the aircraft represented during the display season. Note the Russian star beneath the word 'strong', to represent the first attack on the *Tirpitz*, flown from the Soviet Union.

of course the surface wind is a major factor at display sites and at the destination. The captain and navigator will have already studied the display folder that has been compiled by the BBMF admin. staff. This information can vary from comprehensive Op Orders, display instructions and multiple maps to a single black-and-white photocopied map with an arrow drawn on as a requested run-in heading. I like to contact each of the venues at this stage just to confirm our time of arrival, get any last-minute changes from the organisers and give them any details they need for their commentaries.

'All the aircrew and groundcrew that will be flying in the Lanc or helping with the start-up gather together one hour before departure for the pre-flight briefing. If we are being accompanied by fighters their pilots will be with us as well. The brief follows a strict format and covers the details of each venue, how we intend to carry out the displays or flypasts, all the appropriate timings and any relevant

safety considerations. Depending on the complexity of the flight, the briefing can take from 10 to 25 minutes, after which it is time to check the authorisation sheet, sign the F700, collect together bags, helmet, gloves etc,, and walk out to the "bomber", as we fondly refer to her. Then for the many thousands of Lancaster fans around the world, as we set foot on the aircraft ladder, we become the most envied men on earth.'

Due to the increasing public interest, and the demand for 'official tours' of the Lancaster at Coningsby, a Visitors' Centre has been established to meet the public demand for visits and merchandise connected with the Flight. The Visitors' Centre has proved a great success. Each year some 20,000 members of the public, of all ages and from all backgrounds, visit the centre. Many visitors are ex RAF from different parts of the world, some of them having wartime experience on the Lancaster. Equally, many of the visitors, young and old, have no connection with the RAF but simply want to see the Lancaster close up and to find out more about it. During the peak season (July and August) the Centre is visited by as many as 300 people per day. The Centre is open Monday to Friday, except public holidays, with tours commencing every hour (half-hourly during the peak season) between 10.00 a.m. and 3.00 p.m. There is a small charge for

a visit to the hangar, with reductions available for senior citizens and children, and there are facilities for the disabled. However, it is important to emphasise that there is no guarantee that the Lancaster will be in the hangar on any specific day.

Like any major RAF display team, the future of the Lancaster and the Flight is reviewed every four years. Obviously, it costs money to run the Flight (approximately £1–2 million per year), and it could be considered by some to be an expensive option to fly and maintain all of the aircraft. Thus in today's current financial climate the future of the Flight is never certain. However, the Flight has brought much pleasure to the thousands who see it every year and it remains a living memorial to the many thousands of airmen who gave their lives in the service of their country . . . 'lest we forget'.

Lancaster Mk VII NX611, East Kirkby, Lincolnshire

Just about ten miles to the east of Coningsby is the former site of East Kirkby airfield, where another fine example of the Lancaster can be found. Owned and maintained by two farming brothers, Fred and Harold Panton, NX611 is kept in magnificent condition and remains a major attraction for the Lancaster enthusiast.

NX611 is a Mk VII built by Austin Motors at Longbridge and completed in April 1945. Although it was delivered too late for operations in Europe, the aircraft was destined for the Far East as part of Tiger Force and was one of the first 150 Mk VIIs finished to Far East standard. With the end of the war in the Pacific, NX611 was put into storage at No 38 MU at Llandow until 1952, when it was one of a number of aircraft bought by the French Government for service with the French naval air arm under a Western Union agreement. Painted in midnight blue and coded 'WU15', it was converted for maritime reconnaissance duties, its mid-upper turret being removed and provision for the fitting of the ASV (anti-surveillance vessel) radar being made. Based in Brittany and Morocco, it served for ten years before having a major overhaul and a new white paint scheme. It was then delivered to New

Left, top: Still in the white paintwork of the French *Aéronavale*, but bearing the British registration G-ASXX, NX611 returned to the United Kingdom on 13 May 1965 following a 12,000-mile flight from Australia. The aircraft's future was uncertain until September 1983, when it was bought by the Panton brothers.

Left, centre: NX611 being dismantled at Scampton prior to its move to East Kirkby in 1988. (John Loveley)

Left, bottom: NX611 during ground running at East Kirkby.

Singapore, Malaya, India, Bahrain, Cyprus and France and had included ten stops.

Restoration work commenced and the aircraft was registered with its original serial, NX611, and coded 'HA-P' (Historical Aircraft Preservation Society)—which was also the original code of a Lancaster of No 218 (Gold Coast) Squadron. It was two years before the aircraft could be flown again and it took to the air on 6 May 1967. However, the high costs of maintaining the aircraft in an airworthy condition, and the fact that PA474 had also flown again, indicated an uncertain future for NX611. In 1969 the aircraft was flown to Lavenham in Suffolk, where it was coded 'GL-C' (after Group Captain Leonard Cheshire VC DSO DFC). The future remained uncertain, but in February the following year NX611 was delivered to Hullavington, Wiltshire, where it was repainted. Inspections revealed problems with the starboard inner engine, which resulted in the aircraft being cleared for one flight only. In June 1970 NX611 was delivered to Squires Gate, where it became the main attraction at the Blackpool Aeronautical Museum. In April 1972 the aircraft was offered for auction but failed to reach its reserve price. However, NX611 was bought by the Rt Hon. Lord Lilford of Nateby so that it could remain in Britain.

It was at this point that a Lincolnshire farmer, Fred Panton, decided that one day he would purchase the aircraft for himself. He persuaded the RAF to preserve the aircraft and the following year Lord Lilford generously offered NX611 on loan. In August 1973 NX611 was dismantled

Caledonia, a French island situated 1,000 miles east of Australia. Operating in the Pacific in the roles of maritime patrol, air–sea rescue and communications, it was one of the last three Lancasters flying anywhere in the world. However, a shortage of spares led to these aircraft being withdrawn from service in 1964.

With the cooperation of the French authorities, 'WU15' was delivered to Sydney, Australia, in preparation for its return to the United Kingdom. In April 1965 it was overhauled and at that time was the world's only airworthy Lancaster. Still in the white markings of the French *Aéronovale*, but now with the British registration G-ASXX, the Lancaster left Mascot on 25 April for the start of its 12,000-mile journey back to the UK. The aircraft was captained by John Hampshire and a volunteer crew, and the journey took nineteen days and 70 flying hours before the Lancaster landed at Biggin Hill on 13 May. The journey had staged through Australia,

The Panton brothers stand proudly in front of NX611 at its home at East Kirkby. Fred (right) and Harold Panton bought the aircraft in September 1983 as a permanent memorial to their elder brother Christopher and all the other Lancaster aircrew who failed to return from operations.

and transferred to RAF Scampton; restoration was completed in March 1974 and the following month the aircraft was placed at the main gate for guardian duties. It remained there for the next ten years.

The future of NX611 was once again in doubt during 1983 as the ten-year loan by Lord Lilford was coming to an end. On 1 September 1983 Fred Panton and his brother Harold succeeded in their original ambition of buying NX611 when they purchased the aircraft from Lord Lilford. For the next five years NX611 remained as a gate guardian whilst plans unfolded for the aircraft to be transferred to East Kirkby. In 1988 the Lancaster was disman-

tled and delivered to East Kirkby, where Fred and Harold Panton had restored the former air traffic control tower on their farmland. The two brothers had grown up near the airfield during the war and always remembered the sound of the Lancasters of Nos 57 and 630 Squadrons which had operated from the base. They also had a more personal interest in the aircraft of Bomber Command as their elder brother Christopher had been killed during the Nuremberg raid on the night of 31 March 1944, when the Halifax bomber in which he was the flight engineer had failed to return.

With the Lancaster housed in its hangar, the Panton brothers completed a Visitors' Centre as part of the Lincolnshire Aviation Heritage Centre, which was opened to the public by Marshal of the Royal Air Force Sir Michael Beetham GCB CBE DFC AFC in July 1989. It was fitting that Sir Michael should be the distinguished guest to open the Centre as he had operated with No 57 Squadron from East Kirkby during the war. The hangar in which the Lancaster is kept is built on the site where No 57 Squadron's Lancasters were housed during the war. In October 1979 a memorial to the two squadrons was unveiled on the site of the guardroom that stood at the entrance to East Kirkby airfield.

Lancaster NX611 remains the main attraction at the Centre but, as well as the restored air traffic control tower, there are other buildings of interest and many other historic items and photographs. The Centre is situated in the village of East Kirkby, on the A155 Sleaford–Spilsby road, and is open from Monday to Saturday throughout the year. Opening hours in summer are 10.00 a.m. to 5.00 p.m. (last admission 4.00 p.m.) and in winter (November to Easter) between 10.00 a.m. and 3.30 p.m. (last admission 2.30 p.m.). Car parking and refreshments are available.

The Airfields

It is virtually impossible to drive around the county of Lincolnshire and not come across the sites of former airfields which once were home to Lancaster squadrons and crews. Although the majority of these airfields have long returned to agriculture, the village names are there as permanent reminders. At first glance many of the sites would remain unnoticed but there are many local people keen to ensure that the memories live on as a lasting tribute to all those who served from 'Bomber County'. Organisations such as the North Kesteven Airfield Trail have been established to enable visitors to locate the former airfield sites. Published routes can be followed in a day or at a more leisurely pace.

The county of Lincolnshire had long been popular for the construction of airfields since the days of the First World War.

Below left: The stripped down starboard outer engine of NX611.

Below right: Nose art on NX611.

This was primarily because of the Lincoln Ridge, which runs north–south, allowing the early aeroplanes to take-off into the prevailing westerly winds and gain height very quickly. Many First World War sites were therefore developed during the RAF's Expansion Schemes of the late 1930s. A total of 27 airfields within Lincolnshire were home to Lancasters during or immediately after the war. Their layouts were often very similar and of a triangular nature, comprising three runways and covering an area of up to 1,000 acres. To operate Lancasters an airfield was developed to 'Class A' standard, with the main runway some 6,000ft in length and the two others about 4,000ft long. A handful of these airfields are still used by the RAF, while others are used by light aircraft flying clubs or gliding clubs or by microlights. The remainder have long become disused and the enthusiast will have to spend time to find clues of their presence.

Metheringham Airfield Visitors' Centre
Metheringham opened in October 1943 as one of many new airfields developed from agricultural land to become part of No 5 Group, Bomber Command. It was unusual amongst Lincolnshire airfields in that it was built in the Lincolnshire Fens, on land which was considered unsuitable for heavy bomber operations. It was built to the standard 'Class A' specification and had three concrete runways. In November 1943 Lancasters of No 106 Squadron moved in to Metheringham from Syerston and for the remainder of the war Metheringham was home to the Squadron. On the night of 26/27 April 1944, a flight engineer of the Squadron, Sgt Norman Jackson, was awarded the Victoria Cross following his bravery in attempting to extinguish an engine fire by climbing out onto the aircraft's wing (see Chapter 11). After the war Metheringham was briefly home to the Lancasters of No 467

Squadron RAAF and No 189 Squadron before No 106 finally left the airfield in February 1946. Metheringham closed in the spring of 1946 and the land reverted to agricultural use.

Fifty years on, there are still reminders of the airfield. Situated approximately two miles from the village of Metheringham, on the B1189 directly opposite the B1191

Below left: The East Kirkby memorial to the Lancaster crews of Nos 57 and 630 Squadrons.

Below right: The memorial on the site of RAF Wickenby, home to the Lancasters of Nos 12 and 626 Squadrons.

Bottom left: The memorial on the site of the former RAF Metheringham.

Bottom right: The memorial to Nos 50 and 61 Squadrons on the site of RAF Skellingthorpe.

Above left: The No 617 Squadron 'Dambusters' memorial at Woodhall Spa, designed to represent the breach of the dams.

Above right: The Petwood Hotel at Woodhall Spa, used as the Officers' Mess by No 617 Squadron during the latter stages of the war.

road to Woodhall Spa, is Westmoor Farm on Martin Moor. Here is located the Metheringham Airfield Visitors' Centre which is open to the public and maintained by the owners of the farm, Mr and Mrs Scoley. The Visitors' Centre is in a former domestic site building and has a wonderful exhibition of photographs and wartime memorabilia commemorating the role of the airfield and No 106 Squadron. There are also other original buildings, while close to the Centre are the remains of the concrete runways and perimeter tracks, and also a memorial to No 106 Squadron.

The Visitors' Centre is open to the public between 10.00 a.m. and 5.00 p.m. every Saturday, Sunday and Bank Holiday during the period from the last weekend in March until the last weekend in October. Visits at other times can be made by prior arrangement with Mr and Mrs Scoley. The Centre is supported by North Kesteven District Council and the Friends of Metheringham Airfield and is a tribute to all who served at Metheringham during its short history.

Skellingthorpe Exhibition and Memorial
Just to the west of the city of Lincoln is the site of RAF Skellingthorpe, the wartime home to Nos 50 and 61 Squadrons. The airfield opened in October 1941 and was home to Lancasters of both squadrons from May 1942 until the end of the war. The airfield has now been replaced by a large residential development which is bordered by the A46 Lincoln by-pass. The last areas of the former airfield con-

tinue to be built upon, but permanent reminders of the airfield and its personnel remain. The school built on the site of the main runway is named the Leslie Manser School after Flying Officer Manser, who was posthumously awarded the Victoria Cross whilst flying a Manchester of No 50 Squadron from the airfield in May 1942. Children attending the school have their own classroom dedicated to all those who operated from the airfield during the war.

Close to the school stands what is undoubtedly one of the finest memorials in the county. Dedicated to the two squadrons, it was unveiled in 1989 and the following year the Squadrons' Association presented a Roll of Honour to the city of Lincoln which is now kept in the RAF Chapel in Lincoln Cathedral. A further memorial is situated outside the Skellingthorpe Village Community Centre, where an exhibition of photographs relating to the airfield can be seen in the Heritage Room. A short distance from the village is Skellingthorpe Moor Plantation, the site of the bomb storage area, and a short walk either side of the by-pass reveals the few remaining shelters.

The Dambusters Memorial and the Petwood House Hotel, Woodhall Spa

Situated in the village of Woodhall Spa is the Dambusters Memorial, a tribute to the men of No 617 Squadron who failed to return from operations during the war. Unique in design, the memorial is set within pleasant surroundings in the cen-

tre of the village. Although the Squadron carried out the famous Dams raid from Scampton, it was Woodhall Spa which became home for the Lancasters of the Squadron from January 1944 until the end of the war.

The Petwood House Hotel is a most spectacular building and stands in 30 acres of woodland and extended gardens in Woodhall Spa. The airfield at Woodhall Spa opened in February 1942 as part of No 5 Group, Bomber Command. As one of the smaller airfields it could only accommodate one squadron and so in January 1944 it was decided that it would be the ideal secure location for the Lancasters of No 617 Squadron which, after the Dams Raid, was employed as a specialist bombing unit. The Hotel was requisitioned by the RAF in October 1943 and then became the Officers' Mess for the Squadron. The house was built at the turn of the century for Lady Weighall on a site chosen by her in the area of her 'pet wood'. Many original features are to be found inside the hotel, together with many reminders of the Lancaster crews who flew from Woodhall Spa. The Hotel's Squadron Bar is dedicated to the men of the 'Dambusters' Squadron.

Appendices

APPENDIX A: LANCASTER CHRONOLOGY 1936–45

1936
Sept. — Issue of Specification P.13/36 resulting in Avro Type 679

1939
Mar. — Issue of Specification B.1/39 resulting in Avro Type 683
25 July — First flight of Manchester prototype L7246 at Ringway

1940
26 May — Maiden flight of second Manchester prototype (L7247)
Nov. — No 207 Squadron re-forms with Manchesters at Waddington
19 Nov. — Authority for the maunfacture of four Type 683 prototypes

1941
9 Jan. — Maiden flight of first Lancaster prototype (BT308) at Ringway
24/25 Feb. — First Manchester operations by No 207 Sqn against Brest
31 Mar./1 Apr. — First use of 4,000lb bomb.
13 May — Maiden flight of second Lancaster prototype (DG595)
11/12 Aug. — Operational trial of Gee
Sept. — Lancaster Production Group formed
31 Oct. — First production Lancaster (L7527) flies at Woodfood
26 Nov. — Maiden flight of third Lancaster prototype (DT810)
Dec. — First operational use of Oboe
24 Dec. — A&AEE declares that Lancaster is ready for delivery
24–27 Dec. — First seven Lancasters delivered to No 44 Sqn at Waddington

1942
3/4 Mar. — Operational début (minelaying) by Lancasters of No 44 Sqn
10/11 Mar. — First bombing operations by Lancasters of No 44 Sqn (Essen)
17 Apr. — Augsburg raid
May–June — 'Thousand Bomber' raids
25/26 June — Last Manchester operations
July — Operational use of Window
11 Aug. — Formation of Pathfinder Force
18/19 Aug. — First operations by Pathfinder Force (Flensburg)
Sept. — First Lancaster Mk IIs delivered to Boscombe Down
Oct. — Delivery of first Lancaster Mk IIs to No 61 Sqn at Syerston; delivery of first Mk III prototype (W4114) to Boscombe Down
17 Oct. — Le Creusot raid
20/21 Dec. — Operational début of Oboe

1943
16/17 Jan. — First use of target indicators (Berlin)
25 Jan. — Formation of No 8 (PFF) Group
30/31 Jan. — First operational use of H2S (Hamburg)
5/6 Mar. — Opening of Battle of the Ruhr
16/17 May — Operation 'Chastise' (Dams Raid)
14/15 June — First use of Serrate
19/20 June — Operational début of Monica
20 June — First use of Master Bomber technique by No 5 Group
20/21 June — First 'shuttle' operation when 60 Lancasters land in North Africa
24/25 July — Operational début of *Window*.
July–Aug. — Operation 'Gormorrah' (Hamburg)
17/18 Aug. — Operation 'Hydra' (Peenemünde)
15/16 Sept. — First use of 12,000lb 'Tallboy' (Dortmund–Ems Canal)
Oct. — ABC fitted to Lancasters of No 101 Sqn
7/8 Oct. — Operational début of ABC (Stuttgart)
22/23 Oct. — Operational début of Corona
3/4 Nov. — Large-scale operational début of G-H (Düsseldorf)
8 Nov. — Formation of No 100 (Special Duties) Group
Nov. — Delivery of H2S Mk III Lancasters to Nos 83 and 97 Sqns
Nov. — Battle of Berlin begins

1944
24/25 Mar. — End of Battle of Berlin
30/31 Mar. — Nuremberg raid
6 June — Operation 'Overlord' (Allied invasion of Europe)
12 June — Beginning of Operation 'Crossbow' (attacks on V- weapon sites)
11 July — First Lancaster-equipped Oboe attack by No 582 Sqn (Gapennes)
Sept. — Operation 'Market Garden' (Arnhem and Nijmegen)
Sept.–Nov. — Operation 'Pavarane' (attack on *Tirpitz*)

1945
13/14 Feb. — Operation 'Thunderclap' (Dresden)
12 Mar. — Largest Bomber Command raid of the war (1,107 aircraft, Dortmund)
14 Mar. — First operational use of 22,000lb 'Grand Slam' bomb (Bielefeld viaduct)
Apr.–May — Operation 'Manna' (drop of food supplies)
May — Operation 'Exodus' (repatriation of Allied PoWs)

An early Lancaster Mk I (W4114), built by A. V. Roe at Newton Heath.

APPENDIX B: AVRO LANCASTER I CUTAWAY

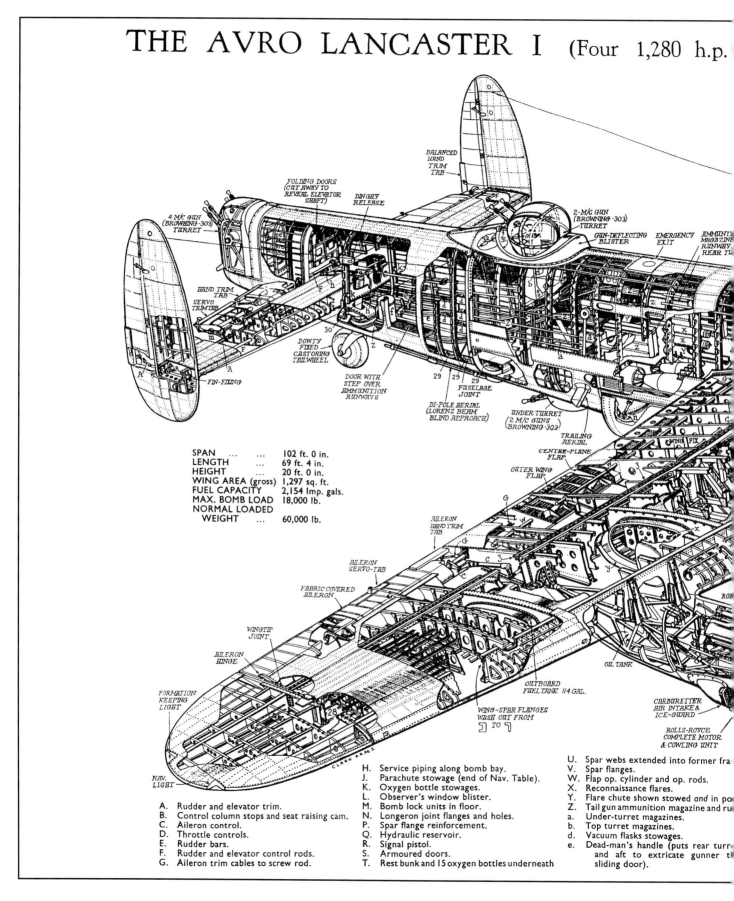

THE AVRO LANCASTER I (Four 1,280 h.p.

SPAN	... ...	102 ft. 0 in.
LENGTH	...	69 ft. 4 in.
HEIGHT	...	20 ft. 0 in.
WING AREA (gross)		1,297 sq. ft.
FUEL CAPACITY		2,154 Imp. gals.
MAX. BOMB LOAD		18,000 lb.
NORMAL LOADED WEIGHT	...	60,000 lb.

A. Rudder and elevator trim.
B. Control column stops and seat raising cam.
C. Aileron control.
D. Throttle controls.
E. Rudder bars.
F. Rudder and elevator control rods.
G. Aileron trim cables to screw rod.

H. Service piping along bomb bay.
J. Parachute stowage (end of Nav. Table).
K. Oxygen bottle stowages.
L. Observer's window blister.
M. Bomb lock units in floor.
N. Longeron joint flanges and holes.
P. Spar flange reinforcement.
Q. Hydraulic reservoir.
R. Signal pistol.
S. Armoured doors.
T. Rest bunk and 15 oxygen bottles underneath

U. Spar webs extended into former fra
V. Spar flanges.
W. Flap op. cylinder and op. rods.
X. Reconnaissance flares.
Y. Flare chute shown stowed and in po
Z. Tail gun ammunition magazine and ru
a. Under-turret magazines.
b. Top turret magazines.
d. Vacuum flasks stowages.
e. Dead-man's handle (puts rear turr and aft to extricate gunner t sliding door).

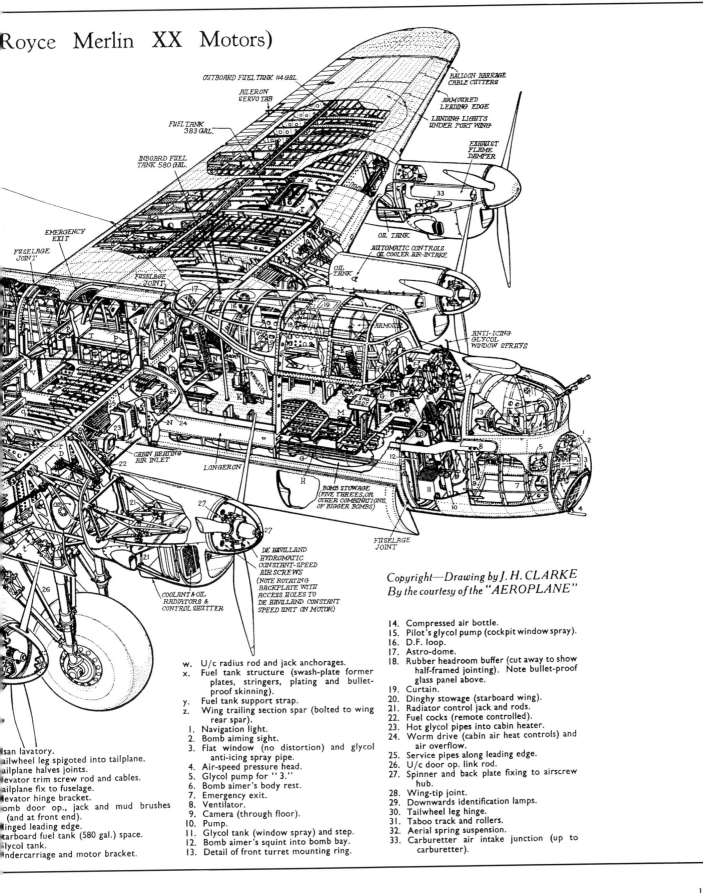

Royce Merlin XX Motors)

OUTBOARD FUEL TANK 114 GAL.

AILERON SERVO TAB

FUEL TANK 383 GAL.

INBOARD FUEL TANK 580 GAL.

EMERGENCY EXIT

FUSELAGE JOINT

FUSELAGE JOINT

BALLOON BARRAGE CABLE CUTTERS

ARMOURED LEADING EDGE

LANDING LIGHTS UNDER PORT WING

EXHAUST FLAME DAMPER

OIL TANK

AUTOMATIC CONTROLS OIL COOLER AIR-INTAKE

OIL TANK

ANTI-ICING GLYCOL WINDOW SPRAYS

CABIN HEATING AIR INLET

LONGERON

BOMB STOWAGE (FIVE THREES, OR OTHER COMBINATIONS OF BIGGER BOMBS)

FUSELAGE JOINT

DE HAVILLAND HYDROMATIC CONSTANT-SPEED AIR SCREWS (NOTE ROTATING BACKPLATE WITH ACCESS HOLES TO DE HAVILLAND CONSTANT SPEED UNIT ON MOTOR)

COOLANT & OIL RADIATORS & CONTROL SHUTTER

Copyright—Drawing by J. H. CLARKE
By the courtesy of the "AEROPLANE"

lsan lavatory.
ailwheel leg spigoted into tailplane.
ailplane halves joints.
levator trim screw rod and cables.
ailplane fix to fuselage.
levator hinge bracket.
omb door op., jack and mud brushes (and at front end).
inged leading edge.
tarboard fuel tank (580 gal.) space.
lycol tank.
ndercarriage and motor bracket.

w. U/c radius rod and jack anchorages.
x. Fuel tank structure (swash-plate former plates, stringers, plating and bullet-proof skinning).
y. Fuel tank support strap.
z. Wing trailing section spar (bolted to wing rear spar).
1. Navigation light.
2. Bomb aiming sight.
3. Flat window (no distortion) and glycol anti-icing spray pipe.
4. Air-speed pressure head.
5. Glycol pump for "3."
6. Bomb aimer's body rest.
7. Emergency exit.
8. Ventilator.
9. Camera (through floor).
10. Pump.
11. Glycol tank (window spray) and step.
12. Bomb aimer's squint into bomb bay.
13. Detail of front turret mounting ring.

14. Compressed air bottle.
15. Pilot's glycol pump (cockpit window spray).
16. D.F. loop.
17. Astro-dome.
18. Rubber headroom buffer (cut away to show half-framed jointing). Note bullet-proof glass panel above.
19. Curtain.
20. Dinghy stowage (starboard wing).
21. Radiator control jack and rods.
22. Fuel cocks (remote controlled).
23. Hot glycol pipes into cabin heater.
24. Worm drive (cabin air heat controls) and air overflow.
25. Service pipes along leading edge.
26. U/c door op. link rod.
27. Spinner and back plate fixing to airscrew hub.
28. Wing-tip joint.
29. Downwards identification lamps.
30. Tailwheel leg hinge.
31. Taboo track and rollers.
32. Aerial spring suspension.
33. Carburetter air intake junction (up to carburetter).

APPENDIX C: LANCASTER VARIANTS

Type 683	Prototypes; 3 built (BT308, DG595, DT810)
Mk I	Standard production aircraft powered by Rolls-Royce Merlin 20, 22 or 24 engines
Mk I (Special)	Modified to carry bombs in excess of 12,000lb
Mk I (FE)	Tropicalised for the Far East
PR.1	Modified Mk I for photo-reconnaissance duties
Mk I (Western Union)	Lancasters supplied to the French *Aéronavale* under Western Union arrangements
Mk I (Egyptian)	Overhauled for the Egyptian Air Force
Mk I (Civilian)	Converted for civilian use
Mk I engine test-beds	Various aircraft used for testing Armstrong Siddeley and Rolls-Royce engines
Mk II	Standard production aircraft powered by Bristol Hercules VI or XVI engines
Mk III	Standard production aircraft powered by Packard-built Merlin 28, 38 or 224 engines
Mk III (Type 464 Provisioning)	Modified to carry 'Upkeep' for dams raid
ASR.3	Converted for air–sea rescue
GR.3	Converted ASR.3 for maritime reconnaissance duties
Mk IV	Became Avro Lincoln Mk I
Mk V	Became Avro Lincoln Mk II

Mk VI	Modified Mk III powered by Rolls-Royce Merlin 85 or 87 engines
Mk VII	Production variant fitted with a Martin mid-upper turret
Mk VII (FE)	Mk VII tropicalised for the Far East
Mk VII (Western Union)	Mk VII supplied to the French *Aéronavale* under Western Union arrangements
Mk VIII	Mark number reserved for Lancaster development but not used
Mk IX	Mark number reserved for Lancaster development but not used
Mk X	Production variant built by Victory Aircraft in Canada
Mk 10AR	Mk X converted for aerial reconnaissance duties
Mk 10ASR	Mk X converted for air–sea rescue duties with the RCAF
Mk 10BR	Mk X converted for bomber reconnaissance duties
Mk 10DC	Mk X converted for drone-carrying duties
Mk 10AR	Mk X converted for aerial reconnaissance duties
Mk 10MR	Mk X converted for maritime reconnaissance duties
Mk 10N	Mk X converted for navigational training
Mk 10P	Mk X converted for photo-reconnaissance duties
Mk 10 (Civilian)	Mk X converted for civilian duties

Top left: PA478 was a Lancaster Mk I built by Vickers at Chester under Contract No 2791 and completed at the end of the war.

Top right: A Lancaster Mk II powered by Hercules VI engines.

Above left: A Lancaster ASR.3 converted for air–sea rescue duties.

Above right: SW338, a Lancaster Mk III built by A. V. Roe at Yeadon under Contract No 1807. (Peter Green)

Below left: NX739, a Lancaster Mk VII built by Austin Motors.

Below right: KB783, a Mk X built by Victory Aircraft in Canada.

APPENDIX D: LANCASTER PRODUCTION

This appendix shows the total Lancaster production. Production figures for each mark are given, followed by the number built by each manufacturing company and at which location, then, in detail, which individual Lancaster was built by which company and under which contract (where known). Also given are the delivery dates for each contract, i.e. the period during the aircraft would have been delivered. The figures quoted in this Appendix may vary from those quoted in other publications. This variation applies particularly to production by A. V. Roe & Co. and Metropolitan-Vickers, where figures may vary by up to six aircraft depending on whether Mk I or Mk III variants are identified. However, the total production figures are correct and agree with those quoted in other sources.

Prototypes

A. V. Roe (Newton Heath)	3

Mk I Production

Metropolitan-Vickers (Trafford Park)	948
Armstrong Whitworth (Baginton, Bitteswell)	911
A. V. Roe (836 at Newton Heath, 54 at Yeadon)	890
Vickers-Armstrong (Castle Bromwich	300
Vickers (Chester)	200
Austin Motors (Longbridge)	150
Total Mk I Production	3,434

Mk II Production

Armstrong Whitworth	300

Mk III Production

A. V. Roe (2,138 at Newton Heath, 642 at Yeadon)	2,780
Metropolitan-Vickers (Trafford Park)	132
Armstrong Whitworth (Baginton, Bitteswell)	118
Total Mk III Production	3,030

Mk VII Production

Austin Motors (Longbridge)	180

MkX Production

Victory Aircraft (Ontario)	430
Total Lancaster Production	**7,377**

COMPANY PRODUCTION FIGURES

A. V. Roe (Manchester area, Yeadon)	3,673
Armstrong Whitworth (Baginton, Bitteswell)	1,329
Metropolitan-Vickers (Trafford Park)	1,080
Vickers-Armstrong (Castle Bromwich, Chester)	535
Victory Aircraft (Ontario)	430
Austin Motors (Longbridge)	330

LANCASTER Mk I PRODUCTION: A. V. ROE & CO.

Newton Heath/Chadderton (839 Aircraft)

Prototypes (3 aircraft)
BT308, DG595, DT810

Contract No B.648770/37 (43 aircraft), delivery November 1941–March 1942
L7527–L7549, L7565–L7584

Contract No B.69274/40 (536 aircraft), delivery February 1942–June 1943
R5482–R5517, R5537–R5576, R5603–R5640, R5658–R5703, R5724–R5763, W4102–W4140, W4154–W4201, W4230–W4279, W4301–W4340, W4355–W4384, ED303–ED334, ED347–ED386, ED389, ED391–ED392, ED394, ED409, ED411–ED412, ED414, ED418, ED420, ED422, ED425, ED430, ED436, ED439, ED443, ED446–ED447, ED451, ED498, ED521–ED522, ED525, ED528, ED533, ED537, ED548, ED550, ED552, ED554, ED567, ED569, ED586, ED591, ED594, ED600–ED601, ED604, ED610, ED622, ED631, ED661, ED692, ED703, ED715, ED732, ED735, ED749, ED751, ED754–ED755, ED757–ED758, ED761–ED763, ED766, ED769–ED770, ED773–ED774, ED777–ED778, ED780–ED782

Contract No Unknown (225 aircraft), delivery October 1944–March 1945
PB643–PB647, PB671–PB674, PB686–PB692, PB695–PB696, PB703–PB705, PB708, PB721–PB727, PB730–PB732, PB734–PB757, PB759–PB768, PB780–PB823, PB836–PB881, PB893–PB922, PB924–PB936, PB949–PB959, PB961, PB981–PB994

Mk I (Special) (32 aircraft), delivery January–March 1945
PB995–PB998, PD112–PD139

Yeadon (54 aircraft)

Contract No 1807 (10 aircraft), delivery November 1942–October 1944
LM301–LM310

Contract No 2019 (54 aircraft), delivery October 1944–March 1945
ME328, ME330, ME350, ME352, ME371–ME374, ME383–ME384, ME419–ME421, ME431– ME440, ME445–ME451, ME455–ME458, ME470, ME475–ME477, ME479–ME480, ME482, ME490, ME495

Total prototype and Mk I production by A. V. Roe & Co.: 893

LANCASTER Mk III PRODUCTION: A. V. ROE & CO.

Newton Heath/Chadderton (2,138 Aircraft)

Contract No B.69274/40 (488 aircraft), delivery November 1942–June 1943
ED362, ED371, ED378, ED383, ED387–ED388, ED390, ED393, ED395–ED396, ED408, ED410, ED413, ED415–ED417, ED419, ED421, ED423–ED424, ED426–ED429, ED431–ED435, ED437–ED438, ED440–ED442, ED444–ED445, ED448–ED450, ED452–ED453, ED467–ED497, ED499–ED504, ED520, ED523–ED524, ED526–ED527, ED529–ED532, ED534–ED536, ED538–ED547, ED549, ED551, ED553, ED555–ED566, ED568, ED583–ED585, ED587–ED590, ED592–ED593, ED595–ED599, ED602–ED603, ED605–ED609, ED611–ED621, ED623–ED630, ED645–ED660, ED662–ED668, ED688–ED691, ED693–ED702, ED704–ED714, ED716–ED731, ED733–ED734, ED736–ED737, ED750, ED752–ED753, ED756, ED759–ED760, ED764–ED765, ED767–ED768, ED771–ED772, ED775–ED776, ED779, ED783–ED786, ED799–ED842, ED856–ED888, ED904–ED953, ED967–ED999, EE105–EE150, EE166–EE202

Contract No 1807 (1,650 aircraft), delivery June 1943–March 1945
JA672–JA718, JA843–JA876, JA892–JA941, JA957–JA981, JB113–JB155, JB174–JB191, JB216–JB243, JB275–JB320, JB344–JB376, JB398–JB424, JB453–JB488, JB526–JB567, JB592–JB614, JB637–JB684, JB699–JB748, ND324–ND368, ND380–ND425, ND438–ND479, ND492–ND538, ND551–ND597, ND613–ND658, ND671–ND715, ND727–ND768, ND781–ND826, ND839–ND882, ND895–ND936, ND948–ND996, NE112–NE151, NE163–NE181, PA964–PA999, PB112–PB158, PB171–PB213, PB226–PB267, PB280–PB308, PB341–PB385, PB397–PB438,

PB450–PB490, PB504–PB542, PB554–PB596, PB609–PB642, PB648–
PB653, PB666–PB670, PB675–PB685, PB693–PB694, PB697–PB702,
PB706–PB707, PB728–PB729, PB733, PB758, PB923, PB960, PB962–PB980

Yeadon (642 Aircraft)

Contract No 1807 (485 aircraft), delivery November 1942–October 1945
LM311–LM346, LM359–LM395, LM417–LM448, LM450–LM493,
LM508–LM552, LM569–LM599, LM615–LM658, LM671–LM697,
LM713–LM756, RE115–RE140, RE153–RE188, RE200–RE222, RE225–
RE226, SW319–SW345, SW358–SW377, TW263–TW273

Contract No 2019 (157 aircraft) delivery October 1944–March 1945
ME295–ME327, ME329, ME331–ME337, ME351, ME353–ME370,
ME375–ME382, ME385–ME395, ME417–ME418, ME422–ME430,
ME441–ME444, ME452–ME454, ME471–ME474, ME478, ME481,
ME483–ME489, ME491–ME494, ME496–ME503, ME517–ME551

Total Mk III production by A. V. Roe & Co.: 2,780

LANCASTER Mk I AND Mk III PRODUCTION: METROPOLITAN-VICKERS

Mk I production: Trafford Park and Mosley Road (948 aircraft)

Contract No B.108750/40 (57 aircraft), delivery January–September 1942
R5842–R5868, R5888–R5917

Contract No B.69275/40 (268 aircraft), delivery September 1942–November 1943
W4761–W4800, W4815–W4864, W4879–W4905, W4918–W4967, W4980–
W4982, DV277–DV282, DV291–DV297, DV299–DV312, DV324–DV345,
DV359–DV407

Contract No 2221 (623 aircraft), delivery November 1943–August 1945
ME554–ME596, ME613–ME650, ME663–ME704, ME717–ME759,
ME773–ME814, ME827–ME868, PD198–PD239, PD252–PD296, PD309–
PD349, PD361–PD404, PD417–PD444,
RA500–RA547, RA560–RA607, RA623–RA627, RA787–RA806, SW243–
SW279, TW915–TW929

Total Mk I production by Metropolitan-Vickers: 893

Mk III production: Trafford Park and Mosley Road (132 aircraft)

Contract No B.69275/40 (132 aircraft), delivery September 1942–November 1943
W4983–W5012, DV155–DV202, DV217–DV247, DV263–DV276, DV283–
DV290, DV298

Total Mk III production by Metropolitan-Vickers: 132

LANCASTER Mk I, Mk II AND Mk III PRODUCTION: SIR W. G. ARMSTRONG WHITWORTH & CO

Mk I production: Whitley, Coventry (911 aircraft)

Contract No 239/SAS/C4(C) (886 aircraft), delivery November 1943–March 1946
LL740–LL758, LL771–LL813, LL826–LL867, LL880–LL923, LL935–
LL977, LM100–LM142, LM156–LM192, LM205–LM243, LM257–LM296,
NF906–NF939, NF952–NF999, NG113–NG149, NG162–NG206, NG218–
NG259, NG263–NG308, NG321–NG367, NG379–NG421, NG434–
NG469, NG482–NG503, RF120–RF161, RF175–RF197, SW296–SW316,
TW858–TW873, TW878–TW911

Mk I (FE) (25 aircraft), delivery June–July 1945
TW647–TW671

Total Mk I and Mk I (FE) production by Sir W. G. Armstrong Whitworth &
Co.: 911

Mk II production: Whitley, Coventry (300 aircraft)

Contract No 239/SAS/C4(C) (300 aircraft), delivery September 1942–March 1944
DS601–DS635, DS647–DS692, DS704–DS741, DS757–DS797, DS813–
DS852, LL617–LL653, LL666–LL704, LL716–LL739

Mk III production: Whitley, Coventry (118 aircraft)

Contract No 239/SAS/C4(C) (118 aircraft), delivery February–June 1945
RF198–RF216, RF229–RF273, RF286–RF326, SW283–SW295

Total Mk I, Mk II and Mk III production by Sir W. G. Armstrong Whitworth
& Co.: 1,329

LANCASTER Mk I PRODUCTION: VICKERS-ARMSTRONG

Vickers-Armstrong: Castle Bromwich (300 aircraft)

Contract No 1336 (300 aircraft), delivery December 1943–August 1945
HK535–HK579, HK593–HK628, HK644–HK664, HK679–HK710,
HK728–HK773, HK787–HK806, PP663–PP695, PP713–PP758, PP772–
PP792

Vickers: Chester (235 aircraft)

Contract No 2791 (235 aircraft), delivery June 1944–September 1945
PA158–PA198, PA214–PA239, PA252–PA288, PA303–PA351, PA365–PA396,
PA410–PA452, PA473–PA478, PA509

Total Mk I production by Vickers and Vickers-Armstrong: 535

LANCASTER Mk I AND Mk VII PRODUCTION: AUSTIN MOTORS

Mk I production: Longbridge, Birmingham (150 aircraft)

Contract No 2827 (150 aircraft), delivery March 1944–April 1945
NN694–NN726, NN739–NN786, NN798–NN816, NX548–NX589,
NX603–NX610

Mk VII production: Longbridge, Birmingham (180 aircraft)

Contract No 2827 (180 aircraft), delivery April 1945–January 1946
NX611–NX648, NX661–NX703, NX715–NX758, NX770–NX794,
RT670–RT699

Total Mk I and Mk VII production by Austin Motors: 330

LANCASTER Mk X PRODUCTION: VICTORY AIRCRAFT

Ontario (430 aircraft)

300 aircraft, delivery September 1943–March 1945: KB700–KB999

130 aircraft, delivery March–May 1945: FM100–FM229

Total Mk X production by Victory Aircraft: 430

APPENDIX E: LANCASTER SQUADRONS

This appendix shows details of all RAF squadrons and units which operated the Lancaster during its history. Details include the mark operated by each squadron, the latter's location at the time and the period during which it operated the type. Wartime squadrons also include the Bomber Command Group in which they served.

No 7 Squadron (No 8 Group): Mk I, Mk III
Motto: 'Per diem, per noctem' (By day and by night)

Oakington	May 1943–July 1945
Mepal	July 1945–July 1946
Upwood	July 1946–January 1950

No 9 Squadron (No 5 Group): Mk I, Mk III, Mk VII
Motto: 'Per noctum volamus' (Through the night we fly)

Waddington	August 1942–April 1943
Bardney	April 1943–July 1945
Waddington	July–November 1945
Salbani, India	November 1945–April 1946 (Mk VII)
Binbrook	April –July 1946

No 12 Squadron (No 1 Group): Mk I, Mk III
Motto: 'Leads the Field'

Wickenby	November 1942–September 1945
Binbrook	September 1945–August 1946

No 15 Squadron (No 3 Group): Mk I, Mk III
Motto: 'Aim Sure'

Mildenhall	December 1943–August 1946
Wyton	August 1946–March 1947

No 18 (Burma) Squadron: GR Mk 3
Motto: 'Animos et fide' (With courage and faith)

Ein Shemer, Palestine	September 1946

No 35 (Madras Presidency) Squadron (No 8 Group): Mk I, Mk III
Motto: 'Uno animo agimus' (We act with one accord)

Graveley	March 1944–September 1946
Stradishall	September 1946–February 1949
Mildenhall	February–October 1949

No 37 Squadron: Mk III, Mk VII, GR.3
Motto: 'Wise without eyes'

Fayid, Egypt	April–August 1946 (Mk III, Mk VII)
Kabrit, Egypt	August–September 1946 (Mk III, Mk VII)
Shallufa, Egypt	September 1946–April 1947 (Mk VII)
Ein Shemer, Palestine	September 1947–April 1948 (GR.3)
Luqa, Malta	April 1948–August 1953 (GR.3)

No 38 Squadron: ASR.3/GR.3
Motto: 'Ante lucem' (Before the dawn)

Luqa, Malta	July–September 1946
Ein Shemer, Palestine	September–December 1946
Luqa, Malta	December 1946–April 1948
Ramat David, Palestine	April–May 1948
Shallufa, Egypt	May –July 1948
Luqa, Malta	July 1948–December 1953

No 40 Squadron: Mk VII
Motto: 'Hostem coelo expellere' (To drive the enemy from the sky)

Abu Sueir, Egypt	January–September 1946
Shallufa, Egypt	September 1946–April 1947

No 44 (Rhodesia) Squadron (No 5 Group): Mk I, Mk III
Motto: 'Fulmina regis justa' (The King's thunderbolts are righteous)

Waddington	December 1941–May 1943
Dunholme Lodge	May 1943–September 1944
Spilsby	September 1944–July 1945
Mepal	July–August 1945
Mildenhall	August 1945–August 1946
Wyton	August 1946–September 1947

No 49 Squadron (No 5 Group): Mk I, Mk III
Motto: 'Cave canem' (Beware of the dog)

Scampton	July 1942–January 1943
Fiskerton	January 1943–October 1944
Fulbeck	October 1944–April 1945
Syerston	April–September 1945
Mepal	September 1945–July 1946
Upwood	July 1946–March 1950

No 50 Squadron (No 5 Group): Mk I, Mk III
Motto: 'From defence to attack'

Skellingthorpe	May–June 1942
Swinderby	June–October 1942
Skellingthorpe	October 1942–June 1945
Sturgate	June 1945–January 1946
Waddington	January–November 1946

No 57 Squadron (No 5 Group): Mk I, Mk III
Motto: 'Corpus non animum muto' (I change my body not my spirit)

Scampton	September 1942–August 1943
East Kirkby	August 1943–November 1945
Elsham Wolds	November–December 1945
Scampton	December 1945–May 1946

No 61 Squadron (No 5 Group): Mk I, Mk III
Motto: 'Per purum tonantes' (Thundering through the clear sky)

Syerston	June 1942–November 1943 (Mk II October 1942–March 1943)
Skellingthorpe	November 1943–February 1944
Coningsby	February–April 1944
Skellingthorpe	April 1944–June 1945
Sturgate	June 1945–January 1946
Waddington	January–May 1946

No 70 Squadron: Mk I
Motto: 'Usquam' (Anywhere)

Fayid, Egypt	April–August 1946
Kabrit, Egypt	August–September 1946
Shallufa, Egypt	September 1946–April 1947

No 75 (New Zealand) Squadron (No 3 Group): Mk I, Mk III
Motto: 'Ake ake kia kaha' (Maori: For ever and ever be strong)

Mepal	March 1944–July 1945
Spilsby	July–October 1945

No 82 (United Provinces) Squadron: PR Mk 1
Motto: 'Super omnia ubique' (Over all things everywhere)

Benson	October 1946–June 1947
Leuchars	June–October 1947
Benson	October 1947
Eastleigh, Kenya	October–November 1947
Takoradi, Kenya	November 1947–March 1949
Eastleigh, Kenya	March–August 1949
Takoradi, Kenya	August 1949–January 1950
Eastleigh, Kenya	January–September 1950

Takoradi, Kenya	September 1950–March 1951
Eastleigh, Kenya	March 1951–October 1952
Benson	October 1952–March 1953
Wyton	March–December 1953

No 83 Squadron (Nos 5 and 8 Groups): Mk I, Mk III
Motto: 'Strike to defend'

Scampton	May–August 1942
Wyton	August 1942–April 1944
Coningsby	April 1944–July 1946

No 90 Squadron (No 3 Group): Mk I, Mk III
Motto: 'Celer' (Swift)

| Tuddenham | May 1944–November 1946 |
| Wyton | November 1946–December 1947 |

No 97 (Straits Settlements) Squadron (Nos 5 and 8 Groups): Mk I, Mk III
Motto: 'Achieve your aim'

Coningsby	January 1942–March 1942
Woodhall Spa	March 1942–April 1943
Bourn	April 1943–April 1944
Coningsby	April 1944–July 1946

No 100 Squadron (No 1 Group): Mk I, Mk III
Motto: 'Sarang tebuan jangan dijolok' (Malay: Never stir up a hornet's nest)

Grimsby	January 1943–April 1945
Elsham Wolds	April–December 1945
Scampton	December 1945–May 1946

No 101 Squadron (No 1 Group): Mk I, Mk III
Motto: 'Mens agitat molem' (Mind over matter)

Holme-in-Spalding Moor	October 1942–June 1943
Ludford Magna	June 1943–October 1945
Binbrook	October 1945–August 1946

No 103 Squadron (No 1 Group): Mk I, Mk III
Motto: 'Nili me tangere' (Touch me not)

| Elsham Wolds | November 1942–November 1945 |

No 104 Squadron: Mk VII
Motto: 'Strike hard'

| Abu Sueir, Egypt | November 1945–July 1946 |
| Shallufa, Egypt | July 1946–April 1947 |

No 106 Squadron (No 5 Group): Mk I, Mk III
Motto: 'Pro libertate' (For freedom)

Coningsby	May–October 1942
Syerston	October 1942–November 1943
Metheringham	November 1943–February 1946

No 109 Squadron (No 8 Group): Mk I
Motto: 'Primi hastati' (The first of the legion)

| Wyton | August–October 1942 |

No 115 Squadron (No 3 Group): Mk I, Mk II, Mk III
Motto: 'Despite the elements'

East Wretham	March–August 1943 (Mk II)
Little Snoring	August–November 1943 (Mk II)
Witchford	November 1943–September 1945 (Mk II until May 1944)
Graveley	September 1945–September 1946
Stradishall	September 1946–February 1949
Mildenhall	February 1949–January 1950

No 120 Squadron: GR Mk 3
Motto: 'Endurance'

| Leuchars | November 1946–December 1950 |
| Kinloss | December 1950–April 1951 |

No 138 Squadron (No 3 Group): Mk I
Motto: 'For freedom'

| Tuddenham | March–November 1946 |
| Wyton | November 1946–September 1947 |

No 148 Squadron: Mk I
Motto: 'Trusty'

| Upwood | November 1946–January 1950 |

No 149 (East India) Squadron (No 3 Group): Mk I, Mk III
Motto: 'Fortis nocte' (Strong by night)

Methwold	August 1944–April 1946
Tuddenham	April–November 1946
Stradishall	November 1946–February 1949
Mildenhall	February–November 1949

No 150 Squadron (No 1 Group): Mk I, Mk III
Motto: 'Always ahead' (in Greek)

| Fiskerton | November 1944 |
| Hemswell | November 1944–November 1945 |

No 153 Squadron (No 1 Group): Mk I, Mk III
Motto: 'Noctividus' (Seeing by night)

| Scampton | October 1944–September 1945 |

No 156 Squadron (No 8 Group): Mk I, Mk III
Motto: 'We light the way'

Warboys	January 1943–March 1944
Upwood	March 1944–June 1945
Wyton	June–September 1945

No 160 Squadron: GR Mk 3
Motto: 'Api soya paragasamu' (Sinhalese: We seek and strike)

| Leuchars | August–September 1946 |

No 166 Squadron (No 1 Group): Mk I, Mk III
Motto: 'Tenacity'

| Kirmington | September 1943–November 1945 |

No 170 Squadron (No 1 Group): Mk I, Mk III
Motto: 'Videre non videri' (To see and not to be seen)

Kelstern	October 1944
Dunholme Lodge	October–November 1944
Hemswell	November 1944–November 1945

No 178 Squadron: Mk III
Motto: 'Irae emissarii' (Emissaries of wrath)

| Fayid, Egypt | November 1945–April 1946 |

No 179 Squadron: ASR Mk 3
Motto: 'Delentem deleo' (I destroy the destroyer)

| St Eval | February–September 1946 |

No 186 Squadron (No 3 Group): Mk I, Mk III
Motto: Not known

| Tuddenham | October 1944–December 1944 |
| Stradishall | December 1944–July 1945 |

No 189 Squadron (No 5 Group): Mk I, Mk III
Motto: Not known

| Bardney | October–November 1944 |
| Fulbeck | November 1944–October 1945 |

Metheringham	October–November 1945

No 195 Squadron (No 3 Group): Mk I, Mk III
Motto: 'Velocitate fortis' (Strong by speed)

Witchford	October–November 1944
Wratting Common	November 1944–August 1945

No 203 Squadron: GR Mk 3
Motto: 'Occidens oriensque' (West and east)

Leuchars	August 1946–January 1947
St Eval	January 1947–April 1952
St Mawgan	April–May 1952
St Eval	May–August 1952
Topcliffe	August 1952–March 1953

No 207 Squadron (No 5 Group): Mk I, Mk III
Motto: 'Semper paratus' (Always prepared)

Bottesford	March–September 1942
Langar	September 1942–October 1943
Spilsby	October 1943–October 1945
Methwold	October 1945–April 1946
Tuddenham	April–November 1946
Stradishall	November 1946–February 1949
Mildenhall	February–August 1949

No 210 Squadron: GR Mk 3
Motto: 'Yn y nwyfre yn hedfan' (Welsh: Hovering in the heavens)

St Eval	June 1946–April 1952
St Mawgan	April–May 1952
St Eval	May–September 1952
Topcliffe	September–October 1952

No 214 (Federated Malay States) Squadron: Mk I
Motto: 'Ulter in umbris' (Avenging in the shadows)

Fayid, Egypt	November 1945–April 1946
Upwood	November 1946–December 1950

No 218 (Gold Coast) Squadron (No 3 Group): Mk I, Mk III
Motto: 'In time'

Methwold	August–December 1944
Chedburgh	December 1944–August 1945

No 224 Squadron: GR Mk 3
Motto: 'Fedele all'amico' (Italian: Faithful to a friend)

St Eval	October 1946–November 1947

No 227 Squadron (No 5 Group): Mk I, Mk III
Motto: Not known

Bardney	October 1944
Balderton	October 1944–April 1945
Strubby	April–June 1945
Graveley	June–September 1945

No 231 Squadron: Mk III
Motto: Not known

Full Sutton	December 1945–January 1946

No 279 Squadron: Mk III
Motto: 'To see and be seen'

Beccles	September–December 1945
Burma	December 1945–March 1946

No 300 (Mazowiecki) Squadron (No 1 Group): Mk I, Mk III
Motto: Not known

Faldingworth	April 1944–October 1946

No 405 (Vancouver) Squadron RCAF (No 8 Group): Mk III, Mk VI, Mk X
Motto: 'Ducimus' (We lead)

Gransden Lodge	August 1943–May 1945 (Mk III, Mk VI)
Linton-on-Ouse	May–June 1945 (Mk VI, Mk X)

No 408 (Goose) Squadron RCAF (No 6 Group): Mk II, Mk X
Motto: 'For freedom'

Linton-on-Ouse	October 1943–September 1945

No 419 (Moose) Squadron RCAF (No 6 Group): Mk X
Motto: 'Moosa aswayita' (Beware of the moose)

Middleton St George	March 1944–September 1945

No 420 (Snowy Owl) Squadron RCAF (No 6 Group): Mk X
Motto: 'Pugnamus finitum' (We fight to a finish)

Tholthorpe	April–September 1945

No 424 (Tiger) Squadron RCAF (No 6 Group): Mk I, Mk III
Motto: 'Castigandos castigamus' (We chastise those who deserve to be chastised)

Skipton-on-Swale	January–October 1945

No 425 (Alouette) Squadron RCAF (No 6 Group): Mk X
Motto: 'Je te plumerai' (I shall pluck you)

Tholthorpe	May–September 1945

No 426 (Thunderbird) Squadron RCAF (No 6 Group): Mk II
Motto: 'On wings of fire'

Linton-on-Ouse	June 1943–May 1944

No 427 (Lion) Squadron RCAF (No 6 Group): Mk I, Mk III
Motto: 'Ferte manus certas' (Strike sure)

Leeming	February 1945–May 1946

No 428 (Ghost) Squadron RCAF (No 6 Group): Mk X
Motto: 'Usque ad finem' (To the very end)

Middleton St George	June 1944–September 1945

No 429 (Bison) Squadron RCAF (No 6 Group): Mk I, Mk III
Motto: 'Fortunae nihil' (Nothing to chance)

Leeming	March 1945–May 1946

No 431 (Iroquois) Squadron RCAF (No 6 Group): Mk X
Motto: 'The hatiten ronteriios' (Warrior of the air)

Croft	October 1944–September 1945

No 432 (Leaside) Squadron RCAF (No 6 Group): Mk II
Motto: 'Saeviter ad lucem' (Ferociously towards the light)

East Moor	October 1943–February 1944

No 433 (Porcupine) Squadron RCAF (No 6 Group): Mk I, Mk III
Motto: 'Qui s'y frotte, s'y pique' (Who opposes it gets hurt)

Skipton-on-Swale	January–October 1945

No 434 (Bluenose) Squadron RCAF (No 6 Group): Mk I, Mk X
Motto: 'In exelcis vincimus' (We conquer the heights)

Croft	December 1944–September 1945

No 460 Squadron RAAF (No 1 Group): Mk I, Mk III
Motto: 'Strike and return'

Breighton	October 1942–May 1943
Binbrook	May 1943–July 1945
East Kirkby	July–October 1945

No 463 Squadron RAAF (No 5 Group): Mk III
Motto: 'Press on regardless'

Waddington	November 1943–July 1945

Skellingthorpe   July–September 1945

No 467 Squadron RAAF (No 5 Group): Mk I, Mk III
Motto: Not known
Scampton   November 1942
Bottesford   November 1942–November 1943
Waddington   November 1943–June 1945
Metheringham   June–September 1945

No 514 Squadron (No 3 Group): Mk I, Mk II, Mk III
Motto: 'Nil obstare potest' (Nothing can withstand)
Foulsham   September–November 1943 (Mk II only)
Waterbeach   November 1943–August 1945

No 541 Squadron: PR Mk 1
Motto: 'Alone above all'
Benson   June–September 1946

No 550 Squadron (No 1 Group): Mk I, Mk III
Motto: 'Per ignem vincimus' (Through fire we conquer)
Grimsby   November 1943–January 1944
North Killingholme   January 1944–October 1945

No 576 Squadron (No 1 Group): Mk I, Mk III
Motto: 'Carpe diem' (Seize the opportunity)
Elsham Wolds   November 1943–October 1944
Fiskerton   October 1944–September 1945

No 582 Squadron (No 8 Group): Mk I, Mk III
Motto: 'Praecolamus designantes' (We fly before marking)
Little Staughton   April 1944–September 1945

No 617 Squadron (No 5 Group): Mk I, Mk III, Mk VII
Motto: 'Après moi le deluge' (After me the flood)
Scampton   March–August 1943
Coningsby   August 1943–January 1944
Woodhall Spa   January 1944–June 1945
Waddington   June 1945–January 1946 (Mk VII)
Digri, India   January–May 1946 (Mk VII)
Binbrook   May–September 1946 (Mk VII)

No 619 Squadron (No 5 Group): Mk I, Mk III
Motto: Not known
Woodhall Spa   April 1943–January 1944
Coningsby   January–April 1944
Dunholme Lodge   April–September 1944
Strubby   September 1944–June 1945
Skellingthorpe   June–July 1945

No 621 Squadron: ASR Mk 3
Motto: 'Ever ready to strike'
Aqir, Egypt   April–June 1946
Ein Shemer, Palestine   June–September 1946

No 622 Squadron (No 3 Group): Mk I, Mk III
Motto: 'Bellamus noctu' (We make war by night)
Mildenhall   December 1943–August 1945

No 625 Squadron (No 1 Group): Mk I, Mk III
Motto: 'We avenge'
Kelstern   October 1943–April 1945
Scampton   April–October 1945

No 626 Squadron (No 1 Group): Mk I, Mk III
Motto: 'To strive and not to yield'
Wickenby   November 1943–October 1945

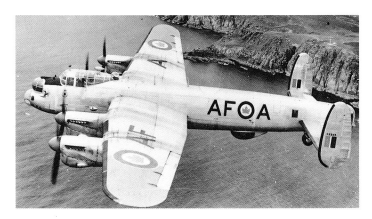

Lancaster Mk X KB959 pictured after the war whilst serving with No 404 Squadron RCAF.

No 630 Squadron (No 5 Group): Mk I, Mk II
Motto: 'Nocturna mors' (Death by night)
East Kirkby   November 1943–July 1945

No 635 Squadron (No 8 Group): Mk I, Mk III, Mk VI
Motto: 'Non ducimus ceteri secunter' (We lead, others follow)
Downham Market   March 1944–September 1945

No 683 Squadron: PR Mk 1
Motto: 'Nihil nos later' (Nothing remains concealed)
Fayid, Egypt   November 1950–February 1951
Kabrit, Egypt   February–April 1951
Eastleigh, Kenya   April–September 1951
Kabrit, Egypt   September–December 1951
Khormaksar, Aden   December 1951–May 1952
Habbaniya, Iraq   May 1952–November 1953

Lancaster Heavy Conversion Units (HCU)

No 1651 HCU	Woolfox Lodge
No 1653 HCU	Lindholme, North Luffenham
No 1654 HCU	Wigsley, Woolfox Lodge
No 1656 HCU	Lindholme
No 1659 HCU	Topcliffe
No 1660 HCU	Swinderby
No 1661 HCU	Waddington, Scampton, Winthorpe
No 1662 HCU	Blyton
No 1666 HCU	Dalton
No 1667 HCU	Lindholme, Faldingworth, Sandtoft
No 1668 HCU	Balderton, Syerston, Bottesford, Cottesmore
No 1669 HCU	Langar
No 1678 HCU	East Wretham, Foulsham
No 1679 HCU	East Moor
No 1678 HC Flight	Little Snoring, Waterbeach

Note: The Heavy Conversion Units often changed location and operated different types of heavy bomber, so exact details are sometimes unclear.

Lancaster Finishing Schools (LFS)

No 1 LFS (No 1 Group)	Lindholme, Faldingworth, Hemswell
No 3 LFS (No 3 Group)	Feltwell
No 5 LFS (No 5 Group)	Syerston
No 6 LFS (No 6 Group)	Ossington

Other Units

Bomber Command Instructors' School (BCIS)	Scampton
Pathfinder Navigators' Training Unit (PFF NTU)	Upwood
No 230 Operational Conversion Unit (OCU)	Scampton

APPENDIX F: LANCASTER ORDERS OF BATTLE

FEBRUARY 1943

No 1 Group
12 Sqn	Wickenby
100 Sqn	Grimsby
101 Sqn	Holme
103 Sqn	Elsham Wolds
460 (RAAF) Sqn	Breighton

No 5 Group
9 Sqn	Waddington
44 Sqn	Waddington
49 Sqn	Fiskerton
50 Sqn	Skellingthorpe
57 Sqn	Scampton
61 Sqn	Syerston
97 Sqn	Woodhall Spa
106 Sqn	Syerston
207 Sqn	Langar
467 (RAAF) Sqn	Bottesford

No 8 Group
83 Sqn	Wyton
156 Sqn	Warboys

Total no of Lancaster squadrons: 17

NOVEMBER 1943

No1 Group
12 Sqn	Wickenby
100 Sqn	Grimsby
101 Sqn	Ludford Magna
103 Sqn	Elsham Wolds
166 Sqn	Kirmington
460 (RAAF) Sqn	Binbrook
550 Sqn	Grimsby, North Killingholme
576 Sqn	Elsham Wolds
625 Sqn	Kelstern
626 Sqn	Wickenby

No 3 Group
115 Sqn	Little Snoring
514 Sqn	Foulsham
622 Sqn	Mildenhall
623 Sqn	Downham Market

No 5 Group
9 Sqn	Bardney
44 Sqn	Dunholme Lodge
49 Sqn	Fiskerton
50 Sqn	Skellingthorpe
57 Sqn	Scampton
61 Sqn	Syerston, Skellingthorpe
106 Sqn	Syerston
207 Sqn	Langar
463 (RAAF) Sqn	Waddington
467 (RAAF) Sqn	Waddington
619 Sqn	Woodhall Spa
630 Sqn	East Kirkby

No 6 Group
408 (RCAF) Sqn	Linton-on-Ouse
426 (RCAF) Sqn	Linton-on-Ouse
432 (RCAF) Sqn	Skipton-on-Swale

No 8 Group
7 Sqn	Oakington
83 Sqn	Wyton
97 Sqn	Bourne
156 Sqn	Warboys

Total no of Lancaster squadrons: 32

JULY 1944

No 1 Group
12 Sqn	Wickenby
100 Sqn	Grimsby
101 Sqn	Ludford Magna
103 Sqn	Elsham Wolds
460 (RAAF) Sqn	Binbrook
550 Sqn	North Killingholme
576 Sqn	Elsham Wolds
625 Sqn	Kelstern
626 Sqn	Wickenby

No 3 Group
15 Sqn	Mildenhall
75 (NZ) Sqn	Mepal
90 Sqn	Tuddenham
115 Sqn	Witchford
514 Sqn	Water Beach
622 Sqn	Mildenhall

No 5 Group
9 Sqn	Bardney
44 Sqn	Dunholme Lodge
49 Sqn	Fiskerton
50 Sqn	Skellingthorpe
57 Sqn	East Kirkby
61 Sqn	Skellingthorpe
83 Sqn	Coningsby
97 Sqn	Coningsby
106 Sqn	Metheringham
207 Sqn	Spilsby
463 (RAAF) Sqn	Waddington
467 (RAAF) Sqn	Waddington
617 Sqn	Woodhall Spa
619 Sqn	Dunholme Lodge
627 Sqn	Woodhall Spa
630 Sqn	East Kirkby

No 6 Group
408 (RCAF) Sqn	Linton-on-Ouse
419 (RCAF) Sqn	Middleton St George
428 (RCAF) Sqn	Middleton St George

No 8 Group
7 Sqn	Oakington
35 Sqn	Graveley
156 Sqn	Upwood
405 (RCAF) Sqn	Gransden Lodge
582 Sqn	Little Staughton
635 Sqn	Downham Market

Total no of Lancaster squadrons: 40

JANUARY 1945

No 1 Group
12 Sqn	Wickenby
100 Sqn	Elsham Wolds
101 Sqn	Ludford Magna
103 Sqn	Elsham Wolds
150 Sqn	Hemswell
153 Sqn	Scampton
166 Sqn	Kirmington
170 Sqn	Hemswell
300 (Polish) Sqn	Binbrook
460 (RAAF) Sqn	Binbrook
550 Sqn	North Killingholme
576 Sqn	Fiskerton
625 Sqn	Kelstern
626 Sqn	Wickenby

No 3 Group
15 Sqn	Mildenhall
75 (NZ) Sqn	Mepal
90 Sqn	Tuddenham
115 Sqn	Witchford
149 Sqn	Methwold
186 Sqn	Stradishall
195 Sqn	Wratting Common
218 Sqn	Chedburgh
514 Sqn	Waterbeach
622 Sqn	Mildenhall

No 5 Group
9 Sqn	Bardney
44 Sqn	Spilsby
49 Sqn	Fulbeck
50 Sqn	Skellingthorpe
57 Sqn	East Kirkby
61 Sqn	Skellingthorpe
83 Sqn	Coningsby
97 Sqn	Coningsby
106 Sqn	Metheringham
189 Sqn	Fulbeck
207 Sqn	Spilsby
227 Sqn	Bardney
463 (RAAF) Sqn	Waddington
467 (RAAF) Sqn	Waddington
617 Sqn	Woodhall Spa
619 Sqn	Strubby
630 Sqn	East Kirkby

No 8 Group
7 Sqn	Oakington
35 Sqn	Graveley
405 (RCAF) Sqn	Gransden Lodge
582 Sqn	Little Staughton

Total no of Lancaster squadrons: 45

JULY 1945

No 1 Group
12 Sqn	Wickenby
50 Sqn	Sturgate
61 Sqn	Sturgate
100 Sqn	Elsham Wolds

101 Sqn	Ludford Magna	195 Sqn	Wratting Common	*No 6 Group*	
103 Sqn	Elsham Wolds	218 Sqn	Chedburgh	405 (RCAF) Sqn	Linton-on-Ouse
150 Sqn	Hemswell	514 Sqn	Waterbeach	408 (RCAF) Sqn	Linton-on-Ouse
153 Sqn	Scampton	622 Sqn	Mildenhall	420 (RCAF) Sqn	Tholthorpe
166 Sqn	Kirmington			424 (RCAF) Sqn	Skipton-on-Swale
170 Sqn	Hemswell			425 (RCAF) Sqn	Tholthorpe
300 (Polish) Sqn	Faldingworth	*No 5 Group*		427 (RCAF) Sqn	Leeming
460 (RAAF) Sqn	Binbrook	9 Sqn	Bardney	429 (RCAF) Sqn	Leeming
550 Sqn	North Killingholme	44 Sqn	Spilsby	433 (RCAF) Sqn	Skipton-on-Swale
576 Sqn	Fiskerton	49 Sqn	Syerston		
625 Sqn	Scampton	57 Sqn	East Kirkby	*No 8 Group*	
626 Sqn	Wickenby	83 Sqn	Coningsby	7 Sqn	Oakington
		97 Sqn	Coningsby	35 Sqn	Graveley
No 3 Group		106 Sqn	Metheringham	156 Sqn	Upwood
15 Sqn	Mildenhall	189 Sqn	Bardney	227 Sqn	Graveley
75 (NZ) Sqn	Mepal	207 Sqn	Spilsby	582 Sqn	Little Staughton
90 Sqn	Tuddenham	463 (RAAF) Sqn	Waddington	635 Sqn	Downham Market
115 Sqn	Witchford	467 (RAAF) Sqn	Metheringham		
138 Sqn	Tuddenham	627 Sqn	Woodhall Spa	*Total no of Lancaster squadrons: 55*	
149 Sqn	Methwold	619 Sqn	Strubby		
186 Sqn	Stradishall	630 Sqn	East Kirkby		

APPENDIX G: LANCASTER OPERATING BASES

During its history the Lancaster operated from a large number of bases, both at home and overseas. This appendix shows alphabetically the location of each base, when it opened and closed (or whether it is still in use) and the Lancaster units which operated at it. Dates during which the unit served are given, which mark of Lancaster it operated from that base and, in the case of wartime units, the Bomber Command Group within which the base and squadron served. It should be noted that the airfield opening and closure dates often vary slightly according to source, particularly when put on care and maintenance after the war. For overseas bases, only units, dates and marks of Lancasters are shown.

Balderton
Nottinghamshire, 2 miles S of Newark; opened June 1941, closed 1954
| 1668 HCU | Aug.–Nov. 1943 | Mk I/III | |
| 227 Sqn | Oct. 1944–Apr. 1945 | Mk I/III | No 5 Gp |

Bardney
Lincolnshire, 10 miles E of Lincoln; opened April 1943, closed 1963
9 Sqn	Apr. 1943–July 1945	Mk I/III	5 Gp
189 Sqn	Oct. 1944–Nov. 1944	Mk I/III	5 Gp
227 Sqn	Oct. 1944	Mk I/III	5 Gp

Beccles (Ellough)
Suffolk, 6 miles SW of Lowestoft; opened 1943, closed December 1945
| 279 Sqn | Sept.–Dec. 1945 | Mk III |

Benson
Oxfordshire, 13 miles SE of Oxford; opened early 1939, still in use by RAF
541 Sqn	June–Sept. 1946	PR.1
82 Sqn	Oct. 1946–June 1947	PR.1
	Oct. 1947	PR.1
	Oct. 52–Mar. 53	PR.1

Binbrook
Lincolnshire, 11 miles SSW of Grimsby; opened June 1940, closed 1988
460 Sqn RAAF	May 1943–July 1945	Mk I/III	1 Gp
12 Sqn	Sept. 1945–Aug. 1946	Mk I/III	
101 Sqn	Oct. 1945–Aug. 1946	Mk I/III	
9 Sqn	Apr.–July 1946	Mk I/III	
617 Sqn	May–Sept. 1946	Mk VII	

Blyton
Lincolnshire, 5 miles NE of Gainsborough; opened November 1942; closed late 1945 (Care & Maintenance until 1978)
| 1662 HCU | Feb. 1943–Apr. 1945 | Mk I/III | 1 Gp |

Bottesford
Leicestershire, 10 miles NW of Grantham; opened September 1941, closed late 1945
207 Sqn	Mar.–Sept. 1942	Mk I/III	5 Gp
467 Sqn RAAF	Nov. 1942–Nov. 1943	Mk I/III	5 Gp
1668 HCU	July 1944–Sept. 1945	Mk I/III	5, 7 Gps

Bourn
Cambridgeshire, 7 miles W of Cambridge; opened early 1941, closed 1948
| 97 Sqn | Apr. 1943–Apr. 1944 | Mk I/III | 8 Gp |

Breighton
Yorkshire, 15 miles SSE of York; opened January 1942, closed 1946
| 460 Sqn RAAF | Oct. 1942–May 1943 | Mk I/III | 1 Gp |

Chedburgh
Suffolk, 8 miles SW of Bury St Edmunds; opened September 1942, closed 1946
| 218 Sqn | Dec. 1944–Aug. 1945 | Mk I/III | 3 Gp |

Coningsby
Lincolnshire, 20 miles SE of Lincoln; opened November 1940, still operational
97 Sqn	Jan.–Mar. 1942	Mk I	5 Gp
106 Sqn	May–Oct. 1942	Mk I/III	5 Gp
617 Sqn	Aug. 1943–Jan. 1944	Mk I/III	5 Gp
619 Sqn	Jan.–Apr. 1944	Mk I/III	5 Gp
61 Sqn	Feb.–Apr. 1944	Mk I/III	5 Gp
83 Sqn	Apr. 1944–July 1946	Mk I/III	5 Gp
97 Sqn	Apr. 1944–July 1946	Mk I/III	5 Gp

Cottesmore
Leicestershire, 10 miles NW of Stamford; opened March 1938, still operational
| 1668 HCU | Sept. 1945–Mar. 1946 | Mk I/III |

Croft (Neasham)
Co. Durham, 20 miles SW of Middlesborough; opened October 1941, closed mid 1946
| 431 Sqn RCAF | Oct. 1944–Sept. 1945 | Mk X | 6 Gp |

434 Sqn RCAF	Dec. 1944–Sept. 1945	Mk I/X	6 Gp

Dalton
Yorkshire, 20 miles NW of York; opened November 1941, closed late 1945

1666 HCU	May–Oct. 1943	Mk I/III	

Downham Market
Norfolk, 9 miles S of King's Lynn; opened: early 1942, closed October 1946

635 Sqn	Mar. 1944–Sept. 1945	Mk I/III/VI	8 Gp

Dunholme Lodge
Lincolnshire, 4 miles N of Lincoln; opened May 1943; closed late 1945 (reopened 1959–64)

1944 Sqn	May 1943–Sept. 1944	Mk I/III	5 Gp
619 Sqn	Apr.–Sept. 1944	Mk I/III	5 Gp
170 Sqn	Oct.–Nov. 1944	Mk I/III	1 Gp

East Kirkby
Lincolnshire, 13 miles N of Boston; opened August 1943, closed February 1948 (Care & Maintenance; reopened 1954–58)

57 Sqn	Aug. 1943–Nov. 1945	Mk I/III	5 Gp
630 Sqn	Nov. 1943–July 1945	Mk I/III	5 Gp
460 Sqn RAAF	July–Oct. 1945	Mk I/III	1 Gp

East Moor
Yorkshire, 7 miles N of York; opened June 1942, closed June 1946

1679 HCU	May–Dec. 1943	Mk II	6 Gp
432 Sqn RCAF	Oct. 1943–Feb. 1944	Mk II	6 Gp

East Wretham
Norfolk, 17 miles N of Bury St Edmunds; opened mid 1940, closed mid 1946

115 Sqn	Mar.–Aug. 1943	Mk I	3 Gp
1678 HCU	Mar.–Aug. 1943	Mk II	3 Gp

Elsham Wolds
Lincolnshire, 11 miles ENE of Scunthorpe; opened July 41 (originally 1916–June 1919), closed early 1947

103 Sqn	Nov. 1942–Nov. 1945	Mk I/III	1 Gp
576 Sqn	Nov. 1943–Oct. 1944	Mk I/III	1 Gp
100 Sqn	Apr.–Dec. 1945	Mk I/III	1 Gp
57 Sqn	Nov.–Dec. 1945	Mk I/III	

Faldingworth
Lincolnshire, 14 miles NNE of Lincoln; opened: October 1943, closed October 1948 (Care & Maintenance; reopened 1957–1972)

1667 HCU	Oct. 1943–Feb. 1944	Mk I/III	5 Gp
No 1 LFS	Dec. 1943–Jan. 1944	Mk I/III	1 Gp
300 Sqn	Apr. 1944–Oct. 1946	Mk I/III	1 Gp

Feltwell
Norfolk, 17 miles NNE of Newmarket; opened April 1937, closed May 1958 (later used as Thor missile site and signals unit)

No 3 LFS	Dec. 1943–Jan. 1945	Mk I/III	3 Gp

Fiskerton
Lincolnshire, 5 miles E of Lincoln; opened January 1943, closed December 1945

49 Sqn	Jan. 1943–Oct. 1944	Mk I/III	5 Gp
576 Sqn	Oct. 1944–Sept. 1945	Mk I/III	1 Gp
150 Sqn	Nov. 1944	Mk I/III	1 Gp

Foulsham
Norfolk, E of Foulsham village; opened May 1942; closed September 1945 (Care & Maintenance; reopened 1954–55)

514 Sqn	Sept.–Nov. 1943	Mk II	3 Gp
1678 HCU	Sept.–Nov. 1943	Mk II	3 Gp

Fulbeck
Lincolnshire, 8 miles W of Newark; opened mid 1940, closed late 1945 (reopened 1953–70)

49 Sqn	Oct. 1944–Apr. 1945	Mk I/III	5 Gp
189 Sqn	Nov. 1944–Oct. 1945	Mk I/III	5 Gp

Full Sutton
Yorkshire, 8 miles E of York; opened May 1944, closed April 1947 (Care & Maintenance; reopened 1951–63)

231 Sqn	Dec. 1945–Jan. 1946	Mk III	

Gransden Lodge
Cambridgeshire, 9 miles SW of Cambridge; opened early 1942, closed early 1950s

405 Sqn RCAF	Aug. 1943–May 1945	Mk III/VI	8 Gp

Graveley
Cambridgeshire, 4 miles S of Huntingdon; opened March 1942, closed September 1946 (Care & Maintenance; reopened mid 1950s–1968)

35 Sqn	Mar. 1944–Sept. 1946	Mk I/III	8 Gp
227 Sqn	June–Sept. 1945	Mk I/III	
115 Sqn	Sept. 1945–Sept. 1946	Mk I/III	

Grimsby(Waltham)
Lincolnshire, 5 miles S of Grimsby; opened November 1941 (originally used in late 1930s); closed late 1945

100 Sqn	Jan. 1943–Apr. 1945	Mk I/III	1 Gp
550 Sqn	Nov. 1943–Jan. 1944	Mk I/III	1 Gp

Hemswell
Lincolnshire, 13 miles N of Lincoln; opened January 1937 (originally 1918 and known as Harpswell), closed late 1970s

No 1 LFS	Jan.–Nov. 1944	Mk I/III	1 Gp
150 Sqn	Nov. 1944–Nov. 1945	Mk I/III	1 Gp
170 Sqn	Nov. 1944–Nov. 1945	Mk I/II	1 Gp

Holme-on-Spalding Moor (Spaldington)
Yorkshire, 20 miles NW of Hull; opened August 1941, closed late 1950s (then used by Blackburn Aviation and British Aerospace)

101 Sqn	Oct. 1942–June 1943	Mk I/II	1 Gp

Kelstern
Lincolnshire, 12 miles S of Grimsby; opened September 1943 (originally used from 1916), closed late 1945

625 Sqn	Oct. 1943–Apr. 1945	Mk I/III	1 Gp
170 Sqn	Oct. 1944	Mk I/III	1 Gp

Kinloss
Scotland, 10 miles W of Elgin; opened April 1939, still operational

120 Sqn	Dec. 1950–Apr. 1951	GR.3	

Kirmington
Lincolnshire, 12 miles W of Grimsby; opened October 1942; closed December 1945 (Care & Maintenance; now Humberside Airport)

166 Sqn	Sept. 1943–Nov. 1945	Mk I/III	1 Gp

Langar (Harby)
Nottinghamshire, 10 miles SE of Nottingham; opened September 1942, closed December 1946 (reopened 1952–68)

207 Sqn	Sept. 1942–Oct. 1943	Mk I/III	5 Gp
1669 HCU	Oct. 1944–Mar. 1945	Mk I/III	

Leeming
Yorkshire, 25 miles SW of Middlesborough; opened: June 1940, still operational

427 Sqn RCAF	Feb. 1945–May 1946	Mk I/III	6 Gp
429 Sqn RCAF	Mar. 1945–May 1946	Mk I/III	6 Gp

Leuchars

Scotland, 5 miles NW of St Andrews; opened April 1920, still operational

160 Sqn	Aug.–Sept. 1946	GR.3
203 Sqn	Aug. 1946–Jan. 1947	GR.3
120 Sqn	Nov. 1946–Dec. 50	GR.3
82 Sqn	June 1947–Oct. 1947	PR.1

Lindholme (Hatfield Woodhouse)

Yorkshire, 7 miles E of Doncaster; opened June 1940, closed 1980s

1656 HCU	Oct. 1942–Nov. 1945	Mk I/III	1 Gp
1667 HCU	June–Oct. 1943	Mk I/III	1 Gp
1 LFS	Nov. 1943–Jan. 1944	Mk I/III	1 Gp
1653 HCU	Oct. 1945–May 1946	Mk I/III	

Linton-on-Ouse

Yorkshire, 9 miles NW of York; opened May 1937, still used by RAF

426 Sqn RCAF	June 1943–May 1944	Mk II	6 Gp
408 Sqn RCAF	Oct. 1943–Sept. 1945	Mk II/X	6 Gp
405 Sqn RCAF	May 1945–June 1945	Mk VI/X	

Little Snoring

Norfolk, 4 miles NE of Fakenham; opened July 1943, closed 1947 (Care & Maintenance; reopened 1950–52, closed again 1958)

115 Sqn	Aug.–Nov. 1943	Mk II	3 Gp
1678 HCU	Aug.–Nov. 1943	Mk II	3 Gp

Little Staughton

Bedfordshire, 4 miles W of St Neots; opened December 1942, closed December 1945

582 Sqn	Apr. 1944–Sept. 1945	Mk I/III	8 Gp

Ludford Magna

Lincolnshire, 20 miles NE of Lincoln; opened June 1943, closed October 1945 (Care & Maintenance; reopened 1959–63)

101 Sqn	June 1943–Oct. 1945	Mk I/III	1 Gp

Mepal

Cambridgeshire, 13 miles N of Cambridge; opened May 1943, closed July 1946 (Care & Maintenance; reopened 1958, closed again 1963)

75 Sqn	Mar. 1944–July 1945	Mk I/II	6 Gp
7 Sqn	July 1945–July 1946	Mk I/III	
44 Sqn	July–Aug. 1945	Mk I/III	
49 Sqn	Sept. 1945–July 1946	Mk I/III	

Metheringham

Lincolnshire, 12 miles SE of Lincoln; opened October 1943, closed spring 1946

106 Sqn	Nov. 1943–Feb. 1946	Mk I/III	5 Gp
467 Sqn RAAF	June–Sept. 1945	Mk I/III	
189 Sqn	Oct.–Nov. 1945	Mk I/III	

Methwold

Norfolk, 11 miles SE of Downham Market; opened September 1939, closed September 1946 (Care & Maintenance; reopened 1955, closed again 1958)

149 Sqn	Aug. 1944–Apr. 1946	Mk I/III	3 Gp
218 Sqn	Aug.–Dec. 1944	Mk I/III	3 Gp
207 Sqn	Oct. 1945–Apr. 1946	Mk I/III	

Middleton St George

Co. Durham, 6 miles E of Darlington; opened January 1941, still open as Tees-side Airport

419 Sqn RCAF	Mar. 1944–Sept. 1945	Mk X	6 Gp
428 Sqn RCAF	June 1944–Sept. 1945	Mk X	6 Gp

Mildenhall

Suffolk, 9 miles NNE of Newmarket; opened October 1934, still in use by US Air Force

15 Sqn	Dec. 1943–Aug. 1946	Mk I/III	3 Gp
622 Sqn	Dec. 1943–Aug. 1945	Mk I/III	3 Gp
44 Sqn	Aug. 1945–Aug. 1946	Mk I/III	

207 Sqn	Feb.–Aug. 1949	Mk I/III
35 Sqn	Feb.–Oct. 1949	Mk I/III
149 Sqn	Feb.–Nov. 1949	Mk I/III
115 Sqn	Feb. 1949–Jan. 1950	Mk I/III

North Killingholme

Lincolnshire, 12 miles NW of Grimsby; opened November 1943 (site originally used 1914–19), closed late 1945

550 Sqn	Jan. 1944–Oct. 1945	Mk I/III	1 Gp

North Luffenham

Leicestershire, 6 miles W of Stamford; opened December 1940, still in use by RAF

1653 HCU	Nov. 1944–Oct. 1945	Mk I/III	7 Gp

Oakington

Cambridgeshire, 6 miles NW of Cambridge; opened July 1940, closed 19??

7 Sqn	May 1943–July 1945	Mk I/III	8 Gp

Ossington

Nottinghamshire, 8 miles NW of Newark; opened January 1942, closed August 1946

6 LFS	Jan.–Nov. 1945	Mk I/III

St Eval

Cornwall, 6 miles NE of Newquay; opened October 1939, closed March 1959

179 Sqn	Feb.–Sept. 1946	ASR.3
210 Sqn	June 1946–Apr. 1952	GR.3
224 Sqn	Oct. 1946–Nov. 1947	GR.3
203 Sqn	Jan. 1947–Apr. 1952	GR.3
	May–Aug. 1952	GR.3
210 Sqn	May–Sept. 1952	GR.3

St Mawgan

Cornwall, 3 miles NE of Newquay; opened February 1943, still in use by RAF

203 Sqn	Apr.–May 1952	GR.3
210 Sqn	Apr.–May 1952	GR.3

Sandtoft

Lincolnshire, 10 miles ENE of Doncaster; opened February 1944, closed November 1945

1667 HCU	Nov. 1944–Nov. 1945	Mk I/III	7 Gp

Scampton

Lincolnshire, 3 miles N of Lincoln; opened August 1936 (site originally used 1916–19), still used by RAF but due to close 1995–96

83 Sqn	May–Aug. 1942	Mk I/III	5 Gp
49 Sqn	July 1942–Jan. 1943	Mk I/III	5 Gp
57 Sqn	Sept. 1942–Aug. 1943	Mk I/III	5 Gp
467 Sqn RAAF	Nov. 1942	Mk I/III	5 Gp
1661 HCU	Nov.–Dec. 1942	Mk I/III	5 Gp
617 Sqn	Mar.–Aug. 1943	Mk I/III	5 Gp
153 Sqn	Oct. 1944–Sept. 1945	Mk I/III	1 Gp
625 Sqn	Apr.–Oct. 1945	Mk I/III	1 Gp
57 Sqn	Dec. 1945–May 1946	Mk I/III	
100 Sqn	Dec. 1945–May 1946	Mk I/III	
BCIS	Jan.–July 1947	Mk I/III	
230 OCU	Feb. 1949–early 1950s	Mk I/III	

Skellingthorpe

Lincolnshire, 3 miles W of Lincoln; opened October 1941, closed 1952

50 Sqn	May–June 1942	Mk I/III	5 Gp
	Oct. 1942–June 1945	Mk I/III	5 Gp
61 Sqn	Nov. 1943–Feb. 1944	Mk I/III	5 Gp
	Apr. 1944–June 1945	Mk I/III	5 Gp
619 Sqn	June–July 1945	Mk I/III	
463 Sqn RAAF	July–Sept. 1945	Mk III	

Skipton-on-Swale
Yorkshire, W of Thirsk; opened September 1942, closed December 1945
424 Sqn RCAF	Jan.–Oct. 1945	Mk I/III	6 Gp
433 Sqn RCAF	Jan.–Oct. 1945	Mk I/III	6 Gp

Spilsby
Lincolnshire, 9 miles W of Skegness; opened September 1943, closed December 1946
207 Sqn	Oct. 1943–Oct. 1945	Mk I/III	5 Gp
44 Sqn	Sept. 1944–July 1945	Mk I/III	5 Gp
75 Sqn	July–Oct. 1945	Mk I/III	

Stradishall
Suffolk, 11 miles SW of Bury St Edmunds; opened February 1938, closed August 1970
186 Sqn	Dec. 1944–July 1945	Mk III	3 Gp
35 Sqn	Sept. 1946–Feb. 1949	Mk I/III	
115 Sqn	Sept. 1946–Feb. 1949	Mk I/III	
149 Sqn	Nov. 1946–Feb. 1949	Mk I/III	
207 Sqn	Nov. 1946–Feb. 1949	Mk I/III	

Strubby
Lincolnshire, 15 miles NNW of Skegness; opened April 1944, closed September 1945 (Care & Maintenance; reopened 1949–72)
619 Sqn	Sept. 1944–June 1945	Mk I/III	5 Gp
227 Sqn	Apr.–June 1945	Mk I/III	5 Gp

Sturgate
Lincolnshire, 15 miles NNW of Lincoln; opened late 1944, closed January 1946 (reopened 1953–64)
50 Sqn	June 1945–Jan. 1946	Mk I/III
61 Sqn	June 1945–Jan. 1946	Mk I/III

Swinderby
Lincolnshire, 8 miles SW of Lincoln; opened August 1940, closed 1990s
50 Sqn	June–Oct. 1942	Mk I/III	5 Gp
1660 HCU	Oct. 1942–Sept. 1945	Mk I/III	5, 7 Gps

Syerston
Nottinghamshire, 6 miles SW of Newark; opened December 1940, closed mid 1971
61 Sqn	June 1942–Nov. 1943	Mk I/II/III	5 Gp
106 Sqn	Oct. 1942–Nov. 1943	Mk I/III	5 Gp
1668 HCU	Nov. 1943–Jan. 1944	Mk I/III	5 Gp
5 LFS	Jan. 1944–Mar. 1945	Mk I/III	5 Gp
49 Sqn	Apr.–Sept. 1945	Mk I/III	5 Gp

Tholthorpe
Yorkshire, 13 miles NW of York; opened August 1940, closed late 1945
420 Sqn RCAF	Apr.–Sept. 1945	Mk X	6 Gp
425 Sqn RCAF	May–Sept. 1945	Mk X	6 Gp

Topcliffe
Yorkshire, SW of Thirsk; opened September 1940, still in use
1659 HCU	Nov. 1944–Sept. 1945	Mk X	7 Gp
203 Sqn	Aug. 1952–Mar. 1953	GR.3	
210 Sqn	Sept.–Oct. 1952	GR.3	

Tuddenham
Suffolk, 8 miles NW of Bury St Edmunds; opened October 1943, closed November 1946 (reopened 1959–63)
90 Sqn	May 1944–Nov. 1946	Mk I/III	3 Gp
186 Sqn	Oct.–Dec. 1944	Mk I/III	3 Gp
138 Sqn	Mar. 1945–Nov. 1946	Mk I	3 Gp
149 Sqn	Apr.–Nov. 1946	Mk I/III	
207 Sqn	Apr.–Nov. 1946	Mk I/III	

Upwood
Cambridgeshire, 8 miles N of Huntingdon; opened January 1937, closed September 1961
PFF NTU	June 1943–Mar. 1944	Mk I/III	8 Gp
156 Sqn	Mar. 1944–June 1945	Mk I/III	8 Gp
7 Sqn	July 1946–Jan. 1950	Mk I/III	
49 Sqn	July 1946–Mar. 1950	Mk I/III	
148 Sqn	Nov. 1946–Jan. 1950	Mk I	
214 Sqn	Nov. 1946–Dec. 1950	Mk I	

Waddington
Lincolnshire, 4 miles S of Lincoln; opened October 1926 (site first used 1916–19), still operational
44 Sqn	Dec. 1941–May 1943	Mk I/III	5 Gp
9 Sqn	Aug. 1942–Apr. 1943	Mk I/III	5 Gp
1661 HCU	Oct. 1942–Nov. 1942	Mk I/III	5 Gp
467 Sqn RAAF	Nov. 1943–June 1945	Mk I/III	5 Gp
463 Sqn RAAF	Nov. 1943–July 1945	Mk III	5 Gp
617 Sqn	June 1945–Jan. 1946	Mk VII	
61 Sqn	Jan.–May 1946	Mk I/III	
50 Sqn	Jan.–Nov. 1946	Mk I/III	

Warboys
Cambridgeshire, 7 miles NE of Huntingdon; opened September 1941, closed January 1946
156 Sqn	Jan. 1943–Mar. 1944	Mk I/III	8 Gp
PFF NTU	Mar. 1944–May 1945	Mk I/III	8 Gp

Waterbeach
Cambridgeshire, 6 miles NE of Cambridge; opened January 1941, closed August 1963
514 Sqn	Nov. 1943–Aug. 1945	Mk I/II/III	3 Gp
1678 HCF	Nov. 1943–June 1944	Mk II	3 Gp

Wickenby
Lincolnshire, 11 miles NE of Lincoln; opened September 1942, closed November 1945
12 Sqn	Nov. 1942–Sept. 1945	Mk I/III	1 Gp
626 Sqn	Nov. 1943–Oct. 1945	Mk I/III	1 Gp

Wigsley
Nottinghamshire, 9 miles W of Lincoln; opened February 1942, closed September 1945
1654 HCU	May 1942–Nov. 1943	Mk I/III	5 Gp

Winthorpe
Nottinghamshire, 15 miles SW of Lincoln; opened September 1940, closed late 1947
1661 HCU	Dec. 1942–Jan. 1944	Mk I/III	5 Gp
	Dec. 1944–Sept. 1945	Mk I/III	5 Gp

Witchford
Cambridgeshire, 2 miles SW of Ely; opened June 1943, closed March 1946
115 Sqn	Nov. 1943–Sept. 1945	Mk I/II/III	3 Gp
195 Sqn	Oct.–Nov. 1944	Mk I/III	3 Gp

Woodford
10 miles S of Manchester; opened 1925, still in use by British Aerospace
On completion of production, Lancasters were transported to Woodford for final assembly and flight testing. Lancasters from operational squadrons and maintenance units made frequent visits to Woodford during the war. At the end of the war Lancaster production was gradually wound down, although the airfield was still used by A. V. Roe for development of other aircraft such as the Shackleton and Vulcan.

Woodhall Spa
Lincolnshire, 18 miles SE of Lincoln; opened February 1942, closed October 1945
97 Sqn	Mar. 1942–Apr. 1943	Mk I/III	5 Gp
619 Sqn	Apr. 1943–Jan. 1944	Mk I/III	5 Gp
617 Sqn	Jan. 1944–June 1945	Mk I/III	5 Gp

Woolfox Lodge
Leicestershire, 6 miles NW of Stamford; opened December 1940, closed August 1945 (Care & Maintenance; reopened 1948–54)

1651 HCU	Nov. 1944–July 1945	Mk I/III	3 Gp
1654 HCU	Mar.–Sept. 1945	Mk I/III	3 Gp

Wratting Common
Cambridgeshire, 8 miles S of Newmarket; opened May 1943, closed April 1946

195 Sqn	Nov. 1944–Aug. 1945	Mk I/III	3 Gp

Wyton
Cambridgeshire, 4 miles NE of Huntingdon; opened July 1936 (site originally used 1916–19), still in use by RAF

83 Sqn	Aug. 1942–Apr. 1944	Mk I/III	8 Gp
109 Sqn	Aug. 1942–Oct. 1942	Mk I	8 Gp
156 Sqn	June–Sept. 1945	Mk I/III	
15 Sqn	Aug. 1946–Mar. 1947	Mk I/III	
44 Sqn	Aug. 1946–Sept. 1947	Mk I/III	
138 Sqn	Nov. 1946–Sept. 1947	Mk I	
90 Sqn	Nov. 1946–Dec. 1947	Mk I/III	
82 Sqn	Mar.–Dec. 1953	PR.1	

Yeadon (Leeds/Bradford)
Yorkshire, on northern edge of Leeds and Bradford; opened October 1931, still in civil use as Leeds/Bradford Airport

Used during the production of Lancasters from April 1942 until the end of the war.

Abu Sueir, Egypt

104 Sqn	Nov. 1945–July 1946	Mk VII
40 Sqn	Jan.–Sept. 1946	Mk VII

Aqir, Egypt

621 Sqn	Apr.–June 1946	ASR.3

Digri, India

617 Sqn	Jan.–May 1946	Mk VII

Eastleigh, Kenya

82 Sqn (various detachments)	Oct. 1947–Oct. 1952	PR.1
683 Sqn	Apr.–Sept. 1951	PR.1

Ein Shemer, Palestine

621 Sqn	June–Sept. 1946	ASR.3
38 Sqn	Sept.–Dec. 1946	ASR.3/GR.3

18 Sqn	Sept. 1946	GR.3
37 Sqn	Sept. 1947–Apr. 1948	GR.3

Fayid, Egypt

178 Sqn	Nov. 1945–Apr. 1946	Mk III
214 Sqn	Nov. 1945–Apr. 1946	Mk I
37 Sqn	Apr.–Aug. 1946	Mk III/VII
70 Sqn	Apr.–Aug. 1946	Mk I
683 Sqn	Nov. 1950–Feb. 1951	PR.1

Habbaniya, Iraq

683 Sqn	May 1952–Nov. 1953	PR.1

Kabrit, Egypt

37 Sqn	Aug.–Sept. 1946	Mk III/VII
70 Sqn	Aug.–Sept. 1946	Mk I
683 Sqn	Feb.–Apr. 1951	PR.1
	Sept.–Dec. 1951	PR.1

Khormaksar, Aden

683 Sqn	Dec. 1951–May 1952	PR.1

Luqa, Malta

38 Sqn	July–Sept. 1946	ASR.3
	Dec. 1946–Apr. 1948	ASR.3/GR.3
37 Sqn	Apr. 1948–Aug. 1953	GR.3
38 Sqn	July 1948–Dec. 1953	GR.3

Ramat David, Palestine

38 Sqn	Apr.–May 1948	ASR.3/GR.3

Salbani, India

9 Sqn	Nov. 1945–Apr. 1946	Mk VII

Shallufa, Egypt

104 Sqn	July 1946–Apr. 1947	Mk VII
37 Sqn	Sept. 1946–Apr. 1947	Mk VII
40 Sqn	Sept. 1946–Apr. 1947	Mk VII
70 Sqn	Sept. 1946–Apr. 1947	Mk I
38 Sqn	May–July 1948	GR.3

Takoradi, Kenya

82 Sqn (various detachments)	Nov. 1947–Mar. 1951	PR.1

Below left: FM213 converted to Mk 10MR standard for maritime reconnaissance duties.

Below right: A Lancaster of No 683 Squadron converted to PR.1 standard and pictured in the summer of 1951 whilst operating from Eastleigh in Kenya. (Peter Green)

APPENDIX H: SIGNIFICANT LANCASTER MAIN FORCE RAIDS

Statistics show dates and target, the total number of aircraft dispatched on the raid, the number of Lancasters taking part in each raid and the number of Lancasters lost. A record for the total number of aircraft dispatched is shown thus *, a new record for the number of Lancasters dispatched is shown thus **, and record Lancaster losses for a single raid to date are shown thus ***.

RAIDS IN 1942

Date	Target	Total force	Lancasters participating	Lancasters lost
3/4 Mar.	Minelaying	4	4	–
10/11 Mar.	Essen	126	2	–
20 Mar.	Minelaying	19	6	–
24/25 Mar.	Minelaying	35	?	1
25/26 Mar.	Essen	254 *	7	–
8/9 Apr.	Hamburg	272 *	7	–
10/11 Apr.	Essen	254	8	–
17 Apr.	Augsburg	12	12 **	7 ***
23/24 Apr.	Rostock	161	1	–
27/28 Apr.	Trondheim/*Tirpitz*	43	12	1
	Leaflet-dropping	8	3	–
28/29 Apr.	Trondheim/*Tirpitz*	34	11	–
4/5 May	Stuttgart	121	14 **	–
5/6 May	Stuttgart	77	4	–
6/7 May	Stuttgart	97	10	–
8/9 May	Warnemünde	193	21 **	4
19/20 May	Mannheim	197	13	–
29/30 May	Paris/Gennevilliers	77	14	–
30/31 May	Cologne	1,047 *	73 **	1

Note: From 1 June 1942 to 31 December 1943 only raids which included more than 20 Lancasters are shown. This is to highlight the larger Main Force raids, and it is acknowledged that there were many more minor raids, diversionary raids, minelaying operations and specialist raids involving Lancasters which cannot be shown because of limited space.

Date	Target	Total force	Lancasters participating	Lancasters lost
1/2 June	Essen	956	74 **	4
2/3 June	Essen	195	27	2
3/4 June	Bremen	170	?	2
6/7 June	Emden	233	20	–
25/26 June	Bremen	1,067 *	96 **	?
27/28 June	Bremen	144	24	2
29/30 June	Bremen	253	64	–
2/3 July	Bremen	325	53	–
8/9 July	Wilhelmshaven	285	52	1
11 July	Danzig	44	44	2
19/20 July	Vegesack	99	28	–
21/22 July	Duisburg	291	29	–
23/24 July	Duisburg	215	45	2
25/26 July	Duisburg	313	33	2
26/27 July	Hamburg	403	77	2
29/30 July	Saarbrücken	291	?	2
31/1 Aug.	Düsseldorf	630	113 **	2
6/7 Aug.	Duisburg	216	?	–
9/10 Aug.	Osnabrück	192	42	–
11/12 Aug.	Mainz	154	33	1
12/13 Aug.	Mainz	138	?	2
15/16 Aug.	Düsseldorf	131	?	2
17/18 Aug.	Osnabrück	139	?	1
24/25 Aug.	Frankfurt	226	61	6

Date	Target	Total force	Lancasters participating	Lancasters lost
27/28 Aug.	Kassel	306	?	3
28/29 Aug.	Nuremberg	159	71	4
1/2 Sept.	Saarbrücken	231	?	1
2/3 Sept.	Karlsruhe	200	?	2
4/5 Sept.	Bremen	251	76	3
6/7 Sept.	Duisburg	207	?	–
8/9 Sept.	Frankfurt	249	?	–
10/11 Sept.	Düsseldorf	479	89	5
13/14 Sept.	Bremen	446	?	2
14/15 Sept.	Wilhelmshaven	202	?	–
16/17 Sept.	Essen	369	?	9 ***
19/20 Sept.	Saarbrücken	89	68	3
23/24 Sept.	Wismar	83	83	4
1/2 Oct.	Wismar	78	78	2
2/3 Oct.	Krefeld	188	31	1
5/6 Oct.	Aachen	257	74	1
6/7 Oct.	Osnabrück	237	68	2
12/13 Oct.	Wismar	59	59	2
13/14 Oct.	Kiel	288	82	1
15/16 Oct.	Cologne	289	62	5
17 Oct.	Le Creusot	94	94	1
22/23 Oct.	Genoa	112	112	–
24 Oct.	Milan	88	88	3
6/7 Nov.	Genoa	72	72	2
7/8 Nov.	Genoa	175	85	1
9/10 Nov.	Hamburg	213	72	5
13/14 Nov.	Genoa	76	67	–
15/16 Nov.	Genoa	78	27	–
20/21 Nov.	Turin	232	86	–
22/23 Nov.	Stuttgart	222	97	5
28/29 Nov.	Turin	228	117 **	–
2/3 Dec.	Frankfurt	112	27	1
6/7 Dec.	Mannheim	272	101	1
8/9 Dec.	Turin	133	108	1
9/10 Dec.	Turin	227	115	1
11/12 Dec.	Turin	82	20	–
20/21 Dec.	Duisburg	232	111	6
21/22 Dec.	Munich	137	119 **	8

RAIDS IN 1943

Date	Target	Total force	Lancasters participating	Lancasters lost
4/5 Jan.	Essen	33	29	2
8/9 Jan.	Duisburg	41	38	3
9/10 Jan.	Essen	52	50	3
11/12 Jan.	Essen	76	72	1
12/13 Jan.	Essen	59	55	1
13/14 Jan.	Essen	69	66	4
16/17 Jan.	Berlin	201	190 **	1
17/18 Jan.	Berlin	187	170	19 ***
21/22 Jan.	Essen	82	79	4
23/24 Jan.	Düsseldorf	83	80	2
26/27 Jan.	Lorient	157	11	1
27/28 Jan.	Düsseldorf	162	124	3
30/31 Jan.	Hamburg	148	135	5
2/3 Feb.	Cologne	161	116	3
3/4 Feb.	Hamburg	263	62	1
4/5 Feb.	Turin	188	77	3
7/8 Feb.	Lorient	323	80	3
11/12 Feb.	Wilhelmshaven	177	129	3

Date	Target			
13/14 Feb.	Lorient	466	164	2
14/15 Feb.	Milan	142	142	2
16/17 Feb.	Lorient	377	131	1
18/19 Feb.	Wilhelmshaven	195	127	4
19/20 Feb.	Wilhelmshaven	338	52	4
21/22 Feb.	Bremen	143	130	–
25/26 Feb.	Nuremberg	337	169	6
26/27 Feb.	Cologne	427	145	3
28/1 Mar.	St Nazaire	437	152	2
1/2 Mar.	Berlin	302	156	7
3/4 Mar.	Hamburg	417	149	4
5/6 Mar.	Essen	442	157	4
8/9 Mar.	Nuremberg	335	170	2
9/10 Mar.	Munich	264	142	5
11/12 Mar.	Stuttgart	314	152	2
12/13 Mar.	Essen	457	156	8
22/23 Mar.	St Nazaire	357	189	1
26/27 Mar.	Duisburg	455	157	1
27/28 Mar.	Berlin	396	191	3
28/29 Mar.	St Nazaire	323	50	1
29/30 Mar.	Berlin	329	162	11
3/4 Apr.	Essen	348	225 **	9
4/5 Apr.	Kiel	577	203	5
8/9 Apr.	Duisburg	392	156	6
9/10 Apr.	Duisburg	109	104	8
10/11 Apr.	Frankfurt	502	136	5
13/14 Apr.	La Spezia	211	208	4
14/15 Apr.	Stuttgart	462	98	3
16/17 Apr.	Pilsen	327	197	18
18/19 Apr.	La Spezia	178	173	1
20/21 Apr.	Stettin	339	194	13
26/27 Apr.	Duisburg	561	215	3
27/28 Apr.	Minelaying	160	46	1
28/29 Apr.	Minelaying	207	68	7
30/1 May	Essen	305	190	6
4/5 May	Dortmund	596	255 **	6
12/13 May	Duisburg	572	238	10
13/14 May	Bochum	442	98	1
	Pilsen	168	156	8
23/24 May	Dortmund	826	343 **	8
25/26 May	Düsseldorf	759	323	9
27/28 May	Essen	518	274	6
29/30 May	Wuppertal	719	292	7
11/12 June	Düsseldorf	783	326	14
	Münster	72	29	2
12/13 June	Bochum	503	323	14
14/15 June	Oberhausen	203	197	17
16/17 June	Cologne	212	202	14
19/20 June	Montchanin	26	26	–
20/21 June	Friedrichshafen	60	60	–
21/22 June	Krefeld	705	262	9
22/23 June	Mülheim	557	242	8
23/24 June	La Spezia	52	52	–
24/25 June	Wuppertal	630	251	8
25/26 June	Gelsenkirchen	473	214	13
28/29 June	Cologne	608	267	8
3/4 July	Cologne	653	293	8
8/9 July	Cologne	288	282	7
9/10 July	Gelsenkirchen	418	218	5
12/13 July	Turin	295	295	13
24/25 July	Hamburg	791	347 **	4
	Leghorn	33	33	–
25/26 July	Essen	705	294	5
27/28 July	Hamburg	787	353 **	11
29/30 July	Hamburg	777	340	11
30/31 July	Remscheid	273	82	2
2/3 Aug.	Hamburg	740	329	13
7/8 Aug.	Genoa/Milan/ Turin	197	197	2
9/10 Aug.	Mannheim	457	286	3
10/11 Aug.	Nuremberg	653	318	6
12/13 Aug.	Milan	504	321	1
14/15 Aug.	Milan	140	140	1
15/16 Aug.	Milan	199	199	7
17/18 Aug.	Peenemünde	596	324	23 ***
22/23 Aug.	Leverkusen	462	257	3
23/24 Aug.	Berlin	727	335	17
27/28 Aug.	Nuremberg	674	349	11
30/31 Aug.	München-Gladbach/ Rheydt	660	297	7
31/1 Sept.	Berlin	622	331	10
3/4 Sept.	Berlin	320	316	22
5/6 Sept.	Mannheim/Ludwigs- hafen	605	299	13
6/7 Sept.	Munich	404	257	3
15/16 Sept.	Montluçon	369	40	–
16/17 Sept.	Modane	340	43	–
	Anthéor viaduct	12	12	1
22/23 Sept.	Hanover	711	322	7
	Oldenburg	29	21	–
23/24 Sept.	Mannheim	628	312	18
	Darmstadt	29	21	–
27/28 Sept.	Hanover	678	312	10
	Brunswick	27	21	1
29/30 Sept.	Bochum	352	213	4
1/2 Oct.	Hagen	251	243	2
2/3 Oct.	Munich	296	294	8
3/4 Oct.	Kassel	547	204	4
4/5 Oct.	Frankfurt	406	162	3
	Ludwigshafen	66	66	–
7/8 Oct.	Stuttgart	343	343	4
8/9 Oct.	Hanover	504	282	14
18/19 Oct.	Hanover	360	360 **	18
20/21 Oct.	Leipzig	358	358	16
22/23 Oct.	Kassel	569	322	18
	Frankfurt	36	28	1
3/4 Nov.	Düsseldorf	589	344	11
	Cologne	62	52	–
10/11 Nov.	Modane	313	313	–
17/18 Nov.	Ludwigshafen	83	66	1
18/19 Nov.	Berlin	444	440 **	9
	Mannheim/Ludwigs- hafen	395	33	2
22/23 Nov.	Berlin	764	469 **	11
23/24 Nov.	Berlin	383	365	20
25/26 Nov.	Frankfurt	262	26	1
26/27 Nov.	Berlin	450	443	28 ***
	Stuttgart	178	21	–
2/3 Dec.	Berlin	458	425	37 ***
3/4 Dec.	Leipzig	527	307	9
16/17 Dec.	Berlin	498	483 **	25
20/21 Dec.	Frankfurt	650	390	14
	Mannheim	54	44	–
23/24 Dec.	Berlin	379	364	16
29/30 Dec.	Berlin	712	457	11

RAIDS IN 1944

Note: From 1 January 1944 only raids which included more than 50 Lancasters are shown. It is acknowledged that there were very many more minor raids, diversionary raids and specialist raids involving Lancasters.

Date	Target			
1/2 Jan.	Berlin	421	421	28
2/3 Jan.	Berlin	383	362	27
5/6 Jan.	Stettin	358	348	14
14/15 Jan.	Brunswick	498	496 **	38 ***
20/21 Jan.	Berlin	769	495	13
21/22 Jan.	Magdeburg	648	421	22
27/28 Jan.	Berlin	530	515 **	33
28/29 Jan.	Berlin	677	432	20
30/31 Jan.	Berlin	534	440	32
15/16 Feb.	Berlin	891	561 **	26
19/20 Feb.	Leipzig	823	561	44 ***
20/21 Feb.	Stuttgart	598	460	7
24/25 Feb.	Schweinfurt	734	554	26
25/26 Feb.	Augsburg	594	461	16
1/2 Mar.	Stuttgart	557	415	3
7/8 Mar.	Le Mans	304	56	–
10/11 Mar.	Factories in France	102	102	1
15/16 Mar.	Stuttgart	863	617 **	27
18/19 Mar.	Frankfurt	846	620 **	10
22/23 Mar.	Frankfurt	816	620	26
24/25 Mar.	Berlin	811	577	44
26/27 Mar.	Essen	705	476	6
30/31 Mar.	Nuremberg	795	572	64 ***
5/6 Apr.	Toulouse	145	144	1
9/10 Apr.	Villeneuve-St-Georges	225	166	–
	Minelaying	103	103	9
10/11 Apr.	Tours	180	180	1
	Laon	148	148	1
	Aulnoye	132	132	7
11/12 Apr.	Aachen	352	341	9
18/19 Apr.	Rouen	289	273	–
	Juvisy	209	202	1
	Noisy-le-Sec	181	61	–
20/21 Apr.	Cologne	379	357	4
	La Chapelle	252	247	6
22/23 Apr.	Düsseldorf	596	323	13
	Brunswick	265	248	4
	Laon	181	52	4
24/25 Apr.	Karlsruhe	637	369	11
	Munich	250	234	9
26/27 Apr.	Essen	493	342	6
	Schweinfurt	217	206	21
27/28 Apr.	Friedrichshafen	323	322	18
28/29 Apr.	St-Médard-en-Jalles	88	88	–
	Oslo	55	51	–
29/30 Apr.	St-Médard-en-Jalles	73	68	–
	Clermont-Ferrand	59	54	–
30/1 May	Maintenon	116	116	–
1/2 May	Toulouse	139	131	–
	Chambly	120	96	3
	Lyons	75	75	–
	Tours	46	46	–
3/4 May	Mailly-le-Camp	360	346	42
	Montdidier	92	84	4
6/7 May	Mantes-la-Jolie	149	64	2
	Sable-sur-Sarthe	68	64	–
	Aubigne	52	52	1
7/8 May	Nantes	99	93	1
	Salbris	62	58	7
	Tours	61	53	1
	Rennes	55	55	–
8/9 May	Haine-St-Pierre	123	53	3
	Brest	64	58	1
9/10 May	Coastal batteries	414	180	1
	Gennevilliers	64	56	5
10/11 May	Railway targets	506	291	13
11/12 May	Bourg-Léopold	201	190	5
	Hasselt	132	126	5
	Louvain	110	105	4
19/20 May	Orléans	122	118	1
	Amiens	121	112	1
	Tours	117	113	–
	Le Mans	116	112	3
21/22 May	Duisburg	532	510	29
	Minelaying	107	70	3
22/23 May	Dortmund	375	361	18
	Brunswick	235	225	13
24/25 May	Aachen	442	264	7
	Eindhoven	63	59	–
	Coastal batteries	224	102	–
27/28 May	Coastal batteries	272	208	1
	Bourg-Léopold	331	56	1
	Aachen	170	162	12
	Nantes	104	100	1
	Rennes	83	78	–
28/29 May	Angers	126	118	1
	Coastal batteries	201	181	1
30/31 May	Boulogne	54	50	–
31/1 June	Trappes	219	125	4
	Mont Couple	115	60	–
	Tergnier	115	111	2
	Saumur	86	82	–
	Maisy	68	68	–
1/2 June	Saumur	58	58	–
2/3 June	Berneval	107	103	–
	Coastal batteries	271	136	1
3/4 June	Ferme-d'Urville	100	96	–
	Coastal batteries	135	127	–
4/5 June	Coastal batteries	259	125	–
5/6 June	Coastal batteries	1,012	551	1
6/7 June	Communications	1,065	589	10
7/8 June	Communications	337	122	17
	Forêt de Cerisy	122	112	2
8/9 June	Communications	483	286	3
9/10 June	Airfields	401	206	–
	Étampes	112	108	6
10/11 June	Railways	432	323	15
11/12 June	Railways	329	225	3
12/13 June	Communications	671	285	6
	Gelsenkirchen	303	286	17
14 June	Le Havre	234	221	1
14/15 June	Troop positions	337	223	–
	Railways	330	61	1
15 June	Boulogne	297	155	–
15/16 June	Ammunition/fuel dumps	227	119	–
	Railways	224	184	11
16/17 June	Flying-bomb sites	405	236	–
	Sterkrade/Holten	321	147	?
17/18 June	Railways	317	196	1
21 June	Flying-bomb sites	322	142	–
21/22 June	Wesselring	139	133	37

Date	Target			
	Scholven/Buer	132	123	8
22 June	Flying-bomb sites	234	119	–
22/23 June	Railways	221	111	4
23/24 June	Flying-bomb sites	412	226	5
	Railways	207	203	2
24 June	Flying-bomb sites	321	106	–
24/25 June	Flying-bomb sites	739	535	22
25 June	Flying-bomb sites	323	106	–
27/28 June	Flying-bomb sites	721	477	3
	Railways	223	214	4
29 June	Flying-bomb sites	305	286	3
30 June	Villers-Bocage	266	151	1
	Oisemont	107	102	–
30/1 July	Vierzon	118	118	14
2 July	Flying-bomb sites	384	374	–
4/5 July	St Leu d'Esserent	246	231	13
	Railways	287	282	14
5/6 July	Flying-bomb sites	542	321	4
5/6 July	Dijon	154	154	–
6 July	Flying-bomb sites	551	210	1
7 July	Normandy Area	467	283	3
7/8 July	St Leu d'Esserent	221	208	29
	Vaires	128	123	–
9 July	Flying-bomb sites	347	120	1
10 July	Nucourt	223	213	–
	Vaires	159	153	–
12/13 July	Railways	385	378	12
14/15 July	Railways	253	242	7
15/16 July	Railways	229	222	3
	Flying-bomb sites	234	58	–
18 July	Normandy area	942	667 **	1
18/19 July	Railways	263	253	24
	Wesselring	194	77	–
	Scholven/Buer	170	157	4
19 July	Flying-bomb sites	144	132	–
20 July	Flying-bomb sites	369	174	1
20/21 July	Courtrai	317	302	9
	Homberg	158	147	20
23/24 July	Kiel	629	519	4
24/25 July	Stuttgart	614	461	17
	Donges	113	104	3
25 July	St Cyr	100	94	1
	Flying-bomb sites	93	81	–
25/26 July	Stuttgart	550	412	8
26/27 July	Givors	187	178	4
28/29 July	Stuttgart	496	494	39
	Hamburg	307	106	4
30 July	Normandy area	692	462	4
31 July	Joigny-la-Roche	131	127	1
	Rilly-la-Montage	103	97	2
	Le Havre	57	52	1
31/1 Aug.	Flying-bomb sites	202	104	1
1 Aug.	Flying-bomb sites	777	385	–
2 Aug.	Flying-bomb sites	394	234	2
	Le Havre	54	54	–
3 Aug.	Flying-bomb depots	1,114 *	601	6
4 Aug.	Oil storage depots	288	288	–
	Flying-bomb sites	291	112	2
5 Aug.	Flying-bomb sites	742	257	–
	Oil storage depots	306	306	1
6 Aug.	Flying-bomb sites	222	107	3
7/8 Aug.	Normandy area	1,019	614	10
8/9 Aug.	Oil targets	180	170	1
9/10 Aug.	Flying-bomb sites	311	171	–
	Forêt de Châtellerault	190	176	2
10 Aug.	Dugny	103	98	–
	Ferme du Forestal	80	60	–
10/11 Aug.	Oil depots	215	109	–
11 Aug.	Railways	459	270	–
	U-boat pens	56	53	–
11/12 Aug.	Givors	189	179	–
12 Aug.	U-boat pens	70	68	–
12/13 Aug.	Brunswick	379	242	17
	Russelsheim	297	191	13
	Falaise	144	91	–
14 Aug.	Normandy area	805	411	2
	Brest	159	155	2
15 Aug.	Airfields	1,004	599	3
16/17 Aug.	Stettin	461	461	5
	Kiel	348	195	2
18 Aug.	L'Isle Adam	169	158	2
18/19 Aug.	Bremen	288	216	1
	Ertvelde Rieme	113	108	–
19 Aug.	La Pallice	52	52	–
25/26 Aug.	Russelsheim	412	412	15
	Darmstadt	196	190	7
26/27 Aug.	Kiel	382	372	17
	Königsberg	174	174	4
29/30 Aug.	Stettin	403	402	23
	Königsberg	189	189	15
31 Aug.	Flying-bomb depots	601	418	6
2 Sept.	Brest	67	67	–
3 Sept.	Airfields	675	348	–
5 Sept.	Le Havre	348	313	–
	Brest	66	60	–
6 Sept.	Le Havre	344	311	–
	Emden	181	76	1
8 Sept.	Le Havre	333	304	2
9/10 Sept.	München-Gladbach	137	113	–
10 Sept.	Le Havre	992	521	–
11 Sept.	Le Havre	218	103	–
	Oil plants	379	154	3
11/12 Sept.	Darmstadt	240	226	12
12 Sept.	Oil plants	412	75	4
12/13 Sept.	Frankfurt	387	378	17
	Stuttgart	217	204	4
14 Sept.	Wilhelmshaven	184	51	–
15/16 Sept.	Kiel	490	310	2
16/17 Sept.	Airfields/batteries	282	254	2
17 Sept.	Boulogne	762	370	1
	Flak positions	132	112	–
18/19 Sept.	Bremerhaven	213	206	1
19/20 Sept.	München-Gladbach/ Rheydt	237	227	4
20 Sept.	Calais	646	437	1
23/24 Sept.	Neuss	549	378	5
	Dortmund–Ems Canal	141	136	14
	Münster/Handorf	113	107	1
24 Sept.	Calais	188	101	7
25 Sept.	Calais	872	430	–
26 Sept.	Calais Area	722	388	2
26/27 Sept.	Karlsruhe	237	226	2
27 Sept.	Calais Area	341	222	1
	Bottrop	175	71	–
27/28 Sept.	Kaiserslautern	227	217	1
28 Sept.	Calais area	494	230	–
3 Oct.	Walcheren	259	252	–

Date	Target			
5 Oct.	Wilhelmshaven	228	227	1
5/6 Oct.	Saarbrücken	551	531	3
6/7 Oct.	Dortmund	523	247	2
	Bremen	253	246	5
7 Oct.	Emmerich	350	340	3
	Kleve	351	90	–
11 Oct.	Gun batteries	180	160	1
	Walcheren	63	61	–
12 Oct.	Gun batteries	96	86	–
14 Oct.	Duisburg	1,013	519	13
14/15 Oct.	Duisburg	1,005	498	5
	Brunswick	240	233	1
15/16 Oct.	Wilhelmshaven	506	241	?
18 Oct.	Bonn	128	128	1
19/20 Oct.	Stuttgart	583	565	6
	Nuremberg	270	263	2
21 Oct.	Walcheren	75	75	1
22 Oct.	Neuss	100	100	–
23 Oct.	Walcheren	112	112	4
23/24 Oct.	Essen	1,055	561	5
25 Oct.	Essen	771	508	2
26 Oct.	Leverkusen	105	105	–
28 Oct.	Cologne	733	428	3
	Walcheren	277	86	1
28/29 Oct.	Bergen	244	237	3
29 Oct.	Walcheren	358	194	1
30 Oct.	Walcheren	110	102	–
	Wesseling	102	102	–
30/31 Oct.	Cologne	905	435	–
31 Oct.	Bottrop	101	101	1
31/1 Nov.	Cologne	493	331	2
1 Nov.	Homberg	228	226	1
1/2 Nov.	Oberhausen	288	74	1
2 Nov.	Homberg	184	184	5
2/3 Nov.	Düsseldorf	992	561	8
4 Nov.	Solingen	176	176	4
4/5 Nov.	Bochum	749	336	5
	Dortmund–Ems Canal	176	174	2
5 Nov.	Solingen	173	173	1
6 Nov.	Gelsenkirchen	738	324	3
6/7 Nov.	Mitteland Canal	242	235	10
	Koblenz	128	128	2
8 Nov.	Homberg	136	136	1
9 Nov.	Wanne-Eickel	277	256	2
11 Nov.	Castrop-Rauxel	122	122	–
11/12 Nov.	Harburg	245	237	7
	Dortmund	228	209	–
15 Nov.	Dortmund	177	177	–
16 Nov.	Düren	498	485	3
	Julich	508	78	1
18 Nov.	Münster	479	94	–
18/19 Nov.	Wanne-Eickel	309	285	1
20 Nov.	Homberg	183	183	5
21 Nov.	Homberg	160	160	3
21/22 Nov.	Aschaffenburg	283	274	2
	Castrop-Rauxel	273	79	–
	Mittelland Canal	144	138	2
	Dortmund–Ems Canal	128	123	–
22/23 Nov.	Trondheim	178	171	2
23 Nov.	Gelsenkirchen	168	168	1
26 Nov.	Fulda	75	75	–
26/27 Nov.	Munich	278	270	1
27 Nov.	Cologne	169	169	1
27/28 Nov.	Freiburg	351	341	1
	Neuss	290	102	–
28/29 Nov.	Neuss	153	153	–
29 Nov.	Dortmund	311	294	6
30 Nov.	Bottrop	60	60	–
	Osterfeld	60	60	2
30/1 Dec.	Duisburg	576	126	–
2 Dec.	Dortmund	93	93	–
2/3 Dec.	Hagen	504	87	1
3 Dec.	Heimbach	187	183	–
4 Dec.	Oberhausen	160	160	1
4/5 Dec.	Karlsruhe	535	369	1
	Heilbronn	292	282	12
5 Dec.	Hamm	94	94	–
	Schwammenauel Dam	56	56	–
5/6 Dec.	Soest	497	100	–
6/7 Dec.	Leuna	487	475	5
	Giessen	265	255	8
8 Dec.	Urft Dam	205	205	1
	Duisburg	163	163	–
11 Dec.	Urft Dam	233	233	1
	Osterfeld	150	150	1
12 Dec.	Witten	140	140	8
12/13 Dec.	Essen	540	349	6
13/14 Dec.	Oslo Fjord	59	52	–
15 Dec.	Siegen	138	138	–
15/16 Dec.	Ludwigshafen	341	327	1
16 Dec.	Siegen	108	108	1
17/18 Dec.	Ulm	330	317	2
	Duisburg	523	81	–
	Munich	288	280	4
18/19 Dec.	Gdynia	236	236	4
21 Dec.	Trier	113	113	–
21/22 Dec.	Politz	208	207	8
	Cologne/Nippes	136	67	–
	Bonn	114	97	–
22/23 Dec.	Koblenz	168	166	–
23 Dec.	Trier	153	153	1
24 Dec.	Airfields	338	79	2
24/25 Dec.	Hangelar airfield	104	104	1
	Cologne/Nippes	102	97	5
26 Dec.	St Vith	294	146	–
27 Dec.	Rheydt	211	200	1
27/28 Dec.	Opladen	328	66	2
28 Dec.	Cologne/Gremberg	167	167	–
28/29 Dec.	München-Gremberg	186	129	–
	Bonn	178	162	1
	Oslo Fjord	68	67	–
29/30 Dec.	Scholven/Buer	346	324	4
30/31 Dec.	Cologne/Kalk	470	93	1
	Houffalize	166	154	1
31 Dec.	Vohwinkel	155	155	2

RAIDS IN 1945

Date	Target			
31/1 Jan.	Osterfeld	166	149	2
1 Jan.	Dortmund–Ems Canal	104	102	2
1/2 Jan.	Mittelland Canal	157	152	–
2/3 Jan.	Nuremberg	521	514	6
3 Jan.	Benzol plants	99	99	1
4/5 Jan.	Royan	354	347	6
5 Jan.	Ludwigshafen	160	160	2
5/6 Jan.	Hanover	664	310	8
	Houffalize	140	131	2
6/7 Jan.	Hanau	482	154	2

Date	Target			
	Neuss	147	147	1
7/8 Jan.	Munich	654	645	15
11 Jan.	Krefeld	152	152	–
13 Jan.	Saarbrücken	158	158	1
13/14 Jan.	Politz	225	218	2
14 Jan.	Saarbrücken	134	134	–
14/15 Jan.	Leuna	587	573	10
15 Jan.	Recklinghausen	82	82	–
	Bochum	63	63	–
16/17 Jan.	Zeitz	328	328	10
	Brux	237	231	1
	Wanne-Eickel	138	138	1
22/23 Jan.	Duisburg	302	286	2
28 Jan.	Cologne/Gremberg	153	153	3
28/29 Jan.	Stuttgart	602	258	6
29 Jan.	Krefeld	148	148	–
1 Feb.	München-Gladbach	160	160	1
1/2 Feb.	Ludwigshafen	396	382	6
	Siegen	282	271	3
2/3 Feb.	Wiesbaden	507	495	3
	Karlsruhe	261	250	14
3/4 Feb.	Bottrop	210	192	8
	Dortmund	149	149	4
7 Feb.	Wanne-Eickel	100	100	1
7/8 Feb.	Kleve	305	295	1
	Goch	464	156	–
	Dortmund–Ems Canal	188	177	3
8/9 Feb.	Politz	482	475	12
	Krefeld	151	151	2
13/14 Feb.	Dresden	805	796 **	9
14/15 Feb.	Chemnitz	717	499	8
	Rositz	232	224	4
16 Feb.	Wesel	101	100	–
18 Feb.	Wesel	160	160	–
19 Feb.	Wesel	168	168	1
19/20 Feb.	Bohlen	260	254	–
20/21 Feb.	Dortmund	528	514	14
	Mitteland Canal	165	154	–
21/22 Feb.	Duisburg	373	362	10
	Mitteland Canal	177	165	9
22 Feb.	Oil refineries	167	167	1
23 Feb.	Gelsenkirchen	133	133	–
23/24 Feb.	Pforzheim	380	367	12
	Horten	83	73	1
24 Feb.	Dortmund–Ems Canal	170	166	–
25 Feb.	Kamen	153	153	1
26 Feb.	Dortmund	149	149	–
27 Feb.	Mainz	458	131	–
	Gelsenkirchen	149	149	1
28 Feb.	Gelsenkirchen	156	156	–
1 Mar.	Mannheim	478	372	3
	Kamen	151	151	–
2 Mar.	Cologne	858	531	6
3/4 Mar.	Dortmund–Ems Canal	222	212	7
4 Mar.	Wanne-Eickel	128	128	–
5 Mar.	Gelsenkirchen	170	170	1
5/6 Mar.	Chemnitz	760	498	14
	Bohlen	258	248	4
6 Mar.	Salzbergen	119	119	1
6/7 Mar.	Sassnitz	198	191	1
	Wesel	87	87	–
7/8 Mar.	Dessau	531	526	18
	Harburg	241	234	14
8/9 Mar.	Kassel	276	262	1
	Hamburg	312	62	–
9 Mar.	Datteln	159	159	1
10 Mar.	Scholven/Buer	155	155	–
11 Mar.	Essen	1,079	750	3
12 Mar.	Dortmund	1,108	748	2
13/14 Mar.	Benzol plants	227	195	1
14 Mar.	Benzol plants	169	169	1
14/15 Mar.	Lützkendorf	255	244	18
	Zweibrucken	230	121	–
15/16 Mar.	Misburg	265	257	4
	Hagen	267	134	6
16/17 Mar.	Nuremberg	293	277	24
	Würzburg	236	225	6
17 Mar.	Benzol plants	167	167	–
18 Mar.	Benzol plants	100	100	–
18/19 Mar.	Hanau	285	277	1
19 Mar.	Gelsenkirchen	79	79	–
20 Mar.	Recklinghausen	99	99	–
20/21 Mar.	Bohlen	235	224	9
	Hemmingstedt	166	166	1
21 Mar.	Münster	160	160	3
	Bremen	139	133	–
21/22 Mar.	Hamburg	159	151	4
	Bochum	143	131	1
22 Mar.	Hildesheim	235	227	4
	Bocholt	100	100	–
	Railway targets	102	102	–
23 Mar.	Railway targets	128	128	2
	Wesel	80	80	–
23/24 Mar.	Wesel	218	195	–
24 Mar.	Benzol plants	185	173	3
25 Mar.	Hanover	275	267	1
27 Mar.	Paderborn	276	268	–
	Hamm	150	150	–
	Farge	115	115	–
29 Mar.	Salzgitter	130	130	–
31 Mar.	Hamburg	469	361	8
3 Apr.	Nordhausen	255	247	2
4 Apr.	Nordhausen	244	243	1
4/5 Apr.	Leuna	341	327	2
	Lützkendorf	272	258	6
6 Apr.	Ijmuiden	55	54	–
7/8 Apr.	Molbis	186	175	–
8/9 Apr.	Lützkendorf	242	231	6
	Hamburg	440	160	3
9 Apr.	Hamburg	57	57	2
9/10 Apr.	Kiel	599	591	3
10 Apr.	Leipzig	230	134	1
10/11 Apr.	Plauen	315	307	–
	Leipzig	95	76	7
13/14 Apr.	Kiel	482	377	2
14/15 Apr.	Potsdam	512	500	1
16/17 Apr.	Pilsen	233	222	1
	Schwandorf	175	167	1
17/18 Apr.	Cham	101	90	–
18 Apr.	Heligoland	969	617	–
18/19 Apr.	Komotau	123	114	–
20 Apr.	Regensburg	100	100	1
22 Apr.	Bremen	767	651	2
23 Apr.	Flensburg	148	148	–
24 Apr.	Bad Oldesloe	110	110	–
25 Apr.	Berchtesgaden	375	359	2
	Wangerooge	482	158	2
25/26 Apr.	Tonsberg	119	107	1

Index

191